SUCCESSFUL
EVENT MANAGEMENT
A PRACTICAL HANDBOOK

Anton Shone and Bryn Parry   **Fourth Edition**

CENGAGE

Australia • Brazil dom • United States

**Successful Event Management:
A Practical Handbook, Fourth Edition**
Anton Shone and Bryn Parry

Publishing Director: Linden Harris
Publisher: Andrew Ashwin
Editorial Assistant: Lauren Darby
Project Editor: Alison Cooke
Production Controller: Eyvett Davis
Marketing Manager: Lauren Mottram
Typesetter: MPS Limited,
   A Macmillan Company
Cover design: Adam Renvoize

© 2013, Cengage Learning EMEA

For product information and technology assistance,
contact **emea.info@cengage.com**.

For permission to use material from this text or product,
and for permission queries,
email **emea.permissions@cengage.com**.

British Library Cataloguing-in-Publication Data
A catalogue record for this book is available from the British Library.

ISBN: 978-1-4080-6663-8

Cengage Learning EMEA
Cheriton House, North Way, Andover, Hampshire, SP10 5BE
United Kingdom

Cengage Learning products are represented in Canada by
Nelson Education Ltd.

For your lifelong learning solutions, visit
www.cengage.co.uk

Purchase your next print book, e-book or e-chapter at
www.cengagebrain.co.uk

Printed in China by RR Donnelley
1 2 3 4 5 6 7 8 9 10 – 15 14 13

BRIEF CONTENTS

CONTENTS

DIGITAL SUPPORT RESOURCES

Dedicated Instructor Resources

To discover the dedicated instructor online support resources accompanying this textbook, instructors should register here for access:
http://login.cengage.com

Resources include:

- Instructor's Manual
- ExamView Testbank
- PowerPoint slides

Instructor access

Instructors can access the digital support resources by registering at
http://login.cengage.com   or by speaking to their
local Cengage Learning EMEA representative.

Instructor resources

Instructors can use the integrated Engagement Tracker in CourseMate to track students' preparation and engagement. The tracking tool can be used to monitor progress of the class as a whole, or for individual students.

Student access

Students can access CourseMate using the unique personal access card included in the front of the book.

Student resources

CourseMate offers a range of interactive learning tools tailored to the fourth edition of *Successful Event Management*: *A Practical Handbook* including:

- Quizzes and self-test questions
- Interactive eBook
- Games
- Media cases
- Glossary
- Flashcards
- Links to useful websites
- Extra case studies

PART 1

THE EVENTS BUSINESS

CHAPTER 1
AN INTRODUCTION TO EVENTS

AIMS

- To consider a definition of, and framework for, special events

- To provide a categorization and typology for special events, together with an overview of the historical context

- To identify the key characteristics of events, in order to understand the business of events management as a service activity

INTRODUCTION

Events have long played an important role in human society. The tedium of daily life, with its constant toil and effort, was broken up by events of all kinds. In most societies, the slightest excuse could be found for a good celebration, although traditional celebrations often had strict ceremonies and rituals. In Europe, particularly before the industrial revolution, routine daily activities were regularly interspersed with festivals and carnivals. Personal events or local events to celebrate certain times of year, perhaps related to religious holy days, were also common. This role in society was, and is, of considerable importance. In the modern world some of the historic driving forces for events have changed. For example, religious reasons for staging major festivals have, perhaps, become less important, but we still see carnivals, fairs and festivals in all sorts of places and at various times of year. Many of these events, although religious or traditional in origin, play a contemporary role by attracting tourists (and thus tourist income) to a particular place. Some major events, however, still revolve around periods such as Christmas or Easter in the Christian calendar, and towns and cities throughout Europe often hold major festivals based on these times. Even in those countries where religion is no longer as important as it once was, the celebration of originally religious, and other folk festivals, still takes place; so do older festivals related to the seasons, including the celebration of spring, with activities such as dancing round a maypole, decorating water wells or crowning a May Queen. Harvest time continues to provide a reason for a seasonal celebration in rural locations. At the same time, many historic, traditional or 'folk' ceremonies and rituals are in practice recent inventions or recreations.

special events
The phenomenon arising from non-routine occasions that have leisure, cultural, personal or organizational objectives set apart from the normal activity of daily life, and whose purpose is to enlighten, celebrate, entertain or challenge the experience of a group of people.

We can grasp, therefore, that **special events** were often historically crucial to the social fabric of day-to-day life. In modern times we are often so used to special events that we do not necessarily see them in this context (e.g. Mother's Day). It is also sometimes difficult for the student of events to understand the full extent of these activities, their variety, their role and how they are run. Unlike many industries we cannot say, 'Well, this industry is worth maybe €30 billion a year', or whatever. In fact it is quite difficult to quantify in monetary terms how much events are worth 'as an industry' due to opaque definitions and overlapping market sector boundaries. Such a calculation is problematic, because the range of events is staggering, from big internationally organized sports spectaculars such as the Olympics, to the family naming ceremony of the new baby next door. All we can reasonably say, perhaps, is that we can look at any one event in isolation and see what value it generates. Indeed, certain events have the purpose of creating wealth or economic value in some way, as well as entertaining and cementing society, but these are not the only reasons for holding events.

DEFINITIONS AND FRAMEWORKS

For the student of events, we have to provide some context or framework to begin to understand the nature of the activity and the issues about management and organization surrounding it. This being the case, and for convenience, we need to attempt both a definition and a means of classification.

Special events are that phenomenon arising from those non-routine occasions which have leisure, cultural, personal or organizational objectives set apart from the normal activity of daily life. Their purpose is to enlighten, celebrate, entertain or challenge the experience of a group of people.

Authors such as Goldblatt (2011) have chosen to highlight the celebratory aspect of events:

> *'A special event recognizes a unique moment in time with ceremony and ritual to satisfy specific needs'.*

Although this definition clearly works for events like weddings, parades, inaugurations and so on, it works less well for activities like engineering exhibitions, sports competitions, **product launches**, etc. Getz (2005), in referring to the experience that **participants** have, states:

> *'To the customer or guest, a special event is an opportunity for a leisure, social or cultural experience outside the normal range of choices or beyond everyday experience'.*

This definition, too, has its advantages, but also seems to exclude organizational events of various kinds. Nevertheless, it is a place to start and from it we can begin to look at the vast range of events that take place.

To do so, it helps to have some means of classification (Tum, 2006). Figure 1.1, for convenience, splits events into four broad categories based on the concept (in our definition) of events having leisure, cultural, personal or organizational objectives. It is crucial to bear in mind, when considering this categorization, that there are frequent overlaps. For example, the graduation of a student from university is both a personal event for the student and his or her family, and an organizational event for the university. A village carnival is both a cultural event, perhaps celebrating some aspect of local heritage or folklore and a leisure event, possibly both for local people and tourists. Therefore, overlaps should be seen as inevitable rather than

product launches
A 'show' to introduce an audience, such as the media, to a new product or service. It may also be aimed at an organization's internal management and staff, sales force or external dealers and customers.

participants
A person attending an event who is actively taking part in it, or in some activity related to it.

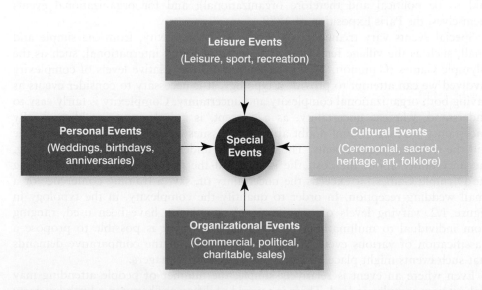

Figure 1.1 A suggested categorization of special events

exceptional and any attempt to categorize an event, even by analyzing its objectives, its organizers or its origins, will have to take account of this, even if we can agree that a particular event does fall into such and such a category.

CATEGORIES AND TYPOLOGIES

In the following section we will begin to consider how this proposed categorization might be developed to take in the great variety of events. It is a useful starting point, one we can adopt to help us look at the context and precedents for modern events and as a means of understanding their breadth and variety.

In looking at the various kinds of special events, whether these are leisure based, personal, cultural or organizational, it is possible to identify a number of characteristics that they have in common, thus helping us understand what special events are and how they work, as well as differentiating them from other activities.

Our definition of events could be given a shorthand version: 'Those non-routine occasions set apart from the normal activity of daily life of a group of people', but this may not necessarily give a feel for the specialized nature of the activity. We can say specialized because of the uniqueness of events, but also because such events may often be celebratory or ceremonial in some way. This is an aspect that other authors including Goldblatt have highlighted. Clearly this approach can be applied to activities such as weddings, product launches, prizegivings, etc. On the other hand, it may be less suited to events such as an exhibition, sports day or annual **conference**, although it can be argued that even an exhibition of paintings or a sales' conference may have an element of ceremony about it, since someone has to open it. However, in so far as exhibitions, conferences and so on are non-routine, the definition is usable. For the purpose of illustrating the four categories and to demonstrate historical progression, this chapter explores four case studies: for leisure events, the ancient Olympic Games; for personal events, a Roman wedding; for cultural events, the Royal Diamond Jubilees of 1897 and 2012 (which, for those interested in the overlaps, could also be said to be political and therefore organizational); and for organizational events themselves, the Paris Exposition of 1889.

conference
A meeting whose purpose is the interchange of ideas.

Special events vary tremendously in size and complexity, from the simple and small, such as the village fête, to the huge, complex and international, such as the Olympic Games (Gammon, 2012). To understand the relative levels of complexity involved we can attempt to provide a typology. It is necessary to consider events as having both organizational complexity and uncertainty. Complexity is fairly easy to understand, whereas uncertainty, as a concept, is a little more problematic. By uncertainty we mean initial doubt about such issues as the cost, the time schedule and the technical requirements. Thus, it can be understood that, at the beginning, the uncertainty about the cost, the timing and the technical needs of organizing the Olympic Games far exceeds the uncertainty of, say, a training conference or a small wedding reception. In order to quantify the complexity, in the typology in Figure 1.2, varying levels of organizational complexity have been used, ranging from individual to multinational. Using this typology it is possible to propose a classification of various events, in order to understand the comparative demands that such events might place on organizers or events managers.

Even where an event is relatively simple, the number of people attending may make it very complex indeed. There is a world of difference between a birthday party

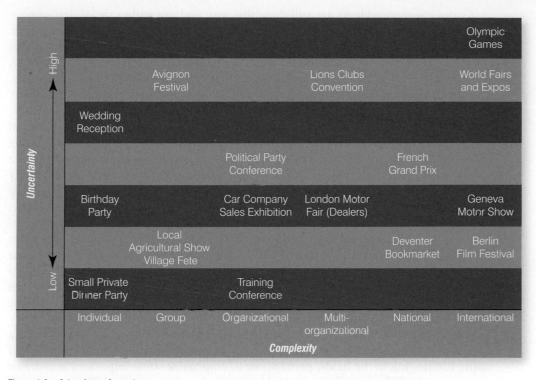

Figure 1.2 A typology of events
Based on Slack *et al.* 2001. 'Operations Management' London, Pitman, 3rd Edition, pp.585-595

for six people and a birthday party for 60 people, even though the format, structure and basic idea may be the same. The typology must be seen with this limitation in mind. Indeed, it is this concept of size which often means the difference between an amateur organizer or a family member running an event on the one hand, or having to employ an event manager, go to a hotel or find specialist advice on the other. Size or number of **attendees** is something that easily catches people out. We can all organize a dinner party for eight or ten people, even a buffet for maybe 20 or 30, but after that the sheer effort involved would overwhelm us: not enough space, not enough equipment and not enough people to help and so on. The events management business in the contemporary world, whether it concerns the annual dinner of the local town council or the organization of the European Figure Skating Championships, is often about the need for trained staff, specialist companies and professional expertise.

attendees
A group of people attending an event, for a range of purposes, from watching the event take place, to actively participating in some or all of the event's activities.

HISTORICAL CONTEXTS AND PRECEDENTS

Events management can be thought of as an art, rather than a science. Historically, the organization of small local events was relatively uncomplicated and needed no extensive managerial expertise. The organization of a wedding, for example, could be done most often by the bride's mother with help from the two families involved and a vicar, priest, religious or other official representative. (In past times, especially up until the Victorian period, 'expert' advice often came in the form of a Dancing Master, employed to give the wedding festivities some formality of style. There were also quite specific local rituals to be observed, which acted as 'checklists' for the activities.) Some weddings are still done this way and are within the ability of non-specialist people to organize and run: the bride and groom deal with the ceremony, the bride's mother orders the cake and a buffet from a local baker, family and friends do some or all of it; the reception is held in one of the family homes or a church hall, flowers come from gardens or are obtained from a nearby flower shop, and so on. All these tasks were, and can still be, coped with in an intimate and sociable way with no great cost or fuss.

While special events by their nature are not routine, pressure for formal organizational or technological skill was not so great in the past for local, family or small-scale events. This is not to say that large-scale events management is a particularly recent development, only that the modern world with its many complexities often requires specialists to do what, in gentler times, could be done by thoughtful amateurs or ordinary people. We should not mistake history, however. The scale and complexity of, say, the Greek or Roman gladiatorial games (which comprised vast numbers of activities, set-piece contests and even theatrically mounted sea battles – the Romans were sufficiently advanced that they could flood their arenas) certainly had what today would be considered as a professional events management organization to run them. This can also be seen in our first case study of the ancient Olympic Games, which helps to illustrate our first category of leisure events.

Looking back in history we can see, however, that events have always had a significant role to play in society, either to break up the dull, grinding routine of daily life (toiling in the fields, perhaps) or to emphasize some important activity or person (such as the arrival of a new abbot at the local monastery). We can trace all sorts of special events far back in time, even if they are the result of some recent 're-invention'. For as long as humanity has lived in family groups there will have been celebrations of weddings, births, religious rites and so on. In following up the categorization suggested earlier of events being leisure based, personal, cultural or organizational in origin, we can consequently seek various historical examples or precedents. That said, we must be careful not to believe that earlier times or other societies had the same cultural attitudes as we have today.

The second category of special events, in our approach, is that of personal events. This includes all sorts of occasions that a family or friends might be involved in. Many modern aspects of family life can be seen to revolve around important occasions: birthdays, namings, weddings and anniversaries all fall into this category, as do many other personal events and celebrations (a dinner party is a special event in our definition). Of all these, weddings can be one of the most complicated to organize, involving friends and family and a whole range of related service activities, from catering to entertainment, as well as the formal aspect of the marriage ceremony itself. This is not to say that all weddings are a 'big performance', some are small, friendly and relaxed, and just as good for it – size is no measure of the success of an event. Almost all cultures known to history have some form of partnership ceremony and in looking for a historical precedent for personal events, the Romans can provide an example.

Special events cover all kinds of human activity, not only sporting and family activities, but also cultural and commercial or organizational activities. Culture, with its associated ceremony and traditions, has a role in all kinds of social activity: and for all kinds of people, organizations and institutions (Robinson, 2010). But it has been especially important for governments and leaders, such as royalty. In cultural events ceremony becomes very evident, often as a way of emphasizing the significance

CASE STUDY 1

Leisure/sporting events: the Olympic Games

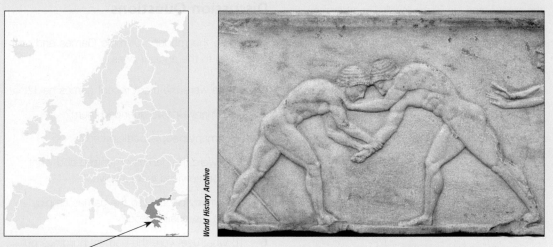

Olympia, Greece

World History Archive

Fragment of a Greek, relief frieze c.500 BC depicting wrestlers in practice

FACTBOX

- Ancient Olympic Games first held in 776BC, last held in 393
- Restarted in modern times in 1896
- Held every four years
- Ancient games were part of the religious festival of Zeus, the chief Greek god
- Modern games are a major economic activity

Learning Objectives

The aim of this case study is to examine the historical background to the Olympic Games with the following objectives:
To consider the historical development of the Games
To highlight comparisons between the ancient Olympics and the modern ones
To understand the differences between the ancient and the modern Games

The modern Olympic Games are loosely based on the games of the ancient Greeks. Those games, first held in 776BC at Olympia, in Greece, had the purpose of celebrating the festival of Zeus, the most important Greek god. They were organized by the temple priests and their helpers, and carried on for many years at four-yearly intervals, even though Greece was normally at war (quite usual in those times). One of the most important aspects of the games was the truce that existed to allow them to take place and to enable the participants, mostly the nobility and professional athletes, together with pilgrims (who were travelling to the temple of Zeus at Olympia), to get to the games safely. The ancient games at first had only one component, the 'stade', a footrace. Later they included not only the stade (about 150 metres, hence the word 'stadium'), but also the pentathlon (the discus, the jump, the javelin, another race and wrestling), together with a chariot race, a horse race and the pankration – a very violent form of wrestling. All of these were performed naked, in the Greek style, although, as the games also celebrated military prowess, the final foot race was performed in full armour. The games lasted for five days and included various religious ceremonies, the main religious aspect being the worship of Zeus, although the women had their own games in honour of the goddess Hera (married women were not permitted at the men's games, even to watch).

The games were organized by the religious authorities of Olympia and involved professional trainers and referees for the events as well as judges. There were also social events and, rather like the modern games, a parade of champions on the final day. The ancient games continued, in all, for about 1200 years and were closed down by the Roman Emperor

Theodosius II in 393. The modern games began again at Athens in 1896, followed by Paris in 1900, and then more or less every four years to the present day (Swadding, 2011; Wallechinskey, 2012).

Discussion Questions

Investigate the modern Olympic Games and compare them to the ancient ones.

1   Where were the most recent games held?

2   How many people attended them?

3   How many people participated?

4   How were the games organized and what support services were involved?

5   How many people did the games employ during the peak period?

6   To what use were the games' buildings put after the games had finished?

7   How much do the modern games differ from the ancient ones?

Websites

Related websites for those interested in the Olympics: **www.olympic.org** and for interesting comment and critique of the Olympics 2012, search: **www.guardian.co.uk/**.

of the event itself or of the person at the centre for the ceremony, the intended effect being to secure support, or to allow as many people as possible to recognize the key individual. For example, the media often show heads of state (kings, queens, presidents) inspecting a 'guard of honour' when arriving at the airport of a country they are visiting; they listen to the national anthem and then walk past the guard of honour. The original purpose of this ceremony was not for the head of state to see the guards, but for the guards to see the head of state, so that the guards would recognize the person they were to protect.

In the Middle Ages, events and ceremonies played a major role, ensuring that a dull daily existence was enlivened and that people were entertained, or at least impressed. There was no TV, video, movies or the internet for entertainment, as all these are less than 100 years old. It was, for example, accepted wisdom in England in the Tudor period (about 1500–1600) that ceremonial was an essential part of showing 'good government'. Government, in this case, being interpreted as the action of the king or queen, was expected to make a good show, or put on a

CASE STUDY 2

Personal events: a Roman wedding

Rome, Italy

Roman marble sarcophagus, 3rd century A.D. with a relief depicting a wedding ceremony

FACTBOX

- The Roman empire covered a huge area of Western Europe, from Britain to north Africa
- Rome was pagan until the AD300s, when it began to become Christian in religion
- Roman weddings had many similarities to modern ceremonies, but also a number of differences

Learning Objectives

The aim of this case study is to examine comparisons between a historical ceremony and a modern one, in this case a wedding, with the following objectives:

To consider how an ancient wedding was conducted and the differences with a modern wedding ceremony (of your choice)

To highlight comparisons between the ancient ceremony and the modern one

To understand that although the ceremony and style may differ the essential purpose remains the same

As with modern weddings, Roman weddings were organized by the families of the bride and groom. A ring was often given as an engagement present, although no ring was involved in the ceremony itself until changes in the ritual after the second century AD (Kamm, 2008). The bride wore a special bridal gown, generally with a flame-coloured veil and garlands of flowers. The wedding would be arranged with the respective families each dealing with various aspects. A legal contract was signed by the two fathers on the day of the wedding. The joining of hands at the ceremony was ensured, not by a priest, but by a married woman, known as a 'pronuba'. At the ceremony, prayers would be said to the family gods and especially to the goddess Juno, with a sacrifice offered to the god Jupiter. This might involve the killing of a donkey, as donkeys were thought to have considerable sexual prowess, and so the sacrifice was thought to ensure a suitably exciting wedding night.

Following the ceremony the guests would make their way to the bride's parents' house, where there would be a major feast in the Roman style, of some excess with large quantities of food and wine being consumed. Once the feast was over, there would be a torchlight procession from the bride's parents' house to the bridegroom's house. It would generally be led by torch carriers, often with children and accompanied by flute players with the families, friends, relatives and other locals joining in. There was a great deal of loud and happy singing during the procession and the cheerful shouting of obscene poetry and jokes, known as 'Fescennine Verses'. This was the Roman equivalent of writing obscene messages on the couple's car with foam and often referred to how 'well equipped' the donkey was. On arrival at the bridegroom's house the bride would anoint the doorposts with oil as a sign of dedication to the gods and the bridegroom would carry the bride over the threshold. At this point we will leave them to it.

Discussion Questions

Perhaps from your own experience of going to a wedding, or from an example of a modern wedding that you have been given:

1 How did it differ from the Roman one?

2 Who organized what?

3 Suppose you have a wedding to organize with 100 guests, how long does it realistically take to get things done?

4 Also, begin to look for possible similarities between the special events in these case studies – what are their common characteristics?

Websites

Related website for those interested in Roman history: **www.roman-empire.net** For further reading see: **http://ablemedia.com/ctcweb/consortium/ancientweddings7.html** (among others).

good display for the people and the people expected to see royalty in all its glory; it was intended to ensure, to a certain extent, respect and allegiance.

One of the things which these historic examples show is that there have long been specialists of various kinds to organize events (the temple priests for the Greek Games, the Lord Chamberlain's department for Queen Victoria). Some events, such as the coronation of a king or queen, have been, and still are, highly complex. Very often, where great ceremony was needed for state events, the military could also be called on to help organize them and army officers were often seconded to do just that, as is still the case with much modern state ceremonial: parades, state visits, pageants and festivals.

Although the organization of historic ceremonial events might be thought of as a matter of the injection of military organizational skills, very often this supposed skill was no such thing. In fact, great historical ceremonial disasters were quite common. The modern events manager has no monopoly on things going **'pear-shaped'**. Many coronations and other great events were famously disorganised. Even where these involved a non-military event, such as the great fireworks held in 1749 to celebrate

'pear-shaped' Description of something which goes wrong or turns into a shambles.

CASE STUDY 3

Cultural events: The Royal Diamond Jubilees of 1897 and 2012

Getty Images/Popperfoto

London, England

The Diamond Jubilee of Queen Victoria

- The Diamond Jubilees of 1897 and 2012
- Involving Queen Victoria (1897) and Queen Elizabeth (2012)
- Main activities were a procession in 1897 and a river pageant in 2012
- The two events provide an interesting comparison over time

Learning Objectives

The aim of this case study is to examine a cultural event and how it has changed over time with the following objectives:

To consider the historical changes both in terms of the event and in terms of the nature of the nation and its outlook in the two periods

To highlight particular issues such as cost and security and how these have been addressed, particularly in the 2012 event by careful consideration of what the event should involve

A royal Diamond Jubilee is that rarest of occasions, it celebrates 60 years of the reign of a monarch and there have only ever been three of them. The most recent being the Diamond Jubilee of Queen Elizabeth II and the previous one being the Diamond Jubilee of Queen Victoria. There have been no others in Europe, though the much loved Queen Wilhelmina of the Netherlands reigned for almost 58 years and would have celebrated her jubilee had it not been for failing health. However, King Bhumibol Adulyadej of Thailand celebrated his Diamond Jubilee in 2006.

The comparison between the two UK Diamond Jubilees is instructive, in so far as they present a picture of the same country, but over a space of more than a century, during which change has been the only constant feature. When Queen Victoria celebrated her Diamond Jubilee on the 22 June 1897, she was Queen of the United Kingdom of Great Britain and Ireland, and Empress of India. When Queen Elizabeth celebrated her Diamond Jubilee on 2–5 June 2012 she was Queen of the United Kingdom of Great Britain and Northern Ireland and head of the Commonwealth. Victoria's Diamond Jubilee in 1897 saw Britain at the very high tide of its powers, as the most important industrial nation of its time and with an empire that included almost a quarter of the population of the world. By 2012 the position of the United Kingdom was of a modest medium-sized European nation.

This change in both national circumstances and national mood was, in effect, shown by the differences in the two Jubilees. Queen Victoria's Diamond Jubilee was described as 'a far grander celebration of her reign than her Golden Jubilee of the previous decade'. A service of thanksgiving took place outside St Paul's Cathedral, so that the Queen could remain in her carriage, as she was too frail to climb the cathedral steps. The scope of the celebrations was expanded considerably in comparison to her Golden Jubilee of ten years before, with a celebration of the British Empire being the central focus. Before leaving Buckingham Palace on 22 June 1897, the Queen issued a telegraph throughout the Empire, saying 'From my heart I thank my beloved people. May God bless them!' Some 47 000 troops from all over the Empire were present for the celebrations, which included not only the main procession on 22 June 1897, but also a review of Colonial troops at Windsor. For example many Indian troops participated in the procession through London, including the Bengal lancers, officers of the Indian Imperial Service Troops, and the Sikhs, who marched alongside the Canadians. The Daily Mail the day afterwards described the troops (in words which were acceptable at the time) as 'an anthropological museum – a living gazetteer of the British Empire'. The military flavour of the jubilee also extended to the Royal Navy with a review of the fleet being carried out by the Prince of Wales at Spithead which included the first ever vessel powered by steam turbines using a propeller, the Turbinia. In addition, a charitable and celebratory lunch was provided for 40 000 poor people by Princess Alexandra.

In comparison the Jubilee of 2012 was a much more restrained affair. The principal focus of the Jubilee celebrations in 2012 was a River Pageant on the Thames in London. From the event manager's point of view, we can consider the advantages of such a choice of main event for the Jubilee. First, it makes use of a range of resources which exist, but are perhaps under-used. For example, the Queen retains 24 Royal Waterman, who are responsible for royal visits on the Thames, normally using a vessel called 'The Royal Nore'. River pageants have been seen on the Thames since 1453 when the Mayor of London, John Norman, first held one: 'having at his own expense built a noble barge, had it decorated with flags and streamers, in which he was rowed by watermen with silver oars, attended by such of the city companies as possessed barges, in a manner so splendid that his barge seemed to burn on the water'. For Queen Elizabeth's Diamond Jubilee, however, a private vessel known as the 'Spirit of Chartwell' was dressed, by an award winning film production designer, for use as the Royal barge and formed the centrepiece of a 1000 strong flotilla of vessels on the Thames. Second, the use of the Thames provides significant advantages in a number of ways, for example, the street congestion caused by Royal or Mayoral processions in London, and events such as the Notting Hill Carnival or the London Marathon, is reduced by using the Thames for such a major event. It also means that the River Pageant can be viewed easily from all the embankments, paths, gardens and buildings along the Thames without the need to put up special seating or viewing areas or block off streets to do so. These advantages also help to reduce the costs (both the direct costs, for example, of temporary seating, and indirect or hidden costs, for example, of time lost through congestion or the need for huge numbers of extra police) of putting on the event. Third, it has an interesting but less obvious security advantage, in so far as it enables everyone to see and greet the Queen, but in so far as she is in the middle of the river, it reduces the opportunities for stupidity or feckless behaviour and mitigates against other more security risks as the river is an unfamiliar environment for potential terrorists, or greater or lesser fools of one kind or another.

In addition to the River Pageant, a service of thanksgiving was held at St Paul's Cathedral, and a concert given at Bush House. Beacons were lit on hills throughout the country in celebration. The celebrations engaged business much more in terms of sponsorship of the event than in seeing it as an opportunity to promote Britain's goods to overseas markets (through visitors) that the 1897 Jubilee had been. In terms of the military aspect, Queen Elizabeth's Jubilee had barely any military overtones. In 1897, we have noted there were 47 000 troops involved, but in 2012, there were no more than 2500 military personnel, barely 5 per cent of those involved in the 1897 Jubilee: an interesting comparison between a nation at the height of its military and industrial prowess in the Victorian age and, the modest one, however proud it might be, in the modern age.

Discussion Questions

Think of a recent ceremonial event you have seen, perhaps a royal or government event, a church event or some ceremony that takes place locally in your town or city, perhaps involving the mayor:

1   What were these events about and what was special about them?

2   Was there much ceremonial or some kind of tradition being enacted?

3   What issues appeared to be important in the choice of a river pageant as the centre piece of the 2012 Diamond Jubilee and why were these relevant to the events' managers?

4   What were the issues of costs and security involved in the 2012 event?

Websites

For a more detailed comparison of the preparations for these two Jubilees listen to: **http://www.bbc.co.uk/programmes/b0194l3j**. You will have to register for BBC I-player to listen and excerpts from the day can be seen on YouTube for example: **http://www.youtube.com/watch?v=zHF7viVJnJg**.

the peace of Aix-la-Chapelle, for King George II, there was no guarantee of success, in spite of the fact that these were organized by George Frederick Handel, the famous composer, and set to his music. The fireworks were to be held in a specially built pavilion in Green Park, London. Handel was designated 'Comptroller of the Fireworks'. This was such a major event that a full dress rehearsal was held, which went perfectly. However, on the night itself Handel had an argument with Servandoni, the pavilion designer, at which swords were drawn, and during the middle of the performance, with 100 musicians playing and a crowd of over 12 000 people watching, half the pavilion burned down.

The modern world is no different. Faster maybe; more complex perhaps; but no less susceptible to things going wrong, falling down, being rained on or flooded out; the guest speaker getting stuck in the traffic; acts of God, both tragic or comic; the groom still drunk after the stag night, fires at weddings, the buffet being dropped on the kitchen floor or the bride falling over the cake at the reception. In some ways, events management is a rather thankless task, one of those roles where everyone notices when something goes wrong, but few people notice the tremendous effort involved in getting even a simple event right. Indeed, some of the things that go

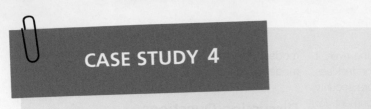

CASE STUDY 4

Organizational events: the Paris Exposition

Paris, France

World History Archive

The Eiffel Tower was a part of the major building programme during the Paris Exposition in 1889

- The Paris Exposition of 1889
- Intended to display France's industrial power
- Resulted in a major building programme in the exposition area, including the construction of the Eiffel Tower
- 32 million people visited the fair

Learning Objectives

The aim of this case study is to examine the nature and purpose of an organizational event with the following objectives:

To consider a historical example of an organizational event

To highlight the purposes of a large scale organizational event

To understand that such an event may leave a legacy

The 1889 Paris Exposition was the idea of the French Prime Minister of the time, Jules Ferry. He wished to see an exhibition that would demonstrate France's industrial might, its commercial activity and engineering skill. The result was the largest, most varied and successful world fair ever held until that time.

The fair was opened on 6 May 1889, a wonderful spring day, by the French president, Sadi Carnot, who rode in a horse-drawn procession from the Elysée Palace. The procession, led by a detachment of mounted cuirassiers, made its way along the Champs Elysées and the Avenue Montaigne among joyful crowds, and entered the exhibition area passing under the arches of the Eiffel Tower, arriving at the Central Dome at 2.00pm. A short ceremony took place at which the Exposition was formally presented to President Carnot: 'This splendid result exceeds all hopes...' Indeed it did. The exposition was huge. It covered the whole of the Champ de Mars and the Esplanade des Invalides, and stretched along the Quai d'Orsay and the Trocadero Gardens to the Eiffel Tower, some 95 hectares, including a huge Ferris wheel. There were almost 62 000 exhibitors from all over the world and by the time an exhausted President Carnot had left at 5.30pm, almost half a million people had streamed in through the 22 entrances to the exhibition, which then lasted 176 days. Some 32 million people visited the fair and among the exhibits was the world's first ever motor car, a Benz (Harris, 2004).

The lasting legacy of the exposition is the Eiffel Tower. When the event was being planned, a member of the French cabinet, Edouard Lockroy, had suggested a thousand foot tower to highlight its importance. The idea of a tower built of iron and steel was not new, as one had been suggested by the Cornish engineer, Richard Trevithick, in 1833, and another by Clarke and Reeves, two American engineers, for the Philadelphia Exposition of 1876. But it was Gustave Eiffel who supervised the building of the Paris tower. It was begun on 26 January 1887, and opened at 11.50am on 15 May 1889, to Eiffel's considerable relief, and has been the symbol of Paris ever since – though for the first 20 or 30 years it was rather disliked by some.

Discussion Questions

Think of a recent event engineering project you have seen launched in public:

1   What was its purpose?

2   How was it organized?

3   In the long term, was there some benefit from having it, did it leave a legacy, such as a building or structure even if that was knocked down later?

4   Does this apply to other kinds of events?

5   How could a town or city benefit from holding an event?

6   Could that event be used to help renovate a rundown area?

7   Who would pay for the event?

Websites

Related website for those interested in the Eiffel Tower: **www.tour-eiffel.fr/teiffel/uk/**. For some images of the event see: **http://www.nga.gov/resources/expo1889-1.shtm**.

wrong at an event may be beyond the organizer's ability to prevent: the weather, the traffic, power failures and so on.

Nevertheless, events can be considerable triumphs of organization and leave lasting legacies. The fourth in our categories is the organizational event; this may be anything from a political party conference to a motor **show**. There are any number of suitable examples. Some of the world trade fairs have left interesting legacies. As trade and commerce developed following the industrial revolution, many countries sought to celebrate and display their industrial achievements. This led to a number of industrial and commercial exhibitions in many major cities. Such exhibitions had often developed out of local trade fairs in towns and cities around medieval Europe. Fairs had been held for many centuries as a way to show off all kinds of products, goods and other wares. One of the first great international industrial fairs was the Great Exhibition of London in 1851 (there had been earlier

show
A full sequence of sets, or more simply, the event itself, in terms of musical, artistic or similar activities.

ones, such as that in Paris of 1849) The Great Exhibition of London was held in a specially built hall, the Crystal Palace, that housed some 13 000 exhibitors from all over the world.

These fairs have taken place at irregular intervals in many major cities ever since. Recent fairs or 'Expos' have taken place in New York, Montreal, Seville, Hanover (2000) and Shanghai (2010). In the Victorian period many cities held fairs; not only London, but also Amsterdam (in 1883 with the International Colonial Exposition and several later fairs), and especially Paris, which held a series of fairs from 1855 to 1900 (and two since, in 1925 and 1937). One such event, which has left a very obvious legacy, the Eiffel Tower, was the Paris Exposition of 1889.

CHARACTERISTICS OF EVENTS

In our definition of special events, we noted key characteristics of events as 'non-routine' and 'unique'. However, events have many other characteristics in common with all types of services and in particular with hospitality and leisure services of many kinds.

These characteristics can be grouped together (see Figure 1.3) as being:

- uniqueness;
- perishability;
- labour-intensiveness;
- fixed timescales;
- intangibility;
- personal interaction;
- ambience; and
- ritual or ceremony.

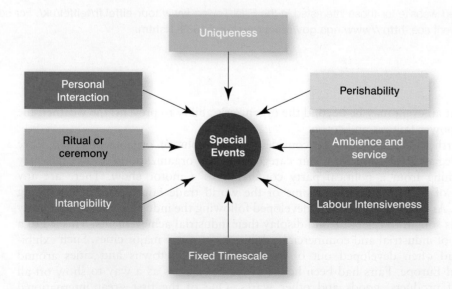

Figure 1.3 Characteristics of special events as a service

Uniqueness

The key element of all special events is their uniqueness: each one will be different. This is not to say that the same kind of event cannot be repeated many times, but that the participants, the surroundings, the **audience** or any number of other variables will make the event unique. Even where we have looked at those special events that are very frequent, such as weddings, all are different because different people are involved, the choice of location, the invited guests, the timing and so on. The same is true of events that may have followed the same format for years and years. The ancient Olympic Games took place at four-year intervals for nearly 1200 years, or put more simply, 300 repeat editions. But each was unique, because each had different athletes, different organizers and a different audience. The format also changed slowly over time. At the beginning, it was a religious festival for the Greek god Zeus and only a 150-metre footrace, the 'stade', was run. At the end, there was no major religious aspect, but the athletics had become the main activity, with 12 or so different sports in the games.

The uniqueness of special events is, therefore, the key to them. We are not doing something that is routine, nor are we producing the same item of work repetitively. Nevertheless, it is important to recognize that certain types of event do recur; they may recur in the same kind of format (such as weddings – each wedding is different but the format or structure is similar), or they may recur on the basis of time interval (such as an annual conference – again the format or structure is the same, but the participants and the subject will be different). Uniqueness alone, however, does not make a special event. Events have a number of characteristics and their uniqueness is closely related to aspects of perishability and intangibility.

audience
The group of people engaged in watching an event or (usually) passively participating in some aspect of the event activities.

Perishability of events

Almost by definition, if we regard events as 'unique', then the event is tremendously perishable; it cannot be repeated in exactly the same way. Two birthday parties at the same location, with the same number of people, will not be the same. Even where a reasonable level of standardization is possible, for example, with activities such as training **seminars**, each will be different and will be very time dependent. They exist briefly and cannot be repeated in precisely the same way. Perishability also relates to the use of facilities for events. Let us suppose we have a banqueting room. It may be used to its peak **capacity** only on Saturdays, for weddings, so the rest of the week its revenue-generating potential may not be exploited. If the room is empty for even one day of the week, the revenue-generating potential of that day is lost for ever – it is perishable. The room can be used on a different day, but the day it is empty cannot be replayed and used for an event.

One of the key issues, therefore, in the events manager's role, is the extent to which facilities and services can be used effectively, given the uniqueness or irregularity (perhaps better to say infrequency) of use. In consequence, events can be expensive to provide. Many items will have to be produced on a one-off basis and cannot be used again. For example, a large banner saying 'Happy Wedding Anniversary Anna and Frederick' would be a unique item and thus (relatively) expensive to provide. On the other hand, a banner saying 'Happy Anniversary' may have a number of potential uses, may be cheaper to produce and could be stored to be used again.

seminars
Describes small gatherings similar to the break-out sessions, where a group, but not the whole plenary, will discuss an issue.

capacity
The maximum number of people who can be accommodated at a venue.

The issue of perishability also means that events venue managers may have to use a variety of techniques, such as differential pricing, to try to encourage activities in quiet periods when a facility or service on offer might not sell. Perhaps a mobile disco can be obtained at a discount for an event on, say, a Tuesday, rather than at a peak period of the week or year, like a Friday or Saturday night or New Year's Eve. This too illustrates the perishability issue; if the disco is not booked one night of the week it will have lost that night's revenue forever.

Intangibility

When you go out to buy a chocolate bar or a pair of socks, you are buying something tangible – you can see it and touch it. With events, however, the activity is more or less intangible. If you go to a wedding, you will experience the activities, join in, enjoy and remember it, but there are only a few tangible things that you might have got from it – perhaps a piece of wedding cake and some photographs, or a video clip you took of the happy couple and the rest of the guests. This intangibility is entirely normal for service activities: when people stay in hotel bedrooms they often take home the complimentary soaps and shampoos from the bathroom or small gifts left for them. These are efforts to make the experience of the event more tangible; a memento that the experience happened and to show friends and family. It is important for **event organizers** to bear this in mind and that even the smallest tangible item will help to sustain people's idea of how good an event has been. A programme, a guest list, postcards, small wrapped and named chocolates, even slightly more ambitious give-aways such as badged glasses or colour brochures help the process of making the intangible more tangible.

event organizers
The individual, or organization, who promotes and manages an event.

Ritual and ceremony

For authors such as Goldblatt, ritual and ceremony are the key issues about special events, the major characteristics that make them special. In our historical examples it was very evident that ritual and ceremony often played an important part. In practice, many modern ceremonial activities are 'fossilized' or reinvented versions of old traditions. The original tradition might have had some key role in the ceremony, now forgotten, but the ritual of doing it (like the inspection of guards of honour) still continues. Often the ritual ceremony is there because it does in fact emphasize the continuity of the tradition, even though the reason for the tradition has gone. In Ripon, England, a horn is blown at dusk to signify the setting of the night-watch. Now it is just a small event for tourists, but in olden days this had real purpose: the town was in open countryside and could be invaded or attacked by barbarians, and the sounding of the horn was to set the guard on the town walls and to ensure that the night watchmen, known as 'wakemen', came on duty. Even this was not thought enough, and because Ripon was a cathedral city, God was appealed to: 'If God keep not ye citie, ye wakemen waketh in vain'. Put in modern English, if God didn't look after the town, the watchmen were wasting their time. Thus, for hundreds of years, this short ceremony has taken place in Ripon and continues on today, every nightfall. The watch is still called to the walls, although the walls are long gone and the last watchman long dead.

Modern events may not, in any way, rely on old tradition and established ceremony. An example of a contemporary specially created event is the Golden Bear awards ceremony in Berlin, an event to recognize good film-making. This 'specially created' event is an example of all kinds of events; in fact, it is often the case that a town or city wishing to attract tourists might do so by creating a new special event, containing a wholly new ceremony, something for the visitors to watch. This can be done for all kinds of special events, making the creation of new ceremonies and 'new' traditions very common. Although it can be argued that for a special event to have a 'traditional' element in it, that element should have some basis – however tenuous – in historical reality.

Ambience and service

Of all the characteristics of events, ambience is one of the most important to the outcome. An event with the right ambience can be a huge success. An event with the wrong ambience can be a huge failure. At a personal event, such as a birthday party, the ambience may be simply created by the people who are there, without the need for anything else – good company among friends can make an excellent event (see Figure 1.4).

Some events, however, may need a little help to go well. At a birthday party, there might be the need for decorations, music and games, as well as food and drink. But it is very important to realize that the presence of these elements does not guarantee that things will go well: there can be a wonderful environment, expensive themed decor, large amounts of excellent food and drink and the event can still be a flop. One of the roles of an events manager is to try and ensure an event succeeds by careful attention to detail and by trying to encourage the desired outcome. Nevertheless, people cannot be compelled to enjoy themselves. If they have had a bad day, or feel grumpy, your wonderfully well-organized event might get them in a better mood, or … it might not.

Personal contact and interaction

In manufacturing situations, customers have no contact with the staff producing the goods, only with perhaps the sales team. In service situations, customers have

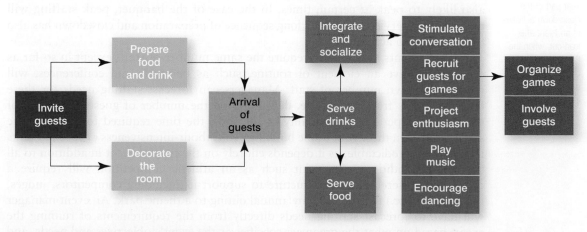

Figure 1.4   Elements in the ambience and service of an event

Based on Berkley, 1996. 'Designing Services with Function Analysis', The Hospitality Research Journal, Vol. 20, No. 1, pp. 73-100

frequent contact with staff and this often determines the quality or otherwise of the experience. People attending events are frequently themselves part of the process. For example, the crowd at a sports tournament is not only watching the event but is helping to create the atmosphere; it is interacting with itself, with participants and staff and is part of the whole experience. Much the same is true of the guests at a Christmas party: it is the guests themselves interacting with each other, with the hosts and perhaps with entertainers, that creates the atmosphere and contributes to how enjoyable the event is. A room decorated for a party may look nice, but will not come to life until it is full of guests.

Therefore, in considering how to make an event successful, event managers must be fully aware that this is largely dependent on the actions and reactions of people attending. It is perfectly possible to have the same event twice in a row, such as a pageant or procession, and one may be a complete success and the other a complete failure, due to audience reactions, interactions or backgrounds. It is vital that event planners have a thorough understanding of their attendees.

Labour-intensiveness

The more complex and the more unique an event is, the more likely it is to be more labour-intensive, both in terms of organization and of operation. The organizational issue relates to the need for relatively complicated planning to enable the service delivery to be efficient, or put more simply, for the event to be a good one (this is why some events may be outsourced to event management companies, caterers or other types of event suppliers). The uniqueness of this type of service implies a high level of communication between the organizer or **client** and the event manager. Such a high level of communication and planning will take time and effort, even where the event may be repeating a well-known formula, or operating within a common framework such as a conference. The operational element may also require high levels of staffing in order to deliver the event properly. A banquet for 300 people will require not only food service staff, but bar and drinks staff, kitchen staff, management and perhaps support staff, such as cloakroom attendants, cleaners and staff to set up and **break-down** the room. Staffing needs are also likely to peak at certain times. In the case of the banquet, peak staffing will take place at service time, but a long sequence of preparation and closedown has also to be taken into account.

No two events are likely to require the same number of staff, except in so far as events that have an element of routine, such as banquets and conferences, will require a known number of staff. Managers can forecast staffing needs for these types of events from experience, depending on the number of guests, the types of service, the experience and quality of the staff, the time required to complete the service and even the layout of the building. The labour-intensiveness of special events is rather less predictable, as it depends entirely on the type of event in addition to all the above conditions. An event such as an athletic competition will require a completely different staffing structure to support it (including competitors, judges, timekeepers, etc.) than a company annual outing to a theme park. An event manager will have to forecast staffing needs directly from the requirements of running the event, based on what the organizer specifies as the event's objectives and needs, and on the experience and forecasts of departmental leaders.

client
The person or organization purchasing or specifying an event.

break-down
That part of the close-down activities of an event after load-out, when the final jobs of site clearance and dismantling of infrastructure are taking place.

Fixed timescale

Events, rather like building projects, run to a fixed timescale, unlike routine activities which can carry on indefinitely. The timescale could be very short, such as for the opening ceremony of a new road; or very long, as with the Paris Exposition noted earlier, where the planning phase took about three years. Even these are not extremes. Many special events are actually composed of a sequence of short bursts of activity, with pauses or breaks in between. Constant ceremony, lasting many hours, might become dull and tiring. The example of the Jubilees show that while these event lasted several days, they were composed of several shorter activities of varying lengths, with breaks, depending on what was going on and why. For those planning special events, this issue of timing must be kept in mind; for an event to be successful and striking, it will need to hold people's attention and interest them, and it is better that this is broken up into sections than it takes place all at once, without a respite. This is not to say that the fixed timescale cannot be varied. Some events, such as a birthday party, may carry on longer than intended because 'it just happened'. Other events may even be extended in a planned way, for some special reason, e.g. to recover the costs or to deal with extra demand, or, of course, they may be shortened because of lack of interest.

SUMMARY

S pecial events have always had a major role to play in human society. In many respects, modern events are not much different from those of ancient times, especially in helping to enliven daily life. In understanding this, we can also see that society has developed and changed. Increasing public knowledge and technology often mean higher expectations of modern events. Whatever role events play in the social context, the management of them can be seen as a service activity. This context helps us understand how events work, what their major elements are and how we can classify them.

EVALUATION QUESTIONS

1 Give a definition of, and framework for special events.

2 Are there other ways we can define Special Events?

3 Provide a categorization for special events.

4 Do these categories overlap, and if so, why?

5 Identify some key characteristics of events.

6 Are some of these characteristics more important than others?

REFERENCES

Gammon, S., in Page, S. J. and Connell, J., (2012) *The Routledge Handbook of Events*, New York: Routledge, pp 104–118.

Getz, D. (2005) *Event Management and Event Tourism*, New York: Cognizant (2 edn) p. 6.

Goldblatt, J. J. (2011) *Special Events: a New Generation and the Next Frontier*, Hoboken: Wiley (6 edn) pp 5–12.

Harris, J. (2004) *The Tallest Tower: Eiffel and the Belle Epoch*, Bloomington: Unlimited (2 edn) pp 1–13, 101–112.

Kamm, A. (2008) *The Romans: An Introduction*, Abingdon: Routledge (2 edn) pp 85–92.

Robinson, P., Wale, D. and Dickson, G. (2010) *Events Management*, Wallingford: CABI, p 4–21.

Swadding, J. (2011) *The Ancient Olympic Games*, London: British Museum Press, pp 5–16.

Tum, J., Norton, P. and Nevan-Wright, J. (2006) *Management of Event Operations*, Oxford: Butterworth Heinemann, pp 9–11.

Wallechinskey, D. and Loucky, J. (2012) *The complete book of the Olympics*, London: Aurum Press, pp 10–27.

CHAPTER 2

THE MARKET DEMAND FOR EVENTS

AIMS

- To examine the scope and scale of the events business

- To consider the determinants of demand for events

- To illustrate the structure of demand for events

INTRODUCTION

It is very common for individuals and organizations to wish to quantify things – we like to be able to say that a particular industry or its market is a particular size. There are several reasons why statistical measurement of events activity might be considered useful. First, data is required from which we can evaluate the significance of events to a particular location, whether that is a town, city or some other geographical region. In this respect data helps quantify the role that events play in the economy and in society. Second, data is essential to the planning of facilities and services. This has been shown in the construction of special sporting facilities, for example, but also for the development of tourism and other community facilities. Third, data is particularly needed by organizations and stakeholders in the events business, by government departments and by individual event organizers for the marketing and promotion of events, for the prediction of demand and for statistical comparisons (Yeoman *et al.*, 2004).

There is a feeling that an expansion of events activity is taking place and this is reflected in the increasingly rapid development of specialist events management companies and related service providers. There may be a number of reasons for this. In Europe, increased wealth (and the associated benefits of disposable and discretionary income) and many years of peace in the industrialized countries have strengthened the inclination to travel, to experience new ideas and to enjoy recreational activities. This, coupled with an active awareness of traditions, has seen an increase and in some cases a re-invention of many kinds of events, especially in the cultural field (such as opera at Glyndebourne and film at Deauville). While this is true culturally, it is also true of the commercial, sporting and personal fields, for much the same reasons. As demand has grown, so too have the mechanisms to supply services to satisfy it, hence the reason for major international organizations and companies taking an interest in event activities. (Cause and effect can be argued here: is the increase in the number of organizations providing events services entirely due to demand, or has the potential demand been suppressed because of lack of available services?) Nevertheless, many of these general demand factors are not apparent to the organizers of individual events, who are probably more interested in the individual motives of participants and visitors, to ensure their event is a success.

Whereas demand for a routinely manufactured product is known and largely predictable, demand for any given event is less easy to predict. This is partly an issue of participants' motives to attend an event, but also because demand might be suppressed by factors not immediately obvious to organizers (such as lack of disposable income for the target market group at a particular time of year). This leads to some unpredictability. Latent demand may also be significant. For example, the demand expansion for Eurostar services through the Channel Tunnel significantly exceeded the expected demand, because it tapped latent (hidden) demand: there were always going to be people who wanted to travel between Britain and mainland Europe with ease, in speed and in moderate comfort, without having to bother with a ferry crossing. This latent demand turned out to be very large indeed. Similar demand aspects may be at work in the events business – who knows how successful an event might be if demand is hidden or latent? This leads to the need for adequate market research, analysis and assessment as a tool in our understanding of how to promote and market events in the light of our knowledge about the market itself and its demand for events, or for a particular type of event or even a specific event (Masterman and Wood, 2006).

SIZE AND SCOPE OF THE EVENTS MARKET

The events market is so diverse and fragmented that it is problematic to say what the business is worth as a whole. In fact, to attempt to quantify it might be a fruitless exercise. Although such a quantification might be seen as a challenge by some academics and researchers, the nature of the business and the limitations of data availability have to be appreciated. Imagine trying to accumulate data for attendance at carnivals in every European town and city.

The student of events management would, therefore, be best advised to steer clear of this problem; indeed, even the serious researcher should not regard an assessment of the total value of the market to be a particularly viable exercise given the lack of suitable frameworks. (Although, as better quantitative information becomes available this position may change.) How, then, can we seek to address the issue of the scope and scale of the events business? This can be done to some extent by breaking the business down into small components. We can then say that a certain part of the business is worth a given amount of money, has a certain number of participants or has a particular impact. We could take a geographical region and ask, 'Can we quantify this type of event in this area?' In some cases this is possible. For example, the total wedding business in a country such as the UK is thought to be worth some €2.3 billion. This is based on the known number of weddings (which are recorded officially) and an estimate of the average cost of having a wedding. A similar kind of exercise could probably be done on a European scale, thus giving us a notional figure for the European wedding market. For some categories or types of events (such as the European Grands Prix) estimates have been made on a European scale. At a local level there are 'toolkits' available for event organizers to estimate the economic impact of their event (Getz, 2007), such as that assessed by Jackson *et al.* (2005) which can be found at the Arts Victoria website: **http://www.arts.vic.gov.au** under resources for community project evaluation.

In building up a picture of event activity we are, in effect, 'building a wall'. At present all we have are several bricks, from widely different sources, and not much by way of foundations. As the events industry is not typically seen as a homogenous whole, there has been no drive to seek common statistical information, either by the industry or by other users of statistical data, such as governments and academics. In the range of events activity, the nature of personal events, voluntary events and similar activities means that almost no data is collected for many kinds of events, except by occasional sampling, or perhaps by the event organizers for their own use or for a few household surveys. Even where events are organizational or commercial in nature, the extent of data collection is very limited indeed and often particular to that event alone. There is no common format even for the collection of attendance data, nor, in the foreseeable future, is there likely to be (although some countries, such as Germany, do require certain types of attendance and other data to be collected for tourist-related festival activities). This means that data collection relies predominantly on a few sources and most often on casual estimates. The accuracy of much event reporting tends to be limited, for a whole range of reasons, not least that accurate data is often collected only for admission paid events. Even then the likelihood of publication is small, since many organizations record data mainly for their own internal use, if they record it at all.

Looking at the problem positively, we can focus on individual events. A practitioner, researcher or student could make a fairly accurate analysis of the size and

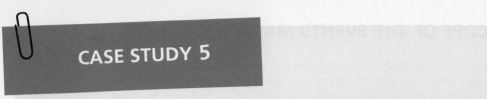

CASE STUDY 5

The size and scope of events: the economic impact study of Edinburgh's festivals

Edinburgh, Scotland

David Lochhead/Shutterstock

Fireworks over Edinburgh Castle at the end of the festival

FACTBOX

- 17 festivals a year in Edinburgh
- Attendance ranges from 400 to 1.5 million people
- The festivals attract over three million people to Edinburgh
- Around €150 million generated by the festivals
- Major local and regional impacts

Learning Objectives

The aim of this case study is to examine the way in which we can assess the economic impacts of an event with the following objectives:

To consider the way in which the economic impact was studied in the Edinburgh examples

To highlight the way in which information was collected and used and so how this could be achieved for other events

To understand what sources of information might be available for the collection of data

A study of the economic impact of the various festivals taking place in Edinburgh was undertaken by SQW Economic Development Consultants and TNS Travel and Tourism in 2005 and several studies have taken place since. The original study provided a framework for studies of a similar type, though other models exist and a comparison of four such models (including the Edinburgh study) was undertaken by Alexandros Vrettos of the University of Maastricht in 2006.

The purpose of the study was to identify the profile of visitors to the various festivals being held in Edinburgh throughout the year and to consider the economic impact in Edinburgh city, its region and Scotland in general. Data was collected from a survey of over 4000 visitors by interview during the various festivals; further material was collected from a survey of performers and participants as well as a survey of hotels and guest participants. In addition desk research was carried out including work on previous economic impact surveys which had been carried out in some previous years. Importantly contact was also made with the organizers of the festivals to obtain details of spending and revenues.

This approach highlights the potential of major surveys to enlighten us about the nature of events. However, it is intensive, costly and time consuming. In this case the funding for the study came from a number of bodies including the City of Edinburgh Council, Scottish Enterprise, Event Scotland and Visit Scotland. Very often our knowledge of the impact of events is limited by the meagre data available and by methodological limitations because professional studies such as this one are quite rare.

In general terms there is a need for a level of uniformity and comparability in the collection and collation of basic statistics for events, and a need for a common framework. This is a task for academics and industry professional bodies (of which there are few). Consequently it may be some time before even the more basic outline of the full scale and scope of the events business is built up.

Discussion Questions

Identify an event or festival in your region and investigate what information the organizers collect about the participants, visitors, income and size of the event:

1 Is this information kept internally or is it disseminated publicly, and if so, how?

2 What key elements of information might help us build up a picture of the events business, how might this data be collected and by whom?

3 What are the current problems and limitations of data collection?

4 For any given event or group of related activities, what sources of information might be available and how might we classify such sources?

Websites

Related website for those interested in this case study: **http://www.efa-aef.eu/** and for event impacts in general: **http://www.eventimpacts.com/**

scope of an event, given time, effort and the co-operation of the organizers. More importantly, in terms of the market demand, once this focus on an event has been made, the market for the event can be analyzed too – we can say what kind of people are likely to attend, or have attended in the past; something of their likely media habits and their motives for going to the event; and what benefits they get from attending or participating. These issues help our understanding of how events and festivals can be planned and marketed and how market information should be recorded. There are five basic areas for continuous monitoring:

- visitor numbers;
- visitor spend;
- visitor activity and participation;
- advertising effectiveness;
- visitor satisfaction.

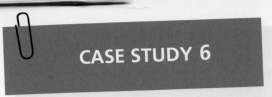

CASE STUDY 6

Estimating market size and scope of events: the UK wedding market

United Kingdom

Harry Page / Alamy

Traditional wedding ceremony

FACTBOX

- UK wedding market
- 283 000 events a year
- Average €8000 per event
- Estimated €2.3 billion market
- Largest components are catering, the reception venue and the honeymoon

Learning Objectives

The aim of this case study is to examine the way in which a sector of the event market is estimated in terms of size and scope with the following objectives:

To consider the nature size and scope of the UK wedding market

To develop an understanding of how the method might be used for other sectors

The wedding market is one of a large number of discrete sectors of the events business, and is also one of a limited number for which there is some assessment of its size and extent. Many component parts of the events business cannot be quantified because of their *ad hoc* nature (e.g. charity events, school sports days, private dinner parties, etc.), and even where there may be potential to collate data about a particular sector of the market it may be difficult to disaggregate the size and extent of the business from other activities.

Both Mintel and Keynote (market research companies) undertake reports on the UK wedding market, as well as a large range of other industry and sector reports on anything from the size of the hotel market to the size of the lingerie market. In attempting to quantify the size and extent of the UK wedding market, Mintel (2009) observes that there is considerable regional, cultural and socioeconomic variation in what a wedding costs. Therefore, even though the national average cost of getting married is thought to be of the order of €8000, this can vary from €5000 to €20 000, depending on location and extent of the celebrations, and comprises a long list of items:

- engagement and wedding rings;
- engagement party, stag night, hen night, evening wedding party, music, band;
- wedding dress, shoes, accessories and bridesmaids' outfits, groom's outfit, going away outfit;
- bride's bouquet, other flowers, posies and corsages;
- cars or carriages;
- registry, church or other venue fees;
- invitations and other stationery;
- photographs, video;
- reception venue or marquee;
- catering and drinks, wedding cake;
- first night hotel, honeymoon;
- various other expenses.

In terms of market demand, the UK wedding market has been gradually declining, with a fall in total number of events from about 400 000 a year in 1981, to 327 000 in 1997 and to 283 000 in 2005, although the average cost of an event has been rising. Some expenditure, such as that on wedding gowns, doubled over a ten-year period to the extent that the average cost of a gown was thought to be almost €1400. The decline, however, in overall demand suggests a change in the social determinants for getting married, in so far as marriage is becoming less popular, and that not only are UK couples getting married later in life, but many are happy not to be married at all. This reflects a change in the family and social structures of the UK, and in the underlying social determinant for being married.

In comparison to many other types of event, the determinants for getting married are primarily social. However, there are a range of secondary motives such as, the ability to have family and friends attend a major life event, and the opportunity, in the case of some types of wedding, to display wealth or status. This change has been somewhat reflected in alterations to English marriage law, whereby couples can now get married in a large number of licensed venues ranging from hotels to castles, whereas prior to 1996 the ceremony itself could only be carried out in a church or registry office. This change has also had some curious side-effects on elements of the wedding market and costs, not only in the changing pattern of ceremonial venues, but also in the perception of suitable clothing for weddings, which has tended to become less formal and more flamboyant.

Discussion Questions

If you have attended a wedding recently:

1   What type of event was it – formal or informal?

2   How many people attended and what was their background: were they family, friends, acquaintances, neighbours, work colleagues – who was involved and why?

3   Was there anything unusual about the event – such as special costumes or a historic venue?

4   Is the market for weddings changing? Is it growing or contracting and why?

5   How is data collected for this type of event, and how do researchers and analysts use the information to produce reports and estimates of size and scope?

6   How could this approach to gathering information and data be used for other sectors, and are there examples of the assessment of size and scope of events available for other sectors? Can you give an example for another sector?

Websites

Related website for those interested in data for the wedding market: **http://hitched-wife.org/**

On this basis, any assessment of the scope and scale of the events business could achieve its ends by looking at the component parts of the business. At an industry level, a note of caution is necessary: we have financial assessments of only a few parts of the total market. The vast majority of elements of the events business have no available estimates of demand, income, expenditure or impact. Indeed, many types of events may never have realistic estimates, especially smaller voluntary events. If we, in our categorization of special events, have included personal events as a key category, there is no way in which the amount of money that is spent on private informal gatherings, such as birthday parties, is ever going to be much more than reasonable estimates, nor for the sake of privacy should this be otherwise. The need for usable statistical data is a key one, however. This being so, event organizers and events management companies need to record more comprehensively the key indicators and publish them in the public domain. This is in order to raise the profile of the industry, assist the planning of facilities, services and training and help focus marketing and promotional efforts.

For an indication of the possibilities of estimating the market for the events business, consider the adaptation of the earlier typology of events in Figure 2.1. From this, readers may wish to insert their own event, or another event known to them, to see how the typology can be applied. Rather like the first periodic table in chemistry, the typology is incomplete, but a means by which we can insert and apply other examples. The vast range of events not listed far exceeds the small number of events that are given as examples of their class. However, there is nothing to prevent an assessment of one event being made in terms of its worth, or of its market. There are even a number of classes of events that could have their worth, market size and market components realistically estimated. This approach, of taking one element (and recognizing it as part of a much greater whole), may be a more useful means of gaining an impression of the scope of the events business.

DETERMINANTS AND MOTIVATIONS

Historically, the demand for events can be seen to have been determined largely by social factors. These included the need for social integration, interaction between individuals and communities, mutual support, bonding and the reinforcement of social norms and structures. In addition there were issues of status, the need for public celebration and the development of religious, civic, trade and community rituals and ceremonies. We might ask why do people attend events, and the answer may simply be that they want to enjoy themselves, celebrate, be happy, be sociable and do something they are interested in.

Events continue to be driven by social and psychographic factors. Human society, while it may have developed technologically, still has the need for integration, interaction and community. In addition to these key social needs, events are also driven by economic, organizational, political, status, philanthropic and charitable needs. The development of events management companies and a larger and more cohesive service infrastructure for events is itself indicative of change in the forces that underpin demand for events activities. In examining the determinants for events we can conclude that the creation of events is also driven by economic factors, an increasing standard of living, changing demographics and the improving education of the population.

Within the European Union a high level of industrial development and general wealth ensure relatively high levels of disposable income, which is increasingly used

Figure 2.1 Assessing market scope and the economics impacts of events

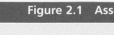

High

Olympic Games:
Full formal
economic and
market Analysis

Avignon Festival
Carnival:
Organizers
economic
and market
estimate

International
Lions Clubs
Conventions:
Informal
economic
estimate

World Fairs
and Expos
Full formal
economic and
market
analysis

National
Wedding
Markets:
Some
analysts estimates

Political
Party
Conferences:
Internal
economic
estimates

French
Grand Prix:
Formal economic
analysis

Uncertainty

London
Motor Fair:
Organizers
economic and
market estimate

Berlin Film
Festival:
Economic
estimate based on
limited data

Local
Agricultural
Shows:
No analysis
No estimates
Little data

Deventer
Bookmarket:
No common
analysis, but
some
estimates

Sales
Exhibitions:
Little analysis,
some estimates,
limited data

Dinner Parties:
No common
analysis or data, and
private.

Village Fetes
and Shows:
No analysis
No estimates

Low

| Individual | Group | Organizational | Multiorganization | National | International |

Complexity

Source: adapted from Slack et al., 2001 Operations Management, London, Pitman, 3rd Edition, pp. 585–95

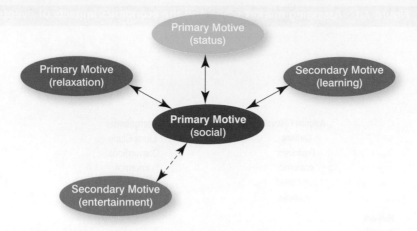

Figure 2.2   A combination of motives for participating in an event, such as an opera gala
Source: adapted from Teare *et al.*, 1994, Marketing in Hospitality and Tourism

towards hospitality, tourism and recreational activities, such as visiting or participating in events. Much the same is true of the commercial sphere of activity (con-
trary to some views of the effect of technology on commercial enterprises) and the
demand for commercial events, such as conferences, exhibitions, product launches
and so on, continues to increase.

In attempting to analyze the key drivers of demand for the events business we can
perhaps conclude that for any given event there is range of motives or determinants.
These motives can be said to be both primary and secondary (see Figure 2.2). For
example, the primary motive for putting on a dinner party may be to entertain one's
friends. However, there may be secondary motives, such as to increase one's status
by showing off a new house where the dinner party is to be held.

The primary motive for holding an athletics competition may be to provide an
opportunity for local athletes to measure their abilities against others; the secondary
motives may be to provide a social integrating mechanism for people with the same
interests, and also, perhaps, to raise money to support an athletics club. We can see from
these examples that there is unlikely to be one single motive for most types of event.

There is a tendency to see the motivation for attending and participating in special
events in terms of personal motivation; indeed Getz (2005) takes this general
approach in considering the satisfying of various personal needs as a mechanism
for getting people to events. Motives for participation in events might be physical,
social or personal, but might also be organizational, and this should not be overlooked (see Figure 2.3). In terms of the primary and secondary motives described
above, the satisfaction of needs can vary considerably from event to event. The
primary need for attending a dinner party might well be the maintenance of friend-
ships, whereas the secondary motive might be to explore the possibility of making
new acquaintances. The primary need for attending a motor show might have
nothing to do with personal needs, but everything to do with the fact that the
organization you work for has sent you for organizational reasons. In this respect,
the classic and often over-quoted theories of motivation, such as those by Maslow do
not provide us with a real picture of why people go to events. Equally, in understanding why people attend or participate in events, a marketing approach that seeks
only to satisfy one single need might not be enough to get people to the event,
without there being some additional benefit or package of benefits.

Figure 2.3 Possible motives for attending events (these may be primary or secondary)	
Examples of Social Motives: Social Interaction with others Creation of community spirit Status or recognition of achievements Philanthropy or charitable contributions	**Examples of Organizational Motives:** The need to make sales The need to have an organizational presence Status or recognition Sponsorship or community support
Examples of Physiological Motives: Relaxation or recreation with others Sexual enjoyment with others Exercise or physical challenge To eat, drink or be entertained	**Examples of Personal Motives:** Seeking new experiences Learning and education Creativity and exploration Fulfilment of ambitions

Source: adapted from Bowdin et al., 2011

Participation in events may be a result of a wide range of potential motives, not just social ones. Personal expectations, tourism, support for other participants in the activity or the propensity to attend events as a form of relaxation or entertainment, may be reasons. In the case of those events for which an admission charge is made, the ability and willingness to pay the price is an issue, and secondary cost implications may also impact on personal events. In the case of the dinner party, whether one's friends attend is not simply a matter of the wish to interact with each other but it is also a question of their ability to do so, in terms of transport to get there, travel costs, distance, time and effort or whether some other personal priority (like the need to look after the kids) exists at the same time as the proposed date for the party.

This does not mean to say that knowing the motives for attendance will necessarily help organizers in trying to discover how many people will actually attend an event. We might find that there is no useful market information whatsoever for an event we are planning, no studies, no collated data. This should not stop us searching for clues. What might be the total market size? What proportion of that total market is in our catchment area? Are there any clues from previous or similar events? Suppose our proposed event is industrial heritage based, for whom might industrial heritage be of interest? How big is the market for it and what might the catchment be? Without research data on market size, we might look initially for other evidence, such as the circulation numbers of popular magazines on the subject (these can be obtained from magazine marketing circulation information, sometimes printed in the magazine itself), although this approach is still little more than guesswork. The same might be true of small events. Our 'first ever' village fête might only have a total potential market of the village population, say a village of 500 people, and not all of these will be there. In short, attendance estimates are just that – estimates. However, the process can, and should, be helped by a little market research: take a sample of the target market and ask them if they are going to attend, but beware – there is a difference between interest and action!

At this point, however, social media may come to our aid. One of the most useful things about the evolution of social media in event marketing is that you can get an idea of attendance in advance of an event from the way people may be talking about it in their social media, whether that is Twitter, Facebook, LinkedIn or other forms. Quite simply, from the personal point of view, knowing that your friends might be attending an event is part of the decision-making process. Although as an event manager or promoter, we may have to consider how to influence decision leaders, in much the same way as we would have to for more traditional marketing methods.

CASE STUDY 7

Motives for attending events: the Berlin Film Festival

Berlin, Germany

cinemafestival/Shutterstock.com

Berlinale Palast, set up for the opening of the Berlin Film Festival

- Berlin Film Festival
- Sells almost 300,000 tickets for a 12 day event
- Screens 240 films
- Attracts major film stars
- Attended by 12 000 journalists and film-makers
- Helps to promote Berlin as an international city

Learning Objectives

The aim of this case study is to examine the development of the Berlin Film Festival and why people attend it with the following objectives:

To consider the historical development of the Festival

To highlight who attends film festivals and why

To understand the differences in motivations of those attending different parts of the event

The 50th Berlin Film Festival took place between 9 and 20 February 2000 in a number of venues and cinemas throughout Berlin. Many of the venues, including the Berlinale Palast, the Cinemax and the Sony complex, were newly opened, as part of the large-scale redevelopment of the city that took place during the 1990s, especially around the Potsdamer Platz, where much of the festival activity goes on. The festival is a major international cultural event for Berlin and attracts not only the movie going public, but also large numbers of celebrities and journalists.

A number of major film festivals have developed over the past 80 years in Europe: 1932 saw the first Esposizione d'Arte Cinematografica in Venice. Held on the terrace of the Hotel Excelsior alongside the Venice 18th International Art Exhibition, as a way of boosting tourism, it attracted some 25 000 people. Later, in 1935, it became an annual event. In the 1930s, Italy and Germany were linked in a political axis and the decision to split the Venice Golden Lion film prize for 1939, between these two countries caused anger in France – which felt that its own film, La Grande Illusion, had lost out to political intrigue. Later that year, France responded by establishing the Festival International du Film in Cannes, although politics made a more dramatic intervention when the newcomer lasted just one day – the day of the outbreak of World War Two.

In 1946, the Association Française d'Action Artistique organized the first full Cannes Film Festival. Then, the festival was a tourist and social event, focused on the few hundred participants who attend a series of parties at hotels along the Croisette and in nearby villas, but as film festivals matured, the commercial aspects began to become more explicit. In 1960, the informal Cannes Film Market, which had grown up alongside the Cannes Film Festival, became an official event; with ten participants (film producers, buyers, etc.) and one screen. By 2002 this part of the event alone attracted 7368 participants, across 29 cinemas.

The Berlin International Film Festival (the Berlinale) was established in 1951, at the Titania-Palast cinema, as part of an initiative to recapture the city's former cultural significance. By 1955, the International Association of Producers, which formally recognizes film festivals, had officially elevated the Berlinale to a status paralleling that of the festivals in Cannes and Venice. In 1978, the Berlinale moved from summer to winter, enabling the expansion of its Film Fair, which became the European Film Market. In 1970 at the Berlinale, a screening of the film O.K. (dealing with the war in Vietnam) caused the jury's resignation and the competition to be halted, prompting the establishment of the International Forum of New Cinema. In 1977, the Berlinale transferred film history retrospectives to the Deutsche Kinemathek and inaugurated the Informationsschau section; the latter evolved into the Panorama. The following year, organizers add the Kinderfilmfest of children's cinema and in 2002, the Perspektive Deutsches Kino section. The 50th Berlinale attracted 390 000 professional and non-professional participants, and 3420 media representatives, from 70 countries, reported the event.

Festivals had to find ways to differentiate themselves, or to respond to changes in festival-goer expectations. So, in 1947, the International Festival of Documentary Films was held at the Playhouse Cinema, Edinburgh, and in its over 50 years' existence it has evolved into the Edinburgh International Film Festival. In 1976, the first Festival Du Cinéma Américain was held in Deauville, Normandy, developing into a competition-based film festival. The Berlin Festival is a means of launching new films, made not only in Europe but also abroad, including the USA. The event is competitive in so far as a jury awards a range of prizes for film-making activities, which are known as Golden Bears (the bear is the symbol and mascot of Berlin). During the 12 days of the 2012 festival 402 films were shown, not only feature films, but also documentaries and shorts. They included some well-known international films and many lesser known ones. Some attracted major audiences not only for the film itself, but also to see some of the stars who attend the festival, particularly where the launch of a new film is taking place. These major films and the presence of their stars can cause chaos, especially with the presence of international celebrities who attract intense attention from fans and journalists.

The Festival not only deals with the main-stream of film-making; there are fringe activities including the 'Panorama' section, which gives advance previews of the next season's films; the Kinderfilmfest (children's film festival); the International Forum of Young Cinema and, separately, the European Film Market, for producers, distributors and other film professionals. Such a major event also attracts political interest, including, in 2011, a visit by the German Federal Chancellor, Angela Merkel, who mingled with the stars at the awards ceremony.

Discussion Questions

1   What kind of people would visit the film festival? If visitors were classified into various categories of, say, film-goers; film-makers; the local public; film stars; film stars' fans; politicians, etc., what

would be their respective motives for going to the festival, both in terms of their primary and secondary motives?

2   How should organizers seek to address the motivations of each category of visitor?

3   Identify a film festival in your region – how many people go to it?

4   How does the distinction between the core festival, 'official' peripheral events and non-official activities, impact on the festival itself? Do the motivations for attending the 'fringe' (the peripheral events) and the motivations for attending the main festival differ (does this also imply different groups or target markets are attending different parts of the event?)

Websites

For those interested in the Berlin and European Film Festivals: http://www.berlinale.de *and* www.filmfestivals.com.

The range of motives can also impact on the attendance for those types of events, such as large-scale festivals, where more than one activity is taking place. In this respect it is highly likely that more than one market segment will be present with more than one motive for being there (see Figure 2.4).

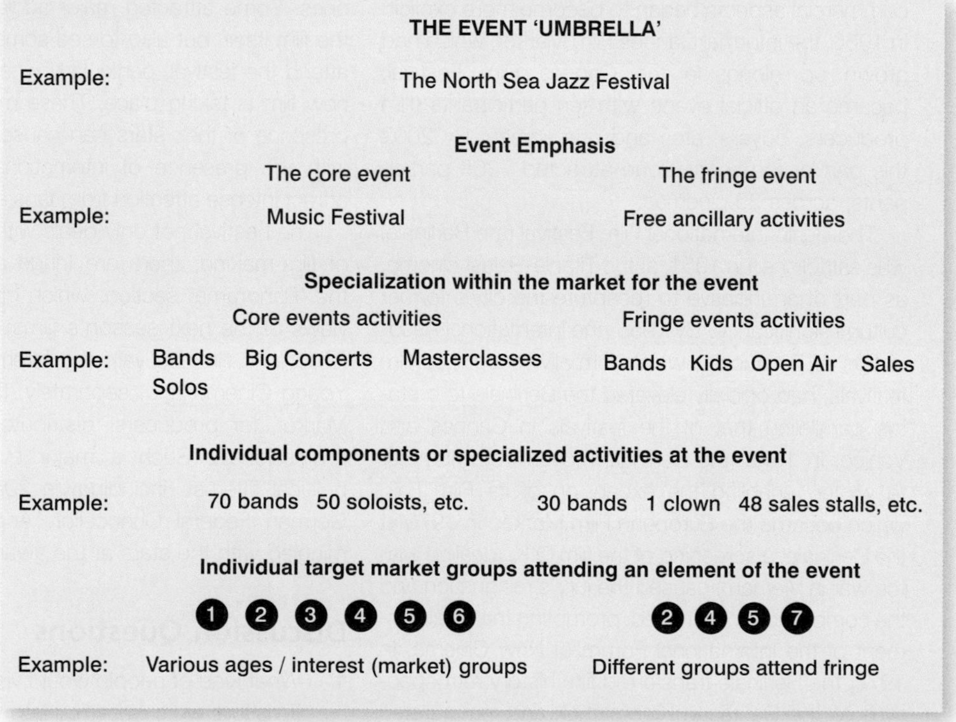

THE EVENT 'UMBRELLA'

Example: The North Sea Jazz Festival

Event Emphasis

The core event   The fringe event

Example: Music Festival   Free ancillary activities

Specialization within the market for the event

Core events activities   Fringe events activities

Example: Bands   Big Concerts   Masterclasses   Bands   Kids   Open Air   Sales
           Solos

Individual components or specialized activities at the event

Example: 70 bands   50 soloists, etc.   30 bands   1 clown   48 sales stalls, etc.

Individual target market groups attending an element of the event

① ② ③ ④ ⑤ ⑥   ② ④ ⑤ ⑦

Example: Various ages / interest (market) groups   Different groups attend fringe

Figure 2.4   Event component mix
Source: adapted from Hall, 1997, Hallmark Tourist Events

In the case of the model, it has been supposed that the event is composed of a number of activities, some of which are core activities and some of which might have 'grown up around it'. This is often true of many kinds of events: conferences, for example, may have associated exhibitions; carnivals may be composed of a large number of different activities linked by the carnival theme. Although an event may be a single activity (such as an anniversary dinner) with one homogenous group of people attending (one market segment), certain types of events comprise a range of activities. These are attended by different groups or segments, possibly with different motives for being there.

THE STRUCTURE OF DEMAND FOR EVENTS

In general, for the event organizer, an interest in the potential sources of demand is key to providing a successful event, because without this knowledge it will be impossible to provide what the target market expects (Swarbrooke, 2002). Indeed, the target market for the event, even if properly promoted, might or might not materialize. This is because for a number of events we are doing something new, and therefore, the estimate of the potential market is just that – an estimate. On the other hand, there are events where the market is known and fixed, personal events being one example. Equally, there are events that, while retaining their uniqueness, recur at intervals, such as annually or biannually, and in this case the market is relatively well known from previous experience. If 5000 people came to a town's firework fiesta last year, and have done so for the past five years, then, assuming all other factors remain more or less the same, there can be a reasonable degree of certainty that 5000 people will come this year. Here, though, is a limitation to the marketing theory that people will come and buy your product or attend your special event provided you have done everything right – it might, for instance, rain on your firework fiesta. To take up a point made in Chapter 1, events are perishable. A one-day event might well suffer from an unexpected external factor, the weather (as with the British Grand Prix at Silverstone both in 2000 and 2012, when rain made access by car to the car parks, which had become muddy fields, impossible; since Silverstone had, and still has, no public transport facilities worth mentioning, the event attendance on both occasions was very nearly ruined), the traffic or a clash with another event; all factors beyond the control of the organizers.

In consequence, there may be all kinds of reasons why an event might not attract the numbers its organizers expect. People might not wish to come to the event at all. On the other hand, the assessment of the market for an event could be based simply on known 'current' demand. This kind of demand may only be part of the event's potential. In terms of new events we may be tapping demand that has been latent or suppressed in some way. There are, in the sense of demand potentials, four kinds of demand (shown in Figure 2.5):

- current;
- future;
- latent; and
- suppressed.

CASE STUDY 8

The event 'Umbrella': North Sea Jazz Festival

Rotterdam, Netherlands

PhotoHouse/Shutterstock.com

Wayne Shorter performs on the opening night of the North Sea Jazz Festival

FACTBOX

- North Sea Jazz Festival – originally at The Hague – held in Rotterdam
- Total participants and visitors: 150 000
- Number of musicians: 1200
- Three-day festival in July
- Held in the Ahoy arenas
- Predominant market: jazz fans aged 35–55

Learning Objectives

The aim of this case study is to examine the North Sea Jazz festival and its 'fringe' from the point of view of who attended and why with the following objectives:

To consider the target markets for this event – why there is more than one market and why do people attend?

To highlight the differences between the main festival and its 'fringe' that is, what may be quite different groups of people attending

To understand how broadly based a festival can become, beyond its original key and central purpose or theme.

There are a very large number of cultural and arts festivals held every year throughout Europe, ranging from folk festivals to poetry festivals, from highland dancing to classical music. Jazz is a major music medium, and there are perhaps some 300 major and minor jazz festivals and events across Europe each year. These are held in all kinds of places, from major cities to small villages, and attract both jazz fans and the general public. There are well known jazz festivals in Glasgow, Scotland; Cork, Ireland; San Sebastian, Spain; Aanekoski, Finland, to name only a few. One of the major European jazz festivals, however, was that held originally at The Hague in the Netherlands: the North Sea Jazz Festival, this moved in 2005 to Rotterdam, having been at The Hague for 30 years.

The Festival attracts, directly, some 70 000 people. It is a three-day event held in July. The programme of jazz bands, groups and musicians is one of the major cultural events in the European calendar, and includes not only the main festival programme at the Ahoy Centre, but also activities for children, supporting sales activities and exhibitions and an additional programme for the public in the city centre, called North Sea Around Town. This part of the festival is held in the afternoon and evenings until midnight, in the form of summer open-air concerts in the city. This open-air programme attracts a further 75 000 people, and adds much to the general atmosphere of celebration and relaxation. It also serves to bring jazz to a wider audience than just jazz fans.

In total, the festival, in its 37th year in 2012, reached almost 150 000 people and was declared the 'Best Jazz Festival of Europe' by *Jazz Times* magazine. The programme, over its three days of events, concerts and open-air entertainment, is provided by almost 1200 musicians. The target market for the event comprises people from all age groups, with the key age group for jazz fans being 35–55 years old. But the event also attracts people from all age groups: families, tourists and people living in Rotterdam itself, from office workers to government ministers. Many of the visitors stay in the city's hotels and guest houses, for which this is a peak period.

Discussion Questions

1 What might be the primary and secondary motives for a jazz fan attending this event or a family attending one of the summer evening open-air concerts?

2 What are the marketing benefits, to the main festival at the Ahoy, of having three days of free evening open-air concerts in the city, for the public? What kinds of businesses in and around Rotterdam benefit from the festival?

3 Do these extra events help create demand for the main event?

4 How does Social Media impact on the demand for an event such as the North Sea Jazz Festival, how does it assist with marketing, and what might be the effect on individual decision making, for example, of finding that your friends are thinking of going to this event through, say, Facebook?

Websites

Related website for those interested in the North Sea Jazz Festival: **www.northseajazz.nl and http://www.northsearoundtown.com/** and you tube: **http://www.youtube.com/user/northseajazz?v=j2bae9lFT-E**

Suppose a town has a range of cultural and sporting events in its calendar. These events take place every year and will often attract different target market groups: those who attend the regional football tournament might not be the same people who attend the annual early music festival. The market for events is, therefore, diverse and changing, and some of the demand is latent or suppressed. Some events will also be more popular than others, some will be new that year, some may not, for a range of reasons (from costs to popularity, or shortage of volunteer expertise), run again next year.

Figure 2.5 Demand potentials
Current demand – that demand which our event satisfies at the moment
Future demand – that demand which our event could satisfy over a normal growth period
Latent demand – that demand which is sleeping until you provide an event for it
Suppressed demand – that demand which exists for our event but which cannot get to it due to being frustrated by price, time, availability, lack of disposable income or other reasons.

So the issue about running an event is not simply about the current market, it is also about whether the expertise, inclination, funding and support exists for an event to be planned and run. In the case of the North Sea Jazz Festival, the event began in 1975 with a small number of visitors, a few venues and fewer than 300 musicians. The level of demand was relatively small, but in each successive year the event has grown, and the level of demand to visit and participate in the event (150 000 visitors and 1200 musicians) could not have been foreseen 25 years ago. At that time, demand for a jazz festival in this location was latent. Rather like building Eurotunnel between Britain and France, the effect was to create a new market and then expand on it. Equally, it is perfectly possible that there might be further potential and unexploited demand for the jazz festival, which is not being tapped for a variety of reasons. This is true of many types of event.

SUMMARY

In examining the scope and determinants of demand for events, we have concluded that due to the unusual and fragmentary nature of the events 'industry' (which includes anything from private dinner parties to the Olympic Games), an overall assessment of the market size of the business is a difficult process. It is preferable to look at individual events or groups of the same kinds of events, to assess their scope, impacts and extent; and although it is possible to make some estimates for certain sectors of the events business, this is not sufficient to provide a picture of the whole. People attend special events for a whole range of reasons; these may be social, organizational, physical or personal. In general, however, events are largely social occasions, and it is in this light that they should be understood.

EVALUATION QUESTIONS

1   Is the events business one unified 'industry' or should it be regarded as having a large number of component parts which differ somewhat from each other?

2   Why do people attend events, what motivates them and how do event marketing staff attempt to influence this?

3   Identify and compare two events you are familiar with from the point of view of who attends them (the demand): what are the differences in the groups attending, why are they different and what implications does this have for the marketing of the two events?

REFERENCES

Bowdin, G., Allen, J., O'Toole, W., Harris, R. and McDonnell, I. (2011) *Events Management*, Oxford:Elsevier Butterworth Heinemann, pp 382–286.

Getz, D. (2005) *Event Management and Event Tourism*, New York:Cognizant, pp 1–23.

Getz, D. (2007) *Event Studies: Theory, Research and Policy for Planned Events*, Oxford:Elsevier Butterworth Heineman, pp 80–89.

Jackson, J., Houghton, M., Russell, R. and Triandos, P. (2005) 'Innovations in Measuring Economic Impacts of Regional Festivals', *Journal of Travel Research* 43(4):360–76.

Masterman, G. and Wood, E. (2006) *Innovative Marketing Communications: Strategies for the Events Industry*, Oxford:Elsevier Butterworth Heinemann, pp 17–35.

Mintel (2009) *Weddingwear Report*, London:Mintel Consumer, Media and Market Research (Accessed 26 July 2009).

Swarbrooke, J. (2002) *The Development and Management of Visitor Attractions*, Oxford:Butterworth Heinemann, pp 58–84.

Yeoman, I., Robertson, M., Ali-Knight, J., Drummond, S. and McMahon-Beattie, U. (2004) *Festival and Events Management: an international Arts and Culture Perspective*,Oxford:Elsevier Butterworth Heinemann, pp 14–31.

CHAPTER 3

THE EVENTS BUSINESS: SUPPLY AND SUPPLIERS

AIMS

- To consider the nature of the events business

- To provide an overview of events industry bodies

- To examine the role of various providers in the industry

INTRODUCTION

The reader will have observed that we have, so far, tended not to refer to the events business as 'an industry'. This is mainly because of the fragmented nature of the activities that make up the huge breadth and range of this business. There is comparatively little explicit structure to it, unlike many industries which perceive themselves as a cohesive whole, for example, banking or retail. There is no one single major supply element to events, although there are some representative bodies, and some understanding that events are a major economic activity, however difficult to quantify.

In contrast to many industries, the events sector is not wholly driven by the need to make money. Indeed, the sector has a very large element of personal, voluntary, charitable and philanthropic activity in addition to what might be considered conventional business aspects and commercial activity. The broad range of events allows all kinds of organizations and individuals to participate in an enjoyable way for the mutual benefit of all concerned. The social benefits of this approach are very considerable, not only in terms of social integration and the contribution that people can make to their community, but also in terms of friendship and good neighbourliness.

This is not to say that a large commercial sector does not exist; it has developed rapidly during the last 20 years and will continue to do so. The market for events has also expanded to the point where the need for a much greater professional input is evident. The increasing number of events management companies and professional events organizers is an indication of this. Events management did not, however, suddenly appear out of nowhere. These businesses have long existed as part of the tourism and hospitality industries, but events management as a stand-alone activity is now seen as commonplace.

As the events sector has developed, the levels of specialization and technical requirements have increased, due to greater expectations on the part of organizers and participants. This has led to a rapid development at venues in event-related services and support organizations (Hassanien and Dale, 2011). While it is still the case that a small personal event, such as an anniversary, may be a comparatively simple affair, with little need of organizational or technical support, larger activities, **VIP** events, launches, **corporate hospitality** activities, competitions or large sporting or recreational events often require a great deal of support from conception onwards (Masterman, 2004). The extent of these services may initially be rather surprising, but think of all the activities that are involved in a carnival, and the potential for complexity in the support of the larger events sector becomes more evident.

VIP
Very Important Person

corporate hospitality
Inviting groups of people, usually clients of a company or high profile organization, to public events.

GOVERNMENTAL SUPPORT INFRASTRUCTURE, INDUSTRY ASSOCIATIONS AND PROFESSIONAL BODIES

A developing support infrastructure exists, which in Europe takes in EU and national government departments responsible for tourism (or sport, culture or the arts, depending on the type of event). For example: the Tourism Division of the UK Department of Culture, Media and Sport; the Ministerio de Industria, Turismo, y Comercio (the Spanish Government Ministry of Industry, Tourism and Trade) and similar government departments exist throughout Europe. This structure also includes national (and regional) tourist organizations (NTOs) responsible for developing and marketing tourism, event and **convention** activities: for example, the British Tourist Authority (BTA), known as 'Visit Britain'; the Netherlands Board of Tourism and Conventions (NBTC) and similar national authorities, who collate information on events and promote and support some of them. National trade associations and industry professional bodies are part of this infrastructure: the Association of Events Organizers (AEO), European Cities Marketing (ECM) and the International Festivals and Events Association (IFEA Europe) are examples. Indeed, there are the best part of 40 industry-related associations in the UK alone and there are probably several hundred such bodies throughout Europe. In addition, regional or local tourist offices and visitor and convention bureaux play a role. Examples are: Visit Birmingham and the Birmingham Convention Bureau; the Scottish Tourist Board; or the Dutch VVV (Vereniging voor Vreemdelingenverkeer); and local or regional tourist information offices in most European towns and cities. Finally, educational institutions, including colleges and universities teaching events management can be regarded as part of this developing infrastructure (see Figure 3.1).

In many cases, especially with professional bodies and with events education, these are still at a fairly early stage of development, largely because of the current rather fragmented nature of the events sector, but the provision is expanding and maturing quite quickly. Indeed, as the sector matures, it is likely that infrastructure organizations will play a greater role (especially where there may be a public agenda for social inclusion or tourism, sport or cultural development activities). Clearly, at the moment, some types of organizations are better developed in some countries than others. Bowdin *et al.* (2011) note the range of associations within the events business is actually quite large, but rather unconsolidated in comparison to other industries.

convention
A conference gathering of greater importance, size and formality; perhaps with more than 300 people in attendance.

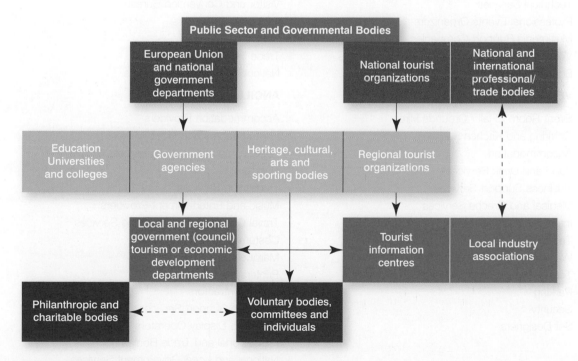

Figure 3.1   Infrastructure of the events business
Source: adapted from Tribe, 1999, *Economics of Leisure and Tourism*

COMMERCIAL EVENT AND EVENT SUPPORT ORGANIZATIONS

logistics
The discipline of planning and organizing the flow of goods, equipment and people to their point of use.

The events sector is not solely concerned with the provision of activities, entertainment, refreshment and **logistics**; it also encompasses a wider range of interlinked services and goods. The larger and more elaborate an event becomes, the greater the need for increased technical and logistical support of one kind or another. With an increasing complexity of needs and demands, the standard of organization required for large-scale events is very high and a whole series of specialist activities has grown up to service these needs. Although many of the organizations in production, distribution, venue and ancillary services might be thought of as private sector, this is not entirely the case, as the quadrant diagram (Figure 3.2) shows.

These organizations typically either package services and provide the whole thing or provide one element of the service needed by an event organizer or organizing

Figure 3.2   Events organizations (commercial and others)

PRODUCTION

Event Management Companies
Event Catering Companies
Party Planners
Production Companies
Exhibition and Theoretical Contactors and Designers
Technical Services
Professional Events Organizers
Multimedia Support Companies
Voluntary Bodies, Committees and individuals
Education and Training

DISTRIBUTION

Individual Events and Venues
Events and Conference Agencies
Trade Media
Hotel Booking Agencies
Incentive Travel Agencies
Visitor and Convention Bureau
Exhibition Organizers
Ticketing Agencies
Trade Exhibitions
National Local Tourism Bodies

VENUE SERVICES

Event Room / Hall / Grounds Hire
Catering and Kitchen Facilities
Accommodation
Food and Drink Services
Business Support Services
Medical and Creche Services
Information and Customer Services
Technical Support
Waste Disposal and Ground Clearance
Toilets, Washrooms and Public Facilities
Parking
Security
Set Designers

ANCILLARY SERVICES

Accommodation Providers
Photographers and Video Makers
Logistics and Transport Services, Ground
Handlers
Translation Services
Music and Entertainment Providers
Travel Companies and Guiding Services
Costume Hire Services
Marquee Hire Services
Printers
Floral Contractors
Database Support Services
Fireworks Display Operators
Professional and Trade Bodies
National and Local Government Services

committee (who may wish to do the rest for themselves). The types of organizations capable of providing complete packages for events are normally:

- Event management companies
- Production companies
- Event catering companies
- Party planners and professional events organizers.

A wide range of companies provide other services which can be hired in, contracted or purchased (depending on the service). These cover directly related services such as the provision of hospitality, or indirect services that exist not only to provide something for the events business, but also perform a function for the local community. For example, transport and guiding services, whose role is to get participants and audiences from the point of arrival to, and sometimes around, a venue; Then there are various other services such as retailing, medical support, administration, secretarial and travel. It can be seen from this approach that a matrix of distribution activities already exists in the events business (see Figure 3.3). There is a range of distribution channels, as found in many industries. For example, when buying a

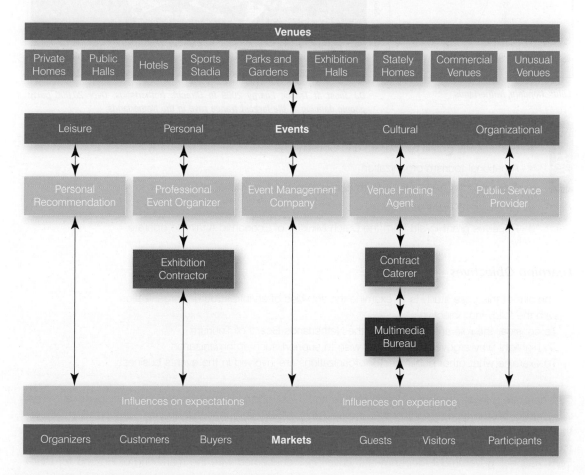

Figure 3.3 Matrix of sample distribution channels and activities
Source: adapted from McIntosh et al., 2009

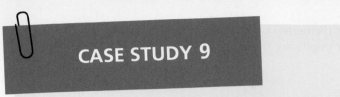

CASE STUDY 9

An infrastructure organization: the Netherlands Board of Tourism and Conventions

Leidschendam, Netherlands

Fotograferen.net / Alamy

DJ Joost at Trance Energy 2009 in Utrecht, Netherlands. Over 20,000 party people dancing at the largest trance rave in the Netherlands

FACTBOX

- Netherlands Board of Tourism and Conventions
- A national tourism organization
- Promotes the Netherlands both domestically and internationally
- Employs 160 staff worldwide
- Receives grant-in-aid from the Dutch Ministry of Economic Affairs to operate

Learning Objectives

The aim of this case study is to examine the activities of an infrastructure organization with the following objectives:

To consider the role and functions of the Netherlands Board of Tourism

To highlight why a government would wish to support such an organization

To examine what other public sector organizations are involved in the events business

There are a large number of infrastructure and public sector type organizations involved in the events sector and the related activities of tourism, leisure and conferencing. These range from national government departments covering tourism, to small voluntary bodies or committees set up to provide or promote a single event. The NBTC is a national tourism organization whose purpose is to promote Holland to visitors both domestically and internationally. It is especially concerned with the marketing of Holland for tourism and events.

The NBTC head office is in Leidschendam with a further 12 offices in its worldwide network including those in Belgium, Germany, Italy, France, Spain, Britain, India, China, Japan and the United States. The NBTC has 160 staff in total and its grant-in-aid for 2009 amounted to €16.5 million for it to operate.

The NBTC is the leading destination marketing organization for the promotion of leisure and business travel to and within Holland. Its marketing strategy, contained in a Strategic Marketing Plan, identifies the target markets which it is seeking to develop by a mechanism known as Product Market Partner Combinations and these include leisure markets such as 'Holland Country Fun' or 'Holland City Style' and business markets such as 'Holland – Be Inspired'. Each year the NBTC promotes a theme or international event, whose purpose is to create greater awareness of the Holland 'brand' and to generate positive public relations and press coverage.

The international event for 2009 was called 'Holland Art Cities' in which the four largest cities in Holland took part in a large scale art and cultural event involving ten major museums in Amsterdam, Utrecht, Rotterdam and The Hague. For example, in Utrecht, a city well known for its architecture, shopping and clubbing, there were special exhibitions at both the Central Museum and the Catherine Convent Museum looking at art and painting, historic manuscripts and architecture and design. These exhibitions were supplemented by related activities including the monthly 'Cultural Sunday' each which featured music, dance, theatre and film in unusual locations.

Discussion Questions

1   Identify one or more infrastructure organizations with an interest in the events business, see what they do and find out why?

2   Why does the Dutch Ministry of Economic Affairs support the promotion of tourism and events and what benefits do these bring nationally to a country?

3   What other national or major public sector organizations may be involved in events and why?

Websites

Related website for those interested in the NBTC: **www.holland.com** and for a thoughtful view of the issue of tourist and events development: **http://www.propoortourism.info/documents/toolbox091106.pdf**.

holiday, the purchaser may go to a travel agent, who might provide a whole package holiday (in the same way that an event management company can provide a whole event package). Alternatively, the purchaser could put together a holiday from various component parts, such as a flight and a hotel, having chosen the destinations using information from a tourist office (thus, in the same way, a client wanting an event could do it themselves by assembling the various parts, a venue, a caterer, an entertainer and so on) (Davidson, 2003). The distribution channels are, therefore, the mechanism by which venues, markets and events activities are put together. The choice of channel depends on the experiences and expectations of the buyer and, by influences such as marketing and public relations that the various companies or other sellers can exert.

The use of these various organizations is a matter not only of budget, but also of the experience (or lack of it) on the part of buyers, of the standard to be achieved at a given event, of the time available to make arrangements and of the requirements of the organization making the booking and completing the planning process. Needs and, therefore, the approach vary.

Event management companies

Event Management Companies (**EMCs**) are a quite recent innovation (but there are historical precedents) and these have often grown out of related service or hospitality providers, which have specialized in providing the complete event.

Events, as we have noted, may range from product launches and dinner dances to themed gala evenings or charity sports competitions. Usually EMCs tend to be involved where the organizers have a requirement for major or VIP events, corporate hospitality or where, for example, a product launch demands specialist design and innovation. The benefit of having an EMC is the range of expertise, ideas and experience they can draw on. Taking the case of a gala evening, such as a themed dinner, the EMC should be capable of providing the expertise for almost any theme the organizer may choose. This will include the planning, menu and theme design; in terms of identifying a suitable menu to go with the theme, as well as full catering support in food production and service at the event. Development of a theme might include specialist sets, props, costumes for participants, and all the range of support requirements from special effects and lighting, to music and entertainment.

The creation of special events of this type is highly complex and, above all, requires extremely careful planning and costing. The choice of the theme itself should be a matter of careful discussion between the event management company and the buyer or client. A great deal depends on the objectives, the venue, the nature of the facilities (such as kitchens and even wash-up areas), the size of the venue, its design features and elements such as the availability of licensing, parking, loading, power and access. However, all these things are within the expertise of an EMC to arrange and sort out, so that a client does not have to do the hard work of organizing an event themselves, but simply employs the EMC, gives them a **brief** and lets them get on with it.

Production companies

Organizers are often confronted by unique problems when seeking to create an event of a professional standard. This is particularly the case for high profile events. The ability to develop such events may be beyond the knowledge of the average organizer who may have been delegated to do the job within a committee or a voluntary organization. Nevertheless, high profile events, VIP ceremonies, **roadshows**, major competitions or product launches, all require specialist technical facilities and knowledge. Increasingly, events of this kind are put into the hands of production companies. These companies are able to package together the wide range of technical support that high profile activities often require. This technical support might range from set design to the training of presenters.

A production company will probably be able to undertake most, or all, of the following activities:

1 Project management, in the case of large-scale projects where the whole event is delegated by the organizer to the production company as a contractor (especially those events that might also involve building or construction, either of the permanent or temporary kind).

2 Design, including set and backdrop design, staging, lighting and all the range of audio-visual support needed for high quality presentations.

3 Venue management, where an organization may, for example, wish to take over a unique venue, such as a castle or stately home, to use for its event and which therefore requires expertise to be brought in that the venue itself might not normally possess (outsourcing).

4 Participant or audience handling, which ranges from the simplest issues of ticketing and security to the full provision of VIP seat booking or allocation of accommodation or pavilion space.

5 Technical support, ranging from simple provision or hiring in of equipment to the full preparation of computer graphics, slide or video production and related facilities.

6 Training of presenters and speakers, often including not only the basic training but also scriptwriting and video production.

Naturally, the packaging of the whole production process does not come cheaply, but production companies have a level of expertise and contacts within the sector that most ordinary organizers may not possess. So that while it might be possible for an organizer to put together a highly complex upmarket event, the organizer would have to be both well trained and extremely experienced to do so. Given that few organizations, especially volunteer ones, possess experienced organizers, it is often necessary to bring in production companies for high profile events.

Events catering companies

One of the most important inputs to the events business is probably the need for catering. This covers all aspects of refreshment for participants, audiences, crew and staff. Catering and hospitality can be provided in three main ways. It is undertaken either:

- in-house (i.e. by an organizer or venue); or
- by contractors permanently employed at the venue; or, alternatively,
- on an *ad hoc* basis at the venue, (i.e. sourced according to the event).

Some venues might not be able to provide specialist catering for an event. For example, for a village fair, the village hall might have a kitchen but no caterer to run it so a contractor or local food provider may have to be found. For these situations the catering arrangements will have to be determined well in advance.

Catering operators range in size and in the types of service they provide and EMCs were earlier mentioned as sometimes having developed from catering operators. The larger contract catering companies also run the in-house services of a number of venues and *ad hoc* provision for conferences, exhibition and other events including corporate hospitality. Independent caterers also have a share of the smaller conference and meeting market. In the price-restricted part of the market, such as for charitable events, there are small independent caterers who provide basic, but sound, catering in the form of buffets. This type of catering for small events may be unserviced, that is to say the food/drink is delivered with disposable plates, etc., and the organizer simply lays it out for participants or guests to eat. Bakeries often provide this kind of unserviced buffet, simply delivered and paid for on the spot and perfectly adequate for the job. A similar service is sometimes provided by supermarket companies.

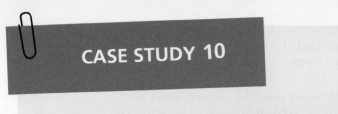

CASE STUDY 10

A commercial organization: Coeva

Paris, France

PsyComa/Shutterstock

French flag on an electric guitar set in front of speakers at a concert

- Coeva, Paris, France
- Specialist events management company
- Provides event and destination planning and management services
- A business partnership
- Specializes in set and scene artwork and design

Learning Objectives

The aim of this case study is to examine the activities of an event management company with the following objectives:
To consider the advantages and disadvantages of using an EMC
To determine why a given event or event organizer would wish to use an EMC
To understand that not all events are suited to a single type of organization

As organizations have begun to concentrate on their core activities, they may not have the staff to do their own event organizing and therefore need an external event organizer, company or agency to do it for them. The task of putting together often complex event activities is taken on by the EMC, which has the necessary expertise and time to achieve a better result. Sometimes this can be via a single professional event organizer, or a company or agency can provide the total package of event organization.

Coeva is a small Paris-based commercial events management organization run by partners Cyril Megret and Julien Potier. Coeva deals with events management activities by co-ordinating collaborators, sub-contractors, artists and other assisting organizations and people, thus operates a network of the support services which may be involved in any one event. This method of organization can be compared with large single company organizations which might undertake all aspects of an event within the company itself.

Effectively, Coeva is a professional services organization with extensive local knowledge, expertise and a network of resources to draw on. The background of the partners is in marketing, communications and the art and design world. Coeva, therefore, specializes in the design and implementation of events, tours and related logistics, so can also operate as a Destination Management Company, providing support for a client's event at any given location within France. Typically Coeva is able to provide events management services for a fairly typical range of events from gala dinners to **trade shows** and from award ceremonies to product launches for different clients of all kinds.

Discussion Questions

1 What are the advantages and disadvantages of an organization using an Event Management Company?

2 As an event organizer, what choices do you have to organize your event – who else could you go to besides either doing it yourself or getting an EMC to do it?

3 List ten events of different types. Which, if any of these events might benefit from the use of an EMC and why? Is the use of an EMC appropriate (or not) to all kinds of events? What other kinds of event organizations exist?

Websites

Related website for those interested in Coeva: **http://www.coeva.com**

Many major hospitality or catering companies have divisions dealing with events catering, sometimes – perhaps wrongly – known as 'Outside Catering'. Events catering companies range in size from small family businesses, which look after things such as local weddings or village fêtes, up to major international caterers which hold contracts for significant large-scale events such as international air shows and sports tournaments, major 'society' weddings, VIP dinners, major corporate hospitality and so on. Consider the complexity and size of the catering provision for the Munich Oktoberfest, the Wimbledon Lawn Tennis Tournament, the Paris Air Show or the Olympics, and it can be seen that this is a very large business indeed.

An organizer may choose any one of the above 'packaging' organizations depending on the requirements of each particular event: what are the event's objectives? Who are the participants? How large will the event be? How complicated will the catering provision need to be? In some cases, it might even be conceivable that all three types of company are needed together, but this is not very common and one will probably have to be the 'lead' organization.

> **trade shows**
> A gathering for a trade or competitive exhibition, often with accompanying social events, a conference or workshops and entertainment, which is probably not open to the general public.

Party planners and professional events organizers

Although major companies, like those above, are common in the events business, so too are a wide range of smaller organizations and individuals willing to provide events-related services. The most common of these are probably party planners and professional events organizers. The first tend to offer a range of services particularly for the personal events market, the second, for the corporate market. This would include the organization of parties, celebrations, weddings, anniversaries and many other similar events. While many people are happy to organize their own events on this small and more intimate scale, not all have the time or wish to expend the effort on doing so, and are happier to pay a professional to come along and deal with all the nitty-gritty detail of planning, organizing, operating and managing an event so that everything goes smoothly. Professional party planners or event organizers are obviously more used to doing this than is the average person, who might only have to put on a biggish event occasionally, and might otherwise have to rely on friends and family to help.

Event promoters

There is a well established group of individuals and companies involved in concert and sport event promotion. Promoters can work for individuals, a company or a particular venue and their role is to contract artists, entertainers or groups either for a single concert, **gig** or event or for a tour (Waddell *et al.*, 2007). This involves having to identify the venues, book dates, deal with the contracting arrangements, market the event in terms of advertising and ticketing, make the necessary licensing, staging, equipment and support arrangements. Most commercial promoters are taking a risk, that is to say they may guarantee an artist or group a fee to perform, they sell the tickets and then they take a share of the profit or have to deal with the loss. It is the promoter who is contractually liable to ensure the various activities take place and therefore, they are also involved in negotiating contracts, advising on legal matters, liaising with designers and printers and dealing with administrative issues such as financial control and record keeping.

gig
A concert of rock, pop, house or other popular musical style.

Exhibition and theatrical contractors

Exhibition (and some theatrical) contractors are a surprisingly mature part of the industry and have existed for many years. Their function is to provide exhibition (or backdrop) services of one kind or another ranging from design and management for large exhibition-type events to the provision of relatively simple one-off stands. Some venues in the field are able to provide in-house services, but may rely on exhibition contractors to create and supply complete shell schemes for exhibitions. Given that some parts of the events market (manufacturing companies, for example) have a long history of organizing combined launch and exhibition events, a number of exhibition contractors also have expertise in events production. However, some specialize and act as suppliers of systems, either for hire or for purchase. Typically, contractors will provide the shells (exhibition booths) in a venue and individual exhibitors will fill a shell with their own material, displays and staff for the duration of the exhibition or show. The contractor will then come in and break down the shells and clear the area.

Technical services and multimedia support

In addition to catering, technical services may be bought in. Not all venues have the technical support or equipment to cope with the full range of services sometimes demanded by organizers. Indeed, the small hotel, marquee or village hall used by parts of the market may have no facilities at all beyond the space and the furniture. Equipment and technical support can be hired in from a range of companies, some of whom simply provide equipment; not, some of whom provide equipment, training and technical support. Presentation equipment can be hired in, ranging from data projectors to computerised and digital display equipment. The higher levels of technology can also be hired in to provide complete presentations on anything from multimedia to video walls. Print shops are capable of copying for guest packs, tickets, hand-outs and support material such as badges or place cards. Video production companies are also common and are used for recording the proceedings themselves, and often have their own recording, sound editing and production facilities. The range of technical facilities provided by the companies in this field is extremely wide and reflects the importance that organizers, particularly of high profile and VIP events, attach to the need for technical facilities, whether this is data or video projection, voice or prompting systems (autocues), or any other of a wide range of technology to support a presentation, a ceremony or commentary at an event.

VOLUNTARY BODIES AND CHARITIES

It must not be overlooked that many events are organized by voluntary bodies, committees, or individuals (either amateur or professional). Voluntary bodies often organize entire events based on voluntary help, or a mixture of voluntary help, support from local authorities and other organizations, or with partial use of commercial organizations in some roles. Essentially, personal events such as dinner parties follow this 'voluntary' framework – you do it yourself or receive help from friends and family to do it and buy your own food from the shops. Another type of organization is the voluntary organization supported by the public sector, as noted earlier – a town carnival might be organized by a voluntary committee, but it also might be helped by the local council's events or tourism department (or a combination of these). Special events organizations should not be seen simply as the province of commercial companies or individuals – these are only part of the whole.

A particularly important category of events often run on a voluntary basis are those undertaken by charities. These can range from activities such as fun runs, money-raising dinners, sponsored events (anything from charity skydives to sponsored bike rides), gift auctions and so on, to organizational support events such as conferences, skills development days, **workshops** and team training for the charity's own volunteers. Charitable events are very wide ranging: money may be needed not just to fund the core charitable activity, but to support the operation of the charity itself such as for:

workshops
A small gathering of people to discuss a specific topic, exchange ideas or solve a particular problem.

- the recruitment of volunteers;
- the provision of funding to make bids for grant aid or sponsorship;
- the payment of expenses;
- the provision of a small permanent secretariat.

In many cases the charity concerned may well organize these within their own resources. Charities often have their own fund raising officers, but in some cases grant-aid may support the provision of a professional event organizer for an ambitious event the charity wishes to put on. In a very few cases, a major fundraising

CASE STUDY 11

Voluntary and charitable events: May the Road Rise

Mediterranean coast

Paul Shawcross / Alamy

Walkers on the the Sentiero Azzurro or Blue Path near Monterosso in Northern Italy

FACTBOX

- A charitable fundraising walk
- 8000 kilometres from Croatia to Spain
- To raise money for three charities
- Involves two people walking barefoot
- Uses social media to help fundraise

Learning Objectives

The aim of this case study is to examine a voluntary and charitable fundraising activity, which uses social media as a method of promotion with the following objectives:

To consider the how charitable funds have been raised in this example

To highlight why the method has been a success

To examine whether it is suitable as a concept for all types of voluntary or charitable organizations

May the Road Rise was a charitable endeavour by two volunteers, Chris Brown and Nick Matthews, to walk 8000 kilometres from Dubrovnik in Croatia to Tarifa in Spain along the north coast of the Mediterranean Sea. This 8000 kilometre walk took them through Croatia, Slovenia,

Italy, France and Spain, with a plan that involved them walking barefoot and sleeping in only the most basic of places en-route.

The walk was intended to raise money for three charities, being The Willow Foundation, Kids for Kids and Epilepsy Research UK. The hope was to raise almost € 1 200 000 to be divided between the three charities, and funds were raised not only through some major single donations but through a large number of small individual ones.

The name of the walk is taken from an old Irish blessing which says:

'May the road rise up to meet you.
May the wind be always at your back.
May the sun shine warm upon your face;
the rains fall soft upon your fields and until we meet again,
may God hold you in the palm of His hand'.

The fundraising method is one based in social media, where donations could be made through the website of the walkers themselves and where their progress and support was given on a Facebook community page 'May the Road Rise'. This method of using the internet to enable people to make donations and social media to help support a charitable cause is increasingly used because of its relative simplicity and its ability to connect charitable activity with support, both financial and moral.

Discussion Questions

1 How were the charitable funds raised in this example and why was the method a success?

2 Could this success be replicated in all cases, or should voluntary and charitable organizations consider other methods of fundraising, if so, why might other methods be better?

3 May the Road Rise is an example of a voluntary project to fundraise, could this type of fundraising be organized in other ways, such as by an EMC. If this were so would there be a financial impact on the actual funds raised for the charity or charities concerned?

Websites

Related websites for those interested in this case: **http://www.maytheroadrise.co.uk/** and Facebook community page, May the Road Rise. For a more general background, discussion papers and material on charitable fundraising see: **http://www.fundraising.co.uk/**

event or activity at national or regional level may involve employing an EMC. However, this is rare, because to do this would mean funding the EMC from within the charitable donations being sought in the first place or from within the charity's perhaps limited sources of revenue. It is much more common, then for charities to operate with volunteers than commercial or private sector event organizations do.

Event management is one of those activities in which there is a large and active voluntary input. Many events, ranging from charity functions to village sports days, from birthday parties to local traditional events, are undertaken by volunteers. This might be family or friends, or a volunteer hobby or recreational club. It might be a small committee set up for the purpose of running the event – anything from an annual rose-growing competition to the recreation of a historic battle in full costume. These types of organization are often overlooked in studies of events activity, as there is a tendency to look at larger-scale commercial professional events as the model for events management. To take such a restricted view would be wrong and would ignore the long social history of events, festivals and traditional folklore activities. A typical voluntary committee might be made up of six or so people interested in putting on a particular event. This group might be already elected to perform some task, in, say, running a voluntary society, as a hobby or recreational club, or might be formed specially to do the job. The effectiveness of voluntary bodies is often very high, due to the commitment, work and effort that the volunteers are willing to put into the activity, and also because of the lengths to which they might go to obtain resources, help, facilities and services for their event.

It is also the case that, for larger or more important events, these might be planned and managed through co-operation between volunteers and professionals. An event might be volunteer managed, through an executive committee, but employ a professional events organizer to plan and run the event. On the other hand, a professionally managed event might still need to use volunteers as staff, but might also need to co-ordinate the activities of a range of voluntary bodies to produce an event such as at a carnival (where the professional organizers might be the city council tourism department, co-ordinating the efforts of everyone from the city band to the local majorettes). The organization structure may, therefore, vary from event to event depending on factors as diverse as the objectives of the event or the resources (in terms of staffing and management, for example) available to run it. (Goldblatt, 2011)

It is often the case that the running of events involves some outsourcing of activities and there are advantages to this such as the bringing in of professional support or new ideas. However, outsourcing has some clear disadvantages and these need to be considered, especially if an event organization is still capable of providing the key or core activities itself. Outsourcing often leads to a loss of direct management control over the activity. Let us suppose a hotel currently does its own room cleaning through its own room attendants (chambermaids), but is persuaded to outsource this key activity to a contractor. The intention behind this move may be to provide the room cleaning more cheaply via a contractor. But we have to bear in mind that a contractor has to make a profit above providing the service which was originally provided internally with no such requirement before. How is this done? The answer is usually that capacity is stripped out in order to make the service cheaper and give the contractor the profit. This may seem acceptable until the outcomes become clear over time. For example, the results may be for example a poor quality of cleaning, lack of commitment to the host organization (that is to say the contractor's staff have no loyalty to the hotel), or a failure to deal with guests properly because the contractor's own staff have no stake in the success of the hotel. This translates as the "Where is the bar?" question – when the hotel employed its own maids, they could always answer this question and many others which guests may put to them. With contracting staff, they have no stake in doing so, so the answer may become "I don't know", which then results in reputational damage for the hotel.

Other implications of the failure of outsourcing were spectacularly illustrated by the G4S scandal during the London 2012 Olympics, where the contractor failed to provide enough security staff and the UK army had to be called in to cover the shortfall. The lessons drawn from this outsourcing failure were that not only was there a loss of management control, but the outsourced company did not have the capacity to make up for the problem. Indeed the capacity failure was highlighted more clearly when it became clear that only the army was funded and staffed sufficiently to cope with the problem, that is to say it had capacity slack or spare inbuilt capacity. In some cases where an organization provides a service internally, the spare capacity or capacity slack which is inherent to it is not obvious until there is a crisis: which the organization can still cope with. If all inherent capacity is stripped out in the name of short-term profit, the resulting outsourcing failure may have the potential to crash the event.

SUMMARY

The events sector has seen the increasing development of commercial companies with specialist roles in management, production and hospitality. Some of these companies, such as exhibition contractors, have been around for many years; some, such as production companies and events management companies, are relatively recent. The governmental infrastructure of the events sector is also becoming more evident, with an expansion of interest from tourist authorities and government departments, and an increasing number of trade and professional bodies. The breadth of the events sector is such that there is also a very considerable voluntary element, organizing anything from small personal events to local shows and sporting competitions. The size of this voluntary element is difficult to judge, but it is as much a key component of events activities as the developing, commercial and public or governmental infrastructure elements.

EVALUATION QUESTIONS

1   The events business is composed of a wide range of different organizations: identify those that you might regards as 'commercial' and those you might regard as 'non commercial'.

2   What government support or 'infrastructure' does your country provide for the events business and why?

3   Voluntary organizations, groups and committees are important to the organization of many events, especially community and charitable events, why is this and why do people put such efforts in?

4   Identify the advantages and disadvantages of outsourcing.

REFERENCES

Bowdin, G., Allen, J., O'Toole, W., Harris, R. and McDonnell, I. (2011) *Events Management*, Oxford: Elsevier Butterworth Heinemann, p 29.

Davidson, R. and Cope, B. (2003) *Business Travel*, Harlow: Pearson, pp 42–55.

Goldblatt, J. J. (2011) *Special Events: A New Generation and the Next Frontier*, Hoboken: Wiley, (6 edn) pp 17–35 .

Hassanien, A. and Dale, C. (2011) 'Towards a typology of events venues', *International Journal of Event and Festival Management* 2(2):106–16.

McIntosh, R. W., Goeldner, C. R. and Ritchie, J. R. B. (2009) *Tourism: Principles, Practices & Philosophies*, New York: Wiley (8 edn) p 182–208.

Masterman, G. (2004) *Strategic Sports Event Management*, Oxford: Butterworth Heinemann, pp 7–24.

Waddell, R. D., Barnet, R. and Berry, J. (2007) *This business of Concert Promotion and Touring*, New York: Random House Watson-Guptill, pp 3–26.

CHAPTER 4

SOCIAL, ECONOMIC, POLITICAL AND DEVELOPMENTAL IMPLICATIONS

AIMS

- To consider events in the context of the environments in which they operate

- To examine the social, economic, political and developmental factors which impinge on the running of events

INTRODUCTION

It would be very easy for us to see special events purely in a social context. In the past, many events were mainly personal and private affairs and the implications of having a special event in a community were largely social. An event such as a village wedding was both a cause for celebration and a means by which the whole village could interact together. Indeed, events of this type often involved the whole community in some way, in addition to the immediate families of the couple to be married. There were often local rituals to be undertaken; these varied from place to place and were part of the social fabric and history of the area. Such rituals, now often long forgotten, served to reinforce community ties and to make events different in many small ways from those of their neighbours. Local village events, for example, were sometimes much rowdier and more spontaneous than today (e.g. May Day), but many of these local traditions faded away during the Victorian era as the nature of society changed, to be replaced by a rather more constrained way of doing things. The reason for this loss was the rather fossilized nature of Victorian society and a tendency in our modern society to regard spontaneity as odd or out of place; as such we had forgotten many of the traditions and differences that characterized our communities until the 1840s. However, the social context is only one element of events and there are many other implications in the modern world (see Figure 4.1 below).

We may regard events only in one particular way, but if we are to take the events business as a whole, it operates within an environment of constant change, and a number of methods of gauging or assessing this exist. We will examine the context in terms of examining the social, economic, political and developmental factors of the world in which events operate, There are, however, other methods, and we will note some of them. A tool used commonly in management and marketing fields is the PEST analysis, which is a mechanism for assessing the market in which a business as a whole operates. Other techniques can be used, such as SWOT analysis, which is a mechanism for assessing how a business unit, an idea or a proposal for a new product (or event) would operate or to judge whether it would succeed or not. In so far as we are looking at events in context in this chapter, we have tended to use the PEST approach, as it can be taken in its component parts to show how different events may have different or mixed implications.

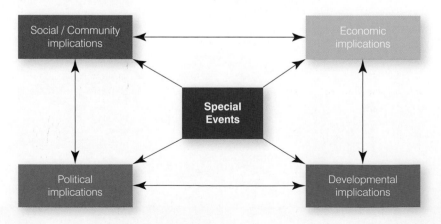

Figure 4.1   The implications of special events

The main components of PEST analysis are Political, Economic, Social and Technological issues and implications. To these can be added a number of other components, and these vary depending on the nature of the assessment being carried out, for example if this were a financial assessment, then a Finance component could be added; if this were an assessment of Industrial change, then an Industry component could be added. However, we are tending to approach our assessment within a framework of looking at the implications of events within their operating or marketing context. So we could use the PESTELI approach, which assesses events or the events business in terms of Political, Economic, Social, Technological, Environmental, Legal and International issues and implications. But bear in mind, importantly, that this approach does not work for everything. Small events (which form the very basis of the business and the vast majority of activities) simply do not require this level of consideration. Nor do most small events organizations or individual organizers have the time or inclination to undertake complicated assessment, they would be perfectly happy with their own instinct about their own local area, its needs and issues. Only when we are considering major events AND have sufficient management expertise available are managerial assessment techniques used.

Returning then from the dizzy heights of management assessment, we can consider smaller scale issues. Local events, for example, are frequently seen in terms of the community, and event managers often go to some lengths to involve the local community. Social integration is not the only outcome of many modern events, because as the size and complexity of events have increased (especially in organizational and sporting events), so have the potential impacts on the economic and political life of the area, or community, whether that is a town, city or region. For example, tourist towns and resorts have long understood the benefits of running special events during the tourist season, perhaps to bring more people to the town (and thus encourage further spending in local shops and businesses) or to extend the season in some way. The Blackpool illuminations, that great triumph of light and colour, with its several kilometres of lights, displays, tableaux and illuminated trams, were intended to extend the tourist season. In this it has very much succeeded, and the event attracts a huge number of people from all over the North of England and Scotland every year, giving the resort's economy a very significant boost.

Looking again at major events, some of these, especially national or international sporting events, play a political role, in addition to the social and economic roles. The Olympics are a prime example of this. There is considerable international competition to stage the games; on the one hand because of their perceived economic and developmental benefits, but on the other because there are also positive political impacts. Impacts such as improving the international image of a country or, in the case of some types of event, as a means of gaining other political benefits such as kudos or public exposure. For this reason politicians often attach themselves to activities such as the Oscars or award ceremonies, as they gain from the reflected glory of the celebrities and the winners attending such events.

SOCIAL AND COMMUNITY IMPLICATIONS

Human society is complex and interactive, and all human societies celebrate, whether they are modern and technological or old and traditional. The means of celebration is very diverse. Sometimes special events are spontaneous – your friends at work find out it's your birthday, and almost straight away they've got you a card, found a cake (even if it's just a muffin with a candle), and opened a bottle of wine (which, being alcohol, is banned from the premises by the tedious management, but hidden by the wise staff). These events serve to strengthen social bonds as well as to spread enjoyment around. Many events are less spontaneous and more carefully planned, but those events whose progress is frequently planned down to the last detail, such as weddings, have significant social implications (Bowdin *et al.*, 2011). They have an impact on participants' emotional and intellectual outlook, in terms of pleasure, social interaction, stimulation of the mind and the senses – ranging from the consumption of food and drink, to enjoying the atmosphere (or not enjoying it, since not everyone likes every event), participating in activities such as games or dancing, or doing unusual or sometimes outrageous things.

There are a number of more general social implications of having a special event. In community terms, many events, particularly personal ones and events run by the community itself, have the benefit of improving social ties and are an opportunity for the community to demonstrate that it can pull together for the greater good. These can be anything from local arts festivals to the Eurovision Song Contest. Even a tree planting day or street party can provide such opportunities. The role of events in encouraging social interaction and the celebration of happy occasions is probably more important in a society which, as a result of modern media, modern work methods and the relative decline of the 'traditional' family structure, feels a greater need to maintain social contact. Without the social contact that events often give, the feeling of social isolation in a society where even work can be conducted in a solitary way, such as from a computer in the home office, can be very great. Human beings are social animals (an issue typically overlooked in the hype that often goes with new technological innovations), and the growth of the events business may in part be due to the need to increase opportunities for social and physical interaction in the community, at a time when less interaction is possible in the work or home environment than at any time in the past. In such a case, organizations (particularly those that rely on technology) may have to give more serious thought as to how to help their employees interact and develop the social skills and interests that are the key to maintaining a cohesive social structure.

Social impacts can also be seen in a wider context, perhaps as a potential mechanism for strengthening weak community structures in a particular location. The Notting Hill Carnival in London was one of the major driving forces behind improvements in relations between local communities with different ethnic backgrounds and ultimately helped to drive forward many community social and political initiatives. But care must be taken not to see special events as some kind of panacea for local social or economic problems. Events may provide positive impacts, but there may well also be some negative impacts, which may be unexpected or unplanned (Deery, 2010). There are no panaceas, only a range of tools which, if handled correctly, and if well received on the part of local people, might work positively for the benefit of all. You cannot impose a special event and say: 'There you are, enjoy that'.

It is very easy and very common for events only to be understood in, say, economic terms, because these are the easiest to measure. However, many events have only modest economic or general impacts or none at all. For example, small community events, which form a large percentage of events staged, should be seen in terms of a wide range of implications, of which the economic ones might only be of the most minor kind. Let us suppose a local hobby club such as a hockey team wishes to gain new members. It may be that the way of doing this is to hold a 'new

CASE STUDY 12

Community implications of events: Giant Mountain's Beer Festival

Vrchlabi, Czech Republic

Beer and wine festivals are popular in many European towns and cities

FACTBOX

- Giant Mountain's Beer Festival, Vrchlabi, Czech Republic
- Annual event
- Typical small community event
- Attracts local people and tourists

Learning Objectives

The aim of this case study is to examine the social and community context of an event with the following objectives:

To consider the role and functions of the Beer Festival in the life of the small town of Vrchlabi

To highlight why small community events remain important

To examine some positive and negative effects of events

The small town of Vrchlabi, north west of Prague in the Czech Republic, is typical of many communities throughout Europe, which run modest local events and festivals. The town has a population of about 13 500 and was historically known for the mining of stone and gems. It is in a pleasant mountain area which is now popular for winter sports such as downhill and cross-country skiing, as well as hiking, walking, mountain biking and hang-gliding in the summer. The town's chief features are its Baroque town hall, Renaissance castle and the monastery of St Augustine.

The town holds a number of events each year, of which the most well known are the Medieval Festival and the Giant Mountain's Beer Festival. The beer festival has (up to 2012) been running for 15 years and attracts not only local people but also visitors to the Krakonos region, as well as tourists from further afield including many from other countries. This is not a huge affair though, at most perhaps 1000 people may attend at any one time and the event is essentially a day event, starting at 09.00 on the Saturday (usually the second weekend in August) and finishing at 02.00 on Sunday morning. The Festival is organized by the local civic association, a role which might be performed in other towns by all kinds of community bodies such as the Chamber of Commerce, the tourist office or the town council itself. Often, though, in small towns, the town council has too little money and too little time to put on events and so, like in Vrchlabi, event organizing is down to willing volunteers with the council and other local bodies acting as partners. Two members of the Vrchlabi Civic Association split the task of organization between them, with assistance from a small group of other people and local volunteers. The two main tasks comprise the organization of the programme, the bands, performances and security on the one hand; and arranging the provision of the beers, catering and sales stands on the other.

The beer festival naturally offers beer and in the 2012 event beer was available from eight different breweries for visitors to taste, drink and compare. The event also provides an opening ceremony with the town mayor and the mythological figure of Krakonos (King of the Mountain) doing the honours. For the rest of the day, the town square hosts the event, and in addition to the provision of beer, there are stands and side booths which sell food and other refreshments as well as local items and craft goods. By way of entertainment there is a competition to judge the best beer, which appears to operate by the simple technique of people voting on a voting paper: the beer with the highest pile of voting papers (measured with a micrometer if necessary) wins. In addition there are other activities such as a beer barrel rolling competition and throughout the day entertainment is provided by a series of local bands including the town and local brass bands, visiting bands and tribute artists.

As with many small community events, the implications and issues of running such an event are modest. The event brings in visitors and money to the town, but being a one-day event we probably shouldn't think in terms of 'economic impact' (this often implies something bigger) but more in terms of the modest income to the event, the town and its businesses (Hall and Sharples, 2008). The Giant Mountain's Beer Festival pays for its costs and makes a small profit or contribution for the organizers. The brewers and the bands, the stall holders selling food and other items all make some money. Local shops, cafés and other businesses, such as guest houses, self-catering chalets and suppliers in general all benefit. Some visitors to the beer festival will stay the whole weekend and their contribution to the local economy will therefore be greater than those just attending for the day. Not only because they are staying overnight, but also because they may undertake some other activity on the Sunday, perhaps visiting other local tourist attractions, hiring mountain bikes and again buying things in the shops, cafés and inns of Vrchlabi. The negative effects of running the event are wear and tear (small routine damage) associated with increased numbers of visitors, additional litter, issues of traffic congestion, parking and noise, and maybe a few drunks to take home in wheelbarrows at the end of the night. These small negative effects are part of the price we expect to pay for the enjoyment and greater benefits of an event: even if you have a dinner party for friends at home, you still have to do the washing-up and tidy the house in the morning.

Discussion Questions

1   From your experience of events, make a table showing the positive and negative effects of an event. How can the positive effects be increased and the negative effects contained? (Remember you are never going to eliminate negative effects completely, any more than you can avoid tidying up after a party!)

2   'Economic impact' is a term which we often associate with large-scale events. Can this term be applied to local events, and if so how?

3   In small towns and communities, can events be of genuine help in maintaining community spirit, strengthening social ties and promoting the economic well being of a place?

4 Events alone would not be enough to sustain the economic and social life of a community. Why is this and why might events be seen as only part of the means of keeping a small community going?

Websites

Related website for those interested the Giant Mountain's Beer Festival: **http://www.krkonosskepivni slavnosti.cz/dear-visitors/**

For a quick list of 'important' things for a beer festival see: **http://www.morningadvertiser.co.uk/ Business-Support/How-to-organise-a-beer-festival**.

members' day' event which will attract public attention, and thereby generate interest and the desired new members. The event may make no money, because it isn't intended to do so, and have no other measurable impacts, but it still has to be organized, be promoted and be interesting to fulfil its purpose.

We can look at many small community events in this way. A local brass band competition may be held for the pleasure of competing and entertaining the public. Its economic impact may be non-existent and the only monetary implication might be that a small admission charge is made, or a raffle held to raise enough money to pay for the venue or contribute to some new instruments, the upkeep of the band room or help pay the routine bills. In small communities, villages and towns, events are often a social exercise. They are put on for the pleasure and enjoyment of the community and they might be socially or charitably orientated (Raj, 2003). Annual village fairs and festivals often fall into this category, their primary purpose is not to attract visitors or tourists; the event simply serves to provide some social cohesion and interaction for the local people and to generate a spirit of goodwill and happiness. We can look at the many kinds of events put on by a local village or town and study what the implications are. You could do this for a place near you: put together a list of all the events you can find which occur there and then consider what they are for, and what the implications are. In all probability there will be a range of events, some social, some charitable, some sporting, some celebratory and so on.

Events can be seen in terms of performing a social role and acting as a stimulus for other related activities, such as tourism. For a town or city wishing to become a tourist destination, elements such as attractions, accommodation, transport, infrastructure and facilities must be present. In looking back at the historical development of some major destinations, it can be seen that all these are present, although the destination may not have had anything to offer in the beginning apart from a natural attraction (such as a beach or a rural landscape). This has been the case for resort towns such as Brighton (England), Howth (Ireland) or Scheveningen (the Netherlands). In addition to the attractions of the seaside or countryside, some towns have relied for their tourist development on the architectural attraction of a great building, such as a castle or stately home, or of an event such as a market, fair or religious festival. Some destinations developed simply because royalty or the upper classes visited them, such as Brighton, where the Prince Regent kept his mistress (see Figure 4.2).

Figure 4.2   Development of tourist destinations: some examples

Location	Origin of Tourist Interest	Type of Attraction
Brighton, England:	Sea bathing, Prince Regent's Mistress	Natural/Man–made attraction
Salzberg, Austria:	Historic medieval city	Man-made attraction
Scheveningen, Holland:	Sea bathing, proximity to the Hague	Natural attraction
Interlaken, Switzerland:	Lake views and scenery	Natural attraction
Galway, Ireland:	Galway Arts Festival, Galway Races	Event attraction
Gleneagles, Scotland:	Golf and golf tournaments	Event attraction

A destination was often intended to build on existing elements such as a pleasant location, warm climate or tourist attraction in or near the town; and the availability of local accommodation, places of refreshment (restaurants and cafes) and good transport networks (by road or rail) also helped. In many tourist resorts there was no major physical attraction, such as a museum or theme park, but often the tourist season could be driven entirely by special events, anything from a carnival to a jazz festival or air show (see Figure 4.3).

In looking at the social implications of events, we have seen that the main impacts are for events to create better social interaction, help develop community cohesion, increase cultural and social understanding, and improve the community's identity and confidence in itself. These are very important gains for many communities. We must, though, sound a note of caution, particularly for large scale, mega-events. As with some of the issues of sustainable tourism, depositing a major international event on a small undeveloped community could do some damage to that community, perhaps resulting even in the destruction of its identity, particularly if the activity is badly handled, organized without thought for the outcomes, or without regard to the occupant capacity of the location (i.e. how many people the location can cope with). Nevertheless, the vast majority of events have tremendous positive outcomes: they serve to celebrate and to entertain, to strengthen and improve social bonds, and they increase community involvement and confidence.

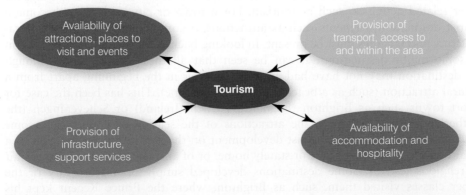

Figure 4.3   Elements of tourism

ECONOMIC IMPLICATIONS

The impacts on a community of a major event, be it a sporting event, or a large cultural event such as a festival, can be looked at in terms of cost–benefit analysis or through economic multiplier analysis (Lilley and DeFranco, 2003). An event itself may not, for example, provide huge direct employment or income, but the indirect effects on local businesses, local services and local infrastructure and environment could be extremely significant. A number of festivals have had this type of analysis carried out, such as the Edinburgh Festival, where about 85 per cent of income came from tourists, making the impact rather greater than if the money had simply been 'recycled' by local people (i.e. spending money on a festival, art activity or event, rather than on some other local activity such as day-to-day shopping). (For a summary of the recent economic impact reports see: **http://www.festivalsedin burgh.com/content/festivals-far-reaching-impact-revealed.**)

The indirect effects of incoming spending of this kind may include the support of activities such as retailing (visitors buying anything from magazines to clothing) and catering (visitors using restaurants, coffee shops and pubs), to less obvious visitor support of services such as transport, taxis, printers, technical equipment, local musicians and entertainers, marquee contractors, photographers and many other types of supplies and suppliers. Some towns, cities and resorts have seen events as their economic salvation when other forms of tourism, such as business, or heritage tourism, might not be appropriate to their area. It is also thought that events that have many participants, as opposed to many spectators, have a greater economic impact on a destination. Thus, it might be quite reasonable to say that a fairly low-key event, such as a three-day international conference of dentists, might have more economic impact than, say, a premier league soccer match, because even though the soccer was higher profile, its spectators are more transient. A number of event-stimulated developments have been undertaken on this economic basis, such as the construction of Symphony Hall in Birmingham or the Exhibition and Congress Centre in Maastricht.

This is not to say that the running of a major special event is the correct solution to the economic problems of any town, city, region or resort. If a public body, such as a city council, invests in an event, or in the physical event facilities, it must perhaps forego investing in something else, say an industrial or retail development. There is an opportunity cost, and even a danger that the event might itself run at a loss. In considering the possibilities for the economic regeneration of an area, the running of a major event is only one option, not a panacea, and may be a significant cost or burden on the sponsoring organization, such as a city council. For this reason, special events are often used as part of some wider initiative, so that an element of synergy can be gained from the event in conjunction with, say, building a new arena. Equally, it might be recognized that the objectives of a particular event are to provide short-term, not long-term, gain. This objective alone might be worthy enough.

In the context of a community, the running of a major event is often perceived as having a positive social and economic impact, in much the same way that the construction of a factory or tourist attraction would. This economic impact is not very well documented, but some studies, especially of sporting events, such as games and Grands Prix, give various clues as to the benefits of events. In the case of some events, the operation and running of them is seen as a matter of civic business. That

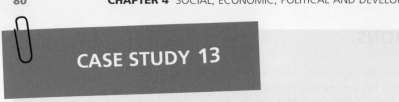

CASE STUDY 13

Economic implications of events: Liverpool European Capital of Culture

Liverpool, England

PAUL ELLIS/AFP/Getty Images

The Kaiser Chiefs perform at Anfield, the home of Liverpool football club, during the Liverpool Sound Concert on 01 June 2008 in Liverpool, north-west England

FACTBOX

- 7000 events and 10 000 artists
- 15 million visits to a cultural event or attraction
- 13 Royal visits, two Presidential visits and one EU Commissioner visit
- €250 million global media value
- Estimated €1 billion economic benefit to the Liverpool City Region

Learning Objectives

The aim of this case study is to examine the economic context and implications of an event with the following objectives:
To consider the effect of a major cultural event
To discuss how the economic effects of an event might be measured

In 2003 the city of Liverpool (England) bid to be the European Capital of Culture, as part of an initiative by the European Union. Liverpool represented the EU area and Stavanger (Norway) represented the non-EU area. Liverpool invested some €150 million from 2003/04 to 2008/09, with some €15 million in sponsorship revenue.

The Chair of the Judging Panel, from the UK Government, noted that: 'there was a greater sense ... that the whole city is involved in the bid and behind the bid'; hence, the bid's success came as less of a surprise to the locals than it did to those linked to the 11 rival bids. After this promising start, there were concerns over the planned events and the original Artistic Programme Director left, before local TV executive Phil Redmond came in as Creative Director.

The Liverpool 08 opening ceremony attracted some 50 000 people and was held at the popular and recently restored St George's Hall (itself built as a venue for music festivals), but became sunk in a controversy when, rather tactlessly, Ringo Starr, formerly of The Beatles, said, after his performance at the event, that he missed nothing about the city.

The University of Liverpool and Liverpool John Moores University established the 'Impacts 08' initiative, to undertake qualitative and quantitative research into the impacts of the year. They estimated that the Tall Ships event brought in some €10 million and the Liverpool Sound concert, featuring Sir Paul McCartney, a further €7 million. While some 75 per cent of new visitors are said to have cited the 'Capital of Culture' as influencing their decision to visit. The Impacts 08 team sought to adapt the framework into an international model that can be replicated for future Capital of Culture research.

Some 67 000 schoolchildren are said to have participated in around 7000 events, some 3.5 million first-time visitors are claimed to have been attracted and both an 08 Volunteer programme and an 08 Ambassador scheme were established. Supporters pointed to the inclusive nature of events, detractors spoke of a limited geographical and social focus. The 125 'Superlambananas' that were designed by artists and community groups, though, demonstrated how such events can unite communities and visitors; the original Superlambanana sculpture

[part lamb, part banana] was first loaned for a previous cultural event, but became a popular part of the city's street scenery.

As with many events of this type, Liverpool had to cope with the fact that the large-scale urban regeneration that was partially designed to attract visitors often took place during the event itself, with the need for the city to avoid having all the first-time visitors needing to navigate a building site. The €1.25 billion, 42 acre Liverpool One retail-led complex, that looked to both benefit from the Capital of Culture initiative and provide a focus for post-event developments, found itself opening just as a recession hit, time will tell if it will prove an overall benefit in the longer term. Claire McColgan transferred from the Culture Company, to become head of culture for Liverpool City Council, in order to lead a team of 25 people and distribute some €6 million in funding for cultural events in 2009, to continue the event's cultural legacy – in line with the aim of repositioning Liverpool as a world-class city. Post 2008 sustainability was also sought for tourism and community engagement.

Discussion Questions

1 How should you measure the impacts of events – in what terms and over what time period?

2 Could you adopt the same approach for both Liverpool and Stavanger?

3 How do the issues above compare with other events, of all sizes, that you have looked at?

Websites

Related website for those interested in the impact of events:
Liverpool Culture Company final report: **http://www.liverpool.gov.uk/Images/tcm21-160685.pdf**
08 Impacts website: **http://www.liv.ac.uk/impacts08/**
BBC News: **http://news.bbc.co.uk**.

is to say, the event may be organized or even sponsored by the city or town council and based at least in part on the economic and social benefits that it brings to the community, in terms of increased numbers of visitors or an increased visitor spend. Given the size and extent of some events, the economic and social benefits may be very great.

POLITICAL IMPLICATIONS

In past times, it might be thought that the political implications of events were relatively modest. However, this is clearly not so. For example, the political nature of the Roman gladiatorial games was well understood, and the ability of the Roman emperor or members of the Roman upper classes to put on a major spectacle contributed much to their status. Similarly, in medieval times much political status was attached to royal events such as jousts and tournaments. Therefore, certain types of events do have political impacts, even if that impact is only to provide a mechanism to indicate some form of political status. The opening of the town's festival, or a civic reception to celebrate some new feat of progress, are opportunities for the mayor and council to be seen in public, officiating at the ceremony with appropriate purpose and dignity. The political implications are simply that the town's dignitaries are expected to be seen doing what the townspeople elect and pay them to do. In this respect many modern events fulfil the same purpose, and politicians gain the benefit of being associated with useful civic activities and positive special events.

The genteel pride with which civic dignitaries were regarded is sometimes neglected today, but towns and cities often organized events or constructed things that demonstrated their commitment to the good of the general population and to mark some technical or civic progress. This might be anything from the construction of a new hospital to the maintenance of some curious quirk of local tradition (such as 'cheese rolling' in Brookworth, England; 'phallus dancing' in Tyrnavos, Greece; 'raisin weekend' in St Andrews, Scotland; or any number of other weird traditions still taking place around Europe). Old photographs of ceremonies and celebrations often focus on this aspect of civic pride, something that, in our modern age, can be overlooked in an effort to seem 'modern', but which was, in past times, crucial to the ritual and traditional nature of events and added to the political status of those dignitaries involved.

Today, it is major events which tend to attract the attention of politicians (and media). and we may observe the very political nature of events such as the Olympics as well as events designed to influence public opinion about a particular politician or ideology.

public events
An event attended by members of the general public.

High-profile **public events** are attractive as mechanisms for producing social and economic benefits of the type noted earlier, and can focus and stimulate political will to promote and run them. Many events can be extremely positive in creating useful outcomes for the nation, region or area concerned. Nevertheless, political interest (see Figure 4.4) in an event may not be related to the good of the community or the local population, and there may be a hidden political agenda behind the event (such as influencing the programme or types of performance allowed). Indeed, there are examples of dictators and corrupt politicians attempting to use events to distract attention from some political problem they have created, or as a mechanism to improve their negative image. It is, therefore, important to understand that some types of events may well have a political element, and the student and practitioner of event management needs to be able to recognize when that political element may or may not be positive.

Having sounded this note of caution, the most common political outcomes of events are positive and useful. A major event held in a town or city might not only help provide social and economic benefits such as community cohesion, jobs and

CASE STUDY 14

Political implications for events: Salzburg festival

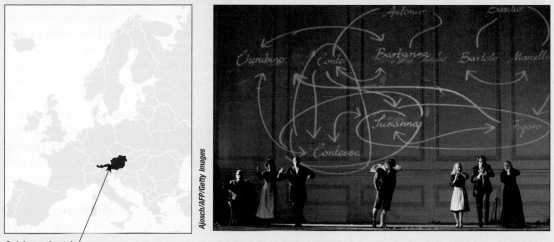

Salzburg, Austria

Ajosch/AFP/Getty Images

Dress rehearsal of the opera 'Le nozze di Figaro' by Mozart during the Salzburg Festival

FACTBOX

- Salzburg International Festival, Austria
- Established in 1920
- In 2008, 250 000 visitors attended the 189 events comprising the festival and spent €21.8 million
- 4876 journalists from 30 countries attended
- 75 per cent of visitors were from outside Austria

Learning Objectives

The aim of this case study is to examine some political implications seen over the long history of the Salzburg Festival with the following objectives:

To consider the creation, development and expansion of the Festival under different political conditions

To examine what impacts the decisions of a sponsor might have on the style, atmosphere and success of a Festival

To examine what might be gained by having a range of funding sources for an event

After several years' work, Max Reinhardt, with several friends and colleagues, succeeded in establishing a music festival in the Cathedral Square, Salzburg, Austria, during 1920. Although a lack of finance caused a break in 1924, the festival grew, under Reinhardt's volunteer directorship, into an international event, expanding into several venues and beyond music into drama. Quickly moving onto the international stage, the festival began radio broadcasts within five years (radio being relatively new at that time). The festival has continued to the present day, despite various political difficulties in the 80 years of its existence. Today a public square in Salzburg is named after Max Reinhardt.

In 1950, the Salzburg Festival Foundation was set up, which put the event onto a formal and professional basis with a board of directors, and in 1952 the festival became a founding member of the European Festivals Association. The Festival benefits from the efforts of a broad base of supporters, ranging from high-profile managers to experienced arts patrons, who, since 1961, have operated under the umbrella of The Association of Friends of the Salzburg Festival. In 1983, performances were relayed live for the first time to visitors in the Cathedral Square. During the 1990s organizers began long-term co-operation with sponsors such as Nestlé, ABB and Allianz, and a reorganization of the festival's board and activities took place, introducing such innovations as subscription tickets for young people and 'Curtain Up' access to rehearsals.

The expanding 'festival district' now encompasses permanent venues, e.g. the Festival Halls; historic properties, such as the Felsenreitschule or Summer Riding School; open air and temporarily covered spaces, including the Cathedral Square and the courtyard of the Residence. This evolution in its organization demonstrates both the financial scope of large festivals and the civic pride that they can build upon. The festival, during its long existence, has contributed significantly to the revitalization of Salzburg as a cultural centre (together with the city's association with Mozart), and to the imaginative use of many of its fine historic buildings for public activities.

The importance of the Festival to Austria's image has, however, resulted in the rather unusual outcome that the Festival is subsidized extensively by the Austrian Government, and the county and city councils of Salzburg. This may seem an excellent arrangement, and for some festivals, the availability of a modest subsidy has a financial, artistic, sporting or community benefit out of all proportion to the amount of the subsidy. The strangeness of the Salzburg Festival subsidy is that it is provided by law (a political decision) – the Government and the councils have to pay for any deficit the Festival makes.

This may seem a wonderful idea (for the taxpayer to comprehensively support a Festival in this way) but the unintended consequence has been that the Festival Board has no incentive whatsoever to manage costs terribly well, nor has it any incentive to manage demand properly. In the case of demand, this has resulted in low ticket prices and big demand, so although the tickets are attractively cheap, many people can't get them because they run out (Frey, 2000). After all, there is limited capacity of seating at many venues, so what is happening with ticket prices is that capacity is not being managed by adjusting the price elasticity of demand to match capacity, but simply by running out of tickets. The consequence of this is a black market in tickets and that many tickets only reach potential visitors in a discriminatory way, that is you may have to 'know someone' at the Festival to have a chance of getting a ticket.

Another consequence of obtaining government or other subsidies for festivals and events (and this is a general point) is that such subsidies will normally come with some kind of string attached. That is to say, the subsidy giver will probably want to exercise some influence over the festival or event. Although such an influence may appear harmless and benign, one has to bear in mind that politicians, in particular, have their own wishes and agendas. What may result is some constraint on the festival, its programme, its venue or its visitors, which was not foreseen by the festival's organizers and which is ultimately detrimental to the event.

Discussion Questions

1 What benefits has the festival brought to Salzburg, and for whom?

2 What problems might be associated with the success of a festival and how might they be addressed?

3 What kind of influence might a subsidy giver (or a sponsor) wish to have over an event? Could such an influence grow over time to the extent that the freedom of action of the event organizers was constrained by political or bureaucratic influences? What might these influences be?

4 Different events are funded in different ways (e.g. ticket revenue, sponsorship, advertising, subsidies, income from support sales and commercial activities such as catering). Is having more than one kind of funding stream important, and if so, why?

Websites

Related website for those interested in the Salzburg Festival: **www.salzburgfestival.at**, and for those of you who are looking for something more casual in Salzburg, here is the flashmob: **http://www.youtube.com/watch?v=WKAJ3GacO2Q&feature=related**.

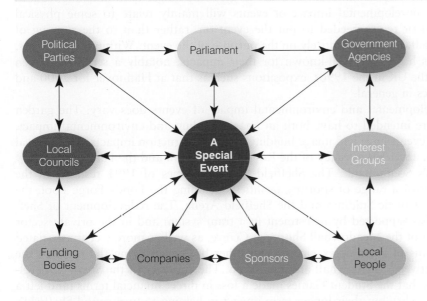

Figure 4.4 Political stakeholders for events

income to local people, but it might significantly alter the image of the place in the long term. This can be a useful outcome especially for those locations that might have endured a long period of economic decline or social drift, for which a major special event could not only rekindle community involvement and civic pride, but also transform visitor perceptions of the place from negative to positive. This role is often performed by the designation of a city as a European City of Culture or similar local initiatives to change an old image.

DEVELOPMENTAL IMPLICATIONS

By their nature, the vast majority of special events are fleeting, with little or no developmental impact. It is necessary only to consider the large number of, say, weddings that take place, to recognize the limitations of most kinds of event in terms of developmental and environmental impact – there is no impact, apart from having to sweep up the confetti. This is true of most events. Even some larger-scale events, such as a horse-racing day, might have little long-term impact except to provide some manure for the roses. It is therefore important not to get carried away on the bandwagon of environmental impacts, sustainability and disturbance. To do so would demonstrate a poor understanding of the real nature of most events as modest, passing affairs.

A few events, however, have some developmental impact, usually because this is a specific aim of their creation. Developmental events may be used as one tool in a toolbox of potential mechanisms for redevelopment, image-building and regeneration, as a means of producing some positive outcome. This outcome might be to support tourism or to improve the environment of a given location. There could be other ways of achieving this. It might be easier and more cost-effective to construct a new business park, hospital or conference centre, rather than to invest time and money in a developmental event in order to get some longer-term outcome from it. Indeed, the developmental impact of events will mainly relate to some physical construction or re-use needed to put the event on, rather than to the running of the event itself. It depends entirely on the purpose of the event. Within these caveats, some events have been well-known for their impacts, notably a series of garden festivals in the UK in the 1990s, expositions such as that at Hannover for 2000 and the Olympics in general.

The developmental and environmental impact of events does vary. The garden festivals were intended to have both an image-building and environmental impact, while other events have had image building and reconstruction impacts. The Festival of Britain of 1951 left a legacy of the Royal Festival Hall and the Hayward Gallery on London's South Bank. The Sheffield Student Games of 1991 resulted in the development of a range of sporting facilities, including the Ponds Forge Pool, the Don Valley Athletic Stadium and the Sheffield Arena. The redevelopment of Sheffield was also supported by investment in a tram system and in the private sector construction of the Meadowhall Shopping Centre, as well as more recent associated work in terms of a multiplex cinema and other businesses along the route of the tramway between Meadowhall and the Arena. The curiosity of the Sheffield development was that the Student Games made a loss in direct financial terms (and left a €64 million debt), but their longer-term impact in helping to turn round Sheffield's once grim image and stimulate other developments has been substantial. The exhibition ground of the Hannover Expo 2000 is still in use for major fairs in Germany and the area around the Expo Plaza has been turned into a centre for information technology, design, media and the arts. Further Expos have taken place in Japan (2005) and at Zaragoza, Spain (2008). Yet the scale of development Expos or of the Olympics, for example, is unusual: most special events have no such impacts, and do not need to, as these are not part of their objectives.

Our assessment of the context of events has been based around the four factors of social, economic, political and developmental issues. However, we should for the benefit of those familiar with other methods, touch on some other contexts. These include Technological, Legal, Environmental, International and Industrial contexts. For example, we have noted that in PESTELI analysis (see Figure 4.5), the most common components are Political, Economic, Social, Technological, Environmental, Legal and Industry implications. Readers may wish to choose a method of assessment, based on the components we have given in detail above and add (or subtract) different contexts depending on what kind of assessment they wish to carry out. Let us suppose it is PESTELI. We already have some details for political, economic and social impacts, and it might be considered that we have touched on environmental issues when discussing developmental implications.

Developmental implications: the Olympic Games in context

London, England

The Olympic flame is lit during the 2012 Olympic Games opening ceremony in London

ALLSTAR Picture Library / Alamy

- Ancient Olympic Games first held in 776BC, last held in 393
- Restarted in modern times in 1896
- Held every four years
- Modern games are a major economic activity
- A key issue in the London 2012 games was the redevelopment legacy

Learning Objectives

The aim of this case study is to consider the development of the concept of the Olympic Games over time with the following objectives:

To consider the history of the Games from earliest times and major steps in the development of the Games towards their modern incarnation

To highlight how the Games have changed over time and how decisions made at different points in time have affected the nature of the modern Games

To examine why legacy now seems to be an important aspect of the planning of the Games

The Olympics are a global phenomenon in the events management firmament, seen as boasting a global reach that none can match and a heritage that stretches back to the ancient world. Yet, as recently as the run up to the 1984 games, it was seen as a poisoned chalice and many of its traditions are fairly recent additions.

Emperor Theodisius abolished the original Olympic Games, along with other pagan festivals within the Roman Empire during 393 AD, though there were irregular attempts to revive them. In England, Robert Dover is credited with establishing the 'Cotswold Olimpicks' including a shin-kicking contest, the day before Scuttlebrook Wake Fair in 1612; while an 1833 poem by Alexandros Soutsos, in the Helios newspaper, recalling the glory of the ancient Olympic Games, encouraged moves towards a revival in their homeland of Greece.

In 1850, Dr Brookes established the Wenlock Olympian Class, within the Wenlock Agricultural Reading Society, Much Wenlock, England, and is credited with organizing the 'Wenlock Olympian Games', as an attempt to revive the Games; the events were a mixture of athletics and traditional country sports such as quoits, football and cricket and awarded small cash prizes. By 1859, Evangelos Zappas inspired by Soutsos' poem was organizing the first of four 'Zappian Olympic Games' which are said to have combined: a fair, trade exhibition and athletics meeting in Athens – again athletes compete for cash prizes, including one donated by Dr Brookes. In 1865, Dr Brookes and others established the National Olympian Association and, the following year, organized a version of the Games at the Crystal Palace, London. In Greece in 1870, the Panathenean Stadium had been restored in Athens, for the second 'Zappian Olympic Games' – 31 athletes competed across nine sports.

From 1875 to 1881 archaeological excavations of the original site of the Games at Olympia further boosted interest in reviving them and in 1894 Baron Pierre de Coubertin helped to found the International Olympic Committee (IOC); intending the games to coincide with the 1900 Paris International Exposition. Greek honour was aroused however and in 1896 the IOC organized the first modern Olympic Games in Athens. Underwritten by George Averoff and held in the restored 45 000 seat Panathenean Stadium, the games attracted some 285 male athletes from 13, mostly unofficial, national teams competing across ten disciplines – the opening ceremony being held on the 75th anniversary of Greece's independence from Turkey.

The IOC then held the Games as part of the 1900 Paris International Exposition, at the Parc Vincennes, welcoming the first women athletes. Some 1066 athletes, from 22 national teams competed, across

15 disciplines, and attracted around 48.1 million visitors – but, the Games returned a loss of some FF (French Francs) 82 000. Originally scheduled for Chicago, the next Games formed part of the 1904 Louisiana Purchase Exposition. Some 680 athletes, from 12 nations, competed across 17 disciplines, but the event was sparsely attended and the US team won all but one event. In 1906, having refused an application for the Games to be based permanently in Greece, the IOC allowed the Interim Olympic Games (or 'intercalated' games) to be held in Athens; celebrating the 10th anniversary of the modern Games – the last time that they were not held in the first year of a four year Olympiad.

The 1908 Olympic Games were scheduled for Rome, but had to be relocated after the 1906 Mount Vesuvius eruption. The breadth and depth of sports administration made Britain an ideal last-minute replacement and, so, the Games were held at the Shepherd's Bush Stadium ('the Great Stadium'), London, following on from the Franco-British Exhibition; while other events were held at Henley (rowing), Bisley and Uxendon (shooting), the Solent (motorboats) and River Clyde (yachting). Allegations of domestic bias did, though, prompt a series of protests and saw these as the last games that a host country had jurisdiction over. The 1906 Games also introduced a system of Gold, Silver and Bronze medals and saw the first winter games represented – these not being separated until 1911, and the later success of the 1924 International Winter Sports Week at Chamonix.

The Olympic flag and oath appeared at the 1920 Antwerp Games, while Citius, Altius, Fortius (Faster, Higher, Stronger) became the official Olympic motto, at the 1924 Paris Games. An Olympic flame was kept burning, for the first time at the 1928 Amsterdam Games; while the Olympic logo and Olympic Village first appeared at the 1932 Los Angeles Games. The 1936 Berlin Games were a particular milestone. Not only were the Games televised, but Leni Riefenstahl made the influential 'Olympiad' documentary – for which several ceremonies (e.g. the torch-relay from Olympia, carrying the Olympic Flame lit by the rays of the rising sun) were introduced and in which several sports-filming techniques (e.g. cranes, tracking rails, cameras in pits or rising up flag poles) were pioneered. The 1948 London Games were the first to be widely televised, when the BBC paid some £1500 for the rights.

Following the riots ahead of the 1968 Mexico Games, the tragedy at the 1972 Munich Games and the debt left by the 1976 Montreal Games, the movement entered a low period. Innsbruck hosted the 1976 Winter Games for the second time, after Denver defaulted; the 1980 Moscow Games prompted a widespread boycott and not only was Los Angeles the sole bidder for the 1984 Games, but it was not even the city itself which bid. The organization of the 1984 Los Angeles Games, though, was seen as demonstrating that the event could be both profitable and beneficial; after that, an increasing number of venues vied for the Games. After the 1994 Lillehammer Winter Games, the Winter Games and Summer Games now alternate, biennially.

The heightened profile that followed the successes at Barcelona in 1992, and Sydney in 2000, was overshadowed by governance issues linked to the awarding of the Winter Games to Salt Lake City and a judging debacle in its ice dancing competition. The expenditure of the Beijing Games and violent clashes during the torch-relay in 2008 heightened the challenges that the London 2012 games faced, in terms of raising finance during a recession and ensuring the promised 'legacy'. The movement faces further challenges, as it wrestles with doping regulation, regulating athletes' clothing and equipment, rationalization of the participating sports and risk management issues in the future.

The 2012 London Olympics ran for 17 days from the 27 July to 12 August, after over five years' preparation work, planning and reclaiming a site situated along the Lower Lea Valley at Stratford, planting it as gardens, parkland and countryside, constructing the Olympic Stadium, Olympic Village, sporting facilities and infrastructure. Key issues were not simply the provision of the games themselves, but also the encouragement of young people's involvement in sport, and from the developmental point of view, the legacy of the games in terms of

its potential to regenerate the area covered by the Olympic Park and other local development outcomes (Clark, 2008, Maennig and Zimbalist, 2012).

Clearly, the objective of land reclamation had already been achieved: the area of the Games had been transformed from its almost unusable derelict state as largely former industrial land to a condition where it was pleasant and suitable for further re-use once the Games finished. Second, the image of Stratford and adjacent areas such as Hackney benefited considerably, as people visited the Games who would otherwise previously never have gone to such a run-down area. The change of image helped stimulate the third and final aim, that of economic regeneration and achieving inward investment (i.e. attracting new businesses and thus providing jobs). The Olympic Park's legacy is a reclaimed area, with good transport infrastructure capable of supporting modern housing, new schools and community areas with some of the reclaimed land remaining in use for a shopping centre and a park with nature trails, a lake, gardens and woodlands, and a number of the features that were originally in the Olympic Park itself. The outcome resulted in economic regeneration, the provision of an improved local environment capable of attracting visitors and one of the largest urban parks built in Europe, with a lasting legacy of sports facilities both for local use and for national and international athletes.

Discussion Questions

1 How has the perceived legacy of the Olympic movement contributed to the modern Games?

2 What organizational issues determine the success of such a global, migratory event?

3 Which cities and countries could/should host future Games?

4 Are such events necessary, or are there other methods of improving the environment in run-down or derelict areas?

Websites

Related website for those interested in the Olympics: **www.olympics.org** and for interesting comment and critique of the Olympics 2012, search: **www.guardian.co.uk/**.

Figure 4.5   PESTELI analysis factors

Technological implications are those issues which impact on events in terms of technological change. On the one hand we can see that the rate of technological change in the events business is relatively slow. The Olympic Games of 2000 years ago would still be recognizable to us today, events, are in essence activities in which the main component is people, and we would hope, happy people. Having said that there are changes in technology which have implications for participants, organizers and managers and these might, for example, be new technologies in ticketing, communications, marketing, energy use, mobile technology, lighting, sound and ancillary systems. New inventions and developments are taking place all the time and technology transfer from other industries (e.g. till systems, or display methods) is quite rapid. The development and expansion of renewable energy sources such as solar and wind power also falls into this category. It might have been virtually impossible 20 years ago to provide a major power source in the middle of a remote event location (a field or mountain) without bringing in major infrastructure. Today a few solar panels, their battery or storage support and accompanying switching might easily be provided to power a remote location at very little cost to the event organizers.

Legal issues cover changes to the context in which events operate in terms of changes to the law and legislation, which might originate at an international, national or local level. This can include anything from impacts on employment of paid staff, the use of volunteers or charitable support staff, to implications about the use of different types of material and equipment (some older materials might be banned, some new ones introduced). It also includes the introduction of legal controls on a whole range of issues from the supervision of children to the signing of contracts for supplies and facilities.

Industry implications are often about changes to the structure of an industry or the market in which it operates, and in some cases such change is very rapid. Think, for example, of the decline of the nuclear power industry in the face of the faster development of clean renewable energy, or the centralization or contracting of a manufacturing industry in response to difficult economic circumstances. These changes might be at a global, national or local level and might be linked to several of the other contexts, notably the economic and political contexts.

SUMMARY

The extent to which special events impact our lives may surprise the uninitiated. Daily life is improved in many ways. If this were not so, events would have had little or no impact on the cohesion of human society. In fact, events have a major impact and have been a feature of society from its earliest beginnings. Events serve to strengthen social bonds, to bring enjoyment and celebration to individuals, families, communities and society as a whole. There are also economic and political benefits, including the provision of direct and indirect employment, the enhancement of facilities and the improvement of local services, which are often stimulated by events. While some large-scale or developmental events may give us pause for thought about their wider impacts, especially culturally or politically, the vast majority of events serve to improve and enhance our society, at a time of significant social change.

Events can also be seen in the context of promoting and sustaining tourism. Not all tourist destinations have physical attractions; consequently, some destinations rely on a continuing programme of events during the tourist season to sustain them. This ensures both the provision of short-term events-related jobs and, crucially, helps to secure permanent jobs, which a small town might not otherwise be able to retain without the continuing stream of events visitors and tourists. In this respect, the involvement of locals, for example, in running their own small sales-stands at fairs and shows, in catering, and in casual employment in key activities, helps to keep tourist spending in the local economy (much more directly than it would if tourists simply spent their money at national chain retailers in the town). The focus on community involvement in events is, therefore, important and methods of engaging the community need to be carefully considered, especially by event tourism providers.

As a generality, we can assess or examine the events business in a number of way and with a variety of management tools. Not all parts of the events business would do this, for small local or community events there is no need and no management expertise to do it, and nor should we expect it to be done. However, on a larger scale, for major or international events, or for the business as a whole it is possible and perhaps useful, to assess the context or contexts in which we operate and it may be a useful and thought-provoking exercise to do so.

EVALUATION QUESTIONS

1 Identify the range of contexts in which major or international events operate.

2 Consider a major international event you are familiar with and list the factors which might impinge on that event using the PESTELI framework as your guide.

3 Why are advanced management techniques of various kinds unsuitable for all events, especially small community or personal events?

REFERENCES

Bowdin, G., Allen, J., O'Toole, W., Harris, R. and McDonnell, I. (2011) *Events Management,* Oxford: Elsevier Butterworth Heinemann (3 edn) pp 64–69.

Clark, G. (2008) *Local Development Benefits from Staging Global Events,* Paris:OECD, pp 23–30.

Deery, M. and Jago, L. (2010) 'Social impacts of events and the role of anti-social behaviour', *International Journal of Event and Festival Management* 1:8–28.

Frey, B. S. (2000) *The Rise and Fall of Festivals: Reflections on the Salzburg Festival Working paper,* Institute for Empirical Research in Economics:University of Zurich.

Hall, C. M. and Sharples, L. (2008) *Food and Wine Festivals and Events around the World,* Oxford: Elsevier.

Lilley, W. and DeFranco, G. (2003) *The Economic Impact of the 2002 British Grand Prix,* Motorsport Industry Association.

Maennig, W. and Zimbalist, A. (eds) (2012) *International Handbook on the economics of mega sporting events,* Cheltenham: Edward Elgar Publishing, pp 541–547.

Olympic Delivery Authority (2007) *The Sustainable Development Strategy for the 2012 London Olympics Executive Summary,* pp 2–27.

Raj, R. (2003) *The Impact of Festivals on Cultural Tourism,* Leeds: Leeds Metropolitan University, Paper for the 2nd DeHaan Tourism Management Conference.

PART 2

MANAGING EVENTS

CHAPTER 5

MAKING A START AND PLANNING THE EVENT

AIMS

- To introduce some of the ways you can get organized

- To consider the process for screening event ideas

- To discuss the potential objectives of running events

- To examine the planning process for events

INTRODUCTION

This chapter is the first in the sequence of chapters dealing with how to run an event. We have tried to present this as a series of steps. In practice, though, as the event begins to come together many of the parts of the process will overlap, so if you are using this book for the first time you might want to follow the order of the chapters, or you may simply want to dip in and look at the elements you need.

We may wish first of all, to consider why we are planning an event, what is the purpose? Now the answer to this may lie in the type of event. If we are planning a dinner party for our friends or to go to a cafe, bistro or restaurant to celebrate someone's birthday, which we may have organized through Facebook, then the answer is that we want to enjoy ourselves and be with our friends. There is no complicated purpose beyond this, and there is no need for one. On the other hand we may be part of a group or committee planning an event for fund raising or to make a profit to support some charitable objective. Indeed making a profit might be a key element of commercial type events, in order to fulfil a contract, put on a display or satisfy a particular request or market demand, the money made in the process of doing this may help provide employment and increase local wealth or go towards helping to fund a local service. Very often, festival type events cover several of these issues, they need to make a profit each year to continue, so they are self-sustaining from each year's income and they are there for the enjoyment of participants or to celebrate some local tradition. Alternatively, the purpose may be to restore the reputation of an event or re-start one that had failed or lapsed. In this case the issues of why need to be considered very carefully, there may or may not be legitimate reasons for failure or for the need to begin again (Carlsen *et al.*, 2010). These issues need to be considered at the early planning stage – in short, why are we doing this event – what is it for?

For most events, time, money, people and effort could be in short supply and the end result needs to be the best possible blend of resources available. However, some of those resources may be quite limited, such as time, funding, staff or expertise. It is also necessary at the beginning to recognize that existing organizational structures (such as a company management hierarchy) that serve an organization very well ordinarily, might not be suitable for the non-routine activity of organizing and running a special event. At a professional level, and for those organizations and individuals involved in the production of events, there is a need to use techniques that will ensure an effective, enjoyable and safe outcome. Tthis will require a more organized and structured approach than the cheerful informality of a family party (Tum, *et al.*, 2006).

Getting started has two aspects: finding people to do the job, which might be you and some friends, or a committee of some kind; and sorting out or screening the idea. The idea might be ready made – you might have been set a task: 'Your job is to organize this year's flower show' or the task might not yet be known, except that it has to solve some problem or other: 'We need to raise some money to paint the village hall'. So the first few steps in getting started are deciding who will do the job, what the idea is and whether it is feasible. Once you have a feasible idea or brief, the real work of planning begins.

Events are, by their nature, non-routine. The techniques used to organize and manage them, though, are just the opposite. Planning is vital to the success of events, because of their complexity, their unusual requirements (which may be considerably different from the routine activities of an organization), and because of the possible unfamiliarity of those organizing an event with what is required. However, care may be needed as organizations sometimes get so locked into the planning process that they never get to the doing part ('analysis paralysis'), or the plan itself becomes a cage from which they cannot escape. No plan will survive its first contact with reality, however good it is. Some change, no matter how small, will be needed. Nevertheless, a plan is a guide and a tool against which progress can be measured, and should not be lightly disregarded.

It can be argued that the planning process itself is the real key to what will happen (Raj, 2008). In having to sit down and prepare a plan, you have to think ahead about the event you are going to undertake, and therefore to identify the elements and issues that need to be sorted out. For this to work well there has to be a systematic approach, because unless you break the plan down into smaller component parts, something important could easily be missed. The planning process, consequently, reveals problems, risks and opportunities; it should serve to get people involved and act as a mechanism to search the environment for information. Having got some basic information together, planning has a number of benefits. These include better co-ordination, the creation of a focus, the experience of thinking ahead and the provision of a device (the plan) for effective control of the progress and outcome of the event. However, planning is time-consuming and involves much thought and effort. Things may still go wrong, but this is a reason to plan, not to fail to plan.

GETTING ORGANIZED

The initial stage of getting an event started depends on what kind of activity is going on, or put more precisely, what the objectives are (and whether there are primary and secondary objectives). The event can be personal, leisure-based, cultural or organizational. It may be organized by volunteers or by professionals. Some events are organized by a single dedicated individual with comparatively little support and encouragement, others are organized by committees or large groups of enthusiastic people. Getting started partly depends on what we know about the event and who will be doing it. In some cases we know what the event will be, but not who will do it; in others we might have people who can organize it, but we don't know what sort of event can be offered. For convenience, and because we have to start somewhere, let's start with who is going to do it.

If you are reading this book, it might be you. You may not be doing it alone, but have other people to help, or you might be part of an organizing committee looking for ideas, or your job might be to organize the organizers. Mostly, a group of people will be involved (see Figure 5.1). Sometimes the group may already exist; a committee that runs a club of some kind, perhaps a sports club, social club or hobby club, will also help run the event. This has the benefit of using an existing committee, whose committee members know each other and know their respective strengths and weaknesses. For a special event, the committee might want to add one or two extra members or advisers: people who have arranged similar events before. Or the committee might want to form a smaller sub-committee to deal with the event, rather than the 'parent' committee doing it. A useful size for a committee is thought

Figure 5.1   Example of an events management committee

one Chair / President

two Operations Officers

one Finance Officer

one Marketing Officer

one Health Safety and Legalities Officer

In addition, various other people might be invited to attend some of the meetings, depending on the type of event and agenda of the meeting:

Representatives from the venue / Licence holders / Sponsors / Police / First Aid / Fire Service

Local council member / Reps from local associations related to, or attending, the event / Bank manager / Chamber of commerce member / Insurance advisor / Professional specialists

to be about six key people; but group size does vary, although the larger the group the more difficult it may be to achieve an integrated approach. Even with a small group there may be problems of cohesion, or difficulties in getting people to work together, so that careful leadership might be essential to the group's progress.

Equally, a new organizing committee may be required. Forming this group from scratch may not be easy, because of the range of expertise that may be needed (and not necessarily available). It is possible to make a number of points about finding suitable candidates: our initial instinct may be that we can get our friends to be on the committee, but they may not have the right kind of skills needed, or have the time or inclination. The search for people will need to consider:

- How much time will organizing the event need from each person – can they spare this time to do the job properly?
- Do they have previous experience – have they done anything similar, do they have a reputation for good work in an activity we might need, e.g. as a good organizer or good at finding resources?
- Do they have good working relationships with other people – will they pull their weight and do they get on well with others?
- If they have weak organizational skills, does another member of the committee have this as a strength, so that the committee has a balance of expertise?

Most of all, the composition of the committee needs to be such that it is able to deal with the key jobs, whether these are organizing, marketing, finance, finding resources, recording data or just plain 'being enthusiastic and keeping things going'. In essence, the organization structure, whether it is a committee, a working party, an advisory group or a co-ordinating team, will need to be able to achieve the requirements of the job. It must be noted that, especially for volunteer groups, the pool of expertise may be limited and that this can act as a constraint on how fast things can be done, how well they might be done and perhaps how good the outcome will be (see Figure 5.2).

The organization of events can also vary according to how an event has grown. What was originally a one-off volunteer-organized event may have grown to the point where it is annual and organized by professionals. As events grow and their organization possibly changes, there may also be changes in the culture of the organizing body for example, from informal to formal or from amateur to professional. Sometimes this

Figure 5.2   Development of organizational structures in events

Based on Hall, C.M. (1997) Hallmark Tourist Events: Impact, Management and Planning, London, Belhaven, pp. 100–17 and p. 120???

kind of change may lead to conflict about how the event is to be run. This also implies that there is a continuum of organizational types, perhaps dependent (although not entirely so) on the growth stage of the event.

As a starting point, we will assume an early stage of development of the event, and that there is a largely volunteer committee doing the work. Indeed some events organizations do not get beyond the volunteer approach, nor do they need to. However, once the organizing committee has met and people have got to know each other a little, perhaps informally as well as formally, the first issue is what the event is going to be. As noted earlier, we might already know, but perhaps we don't know, and have no ideas, so what happens next?

ORGANIZATIONAL ISSUES IN EVENTS OF VARYING SIZES

The nature of organization between small local events, medium-sized events and large-scale international mega events is not especially one of differences in management functions; but is about differences in scale, sophistication of techniques, intensity and detail of planning and questions of the division and allocation of responsibility. It is entirely reasonable to suppose that the organizing committee of a local town festival would be composed of people who wish to be part of the event, who want to contribute something to the community or feel that they have the skills to contribute to the success of the event, and are doing so as their hobby and as a volunteer. The management functions of this committee, which might be no more than five or six people, would be planning, organizing and controlling the event, raising money, undertaking publicity, obtaining resources and support, liaising with other local groups who would be participating in the festival and so on.

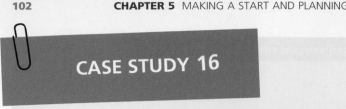

The professionalization of events: Avignon Festival

Avignon, France

Rehearsal of the opera 'Turandot' in 2012 during the Choregies d'Orange Festival in France

FACTBOX

● Avignon Festival
● Established in 1948
● Attendance in excess of 100 000 visitors
● 20 year-round permanent staff; 600 seasonal staff during Festival time

Learning Objectives

The aim of this case study is to examine the development of the organization of the Avignon Festival with the following objectives:

To consider the historical originals and development of the Festival

To highlight comparisons between the Festival as it began and its modern incarnation

To understand why professionization often takes place as Festivals or events increase in size and complexity

In 1947 theatre director Jean Vilar, with only a little additional help, organized a week of dramatic art in Avignon; this became the Avignon Festival a year later. The Festival has a history and origins in performance art, rather than one of music or folklore, and the modern Festival still reflects these origins, with many of the Festival's productions being theatrical in nature. However, the Festival's artistic programme in 2007, for example, covered performance arts, music, readings, exhibitions and films. There is also a festival 'fringe' known as the 'off' where smaller performances and informal activities take place on the sidelines of the main Festival.

In the early days of the Festival, Jean Vilar undertook the work of organizing the Festival at a time when he was still Director of the National Popular Theatre in Paris, a post he relinquished in 1963 to devote all his time to the Festival. Until 1963, the Festival struggled for finance and was dependant on ticket sales and often on private support and sponsorship. This limited the extent of the programme which could be put on. Jean Vilar introduced dance (ballet) to the Festival in 1966 and film in 1967. In this period, the Festival had effectively been administered and supported somewhat by the city council of Avignon, with Jean Vilar as Director. He continued as head of the Festival until his death in 1971, after which a new Director, Paul Puaux, took over.

By 1980 the arrangement with the city council was becoming difficult to continue and given the size of the event a better funding structure was needed, other than that of just ticket sales and private funding. Professionalization of the Festival effectively took place in 1980, when the Festival was set up as a not-for-profit organization with an Executive Board of seven people, made up of representatives from the French Government; the City of Avignon; the Vaucluse County Council and the Provence-Alpes-Cote D'Azur Regional Council, as well as the Artistic Director. The Board meets two or three times a year and its responsibilities cover general trends, the Festival programme, voting on the budget and dealing with major administrative issues. The budget is now split like so:

- 60 per cent comes from government subsidies and contributions from the various councils;
- 35 per cent from ticket sales; and
- 5 per cent from sponsorship and other private funding.

The Festival employs about 20 permanent staff (not all full-time) and at peak periods, in the three weeks from the second week in July, there are about 600 people working for the Festival. There might typically be 40 productions, with 300 performances ranging over 20 venues, from the Pope's Palace, through concert halls and theatres, to monasteries and even a disused stone quarry.

Discussion Questions

1 Is professionalization an inevitable consequence of the organizational progress or growth of an event?

2 Why should the various city, county and regional councils have become involved in funding this event, why might it be important to them?

3 What benefits will this Festival have brought to Avignon since its beginnings over 60 years ago?

4 What problems might be associated with an event which attracts 100000 people to a historic city with many old buildings and finite resources in terms of, say, accommodation and parking?

Websites

For those interested in Avignon Festival go to: **www.festival-avignon.com** and **www.avignonleoff.com** and dance at the festival **http://www.youtube.com/watch?v=VKosH7WFuao&feature=related**.

In a small committee you might expect there to be a chair, secretary, treasurer, publicity officer and a couple of other committee members with general organizing roles. For a larger event there may be specific aspects of the event which need attention, these may include:

- co-ordinating the programme of activities;
- accreditation or training of teams;
- co-ordination of attendance and accommodation arrangements;
- transport;

- arrangements for the opening and closing ceremonies;
- facilities and services for the spectators and the media; and
- provision of funding and identification of sources of sponsorship.

If we just break one of these activities down into its component parts, such as the programme, we begin to find the level of complexity involved. The programme may include:

- the briefing of staff;
- the technical rehearsals;
- the organization of practice sessions;
- time trial tests;
- meetings for stewards, officials or judges;
- finding performers or participants;
- preliminary and main team meetings.

The programme then has to deal with the event schedule itself perhaps including several sessions, sequences of activities or even competitions. In addition to the core activities, the planning and organization of the programme may also cover opening and closing ceremonies and the social and support features such as local outings, a gala dinner or a farewell crew party. This is a lot to cope with and may take a whole year's planning or more, and is one reason why many large sporting and cultural events rotate around different locations or countries, so that the burden of the work only falls on one place in any one year, not the same place every year. The larger the event, the larger the effort and the strains which the host organization or community has to cope with.

For mega events, we have said that the essential organization issues are really a matter of scale, so that what would be an organizing committee for a small event would not be adequate to take on the task of organizing a large event. For this reason, mega events generally have an Executive Board, but it would be unwise for such a board to have more than 12 members, as the differences of opinion where there are large numbers of people involved could result in failure. This being the case, the normal approach at mega events is for there to be an Executive Board of quite small numbers, to which various working parties or sub-committees report. These sub-committees could be dealing with a wide range of operational requirements:

- fundraising and sponsorship;
- logistics and transport;
- visitor services and facilities;
- publicity and promotion;
- first aid, safety and security;
- staffing;
- the programme and participant activities;
- properties and venues, etc.

In some cases there might be as many as 25 or 30 committees involved in a mega event (whereas a small event might only have one or two). The co-ordination of these is more likely to be via a regular meeting of Heads of Department or committee chairmen, than through the Executive Board, which would be there to oversee the strategy of the event, not to worry about how many portable toilets are required. This may seem a facetious comment, but as experienced practitioners and authors have noted: a major myth about events is that they are planned according to a rational process. Often, the bigger the event, the worse the planning process is and the more interference it is subjected to from politicians, sponsors and other stakeholders. An event manager may then not have the level of control which many suppose. At mega events, the brief may well have been determined and handed down before professional advice is sought. The process in a case like this, first identified some vague need for a specific project; has then seen the development of a cursory report promoting the idea; following which a range of decisions have been taken requiring the development of a plan to justify the project afterwards. Consequently, the event manager, or the Executive Board role is to sort out a way of providing it. This process may, of course, be successful, occasionally though, it isn't and a spectacular and expensive flop follows. Or much more often, the event is a success, but there are a long list of cost over-runs which originate from the haphazard vagueness of the original idea.

EVENT FEASIBILITY: FINDING AND TESTING AN IDEA

The feasibility of an event might not have been considered at all, because it seemed 'such a good idea'. But without a doubt, most event planning would benefit from a brainstorming phase when various ideas are thrown in and tossed around to 'see which is best'. Unfortunately, this often involves little more than the organizing committee having a couple of beers and saying, 'Yeah, we've got it, it's going to be fantastic'. To a detached observer, this conclusion will probably result in the response: 'Is it?'

In practice, there is a need for a systematic approach, as with much of events management. Being systematic helps us in situations where we have limited expertise and when the time period in which events have to be scheduled may be quite short, and we have to rely on volunteer labour or community support to achieve our aims. In regard to feasibility, major events might well get into intensive methods of assessment, such as cost–benefit analysis or investment appraisal or related formal assessment methods (O'Toole, 2011). For the more common type of event, perhaps of the kind put on by a town or village or by a voluntary organization, a relatively straightforward series of tests could be applied, in the form of 'screening'. From this first phase, more detailed planning can follow.

There are three screens or filters that we can put suggestions through. These are the marketing screen, the operations screen and the financial screen. All are intended to sort out less viable ideas and help to identify the idea(s) that will work the best when tested against the objectives or criteria set. It is important to recognize, however, because of the varied nature of special events, there may not be one 'perfect fit'. The end of the screening process may still result in several acceptable ideas – or in none. The organizers will finally have to make a choice about what to do. In addition to these processes, once an event has been agreed on, the first of many planning activities must begin. This first activity is about the 'lead time' for the event, or, put more simply, whether there is enough time to get it booked and organized.

In most cases the answer will be yes, it can be done in the timescale, but careful planning and forethought about the critical timing issues will focus attention on whether the event really is achievable in the time available. Many events go badly because of lack of time to organize them properly, and many project management texts argue that a poor level of planning during the early stages, due to a shortage of time, creates problems that will surface later.

We should bear in mind that all special events require a feasibility process, although some events happen simply because they have to. Typically, it is unlikely that personal events require a feasibility process: you obviously don't feasibility-test a dinner party, but you do think about what is needed to get it right. With personal events, the 'feasibility' is not a formal process, but is much more likely to be an informal, even unconscious, decision about what will happen. There may be constraints, such as the availability of money or where to have it, but these may affect just the size or magnificence of the event rather than if it goes ahead or not. In this case the event is predetermined, and the real issue is how to make it happen.

On the other hand, many events do not develop by such a simple process, especially given the vast range of special events that take place. Let us consider the three screens, or filters, that we should put potential events through: the marketing screen, the operations screen and the financial screen. Suppose the scouts need to raise money for a new roof for the Scout Hall: there may be many possible events that could be put on to raise the money, but there has to be some way by which a selection is made. Perhaps a list of ideas of what the scouts could do is put together:

- a car wash day;
- a theatrical play;
- a sponsored swim;
- a sale of pledges (a pledge is a gift contributed, then auctioned);
- a jumble sale or car boot sale.

The criteria for what to do might include what type of event has been successful in the past; what can be organized, given the resources of the scout-pack; what might earn the most money and so on. These are relatively simple considerations, but they still represent a very basic kind of feasibility.

For larger-scale, public and organizational events in particular, there may well be an issue of how to choose from a range of possible activities for, say, fundraising, or for a product launch, and how to screen the choices to identify the one most likely to be effective. It has been noted in the past that: 'However good an idea may seem to be, if it cannot win sufficient support, and if it is unlikely to attract the public of a locality, the best thing to do is to drop it'.

THE SCREENING PROCESS

The process of screening is very important. Not only does the event have to be possible to carry out, it must also attract sufficient support to be successful. Let us consider this process in more detail.

The first stage of the screening is to come up with the initial concept or set of ideas that would be tested (see Figure 5.3). In some cases, a better range of ideas might be obtained by skipping through this general process and simply brainstorming a long

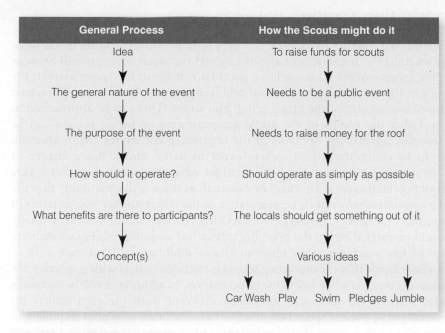

Figure 5.3   Generating ideas

list of (possibly) raucous, heroic, obvious, typical or ludicrous events and then dealing with the list in a serious way through a series of criteria to evaluate what really is feasible. There are several possible ways of doing this, by using evaluation criteria (such as cost–benefit analysis), or concept screening (see Figure 5.4).

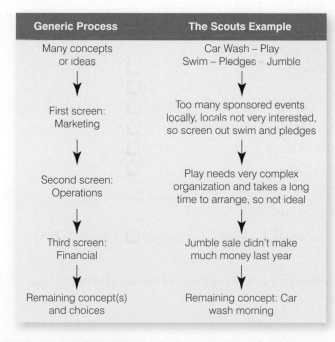

Figure 5.4   Concept screening

The marketing screen

Having identified a number of ideas or concepts for a possible event, there has to be a process whereby the organizers or clients can sort out what concepts will be most suited to the target market. This implies a good knowledge of the target market: the type of people, their demographic or social profile, age group, familiar activities, past experience of events, size of the target group and so on. This can be approached in two ways. Either the results of the initial brainstorming or listing session can be checked roughly against the opinions of the organizing committee (who, after all, will have to be committed to an idea in order to make sure it has a chance of success), or some pilot research can be done to see what the potential market makes of the list of potential events. This may be essential, as there is the possibility that the organizing committee may not be representative of the target market (e.g. in terms of age group, life experiences, gender, etc.). Detailed research about the event finally chosen could be carried out in the planning phase, but an initial pilot questionnaire could explore first reactions to the range of ideas (Goldblatt, 2002) (Figure 5.5).

The essential factor that the marketing screen is intended to deal with is whether the various ideas or concepts will work in the target market. In addition, it will be necessary to consider whether the ideas are sufficiently different from (or even similar to) successful competing events. Special event organizers are often very poor at pulling in information about other events that may be taking place at the same time and targeted

---

SURVEY OF MIDDLEBURG RESIDENTS AND VISITORS

The Middleburg Garden Club is proposing to raise money to revitalize the Arboretum and Venetian Bridge. We would like to put on a suitable fundraising event in the Arboretum walled garden in July and would be most grateful if you would return this questionnaire, either in the post to the secretary (address on reverse), or pop it into the special post box set up in the town library foyer, or vote on our website.

PLEASE PICK TWO CHOICES – 1 FOR YOUR FIRST CHOICE, 2 FOR YOUR SECOND CHOICE.

Suggested Events:

Garden Club Show of Prize-winning Blooms ☐

Evening Fireworks Extravaganza ☐

Summer Dance and Buffet ☐

A production of Shakespeare's 'A Midsummer Night's Dream' ☐

Treasure hunt through the park, finishing at the 'Knobbers Rest' pub ☐

Concert in conjunction with the Middleburg Concert Orchestra ☐

Have you got another idea? _____

PREFERRED TIMING: PLEASE TICK ONE BOX ON EACH LINE:

Monday ☐   Tuesday ☐   Wednesday ☐   Thursday ☐   Friday ☐   Saturday ☐   Sunday ☐

Morning ☐   Afternoon ☐   Evening ☐

Many thanks for your kind help. We look forward to welcoming you at the event, which will be advertised soon.
Name: _____
Address: _____

Figure 5.5   Example pilot questionnaire for proposed events

at the same market as their own concept. This may result in clashes of dates, or two different organizing groups putting on almost the same type of event. The issue of the 'environmental search' is a way of doing this. Identification of competing events can be difficult, but should at least involve compiling a list of dates when similar events take place in the area, obtainable from tourist information, from local What's On publications, magazines, social media or trade press. Put these together with a knowledge of activities in the calendar, or by checking local newspapers for the same period in the previous year, and getting people in the organizing committee to ask their friends and other contacts if anyone is aware of similar events. This should produce a list of what else is going on, which will help serve a number of purposes:

- It will identify dates to avoid (you may not be able to avoid all clashes).
- It will give a feel for what goes on and what the local market likes.
- It may give additional ideas or identify gaps in the market that are not being filled.

In this way it will be possible to create a shortlist of events that will satisfy the overall objectives of the organizing committee or clients (if this is a commercial or paid event), but will also suit the available target market and run at an appropriate time, not competing with other activities. This done, there is the final question of whether the list of 'possibles' fits in with the organizational type. There is not much point in putting on a 'Tarts and Vicars' theme for the Sisters of the Immaculate Conception annual fundraising tea. The marketing screen is intended to identify:

- what will work in a given market;
- what else might be going on by way of competition;
- what an organization would see as appropriate; and most of all
- what demand there should be from the target market.

Having done this, the organizer can move on to the operations screen.

The operations screen

So far, from a list of ideas or concepts screened against the marketing criteria for an event, there will probably still be a large number remaining that might work. However, the event manager also needs to consider what is achievable. All events have various resource needs, based on how adventurous, ambitious or limited the ideas are, what expertise and staffing is available, what locations or venues are available with capacity at the required dates, what timescale and what technology or other equipment will be needed. There may also be risk assessment or risk management issues which may prevent the event going ahead. Due consideration needs to be given to legalities – are licences needed? Will insurance be needed? Are permits required for various activities, etc.? This is the role of the operations screen.

Events often fall into two operational styles, volunteer or professional (although some have parts of both). For example, many events, especially in the personal, sporting and cultural categories, are run by volunteers. A volunteer committee may well consist of people who have had no experience of events before, or who have only their own experience and innate good sense to go on.

On the other hand, there are other events (particularly organizational, but also some sporting, cultural and some personal events) that are to be professionally run, or for which a professional adviser, consultant or Events Management Company (EMC) has been employed. The level of expertise available is then an issue for the operations screen, which indicates what events can be done within the style of organization preferred. However, there are some excellent amateur organizations and some very inadequate professional ones (and vice versa); there is nothing to say that volunteer organizations are necessarily worse off than professional ones in putting on events. They may have less experience and (perhaps) lesser knowledge of what can be achieved, but it should not be assumed that professional organizations or companies know everything or will produce a perfect result. Any number of things may go wrong, including the professionals not paying sufficient attention to the brief or to key issues. Volunteer organizations might be more enthusiastic, more resourceful with limited means, and have a better local knowledge than a professional events company.

For events with a volunteer style of organization and volunteer staff, the matter of achievability is important. Does anyone within the organizing committee have relevant expertise? If so, they must be used to best effect. People with a financial background may be best suited to financial issues, people with design backgrounds best suited to design issues and so on. In addition, volunteer organizations should not only look at members' jobs, but also at personal interests: creative people and good organizers are needed for special events. Clues about people's backgrounds, hobbies, interests and expertise need to be sought and could yield useful experience. However, volunteering is hard work and not everyone wants to do it. In the end, people may not have time to participate in the event, or may be called upon to deal with all kinds of occurrences or emergencies that they may not be equipped to cope with.

Equally important is knowledge of previous activities. For instance, is the event a regular one, say, every year and, if so, who knows what has gone on in previous years? However, we need to recognize the boundaries of volunteer expertise – the person who has attended the annual flower show of a nearby town might be the only one in a volunteer organization who would know anything about how to organize a flower show, but the limitations of this approach must be understood. Going to a flower show (or any other event) as a visitor does not necessarily tell you anything about what goes on behind the scenes, how the event was organized or what effort went into putting it on. This is an issue of expertise and when to know you need some. All kinds of special events have to start somehow and the expertise to run them is often built up over many years, or at least the knowledge about where to obtain the expertise is. This expertise is key when issues of health and safety, legality or technology are important to an event.

The operations screen, then, is all about what can be achieved. From the original list it will have been possible to eliminate some of the activities on the basis that they are too difficult or complicated, or because there isn't the time, the staff or an appropriate venue. This can be done by using an events screening form (Figure 5.6), which will help formalize the screening, and several events might be written up in order to identify major problems and possible unforeseen issues in terms of licensing, regulations and permissions or approvals needed.

The financial screen

Almost all special events will have a budget of some kind, even if that 'budget' is only an approximate figure of what the organizers or clients can afford, based perhaps on similar events. For many events, the financial issues are cost-orientated. For a

CASE STUDY 17

Club Volunteer organizations and event screening: University College, Cork Hockey Club

Luis Santos / Shutterstock.com

Cork, Ireland

University of Cork in Ireland

- University College, Cork
- Founded in 1845
- 12 000 students
- Over 100 student clubs and societies
- A large number of sports clubs
- Men's Hockey Club, run by a committee of seven

Learning Objectives

The aim of this case study is to consider how event idea screening works in an example which might be most familiar to students with the following objectives:
To demonstrate the creation and elimination of event ideas
To highlight issues of selection in choosing an event
To understand that this is not a formal process in all events

Volunteer organizations are extremely common in events management. Clubs, societies, associations and charitable bodies often rely on volunteers to run the organization. Volunteers may have little or no training, but do have enthusiasm about and dedication to what they are doing. Many people have some experience of committee activity and voluntary organizations at college or university, where clubs and societies dedicated to a whole range of sporting, leisure, recreation and special interest activities are common. The Hockey Club of University College, Cork, is one such example. Its primary activity is playing hockey, but it also has an active social role.

The Hockey Club is very typical of many clubs and societies throughout colleges and universities. It plays matches and tournaments and has its own web pages within the website of University College, Cork. The club has an active social life, with its members taking part in a whole range of student activities. Its committee organizes frequent events, both small and (relatively) large scale for its members and their friends and partners.

The choices of activities in any academic year might produce a list of possible events that include a quiz night, a charity horse-race night, a buffet with disco, a formal dress ball, an American-style prom, dinner at a local restaurant or a fancy dress party. As the Hockey Club is a relatively informal kind of organization, these choices are bounced around members of the committee and the team and their friends. There was no complex formal process involved in deciding which event to have, only an informal process that involved the major stakeholders (the team and their friends) in the decision-making process. The choice reached was the result of a general consensus about what event they wanted. For example in 2006 this was a formal dress ball, which members of the committee, together with a few helpers, organized.

The kind of process involved here is very typical of voluntary organizations and the limited market may mean that in-depth research is not required. However, the larger and more diverse the market, or the more unknown the style of event, the more likely will be the need to do a survey, or at least some pilot research work, to ensure the event is what the market is interested in.

Discussion Questions

1 If you are a member of a club, society or association, what is the major event in the organization's social calendar?

2 How is this event organized and by whom, and how are the choices made about what kind of event it will be?

3 Can the process be said to involve any research or confirmation that the event is appropriate?

4 If you were the chair of a committee planning an event that the public has to pay to attend, what steps could you take to ensure your proposals would meet what the public wants to participate in?

Websites

Related website for those interested in University College, Cork and its student life: **www.ucc.ie/about** and **http://www.youtube.com/watch?v=e-H3I8NEPpc&feature=related**.

wedding, there is no discernible financial revenue to set against the balance of what might have to be spent. In this case, the organizers (the parents of the couple to be married and the couple themselves) will have some idea of how much they can afford and if several ideas are being considered (for example, for the reception), the deciding factor might be the cost.

Not all events are 'cost only'; often there is a financial reason for putting an event on, such as fundraising or economic regeneration. There are events that are expected to make sufficient money to cover costs and **break-even**, or to make a small surplus. This is often the case with local volunteer events such as an annual town carnival. The carnival committee will be concerned with putting on a good show at a reasonable cost, and generating enough of a surplus to start next year's carnival properly.

Assuming the event has to make money (say, for fundraising purposes), or at least to cover its costs, then the financial screen is all about identifying which possible events from the shortlist could achieve it. Two or three likely events might be

break-even
The point at which an event's costs equal the revenue received for it.

OUTLINE EVENT DETAILS:

Purpose of event: _____

Suggested location: _____

Is the proposed event: A one off event? ☐   Expected to take place annually? ☐

Have you checked that the venue or location is available?   Yes ☐   No ☐

DETAILS OF THE ORGANIZER OR CHAIR OF THE ORGANIZING COMMITTEE:

Name: _____   Phone number: _____

Email: _____

Address: _____

_____

FUNDING OF THE EVENT:

How do you expect the event to be paid for? _____

What are the major costs of your event and have you included insurance? _____

_____

_____

(A summary of the outline budget should be attached to this form).

ATTENDANCE AT THE EVENT:

How many people do you expect to attend? ☐

How many other people will be there?   ☐   (include organizers, crew, players, ushers, staff, etc.)

LICENSING, PERMISSIONS, EMERGENCY ISSUES:

Have you / will you liaise with any of the following services to establish their input to the event?

          Police ☐   Fire ☐   Ambulance ☐   Red Cross ☐

Licensing Authority ☐   Town Council ☐   Other (specify) _____

Will the event have any implications for local residents: e.g. noise, site set-up, parking, access, crowds etc.?

_____

Will you need any specialist help with the event or other professional advice or input?

_____

_____

Signed: _____   Date: _____

Figure 5.6   Events Screening Form
Source: kindly provided by Tendring District Council

compared using an outline budget. For this to happen, the organizers will need to come up with some basic financial information, both in terms of revenue:

- How many people attend?
- What can they be charged?
- What other ways revenue can be raised during the event? etc.

Also in terms of costs. What are the likely costs of:

- The location or venue?
- The staffing?

- The materials?
- The decor?
- The consumables;?
- The insurance?
- The power?
- The food and drink? etc.

From this you should be able to assess whether a profit or surplus would be made.

In some projects, especially large-scale ones, there are both capital costs and running costs. Think of the Olympics: the capital costs are about building the facilities, the infrastructure, the accommodation, etc. and the running costs are about actually operating the games. Will the revenue cover both of these or, in the case of the capital costs, will some other benefit be the outcome; could the athletes' accommodation be turned into flats and sold afterwards? Could the stadium replace one that is old and needed replacing anyway? Crucially, will the event being planned take place within the appropriate budget?

In short, the purpose of the financial screen is to take the shortlist of possible events, preferably no more than two or three, and prepare an outline budget for each one, to help the decision-making process. A little later, as part of the detailed planning, the outline budget can be turned into something more detailed and accurate. For care in preparation, an outline budget should attempt to slightly underestimate revenues and slightly overestimate costs.

PROGRESSING THE IDEA

In many respects, choosing the event, through the process outlined above, is the easy part. The sequence of brainstorming and then filtering ideas to see if an event is appropriate can be quite enjoyable. Serious financial and operational feasibility, if this were a major project, would then follow from the screening phase. The organizers or clients would also have some feel for the acceptability of the event, given their knowledge of who might be attending. In addition, for any event involving a significant budget or complicated organizational issues, a judgement of risks might have to be made:

- How vulnerable is the project financially and operationally?
- What issues might constitute a risk?
- Are there factors about licensing, fire, health and safety, crowd control, security, hazardous materials or activities that have to be considered?

It may be possible to find useful information to help with this process from a range of sources, not only those published in books and guides, but also from 'toolkits' that can sometimes be found on events-related websites.

Having found the preferred concept, the organizers might then wish to review the proposal again in the light of the objectives, and ask if the proposal still meets those objectives (see Figure 5.7). It is also quite common for events to have additional, subsidiary objectives, such as to educate, or to make money, or to leave a useful legacy. To take the idea forward there would have to be some building on the initial objectives, with a draft of the proposal containing the overall objective broken down

Figure 5.7 Examples of possible events objectives

- Development of public involvement in the arts, sport or other leisure activities
- Fundraising for a special project or charity
- Start a new event to create a tourist attraction extend the tourist season or make better use of a resource
- Introduce a new idea to the market
- Attract more visitors to a venue or tourist destination
- Focus attention on a specified subject or project
- Create a sense of community, involve the community or strengthen its goodwill
- Advance and promote the community for the public benefit
- Promote political and cultural exchange
- Encourage participation in, or support of, an organization

into several aims, and then into the component parts for the event. Even relatively simple events may have several component parts:

- How will these be put together?
- Who will be doing the organizing and who is responsible for what?
- Where will the event be held and has more than one venue been approached?
- When will the event happen and are suitable dates and times available?
- What materials, supplies and equipment might be needed?
- What transport, parking or access is available?
- Why is the time schedule for achieving this important, and what are the deadlines?

All these questions will have to be answered. More work can be done later, but even if this is put into a few pages of notes it will be a useful start, and the planning can then be built from the initial ideas. The most important aspect of this pre-planning phase is to have enough time, not only to work up the detailed plans properly, but also to determine whether the event is achievable in the time available. In general, volunteer organizations may require more time to deal with complex events than professional or full-time organizations, but equally, those professional organizations are likely to have a far more realistic appreciation of the amount of work involved and the likely time it will take to achieve.

There may well be a '**critical path**' of timing issues that will determine whether a project or event can be done in the timescale, which the unfamiliar organizer may think is easy, but may not be. Consider building projects as an example. Builders are often seen as overrunning the time 'allowed' for a project, but frequently this is due to an unrealistic appreciation of the complexity of the job; the need to get planning permission, the logistical problems, the long lead time on deliveries, sourcing unusual materials, etc. Much the same is true of special events. An event that might seem very simple at first glance can become extremely complicated once someone actually sits down to write out all the parts. Nor is there any guarantee that what appears to be the 'critical path' of a project will be so.

critical path
The key time-limited route through a number of time-critical activities in the planning of an event.

Suppose we are organizing a special prize ceremony for the best rose grower in the district. The organizing committee wants this to get some good local publicity, so has decided that the presentation should be made by the Mayor in the famous gardens of a nearby stately home. Several factors impinge on the timing: the event needs the stately home, the mayor and the local media (assuming there is to be no other activity after the ceremony). The 'critical path' will emerge from one of the three elements:

- How long to book the stately home and are the possible dates available?
- How long it will take to get a slot in the mayor's busy diary and will this match the availability of the stately home?
- When is a good day for the local media?

For example, the lead-in to the 'critical path' may be the last of these. Not all days are good days in media terms. If the local newspaper is published on a Friday, then they may be looking for good local stories several days before, probably Monday or Tuesday (not Wednesday or Thursday, as they have to write up a story and get the artwork done in time to meet their own print deadline). This gives a framework for the best days on which to do this particular event. In all probability, both the booking of the stately home and the mayor's diary have long lead times, and whichever is longer (after preliminary enquiries) will have to be done first, as everything else can then follow. As a generality, the larger and more complicated an event, the more detailed the planning process will need to be and the longer the lead times will be. The key lead time is often booking the venue, as popular venues are booked months, sometimes years in advance.

An experienced events organizer will be familiar with those issues that take time to get going, and those that can be done quickly. However, for the person who has never organized an event before, there is the problem of possibly overlooking something. Figure 5.8 gives an initial checklist for various issues and some useful things that can be listed at this stage of the event planning process. Nevertheless, all events vary in some way and the points shown in the list are not definitive, but are a possible source of ideas about what to check and what to do next. The information in the checklist, here called the pre-event planner, and of a type also often found in hotel 'Banqueting Orders', is in three main sections. The first deals with contact information, who is organizing the event, and basic information about the date and type of event. The second deals with information about the possible venue, the event and any requirements for refreshments. The third section deals with requirements for the layout of the venue, design issues, entertainment and support activities, ranging from audio-visual equipment to car parking.

THE PLANNING PROCESS

The diversity and individuality of events can make them very labour-intensive, because of the effort involved in undertaking a non-routine activity. This is not simply a matter of how events are operated on the day, but is also a management and organizational issue. The management input to any event will be far greater than for a routinely manufactured product when management becomes essentially a supervisory function based around quality control, once the development phase is over, because the manufacturing process is being repeated again and again. Planning events, for the uninitiated or for an inexperienced organizer is, therefore, rather more

Figure 5.8 Simple pre-event planner

MIDDLEBURG MUSIC FESTIVAL

Pre-Event Planner

Type of event:	Date(s):
Your organizer:	Phone(s):
Address:	Email(s):
Our contact:	Phone(s):
	Email(s):

Location / Room:	Booking of venue with:
Start time:	Finish time:
Number of participants / guests:	
Number of meals and / or refreshments:	
Menu:	Printing: programme, schedule, menus
	Layout
	Staff plan
Bar / Wine:	Other refreshments:
Booking Deposit:	

Room Layout:	For Event	
	Buffet / Dinner / Refreshment Area	
Room Decoration:	Theme	Lighting
	Colour scheme	Special Items
Entertainment:	Music	Créche
	Disco	
	Other Live Entertainment	
	Games	
Special Equipment:	Audio	Costumes
	Visual	Photography / Video
	Staging	
	Other Items	
Car parking notes:		
This account to be paid for by:		
Any other remarks / special requests:		

important and time-consuming than the equivalent processes for repetitive goods and services. Taking the example of a wedding, the actual wedding may be a ceremony of no more than an hour, followed by a reception and a buffet, but the planning may have taken several months and involved large numbers of people – families, friends, the venue management, the caterers, the florist, the dress hire company, the musicians, the car company, the religious authority or civil registrar and so on. This complexity of planning is typical of events in general and is part of a whole cycle of interrelated activity covering planning, action and control. The increased importance of planning is because of its key role in helping to deal with the uncertainties of events.

Planning is the process by which the manager or organizer looks towards the event, to discover what various courses of action are available to arrange it and which course of action would be the best. This is not to say that a plan is going to appear the moment someone sits down to think about it. The manager, organizer or planning committee may have run many events, or may have run none (see Figure 5.9).

The advantage of having done it before is not only the experience, but also the existence of records and previous plans. On the other hand, with a new event, the plan to start with may be no more than a vague hunch or an organizer's intuition about what might be appropriate. However, this can be worked up very quickly into something more useful and relevant; a plan is essentially a predetermined course of action based on given objectives.

The objectives have to be carefully thought through, and be precise and clear enough to ensure that the purpose of the event is obvious to all those involved in it, from the chair of the organizing committee or clients, down to staff or volunteers at the operational level. Clarity at the beginning also helps the planning process and getting everyone to pull in the same direction. The objectives should not be too complicated, perhaps consisting of only one or two primary objectives, although these can be broken down into a number of detailed aims; but preferably not more than six, otherwise the point may be obscured, and simplicity is best at this stage.

Figure 5.9   Planning as a management activity for an event

OBJECTIVES, ENVIRONMENTAL SEARCH AND INFORMATION GATHERING

The objectives are the starting point for the planning of any event – what is the event intended to do? Is it intended to celebrate, to entertain, to fundraise? Given this, and some view of the feasibility of the event after the screening process, the organizers should have a reasonable idea of the kind of event that can be put on and whether it will suit the type of people coming to it (the target market). However, planning should not be seen as something that starts with a concept and ends on the opening hour. Even after the event has started the organizer is likely to be making changes, sometimes very major changes, in response to problems or to deal with an unforeseen crisis. One of the purposes of planning is to visualize potential problems and to have a plan that will take into account the environment of the event, the stakeholders, the circumstances in which the event is taking place and what might go wrong; or put more simply, there will need to be some contingency planning for emergencies, in addition to the main plan itself.

From the bare bones, an outline plan can be drawn up (see Figure 5.10), perhaps by brainstorming around the event idea and then listing the issues identified. This basic draft can then be added to in a more systematic way by the organizing committee and its advisers and helpers to cover headings such as operations, finance and marketing. This can include an 'environmental search and information-gathering' phase, a part of the process that involves collecting information relevant to the event. Facts such as available dates, suitable times, potential venues and useful staff have to be identified; checking has to take place to ensure there are no clashes with other, similar or competitor events. For major events, checking what else is taking place, or is planned, can also be done using online listing services as well as by methods such as looking at magazine or newspaper event listings (checking the same time in the previous year's reports is also useful in doing this). If the prospective market is not known, market research should be done into what people would like and pay for, building on any pilot research that might have been carried out at the screening stage.

The draft plan is really a place for initial ideas to be recorded, a kind of scrap-box for brainstorming and all your initial thoughts and concepts. Its headings should, importantly, cover six key issues, to give it some structure and form:

- Why the event is being undertaken?
- Who will be involved in the process and the event (and who may not)?
- What will take place and what information or research is needed to make decisions?
- How will it be done?
- Where will it happen (including the main location and any additional locational needs)?
- When will it take place (including dates and expected outline times)?

This is part of the mechanism, like the screening process, by which an organizer seeks to identify potential problems at an early stage. Once all the ideas and information have been 'thrown in', the plan can then be reorganized to give it some proper structure. Always keep the first drafts, though, as sometimes they contain material that might be thought of as not very important, until, nearer the event, a problem of some kind emerges.

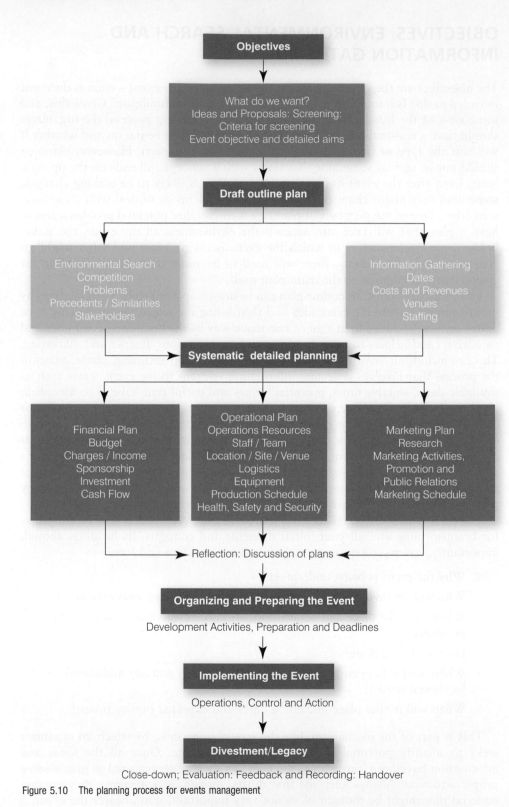

Figure 5.10   The planning process for events management

CASE STUDY 18

Environmental searching: the reopening of the Scottish Parliament

Edinburgh, Scotland

Parliament Chambers, Scottish Parliament

© Scottish Parliamentary Corporate Body

- Reopening of the Scottish Parliament, Edinburgh
- First parliament in Edinburgh for almost 300 years
- Ceremony combined old and new elements
- Parliament opened by Queen Elizabeth
- 'The Scottish Parliament, which adjourned on 17 March 1707, is hereby reconvened'

Learning Objectives

The aim of this case study is to examine the issues which impinge on the environment (in this case the political and cultural environment) in which an event operate with the following objectives:
To consider why local knowledge or understanding might affect the success or failure of an event
To understand the issues which an event organizer or committee might have to take into account when planning an event of a sensitive nature

On the 1 July 1999, the Scottish Parliament met for the first time in almost 300 years. It had been abolished after the joining of Scotland and England had removed political power from Edinburgh in 1707 and made Westminster the only UK parliament. The re-establishment of Scotland's parliament was greeted with considerable enthusiasm in Scotland.

The environment and circumstances of the planning stage

In Scotland the nature of the opening of the parliament was a matter of some controversy during late 1998 and early 1999. There was a feeling that the ceremony would be too short and modern, and that the event would fail to include the heraldic flag-bearers of Scotland, who are traditionally associated with royal Scottish ceremonial events. In public, the reason given for the absence of the flag-bearers was that the ceremony needed to be modern, but the scathing publicity in the Scottish media about their absence suggests that the organizing committee was taken by surprise.

The organizing committee initially failed in two ways: first, it had insufficient experience of Scottish public feeling, and second, they had not undertaken a proper environmental search. It was thought that the committee originally had no idea of Scottish traditions because the reform had been initiated in London and the committee's 'starting point' had been London, not Edinburgh. There was, therefore, little recognition (due to inexperience and inadequate research) that a Scottish parliamentary tradition existed, let alone how it had worked. However, the committee (fortunately) listened very closely to public opinion in Scotland and these issues were addressed carefully and in time.

The stakeholders

The people and groups most concerned with the opening were its organizing committee, the political parties (notably the Labour Party, under whom the reform had been promoted, but other parties as well, including the Scottish National Party), Queen Elizabeth and the Royal Household, the Scottish Office (a government department), the national and local media, the people of Scotland, the army (as escort to the royal family), the Heralds and ceremonial officers of Scotland, The Duke of Hamilton (as Scotland's senior Lord, responsible for the Crown Jewels of Scotland) and a very large number of people and groups involved in the ceremony, such as the orchestra, schoolchildren, poets and so on.

The outcome was an event that was very well received. In the modern (and then temporary chamber) of the Church of Scotland, the ceremony was opened with a fanfare played by the Royal Scottish National Orchestra, following which the Royal Procession entered with the Duke of Hamilton carrying the Scottish Crown on a purple velvet cushion, followed by the Queen, and then the Lord Lyon King of Arms and the Heralds ('more Heralds than were needed to put on a Hollywood movie', the newspapers reported). This was followed by the opening speeches, some poetry and spontaneous singing by the Scottish MPs.

The ceremony was hailed as a major success, not only in style but also in tone. It celebrated the need to open a modern parliament and recalled the traditional way in which the old parliament, 300 years before, had been opened, thus fulfilling its objectives.

Discussion Questions

1 Why is finding out about the environment and circumstances of your event important?

2 How can you identify the stakeholders (those people and groups that would take part or be interested in some way) for an event?

3 Why is doing this important, and what might happen if you do not identify them all?

4 Why is clarity of objectives key to running a successful event, and were the objectives for this event clear from the start?

Websites

Related website for those interested in the Scottish Parliament: **www.scottish.parliament.uk** and for a recent opening see: **http://www.youtube.com/watch?v=DmlNmuEl310**

In many ways the environmental search/information-gathering process is also a search for opportunities (as well as problems). For example, another event in the same area and of the same type as your event might be seen as competitive, but could be complementary. The organizer, or in the case of a very large event, a professional researcher, will be looking for:

- information about demand for the event and the capacity of the market;
- any competition;
- availability of technology, equipment and supplies;
- financing and sponsorship;
- organizations and the availability of staff;
- local cultural or social issues and precedents; and
- time issues in planning.

This information can then be included (or put aside) and helps the organizers to plan and identify what else is needed, but assists also in the organization and running of the event. Sometimes, however, the process of 'environmental searching' is not properly done and results in some major problems or mistakes which embarrass the organizers (see Figure 5.11).

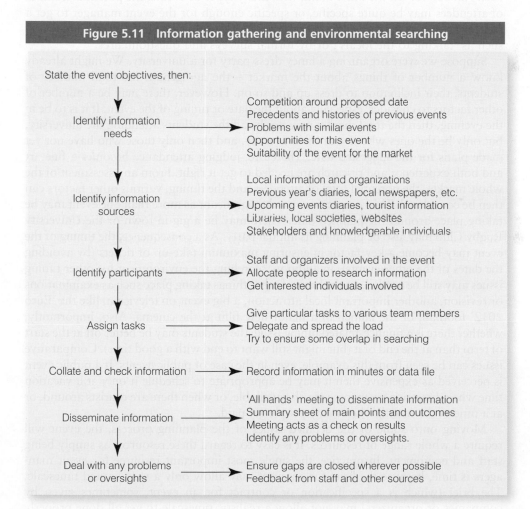

Figure 5.11 Information gathering and environmental searching

State the event objectives, then:

Identify information needs →
Competition around proposed date
Precedents and histories of previous events
Problems with similar events
Opportunities for this event
Suitability of the event for the market

Identify information sources →
Local information and organizations
Previous year's diaries, local newspapers, etc.
Upcoming events diaries, tourist information
Libraries, local societies, websites
Stakeholders and knowledgeable individuals

Identify participants →
Staff and organizers involved in the event
Allocate people to research information
Get interested individuals involved

Assign tasks →
Give particular tasks to various team members
Delegate and spread the load
Try to ensure some overlap in searching

Collate and check information →
Record information in minutes or data file

Disseminate information →
'All hands' meeting to disseminate information
Summary sheet of main points and outcomes
Meeting acts as a check on results
Identify any problems or oversights.

Deal with any problems or oversights →
Ensure gaps are closed wherever possible
Feedback from staff and other sources

Source: adapted from Costa and Teare, 1996, Environmental Scanning: A tool for competitive advantage

OPERATIONAL PLANNING AND DEMAND

For some events, the issue of demand may not seem directly relevant, and for personal events in particular it might be thought that demand is not a significant factor in the planning process, except to know roughly how many people are coming or will be invited to an event, such as a wedding or birthday party. (Yet even for personal events, some checking is needed. You might invite 100 people to your party, but this does not mean 100 people are going to turn up.) For almost all events, demand and the potential market are an issue.

- What sort of people are interested?
- How many might attend?
- When would be a good date or time to put the event on?

It can be difficult to assess this effectively, especially when no similar event has been run before. On the other hand, with many types of events, the potential number of attendees may be quite specific, or specific enough for the event manager to get a feel for the requirements. This can be checked by some research, either informally such as 'talking to the locals', or by formal surveys and questionnaires.

Suppose we were organizing a fancy dress party for a university. We might already know a number of things about the market – the age group, the total number of students, their inclination to dress up and so on. However, there may be a number of other factors to consider, especially about the date or timing of the event. If it is to be in the evening, then the total market may not be all the students attending the university, but only be the ones who live at the university, and then only those who have not yet made plans for the suggested date. Therefore, judging attendance becomes a fine art and both experience and research are needed to get it right. From an assessment of the whole market, the potential total of attendees and the timing, various other factors can then be considered. The competition may be significant as more than one event may be taking place around the planned date. There may be a gig in town or the University Rugby Club may also be planning its annual party. As a consequence, the timing of the event may become a key factor in ensuring maximum take-up of tickets (by avoiding the dates of the other events). In addition, searching the environment for other timing issues may still be needed, on the basis of other things taking place such as examinations or revision, another important local attraction, a big event on television, like the 'Euro 2012' football, or the launch of a major new film at the cinema. Also, importantly, whether there is a finance-related timing issue; the students may be better off at the start of term than at the end of it (but might still want to end with a good time). Comparative issues can be seen from this example, even in the case of public events. If a public event is perceived as expensive then it may be appropriate to schedule it only at a vacation time when discretionary income may be available, or when there are tourists around, or at a time of the month when many people get paid.

Moving onto some of the detailed issues of the planning process, the event will require a whole range of resources. It is easy to regard these resources as simply being staff and equipment. In practice, the single most important resource for event managers is time, because the brief for an event may allow only a very limited timescale. The brief (which is a specification or contract for an event, sometimes given by companies or organizers) may not allow a realistic timescale to get all done properly without incurring very high costs for staffing, resources needed and management time. Professional event managers may turn down some briefs on this basis. There has to be enough time to plan the event properly, to meet deadlines and **cut-off points,** and to achieve the set-up, run the event and break down its various elements afterwards.

Event managers therefore need to be aware of key timing issues. The lead times of various event-related activities are often underestimated; for example the difficulty of getting a large number of volunteer stewards for a big event. But there are many other lead-time issues, from marketing and the production of brochures to the lead time of booking the right venue. Many venues will be booked up well over a year in advance. Popular dates and times of year often take the uninitiated by surprise and almost the first activity in planning will be to identify suitable venues and dates. Bookings can be made provisionally but will usually be subject to a deposit, even if the venue is the village hall. For events that are self-funding this may result in a chicken-and-egg type problem; what to do first, confirm the venue or sell tickets? This is usually resolved by having a **cut-off date** by which the event will be confirmed, and the venue paid for by selling a limited number of tickets early on. If cancelled, no money is lost before the booking cut-off date and it can then be returned to those who booked early (see Figure 5.12).

cut-off points
The points at which something ceases to apply.

cut-off date
The designated date on which an organizer must release reserved but unconfirmed space, or confirm a booking by payment.

FINANCIAL PLANNING

The plan should now be starting to have some shape. The organizers should have been able to quantify the size of the event – how many people are coming, whether there is any competition or synergy and whether the event is convenient in relation to this. Identifying similar events may also have given some feel for the prices people are willing to pay. However, price should not be determined by other events, but by what it will cost to put on your event and whether it has to be profitable (the issue of budgeting is dealt with in more detail later). This issue of pricing is very important, as inexperienced organizers typically underestimate the various costs. It is absolutely essential to sit down and list all the items required and cost them properly: 'a few balloons' may turn into a budget for decorations of several hundreds of Euros.

There is a tendency on the part of everyone to say, 'Oh well, it will cost about ...' without actually checking. When someone does get around to checking, the real amount comes as a shock. A good example is discos: someone on the organizing committee always 'has a mate' who does a disco and it will be 'really cheap'. No, it won't! The 'mate' will either not be able to do the date or will take various liberties with the organizers who will find out, after the event, that they could have had a cheaper disco by getting several quotes from firms advertising on the net or locally. The other serious mistake is for organizers to start off with a ticket price they have picked out of thin air, 'I think tickets should be ...' This method, based on no reasoning whatsoever, is almost guaranteed to land the event in serious financial difficulties. If you decide the ticket price before the costing has been done, you end up cutting back on all the things that make the event special. The ticket price has to be based on accurate costings and only then, considered in the light of competition and what the market will pay (which should also be based on some realistic data, not on what the organizers 'think' the market will pay, which often underestimates reality). A further financial issue that should be included with the budget and cash-flow statement is a calculation about the break-even point of the event. For example, say ticket prices are €10 and costs are €500. For the event to break-even, this means that 50 tickets have to be sold. What if the venue only seats 45? You couldn't make a profit. In essence, once

Figure 5.12 Simple example of marketing lead times: Middleburg Sports Day				

Outline marketing plan: August / September 2012, weeks 1 to 4, to raise money for the church bells. Middleburg Sports Day to take place on Saturday the 8th September 2012, including a sack race, three legged race, tug of war, knockout games and 'guess the weight of the big church bell'. Various traders and stalls will be booked

Week	1 MTWTFSS	2 MTWTFSS	3 MTWTFSS	4 MTWTFSS
Write plan, check costs, etc. Book venue	XXX			
Make sure Mayor Beaumont is confirmed to open the event	X			
Send sponsorship request letter to local businesses		XX		
Promote event competition in the town newspaper, public notice boards, library and halls		XX		
Design a poster		XX		
Write media release		XX		
Send media release			XXX	
Put up posters in key places			XXXXX	
Vicar to go round local businesses to follow up sponsorship letter			XX	
Post out invitations on mailing list			XXX	
Open Sports Day				X
Work out what money was made for the bells fund				X
Have a glass of Alsace with Mayor Beaumont				X
Make a note of any problems for next event				X

the full costs of the event are known, the ticket price can be calculated, bearing in mind that enough tickets have to be sold to cover all eventualities.

There are other hidden-cost risks involved in event management. Breakdown and bottleneck costs can be very severe and not apparent until they occur. The ticketing problems of the 2012 Olympics could be thought of as having breakdown costs, with there being not only negative financial outcomes, such as having to pay compensation for the breakdown, and also the costs of damage to the ticket company's reputation, which might turn out to be so severe that the company may not recover. These failure costs can be thought of as falling into three categories:

● Cost risks related to quality management and standards.
● Cost risks related to the expense of putting on the event.
● Costs risks related to the effective timing and scheduling of events.

CASE STUDY 19

Demand planning: the opening night of the Millennium Dome

London, England

Originally the 'Millennium Dome' now the London 02 Arena

cristapper/Shutterstock.com

- Millennium Dome, Greenwich, England
- Cost: in excess of €1200 million
- The Dome contained 14 zones
- Much of the cost was covered by companies sponsoring the Dome and by Lottery grants
- The opening night was reported as a disaster

Learning Objectives

The aim of this case study is to examine the failures which contributed to the perceived shambles of the opening night ceremony of the Millennium Dome with the following objectives:
To consider the background to the ceremony
To highlight the issues which contributed to the problem
To understand why a large organization failed to react to the problem

The Millennium Dome, at Greenwich in London, took three years to build. The total cost of the building and its operations was some €1200 million. It was opened at a ceremony scheduled to start on the evening of 31 December 1999 and run into the early hours of the morning of 1 January 2000.

The Dome was the culmination of a plan, first suggested in 1994, to celebrate a Christian (religious) event for 2000. Initially it was thought that Birmingham, in the English Midlands, would be the site. However, as the idea began to be adopted by the government, the concept changed from being religious (once the site was selected as Greenwich in east London), to having the purpose of regenerating a large area of derelict land on the Greenwich peninsula, over-looking the River Thames. In this form it was intended to be a trade exhibition, rather like the Festival of Britain of 1951, and its forerunners like the Paris Exposition of 1889 but the idea gradually changed from this to an exhibition celebrating 'time' and the phases of life as its theme. The final outcome was the 'Dome', containing 14 zones, such as the mind zone, the journey zone, the home planet zone, etc., representing various life experiences. Each zone attracted sponsorship from national and international companies; for example, Ford sponsored the journey zone with almost €19.5 million of support, it was reported by the *Daily Telegraph Magazine* at the time.

The opening ceremony, despite every intention to make the event successful, was a shambles of haphazard ticketing, ineptly managed security and the unfortunate late arrival of guests. The results were not only tremendous stress and anger on the night itself, among those struggling to get to the event, but also massive public relations damage to the image of the Dome and to the organizing company. The cause of this shambles was inadequate planning and a lack of awareness on the part of the New Millennium Experience Company (NMEC), of scheduling, especially of the ticketing, together with the apparent lack of a thought-out timescale for the activities of ticket processing and security checks. 10 000 people had been invited to the opening ceremony. A few days before the event, only just over half the tickets had been sent out. At this point, it was discovered that there would not be enough time to post the remaining tickets to the invited guests. The problem was compounded by a lack of a sense of urgency that this was a major material issue that, if not handled well, would cause serious damage.

The NMEC showed no apparent significant managerial concern about the ticketing problem until the issue began to appear in the newspapers a few days before, by which time it was too late to get the tickets out. Consequently, guests were told to get themselves to Stratford underground railway station in east London on the night, where special arrangements would be made to get them onto the Tube (London's metro), which was running special trains to the Dome station at Greenwich. The Dome had been designed with almost no car parking and access was by public transport only; this poor infrastructure was a major cause of low visitor numbers. Indeed, designated parking was often at car parks that were major public transport hubs, such as Luton Airport, some 70 km from the Dome. (In August 2000, after the Dome had further grants and loans of over €100 million, in addition to its original costs, and with continuing low visitor numbers, a car park with a capacity of 1000 car parking spaces was opened at the Dome site, too late to save the peak summer season.)

The opening ceremony was to be performed by the Queen, together with the Prime Minister and the Archbishop of Canterbury, and with a large number of VIPs present, and there was to be tight security. In practice this meant that every guest was supposed to walk through an electronic security gate. The impact of 4000 people turning up at the Stratford underground station, where there were four security gates (only one of which was working properly), had not been adequately thought about or properly checked. As the 4000 ticketless but invited guests began to turn up at Stratford, in their best evening wear, dinner jackets and ball gowns, the outcome was complete chaos. In no way could 4000 people get through one gate and this presented a major issue.

Management locations on the opening night

Senior Management in Greenwich at the Dome

∧

Supervisors at the Dome

∧

Junior contact staff

∧

Operations at Stratford

As the situation deteriorated and with an apparent blasé attitude on the part of the NMEC management, most of whom were already at the Dome and could not understand the magnitude of the chaos at Stratford, partly due to the filtering effect of layers of management and limited communications, as well as the distance, some efforts were made to get the guests to the Dome in time for the main ceremony, scheduled for midnight. Special buses were brought in, and eventually attempts at 'security' were abandoned, in an effort to get people to the Dome. By 10.40 pm, when the 4000 unfortunate guests were at last beginning to arrive, all the food and drink (including 10 000 bottles of champagne) had been either consumed or removed, and further chaos ensued while people tried to find their seats. In this maelstrom the atmosphere of happiness intended for the evening was largely ruined, although the ceremony went ahead.

The following day, the managing director of the NMEC dismissed the chaos as unimportant. Unfortunately for the company, among the 4000 invited guests who had been put through the chaos at Stratford were several national newspaper editors and their wives, the director-general of the BBC and a number of the major sponsors. The company and the event were savaged in the media, and, together with the Government, had to apologize. Within a month, and partly due to 'lower than expected attendances' at the Dome, the chief executive of the NMEC had been replaced. This was the price of inattention to detail in planning and a lack of conviction in management – for example, to avoid jokes about Disney, the NMEC had avoided seeking advice from the amusement park industry, which had the necessary experience of large scale outdoor events. The new chief executive, Pierre-Yves Gerbeau, appointed after the disaster, was from Disney in Europe and an expert in visitor park attractions and ticketing. The Dome closed in December 2000 and the post-event divestment of the site has had all the hallmarks of its dubious pre-event planning. Eventually, after several false starts, the Dome was bought by telecoms company O2 and redeveloped into the O2 arena. It reopened in June 2007 and is now used for music, entertainment and sporting events of all kinds.

Discussion Questions

Identify the key mistakes that NMEC made in its organization of the opening night of the Dome.

1 What are the likely background reasons for these mistakes?

2 What management tools or systems, used in event management, would have prevented the initial ticketing failure?

3 How did the shambles of the opening night impact on the public and media image of the Dome as an attraction?

4 Was this the only reason for lower than expected visitors to the Dome, or did the Dome have infrastructure and content problems as well?

5 What is the accounting convention known as 'sunk costs' and what might its relevance be to the Dome?

Websites

You may search news website archives for commentary on the Dome, such as: **http://news.bbc.co.uk**. For those interested in the arena, go to: **www.theo2.co.uk/** For the Dome's re-incarnation as a major music venue see the Kings of Leon (for example): **http://www.youtube.com/watch?v=GPdgHN-GAvM**.

A tension exists between these issues. For example, for the quality of an event to be assured, both adequate time and money have to be put in; if this is not done, the outcome may not be as intended. This was the case with the Dome's opening night. There was the failure of not having planned enough time and given enough resources (such as expertise, management and staffing) to despatch 4000 tickets. The breakdown resulted in a quality failure and a cost failure (the simple cost in terms of getting people to the Dome by special buses, and the severe and complex cost afterwards of the public relations damage). What action could have been taken to deal with the problem is open to debate, but it should have been possible, for example, to courier tickets out to more than one location for distribution; to arrange for people to meet at more than one place for their onward transport, as well as to have more than one operating security gate at these different locations. Doing this would have cost money to sort out, quite a lot of money. But it would have saved the reputation of the NMEC. The lesson is to pay enough attention to the services being provided for the event and what the participants or guests are saying. In doing so, the cost of solving a problem as it develops may be less than the cost of trying to put the damage right afterwards.

One of the further issues in term of financial planning may be related to legacies. Any legacy of an event may have to be planned from the start. Event legacies are not common for all events, small and personal events don't always tend to have legacies, but some large-scale, national or international events do have legacies (see Chapter 12). These may have major financial implications, indeed it might not be possible to put on an event such as the Olympics without there being a significant legacy: what would be the point of spending hundreds of millions on three weeks of sport unless there were a long-term more permanent gain to be obtained? On a lesser scale this may be true of other kinds of events, the legacy from a village flower show might be that enough money is made to provide flowers or flower baskets around the village for the summer, if so, then the financial implication of the legacy has to be considered in the planning process: how much money is needed for the legacy as well as to run the event again annually? If you want a legacy for an event, it must be realistic and achievable – too heavy a financial burden on the event might mean that it doesn't make enough money to cover both its costs and the cost of the proposed legacy you will have collapsed the event by asking too much of it.

MARKETING PLANNING

All events require marketing planning. We might think some events that are not intended as public activities (such as those for our immediate family and friends), might not need marketing. But think what you do when you invite your friends to a party – you want to make it sound good so people will come, so you are, in effect, doing some marketing. The issue of how to market an event does become significant, even if we are only 'marketing' within a group of friends or neighbours or to a small organization, rather than to the public as a whole. Arguably, we are looking at several marketing-related activities: research (if a public event: who is our market? What will they pay? What are their interests? How will they get to us? etc.); internal marketing, within the organization, both in respect of the people involved in preparing the event and in respect of those people within the organization whom the event would be for; and/or external marketing, for public events or events where some external public relations would be a benefit.

Assuming the event organizers wish to obtain some publicity or public relations coverage, it is necessary to plan the marketing activities that would produce this. For some kinds of activities, such as product launches, the budget available for promoting the event might be very large indeed. For other events, such as a village fête, there might be a modest budget, so, the marketing for it might have to be based on effective public relations and social media rather than on advertising or expensive promotional tools. In working up a marketing plan, the event organizer will have to identify what the available budget is.

There are essentially two ways of doing this. One way is to say, well, here is the income, marketing can have so much (after which the marketing team will take fright and probably have to see what they can get for limited money). The other more preferable way is to look at the event objectives and work up a marketing budget based on what needs to be done.

The next stage will be planning the marketing effort in terms of time. We can call this a marketing action plan, or even a launch plan. It is a schedule of activities leading up to the event (other activities may take place afterwards, such as getting pictures of the event in the local newspapers). The marketing team will need to identify the key lead times for each activity. Suppose a printed programme is required. It will be important to find out not only how long it will take to collect the information to include, but also how long the programme will take to print; how long to be proof read and checked; and how long to be delivered. Many marketing teams have come unstuck with programmes or brochures because a vital piece of information is not ready:

'Oh yes, the committee is meeting next week to decide that'.
'But we need to get the programme proof to the printer today'.
'Oh sorry, you'll just have to wait'.
'But it takes six weeks to print ...'.

In consequence, the key to the marketing programme is to allow enough time and to know who is making relevant decisions and when. Things that often appear simple are not, or take much longer than expected. Comments, which are very typical of the inexperienced organizer, might be:

'I rang up the radio station to tell them about tomorrow's fireworks ... they said they needed to know three weeks ago, in order to get it into the right schedule'.

It is essential, therefore, to find out, genuinely, how long marketing and public relations matters will take, and then to plan accordingly.

There are many lead-time issues that relate to the marketing function. These may include:

- printing of tickets, posters, menus, programmes, banners, etc.;
- ordering of equipment, often the more specialized the longer the lead time;
- advertising and promotion, even local radio may need two or three weeks notification of an event to ensure it is given good coverage;
- liaison issues, where relevant, with police, highways departments, health and safety and so on, especially where large numbers of the public may be attending.

In essence, the longer the lead time you give yourself before an event the better, although this is not to say it is impossible to put on an event very quickly, but to do so may need professional help or may result in higher costs.

We might argue that some types of marketing, especially viral marketing through social media are very fast, but the use of social media such as Facebook, Twitter, LinkedIn and so on are not the simple solution they may seem to be for all marketing issues. They need to be considered in terms of their strengths and weaknesses in just the same way as conventional paid media or advertising. Social media is very useful for personal events and events which take place in a hurry or on the spur of the moment, but most events are not of this type, and consequently the use of social media may best be as one element of the wider marketing mix. Second, social media has a tendency to reveal nasty surprises to inexperienced marketing personnel and even experienced managers. What your organization might have thought was the best idea since the invention of the wheel might expose you to ridicule or insult, because it's not such a good idea or people are resistant to it. Social media has a tendency to allow people to feed back information instantly and if you are disliked, or your event is lousy, or if your organization has a bad reputation then social media, whether its is through Facebook pages or through the use of the **backchannel** at an event, is likely to tell you this very quickly (and possibly in a way you didn't expect or don't like). Social media, therefore, is another tool in the box of tools which can be used as part of your marketing or public relations plan and should be considered just as carefully as any other part of it.

backchannel
An on-line real-time conversation among participants about an event or a presentation in progress.

GETTING IT TOGETHER

At the point at which the organizers have gathered all the information, written the plans and sorted out the major issues, there should be a pause. This may happen naturally between the planning and the event, or it may have to be built in. The pause is needed because there should be time to reflect on the progress of planning the event so far, to check the status of the plans; also time is needed for discussion and feedback and for people and organizations to respond. This is one of those points when everyone should meet to see what else has been done, to discuss what still needs to be achieved and to participate in further arrangements and final checking. Organizers must handle this phase sensitively. It is not necessarily there for them to tell people what will be done, but is to jointly and openly explore progress and is a key characteristic of good events planning: an opportunity to pause and listen.

Throughout this process, the event will be getting closer and closer. There will be deadlines to deal with and in due course the event will take place. With careful planning, modest (or major) success should be the result. After that, a short 'wash-up' session should take place, for feedback on the event, to write up the accounts, complete the records and make any notes of importance to the planning of a similar event in the future.

SUMMARY

A t the beginning of the feasibility phase, a large number of ideas or concepts for an event may have been identified. These various ideas could then be put through a series of screens: marketing, operational and financial, whose purpose is to filter out those ideas that were not really viable. Having done this, the organizers should have a limited number of events to choose from; it is even possible that just one event may have made it. In fact, if the process is done in a very formal way, against set criteria for each part, there might be no ideal outcome, only the 'nearest fit'. Where there is more than one possible event, the objectives can be looked at again and if there is still more than one event on the shortlist, choose the one that would be most enjoyable!

Planning, and the planning process, plays a key role in the organization and management of special events. It is a tool that organizers can use effectively or, sometimes badly. Even the simplest of events, such as a birthday or dinner party, will need to be planned, or at least given some forethought. The larger and more complex events become the more detailed and systematic the planning will have to be. Care, time and effort at the planning stage of an event will yield many benefits, the most important of which is ensuring the most positive outcome for the event.

EVALUATION QUESTIONS

1 How might you organize a committee to put on a small town festival and who might need to be involved?

2 When you have identified several potential ideas for a new event, what screens or filters can you use to test which ideas are best?

3 Different events have different objectives. Identify a personal event, a cultural event, a sporting event and an organizational event and compare their objectives

4 List the main stages in planning an event. Do these stages occur in all types of events, and if not why not?

REFERENCES

Carlsen, J., Andersson, T. D., Ali-Knight, J., Jaeger, K. and Taylor, R. (2010) 'Festival management innovation and failure'. *International Journal of Event and Festival Management* 1(2):120–31.

Goldblatt, J. J. (2002) *Global Event Management in the 21st Century*, New York: Wiley, pp 36–44.

O'Toole, W. (2011) *Events Feasibility and Design: from Strategy to Operations*, Oxford: Elsevier Butterworth Heinemann, pp 261–264.

Raj, R., Walters, P. and Rashid, T. (2008) *Events Management: An integrated and practical approach*, London: Sage, pp 24–33.

Tum, J., Norton, P. and Nevan Wright, J. (2006) *Management of Event Operations*, Oxford: Elsevier Butterworth Heinemann, pp 91–104.

CHAPTER 6

FINANCIAL MANAGEMENT AND THE BUDGET

AIMS

- To provide an introduction to some of the financial planning, control and budgetary issues in running events

- To consider the budgetary organization of events in terms of break-even, monitoring and recording of revenues and costs

- To discuss additional financial issues such as raising income, public funding, concessions and sponsorship

INTRODUCTION

Financial planning and good financial control are important aspects of the event management process. Even if we are only organizing a small personal event, we need to know how much can be spent. For the vast majority of events, there will be both income and expenditure. The careful monitoring, recording and control of these incomes and expenditures is a significant concern of clients, organizers, co-ordinators and finance officers of all kinds. For the professional finance officer, this chapter will seem a very general outline of what has to be done. But for the person new to the job of volunteer treasurer or financial officer of an event, it should prove a helpful starting point. As such, the purpose of the chapter is not to deal with the entire financial management subject related to the area; for this the reader may wish to look at Jagels (2010) or similar texts. The recording of the financial aspects of events, ranging from the purchase of items to the final budgeted accounts, is potentially much more complicated than the summary here. Good financial control is important to the success of events, even those not intended to be profit-making, but there are many useful accountancy practice books and considerable software available for those who wish to expand their expertise.

For events that are revenue generating, as well as those where the recording of outgoings against a client's budget is needed, we can begin to see the necessity of normal accounting processes, rather than simply being able to list the costs on a sheet of paper. Even the scouts of Middleburg with their car wash fundraising idea can serve to illustrate the fact that events exist whose primary purpose is to make money with a minimum expenditure (a few buckets of warm water, some sponges and a large number of happy scouts being all that is needed), but it is still essential to know what money has been made. So while we might have events that are entirely cost-oriented on the one hand, or entirely income-oriented on the other, there are a very large number of events that require both these things and have to be financially managed in a conventional way, with careful assessment of potential income, expenditure and profit, sur-plus or break-even, depending on the type of event.

In all cases, some effort needs to go into providing an overview of the financial aspects of the event, both at the planning stage, during the event itself and at the end. In the case of the wedding or the scouts' car wash, this might simply comprise a list of what has been spent or what has been made (it is better to do two lists – of what is planned and what actually happened – both forecast and actual). Clearly, if the wedding was planned to cost €5000, but €10000 was spent, someone had to find the money. Equally, if the scouts planned to raise €1000 from washing cars but raised only €500, then perhaps the new roof and redecoration of their hut might have to be reduced to the new roof. The function of financial control is to tell us what happened, but it also takes place before and during an event. Beforehand, a budget will be needed so the organizers can judge whether the event is likely to be a success in financial terms, and afterwards as a guide to see whether the event could be judged successful against its financial objectives. Additionally, we will look at ways in which the potential income for an event could be increased, and also at the public funding of events and sponsorship.

OBJECTIVES AND FINANCIAL PLANNING

The setting of objectives is important for the entire event and is also the key to what has to be done financially. Event organizers may be faced with a range of financial choices depending on what has been decided about the objectives (see Chapter 5, about the financial screening process). Care, time and effort will need to be taken at an early stage to ensure good financial management, and that all the possible kinds of expenditure and income have been identified. Small personal events, whose objective is simply the enjoyment of the participants, may have little in the way of financial management, except an awareness of the potential spend in the most general terms. For very large events on a regional, national or international scale, the financial aspects may have to become the subject of financial feasibility studies based on a range of possible techniques, from cost–benefit analysis to assessing the tourism multiplier of a total event project. Such techniques are, however, rather beyond the boundaries of this book and we will concentrate on the more common aspects of financial management in terms of budgeting and control, which are appropriate for the popular range of events.

One key to the effective financial management of events is the appointment of someone responsible for it, in the same way that members of an organizing committee might be responsible for bookings, organization, staff and publicity. It is rather typical of events (particularly those that rely on volunteer staffing, as many do) for their financial aspects to be relatively poorly understood, especially in terms of cash-flow (that is, the relative timing of income and expenditure). Many events organizers do not fully appreciate the financial implications of the decisions they are making and are consequently surprised, when the accounts are done, how little profit has been made or how big a loss has been incurred. Even apparently unrelated decisions can have a major impact on revenue. A good example might be the timing of an event. If this decision is wrong, and perhaps the event clashes with a similar one at the same time, then the target market might not be able to attend both, with a consequent loss of ticket sales, income and other revenue, which may result in a forecast profit becoming an actual loss. For this reason, a numerate and capable person should be appointed to oversee the accounts.

It is also useful to understand the links between the original setting of the objectives and to follow those through into the financial management and budgets. It is no good saying in the objectives (as in the example in Figure 6.1), that a key objective is to raise enough money 'to rebuild the city stadium', if it is not known how much that would cost, and whether the budget for the event will actually be able to cope with it. Similarly, it is no good saying that the objective for a wedding is to spend less than €5000, if this is not properly written into the budget, or if someone goes out and blows €4500 on the pre-wedding party, leaving only €500 for the whole of the actual wedding ('Oh, nobody told me we only had €5000'). The objectives and the financial management are intimately linked. It is essential that the organizers make the links clear – remember the SMART acronym (see page 242): the budget is about measuring.

Cash-flow issues also tend to be serious, particularly for events that involve pre-booking, such as a fundraising dinner. Some expenditure or investment may well have to take place before any income is generated or tickets sold, thus exposing the organizers to risk of financial failure. Venues for events often have long lead times for bookings and require money up front to hold or confirm the booking. When this is the case, the treasurer (or finance officer of the organizing committee) will have to

Figure 6.1   Examples of various event objectives

LEISURE EVENT

International City Athletics Competition

Primary objective: to develop sporting talent in athletics; to bring a large number of visitors to a city to watch or participate; to improve its image.

Financial objective: to make enough money (surplus from the event) to rebuild a city stadium; to provide some additional housing once the competitors have left, based on the financing of the athletes village in conjunction with developers.

CULTURAL EVENT

Village Fête

Primary objective: to hold an enjoyable annual celebration for the village.

Financial objective: to make enough money to break-even and to buy a new bench to put beside the village pond.

ORGANIZATIONAL EVENT

Sales Managers' Team Building Day

Primary objective: to improve the team skills of the sales department.

Financial objective: to keep within the budgeted cost allowed for staff development.

PERSONAL EVENT

Family Wedding

Primary objective: to celebrate the wedding and have a good time.

Financial objective: to cost less than €5000.

ensure sufficient money is available to pay for the various costs before the deadlines, or risk losing the booking and the event. This will mean careful attention to issues such as debt collection and credit periods. For example, if an agent has agreed to take a certain number of advance tickets for an event, when do you, as finance office of the event, get paid for them? If the period between booking the tickets and payment is too long, your event might go bankrupt in the meantime, because you have to pay money out but have not got enough cash coming in (see Figure 6.2).

Suppose a town festival committee has booked a marquee for a medieval banquet as the climax to its annual town pageant. Although the festival might not take place until August, the marquee company, the caterers and the musicians may all want a booking fee. Suppose these booking fees add up to €1000. The capacity of the marquee is 250, and the booking deadline is the end of June. In a very basic way, the financial manager will either have to find €1000 from existing funds (if the event has been run before and generated a surplus in previous years), or, in the case of there being no existing funds, would have to get 250 deposits of €4 per person (or equivalent) to cover the booking costs by, say, a week before the end of June, to have a chance of the event running; or funds from other methods, such as sponsorship, donations or borrowing (e.g. a bank loan, bearing in mind that this would have to be repaid with interest, probably against some form of security). This might be only the first of several financial deadlines and serves to illustrate that cash-flow and deadlines could mean the difference between whether an event runs or not.

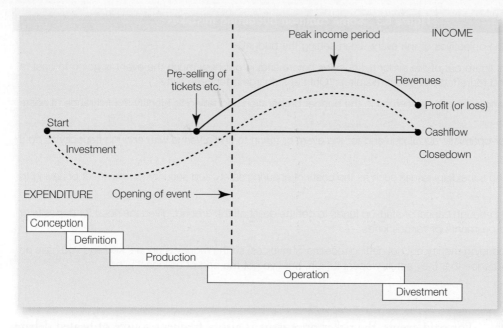

Figure 6.2 Cashflow at events
Based on Morris, W.G. (1994) The Management of Projects, London, Thomas Telford, p. 245

CREATING A BUDGET

In commercial organizations, senior management or a head of department might do the preparation of a budget for an event. However, in the case of many events, run by volunteers, committees, individuals or families, who may have no experience of how to make an event work in financial terms, the preparation of a budget might involve several people, or a volunteer with some financial or organizational background suited to the task. For the person new to the financial aspects of running an event, the planning of a budget may not be as easy as it first appears, since a great deal of information has to be collected, and many new techniques learned, which might not be obvious at the start. However, the time and effort put into careful preparation of a budget is extremely important to the success of the event, and to the financial and general control of what is going on (see Figure 6.3).

The budget for an event may be no more complicated than a list of revenues and costs, or it may be vastly complicated. Either way, it has to be determined with the objectives of the event in mind. It is no good setting a budget in which a large profit is forecast, if the event is supposed to be for public entertainment and only intended to generate a small surplus or to break-even, because making a large profit might result in having to charge too high a ticket price. So, what is the financial objective? Is the event intended to make money or simply to cover its costs? If it is to cover costs, what is the total amount that can be spent, specified either by the clients or by the organizing committee?

It is important to bear in mind that a large number of events, especially corporate events, have a predetermined budget as part of their brief, because the event is not intended to raise money, but to perform some other organizational function (an example being a conference or team building activity), so that 'income' is simply a matter of the use to which the budgeted figure is put.

Figure 6.3   Some common budgeting mistakes

- Ignoring the objectives of the event when setting the budget.

- Plucking a figure out of the air for ticket sales before finding out how much the event is going to cost (a serious and regrettably frequent mistake). ('Oh! Let's charge a tenner!' 'Why?')

- Not involving everyone concerned in the budget preparation and failing to identify the full range of costs accurately.

- Being over-optimistic about demand for the event or failing to find a venue with enough capacity to do it properly.

- Overlooking subsidiary issues such as the costs of ensuring safety and security, or the effect of having to add tax.

- Not having enough capital or start-up funds to get the event off the ground, given the need for deposits or advanced payments of various kinds.

- People spending money but not getting receipts or invoices, so the money is unchecked and you have no control evidence that they actually spent it ('Oh, but I've got the bag of balloons!').

For paid events, the ticket price issue is also a frequent source of heated debate, sometimes before any attempt has been made to identify costs. This is a very common mistake, partly because organizers wrongly see it as the most important issue. The ticket price might be an important issue, but it simply is not good enough to say 'We must make it cheap or no-one will come'. This is usually based on someone's private opinion, not on a carefully budgeted assessment of the costs, let alone on an objective view of what the target market would really pay. In essence, costs need to be listed first and accurately (not just, 'My mate said it would be the same as the one they did last year at the football ground'). Quotes or actual prices need to be obtained for all aspects of the activity. For the football ground, for example, by getting the cost quote from the ground manager, not from 'your mate'. In some cases there would need to be more than one quote. Quotations should be made on a like for like basis, and the criteria decided (do you want the cheapest quotation, or the best quality of goods or services, etc.?). From there, the expenditure can be assessed and then, and only then, should a ticket price be estimated, bearing in mind the numbers expected to come (Bowdin *et al.*, 2011).

In the case of certain types of events there might also be differential pricing of tickets (e.g. at sporting events, where the best seats have a higher price). Differential pricing also allows us to provide a range of tickets at a range of prices, for example, family tickets, group tickets, full price or off-peak tickets. This requires careful understanding. Suppose our event needs to sell 120 tickets at €10 each to make our target profit, but our estimates of what the target market will pay show that only half the people we expect to attend will pay the full price, even though we are expecting an attendance of 120 people. What do we do? Perhaps we might have to cancel. On the other hand, we might find that the rest are willing to pay €6 for tickets (we will call these 'contribution price' tickets). Does this help, even if we have said the ticket price must be €10? It depends on whether €6 will be enough to cover our fixed costs, and if enough people paying full price still want to come. Fixed costs might be €5 per person (this is a simplified example).

Queue to collect tickets from the box office, at the Olympic Park on July 30, 2012 in London, England

The total income would thus be €960 and the event would make a profit, even though we couldn't sell all our tickets at the full price and make the full profit. You will have noticed that I didn't use the word 'discount' in this example. Forget 'discount', as it gives you the wrong idea, since the contribution tickets still have to cover all fixed costs, and we still have to sell enough of both tickets to cover our total costs. This is why you can go to, say, a leisure centre or a theme park at an off-peak period and pay less than you would at a peak period. It is about having differential ticket prices for different times, for different target markets and different groups, in the knowledge that not everyone will pay full price, at any given time. Airlines do it too. You might have got the last two seats on a plane at €50, when everyone else has paid €500 a ticket, but that is because the plane is covering its total costs, and they might as well have two people with cheap seats, rather than two empty seats. On the other hand, if everyone paid €50, then they probably couldn't afford to taxi the plane along the runway. This is also true of events, and can lead you to do some creative ticket pricing, if you have to. But only if you have to.

A major issue for event organizers is to know how many people will attend. In order to prepare a reasonably accurate budget, the estimates of attendance may be based on surveys of the market, attendance at similar or previous events, knowledge of the size of the available customer base and so on. From the point of view of budget preparation, an organizer might want to be optimistic about attendance, but, given the potential problems about booking deadlines and deposits, it is important to be realistic about how many tickets can be sold and whether the venue can be filled, or whether the budget should estimate to break-even, if, say, half the venue is filled. Optimism is very nice, but the real test is often when the organizing committee or sales team go out and try to sell tickets and find that, 'no one wants to buy them yet'. There are ways in which this kind of response can be influenced, such as by asking for a deposit (once people have committed some money they are generally likely to pay the balance when the time comes), or by offering discounts for advance purchase (rather like advance purchase airline tickets), or by selling tickets to key opinion formers as a way of generating interest.

Break-even is a key issue and sometimes not well understood. Say an event will cost €500 to put on, and the venue will accommodate 100 people. At first glance you might say, we need to sell 100 tickets at €5. But if you did this, you would make a loss even if 99 out of the 100 tickets were sold. You have to consider what your realistic break-even point is. To make €100 profit in this case you would have to sell 100 tickets at a ticket price of €6, not €5.

Other difficulties arise due to unforeseen costs or subsidiary issues, a common one being whether tax has to be added to ticket prices. For most small-scale or family events, this is irrelevant, but for big events it would have to be checked with the correct government department, as there is a minimum threshold for payment (in the UK, this is the HM Revenue and Customs and the UK VAT threshold at the time of writing is £68 000 before registration is required).

For those new to events budgeting, the Outline Budget Form in Figure 6.4 will help you understand what is needed and what information may be missing. It may also show that once you have identified all the costs, your first ideas about how much to charge as an entry fee or ticket may be completely wrong. Most important of all, it may also be evident that there is no margin of safety in running the event between its revenue and its forecast costs. In simple terms, there have to be enough people attending and paying to cover the costs and make sure there is a profit or small surplus. (Although some events are not intended to make a profit.)

Suppose our total costs are €1000. We forecast that 100 people will attend, so the cost would appear to be €10 per person. This, however, is not a safe position to be in, as even if 99 people come to the event it will still make a loss. The budget should be worked out based on the idea that more people will come to the event than are needed to cover the costs, for example, 125 people at €10. Or that the ticket price is higher, for example, 100 people at €12.50. In this respect it is also necessary to take into account not only how many people we expect to attend, but whether the venue capacity is appropriate. If the venue will only accommodate 75 people but we need 100 people to attend in order to cover our costs or make a profit, then the event is not viable at that venue. It is possible, on the basis of various cost estimates, for the organizing committee or finance officer to prepare some comparative outline budgets to help the decision-making process, where an issue, like the venue, needs to be compared with others (see Figure 6.5).

This first attempt at providing an adequate outline budget will help us identify what further information is needed to prepare a more detailed budget forecast. The detailed budget can be based on a given number of attendees, or we can have alternatives showing worst case and best case. It is necessary, probably crucial, to have a good idea of the point at which the event will break-even and make a profit. For this we have to bear in mind that some costs are fixed and some are variable (Garrison et al., 2009). For example, for whatever number of people attend, the cost of hiring a marquee for an event would be fixed, let us say €1450. The marquee will still cost €1450 whether one person attends our event or whether 100 people attend – this is a fixed cost. On the other hand, the cost of the food might be variable in relation to the number of people: let us suppose a sit-down meal costs €20 per person. In the case of the meal, if one person attends the cost is €20. If 50 people attend the cost is €1000 and if 100 people attend it is €2000. This is a variable cost (see Figure 6.6).

PRELIMINARY BUDGET FORM

Proposed Event: _____   **Date Today:** _____

Date of Event: _____   **Days to go:** _____

Forecast number of people expected: _____   **(Paying Guests / Paying Visitors)**

Capacity of the Venue: _____

List of Costs

Venue Hire: Total amount: €_____

                    Deposit amount: €_____   **Deposit due by:** _____

Staff/Labour: Number of volunteers needed: _____   **Number of paid staff needed:** _____

Total staffing cost incl. staff meals: €_____

Example Overheads:	Total Amount €:	Best price quotation* given by:
Advertising	_____	_____
Printing / Posters / Tickets	_____	_____
Signs / Place Cards / Menus / Programmes	_____	_____
Custom T-Shirts / Uniform / Badges	_____	_____
Equipment Hire	_____	_____
Food	_____	_____
Drink	_____	_____
Entertainment	_____	_____
Music	_____	_____
Decorations	_____	_____
Linen / Linen Hire	_____	_____
Prizes / Complimentary Items	_____	_____
Floristry / Plants	_____	_____
Security / Crowd Control / Guides / Info point	_____	_____
Insurance	_____	_____
Refuse Removal / Cleaning	_____	_____
Power / Heat / Light / Air Conditioning	_____	_____
Ticket Distribution / Stationery / Postage	_____	_____
Licence / Licence application	_____	_____
Audio Visual / Sound	_____	_____
Phones / Mobiles / Radio Links	_____	_____
Photographer / Video Company / Press Kit	_____	_____
Other items	_____	_____

Total of all costs including venue and staff   €_____

Total costs divided by number of paying guests (including venue hire, staffing and any other items not listed here but known, expected or planned): €_____ **(Costs per person)**

Profit / Surplus Required? €_____ **(Profit per person)**

List any additional deposits or prepayments required:

_____

_____

Figure 6.4   Preliminary (outline) budget form

* Quotations should be made on like for like basis and the criteria decided (do you want the cheapest quotation or do you want the best quality of goods or services, etc.?) Quotes should include VAT.

Figure 6.5   Example of comparative outline budgets for a proposed company party

Venues:	Luigi's Garden Bistro	Rolf's Bar & Marquee	Rumours Nightclub
Venue Capacity:	60	100	120
No of guests expected:	50	50	50
Costs:	€	€	€
Venue Hire	0	1450 (Marquee)	500 (Deposit)
Staffing Costs	0 (Included in meal)	0 (Included in meal)	100 (Door / coats)
Printing	50	50	50
Menus and Place Cards	50	50	50
Food	1250 (Sit down meal)	1000 (Sit down meal)	750 (Buffet)
Reception Drinks	300	300	300
Band	500	500	500
Raffle Prizes	100	100	100
Total Estimated Costs	2250	3450	2350
Ticket price if 40 people attend:	€45	€69	€47

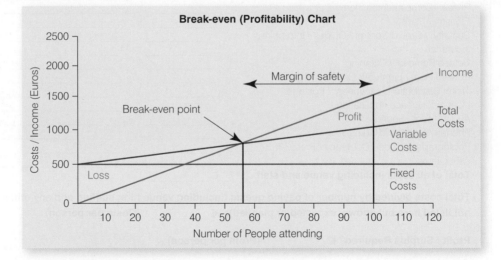

Figure 6.6   Break-even chart

Note that the margin of safety is the amount of capacity or production above the break-even point which you can achieve with the expected demand (as opposed to the maximum capacity of a venue or maximum possible production). In this example, the maximum attendance you expect is 100 people, even though the venue could accommodate 120. To achieve a profit 54 or more people must attend.

In terms of expenditure and costs it is essential that we have properly calculated the total costs and have included every cost that might be involved. It is very important to ensure that all the costs have been checked and that the list is genuinely complete.

THE DETAILED BUDGET

It would be very easy to use the common financial term 'budgetary control' at this stage. However, 'control' often concentrates financial managers' minds only on costs or expenditure, and clearly, in event management terms, revenue generation and the whole picture are equally important. If the event objective is about quality rather than profitability, then over-concentration on costs might well damage the success of the event, because cheap materials would be bought rather than good quality ones. We have already noted that certain types of events can be more revenue-led than cost-led.

A budget is a forecast or plan, which helps to regulate the operation of an event (or any business) over a given period of time. In the case of a business such as a hotel, the budget might be an annual one. In the case of an event, because events are one-off and time limited, the budget will normally be for the time period of that event. A budget is also a management tool by which responsibility for various activities (e.g. sales or the control of costs) can be seen, in much the same way as the general event plan. The budget, both a forecast of what is intended to happen and a record of what is happening (or, after the event, of what had happened), acts as a means of comparing the forecast with the reality and sets targets that the organizers can strive to achieve (see Figure 6.7).

The advantages of having a budget are that it is a detailed forecast of what should be happening financially, and as such it helps planning (Yeoman et al., 2004) but, as with any other element of a plan, it should not be a single controlling factor. A budget is just that, a financial guide, not a straitjacket. The budget should result in better co-ordination between the organizers of an event. For example, the budget could be split into revenue budget, as a target for the ticket sales staff to achieve; a publicity budget for the marketing staff to keep within and an operations budget for the events manager to ensure that he/she has not overspent on printing, decorations, staff, equipment or other resources. The budget is intended to act as a measure of performance between that which is forecast and the actual outcome which the organizers are responsible for. This forecasting may often be difficult for events because of their unique nature, and it may be simply an approximate estimate. On the other hand, some events may have occurred before, in similar circumstances, or in previous years, and a new budget can be created with a little adjustment from the actual outcome of the last event.

Budgeting is also a method of controlling expenses and costs because it should help to establish clear lines of responsibility about who can or cannot spend money. Related to this, the budget should also make managers aware of costs and revenues, so that they do not become over-enthusiastic in spending money, or fail to exploit an opportunity to make money or generate revenue from some aspect of the event. For example, it might be very nice to have a media celebrity open a carnival or present the winners of a sports competition with their prize, but most media celebrities charge a major fee for appearing, and if this has not been budgeted for, it should not be done – it might result in an event that should have been profitable making a loss.

Because it is helping the planning process, the budget should also seek to ensure that the resources available to the organizer are most economically or efficiently used, thus helping to keep costs under control or to ensure a profit or surplus is made. For example, there is no point hiring 20 ushers all day if they are only going to be needed for the first ten minutes, and costs like this might well show up in the

(SUMMARY) EVENT BUDGET

Event: _____

Date of Event: _____　Date of this budget: _____

Attendance (Paying guests)　　　　　　　　Forecast: _____　Actual: _____

_____

Income / Revenue	Budget €:	Actual €:
Ticket Sales	_____	_____
Catering	_____	_____
Income from concession stand rental	_____	_____
Raffle	_____	_____
Other (Specify) _____	_____	_____
Total Income	**€_____**	**€_____**

Expenditure:	Budget €:	Actual €:
Venue Hire	_____	_____
Staff / Labour	_____	_____
Advertising	_____	_____
Printing / Posters / Tickets	_____	_____
Signs / Place Cards / Menus / Programmes	_____	_____
Custom T-Shirts / Uniform / Badges	_____	_____
Equipment Hire	_____	_____
Food	_____	_____
Drink	_____	_____
Entertainment	_____	_____
Music	_____	_____
Decorations	_____	_____
Linen / Linen Hire	_____	_____
Prizes / Complimentary Items	_____	_____
Floristry / Plants	_____	_____
Security / Crowd Control / Guides / Info point	_____	_____
Insurance	_____	_____
Refuse Removal / Cleaning	_____	_____
Power / Heat / Light / Air Conditioning	_____	_____
Ticket Distribution / Stationery / Postage	_____	_____
Licence / Licence application	_____	_____
Audio Visual / Sound	_____	_____
Phones / Mobiles / Radio Links	_____	_____
Photographer / Video Company / Press Kit	_____	_____
Other items	_____	_____
Total Costs	**€_____**	**€_____**
Surplus (Profit) / Deficit (Loss)	**€_____**	**€_____**

Figure 6.7　General budget form

forecast as being out of line with the rest of the budget. The budget can be made more or less detailed depending on the needs of the organizers or clients. For a small event, it might be enough to include minor costs (e.g. cost of ushers) in the budget line about staffing. On the other hand, we might want to have full and complete

CASE STUDY 20

Event break-even: the annual dinner of the Ecclesbourne Valley Railway

Wirksworth, England

© Pcgenius9

Ferrybridge No.3 train on it's first test run the re-openning of the Ecclesbourne Valley Railway

FACTBOX

- The Ecclesbourne Valley Railway
- 14 km heritage railway at Wirksworth, near Derby, England
- Runs a number of public events each year
- Annual dinner targeted at members and shareholders
- Purpose of the event: to raise money for the railway

Learning Objectives

The aim of this case study is to examine the concepts of break-even and profitability in relation to putting on an event with the following objectives:

To consider the way in which break-even is calculated for a known example

To highlight how a main sources of revenue (e.g. tickets) might be supplemented by other sources

To understand that careful control of costs is important to ensure events are profitable or that they break-even (not all events are commercial or intended to be profitable)

The Ecclesbourne Valley Railway is typical of the many heritage railways and railway museums in the UK and in other parts of Europe. It is a 14 km privately owned railway line in the English Midlands, providing a tourist experience for people interested in railway history, steam locomotives, and historic railway equipment and artefacts. As a tourist attraction run largely by volunteers, it not only raises its revenue through ticket sales, retail activities, catering and other commercial means, but also through events of various kinds, charitable grants and donations and local authority contributions. This range of fundraising is necessary to keep the railway operational and to help restore and maintain its historic artefacts.

In the 2009 event season the following annual dinner was costed. This type of dinner, often called a fundraising dinner or 'Sportsman's' dinner, is very typical of this sort of event. Such dinners are common among all kinds of charitable, voluntary and sporting organizations, and in the case of some of the smaller organizations, a dinner of this kind may be the major social event in their calendar. In most cases the objectives are as follows. Primary objective: fundraising (either in general, or for a specific reason, e.g. new kit for a rugby club; refurbishment of the club's premises; new fencing, etc.); secondary objectives: social meeting of an organization's members and supporters; raising of the organization's profile among potential supporters and sponsors; opportunity to invite honoured guests, contributors or sponsors by way of thanks for their interest in or help given to the organization.

In the case of the Ecclesbourne Valley Railway, the primary purpose is to raise funds for the maintenance and repair of historic rolling stock (engines, carriages, wagons, etc.). The secondary purpose is to provide a social opportunity for the railway's shareholders and members, the budget for the event being based on a maximum number of 150 guests and a break-even point of 38 guests.

There are some interesting issues in considering this data:

First, unlike our text examples, the fixed costs for this dinner can be reduced somewhat to lower the break-even point. For example, this could be done by not hiring a guest speaker and so eliminating the expenses allocated. Thus, if demand for tickets were very low indeed, but those attending still wished it to go ahead without having a speaker, some fixed costs could be saved here. Some further fixed costs could be saved by not having the menus and place cards printed professionally, but simply printing one menu per table on a home computer. Also, the cost of mailing out final tickets may fall if there are fewer of them. So if the organization wanted the event to go ahead for secondary rea-

sons (in this case social reasons) this could still be done, even though very little profit could be made.

Second, further money could be raised during the event itself, separate from ticket revenue.

Venue: The Bear Inn, Alderwasley, Derbyshire, England.
Event date: Friday 25 September 2009
Maximum capacity of the venue: 150 diners.
Ticket Price: €45

Fixed Costs	For 150 people €	For 38 people €
Venue hire	300.00	300.00
Guest speaker's expenses	150.00	0.00
Menus and place cards	75.00	2.25
Mail-out to shareholders promoting the event	285.00	285.00
Photocopying of booking form for mail-out	60.00	60.00
Photocopying and mail-out of booked tickets	51.75	30.00
	921.75	**677.25**

Variable Costs		
Cost of dinner per head €26.40	3960.00	1003.20
Total Costs	4881.75	1680.45
Revenue at ticket price €45	6750.00	1710.00
Profit on event	€1868.25	€29.55

This is very common at charitable dinners and is done by holding raffles, playing bingo, having a range of money-raising games (e.g. tops and tails, etc.) or holding auctions of donated gifts or pledges.

Third, the very act of holding the event might bring in new sponsors, advertisers or useful contacts. In consequence, if organizers at any fundraising dinner had to make a decision about whether to run their dinner in the case of only break-even on ticket sales, they might still wish to carry on because of the secondary benefits.

Discussion Questions

1 Suppose the above event had three additional revenue-earning games, a raffle, a bingo game and an auction of a prize, which respectively brought in €350 per activity, what would be the total profit of this event at its maximum capacity?

2 Consider any fundraising activity or dinner you have attended. How has the main revenue been earned and what additional sources of revenue have the organizers found?

3 The guest speaker's expenses in this case were very small, the speaker being a local man with an interest in railway history. What might the costs have been for a 'celebrity' or professional speaker?

4 Might these costs have wiped out the potential profit of this event? How could this be overcome?

Websites

For the related website for those interested in the Ecclesbourne Valley Railway, go to: **www.e-v-r.com**. Also of interest in terms of event budgeting see: **http://eventplanning.about.com/od/eventplanning basics/ht/basicbudget.htm**.

details of all items. To do this, the general budget, with its list of incomes and costs, can be broken down into extra information (see Figure 6.8).

WHO SPENDS WHAT

We have now prepared our detailed budget, it has been approved by the clients or the organizing committee and the serious preparations are about to begin. People will want to go out and spend money, but before they do, it is vital that we have a control system in place to record who is spending what, when and how. Each part of the budget needs to have someone responsible for it (not just the finance officer who wrote it). The revenue part of the budget might be the responsibility of the marketing department, together with their own expenditure. For example, the advertising expenditure budget might be €1000, but in giving the marketing department this amount to spend, we expect them to attract 500 people to the event, paying €10 a ticket. Therefore the marketing department must have its own clear targets about how its money is best spent to attract the 500 people. Similarly, if we expect the catering department to make money, say, €500 on beverages, it needs to have some idea of what kind of beverages it is going to sell, and how many it will have to sell and at what price and profit to make the expected €500.

An important issue is who is allowed to spend money. If a department has a budget, normally it will be the department head that has the authority to spend it, and the key question is how much and who else can authorize this. Events management depends on the ability of managers and events organizers to solve problems, often very quickly. If they do not have the funds to do this, or the ability to take decisions quickly, then the event may fail (the ticketing fiasco at the Millennium Dome opening night is an example – the inability to deal with

DETAILED EVENT BUDGET SUMMARY AND COST BREAKDOWNS

Event: _____

Date of Event: _____ Date of this budget: _____

Attendance	Forecast:	Actual:
Paying visitors / guests	_____	_____
Complimentary / hospitality visitors	_____	_____
VIPs	_____	_____
Press	_____	_____

Opening Balance (At bank): €_____

Income / Revenue	Budget €:	Actual €:
Ticket Sales		
Individual	_____	_____
Family	_____	_____
Group	_____	_____
Discount / Elders	_____	_____
Catering		
Restaurant Food	_____	_____
Restaurant Drink	_____	_____
Arena Coffee Bar	_____	_____
Arena Hospitality Area Extras	_____	_____
Income from concession stand rental		
Ice Cream Stands	_____	_____
Retail Stands	_____	_____
Raffle		
Saturday Raffle	_____	_____
Sunday Raffle	_____	_____
Other (specify): Parking	_____	_____
Total Income	€_____	€_____

Expenditure:	Budget €:	Actual €:
Venue Hire		
Staff / Labour	_____	_____
Staff wages	_____	_____
Staff meals	_____	_____
Staff insurance	_____	_____
Staff uniforms	_____	_____
Volunteers' meals	_____	_____
Volunteers' gift bags	_____	_____
Volunteers' sashes and armbands	_____	_____
Advertising		
Local Radio: 6 adverts (10 second)	_____	_____
The Telegraph: 3 Adverts (1/8 page)	_____	_____
Banners (2)	_____	_____
Newspaper inserts (10 000)	_____	_____
Artwork for leaflets	_____	_____
Leaflets (10 000)	_____	_____
Etc.	_____	_____
Etc.	_____	_____
Total Costs	€_____	€_____
Surplus (Profit) / Deficit (Loss)	€_____	€_____
Closing Balance (At bank)	€_____	€_____

Figure 6.8   Budget: Detailed income and costs – final outcome summary

the problem of not being able to get enough tickets out to enough people might have resulted from the ticketing manager's lack of authority to spend enough money to get the tickets out in time). Also, in normal circumstances, many items for events are pre-ordered, and for this to take place properly not only are purchase specifications needed (which describe what sort of item is being ordered in detail, so you get what you ordered on the day, e.g. 500 blue stacking chairs, not 250 green armchairs), but also purchase order numbers for any item above a given amount (see Figure 6.9). In this way expenditure can be properly recorded (Lucey, 2008).

Middleburg Events Company
Festival Park Street
Middleburg MG56 2RP
00 44 (0) 1786 123456

To: Order Number: 48519
Red Dragon Furniture Hire
Ty Gwyn
Fford Uwd   Date: 14 August 2010
Abertawe, Wales
SW5 6RE

Dear Sir / Madam,

Please supply and deliver the following items to the address and on the date stated below:

Quantity	Size	Description	Cost
500	**Standard**	**Stacking Chairs (Type 2000)** **Blue only**	**€5600 (inc VAT)**

Deliver to	On
Mr Kevin McDonald **Events Co-ordinator** **At: Middleburg Music Festival** **Festival Park** **Middleburg**	**28 August 2010** **(Before 1 p.m.)**

Yours faithfully,

Anna Murray

Purchasing Officer
Middleburg Events Company
(anna@middleburg.co.eu)

Figure 6.9   Purchase order form

Petty Cash

Petty Cash requested for: ______________________________ Amount issued €______

Issued to (signature): ______________________ Date: ______

Print name: ______________________

Authorized by (signature): ______________________

Receipt attached for items Cost: Amount used €______/______Cents

Figure 6.10 Petty cash voucher

Similarly, for small items, petty cash may be needed and a system will have to be set up to issue it (petty cash is a small amount of money for items that have to be paid for in cash, say at local shops, also minor items and those that are too small to be bought in bulk). Normally, an amount of petty cash (perhaps €500) might be held by the **event co-ordinator** and issued on petty cash vouchers (see Figure 6.10), so that people can be sent out quickly for things that are needed. ('Oh, we've run out of teabags.' 'OK, here's a 20, go and get a box. And bring me the receipt.') At the end of the event, the various petty cash vouchers and receipts, together with the major receipts and invoices, will be collated to make up the final accounts.

event co-ordinator The individual who manages an event on behalf of a client.

The budget is also a mechanism for showing what is going wrong. If the budget shows a forecast expenditure of €1000 on seating, but the real cost is €2000, you need to find out why, and to do so quickly. The reasons might be legitimate and necessary, and you might have to adjust the rest of the budget to take account of this, perhaps by increasing prices or cutting back on something else. On the other hand, the reason may not be legitimate and you will have to take very rapid action. Someone may be defrauding you, or theft is taking place, or any number of other problems, which the divergence between the budget forecast and the actual might show.

OTHER SOURCES OF INCOME

So far we have assumed that income is derived from people buying tickets. It is important to bear in mind that there might be other sources of income or revenue besides ticket sales. These sources may be other revenue-generating activities, or sponsorship-related activities.

Special events are such diverse activities that it can be difficult to generalize about them, especially in financial terms. Additional income is often needed for events, even those where there is a defined ticket price. For example, we might wish to run a charity or philanthropic fundraising race night and charge tickets at €15. This might raise a good amount, above and beyond what was needed to break-even. But more money might also be generated for charity by having other activities going on besides

Figure 6.11   Sources of additional revenue in addition to ticket or admission prices
Programmes / Brochures / Guidebooks
Catering / Fast Food / Sales Stalls
Retail / Souvenirs / Clothing / Merchandising
Corporate Hospitality Areas / Lounge Suites / Chill Out Area / Crèche
Photography Charges / Photography Sales / Video
Car Parking / Transport Services
Concessions / Stalls / Stands / Pitches / Franchises / Rentals / Contracting
Raffles / Lottery / Tombola / Games
Broadcast Rights (usually major sporting events only)
The use of 'membership' type subscriptions to encourage repeat visits (where appropriate)

the races. There could be a raffle or an auction of pledges. There could be games such as 'hit the whisky bottle' (with a large denomination coin, whoever gets the closest wins the bottle, and the rest of the coins are collected for the charity). There could be a **cash bar**, in addition to, say, wine included in the ticket price. A little careful thought can identify many good, simple, money-raising activities, thus helping to increase the income of an event (see Figure 6.11). Control needs to be exercised over loose cash, though. Money should be recorded properly if going through tills. If being collected in some other way, e.g. for charity, it needs to be collected in sealed containers, which should only be opened with two people present. In this way it can be counted and recorded legitimately.

> **cash bar**
> A bar set up during a function where the guests or delegates, rather than the host, pay for drinks individually.

This is not to say that the financial manager of an event should not be actively seeking external or additional ways of raising money to support an event. In fact, the generation of additional revenue is often a key failure of many events, especially volunteer events, because it is wrongly seen as less important than financial control. It is easy to see who is responsible for cost control within budgets, but the raising of additional or extra revenues is often overlooked: no one is made responsible for ideas about it or for carrying through such ideas and consequently opportunities to raise extra income streams are lost.

Events vary considerably in how they are funded. It is important to recognize that many events have more than one source of income or revenue – in fact there might be as many sources of income as there are costs associated with the event (see Figure 6.12). Equally, we should not regard the term 'income' as necessarily meaning revenue. The 'income' for operating an event may simply be a budgeted amount that an organization has to spend, funded by the organization itself. Similarly, events put on by government or councils may depend on a budgeted amount, which is funded by tax nationally or locally. The purpose of tax is to provide public services, of which sporting, cultural, ceremonial or tourist events might be examples (in the same way that rubbish collection, street lighting and hospitals are public services paid for out of taxes). Certain types of events can require start-up funding. This can be sought from all kinds of bodies who might have an interest in the event, not just government, councils or agencies, although there are official bodies (and some sponsors) who often have limited funds for this type of activity (but many calls on them).

> ### Figure 6.12   Types of event funding
>
> #### LEISURE EVENT
>
> International City Athletics Competition
>
> Funding: Possible range of funding including government agencies such as sports councils, local government funding for sporting events, support from sports sponsors and broadcasters, together with income generated from ticket sales, concessions selling food, drink and sports related merchandise.
>
> #### CULTURAL EVENT
>
> Village Fête
>
> Major income might be from entrance tickets, parking, income from renting pitches for the various stands, money raised from a raffle and various games, also sponsorship of activities on an organizational or individual basis, charitable donations in money or in kind (gifts).
>
> #### ORGANIZATIONAL EVENT
>
> Sales Managers' Team Building Day
>
> No direct income as such. The event will be paid for within a particular budget determined by the organization and operated by the Sales Department itself (for staff training) or a related department, such as personnel, according to the appropriate organizational objectives.
>
> #### PERSONAL EVENT
>
> Family Wedding
>
> No direct income as such. The event would be paid for by the people getting married and their families, with donations of presents and other useful things 'in kind' e.g. friends decorate the church, or help prepare a buffet, or contribute flowers, etc.

SPONSORSHIP AND PUBLIC FUNDING

One of the common misconceptions in the design of events is the view that an event will easily attract sponsorship. In practice the attractiveness of any given event to potential sponsors is very limited. The time and effort that the organizers might waste trying to get (elusive) sponsorship could well be better used elsewhere, perhaps in developing secondary income streams for the event, such as catering or retailing, as mentioned earlier.

The most important aspect of sponsorship is for event organizers to remember that potential sponsors have to get something out of the event, and are extremely unlikely to provide money for nothing ('Oh, but you can have an advert in our programme …'. 'Really? Why should I need that?'). Therefore, it is important to keep in mind what the event would do for a potential sponsor (Skinner and Rukavina, 2003). There are several aspects to this. First, the event and potential sponsors should be looking at the same target market. It is no good trying to get a hearing aid manufacturer to sponsor an annual student ball. Second, the issue of media exposure: what are the publicity and public relations plans for your event and will the sponsor benefit from them? Third, will the sponsor get some direct benefit besides media coverage? For example, some places at a table in the gala dinner; free admission to the event for the sponsor and a colleague or partner; complimentary VIP seats in the hospitality box. Without some or other of these benefits to give to potential sponsors, events organizers will have significant problems attracting sponsorship.

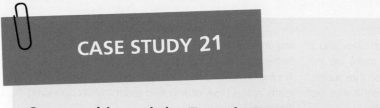

CASE STUDY 21

Sponsorship and the Tour de France

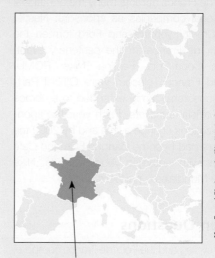

Marc Pagani Photography/Shutterstock.com

Tour de France

The final laps of the 2004 Tour de France in Paris

FACTBOX

- Begun as a newspaper publicity stunt, it celebrated its centenary in 2003
- 22 teams, of nine riders, compete for €3 million in prize money – €400 000 for the winner
- Coloured jerseys (each sponsored) distinguish the leader on time, leader on points, 'King of the Mountains', best climber and best young rider

Learning Objectives

The aim of this case study is to examine the way in which sponsorship may play a major role in event funding and marketing with the following objectives:

To consider the way in which the Tour draws in sponsors and how the Tour benefits from sponsorship

To examine the range of sponsors for a major event and to consider what sponsors get out of their contribution, as well as what benefits or potential pitfalls may exist

The Tour de France began as a 200 km bicycle race in 1903, as a means of boosting sales of *L'Auto* newspaper. Controversy dogged the race from the start and the 'gamesmanship' of the 1904 race (such as fans sprinkling nails in the tracks of their competitors, or competitors using cars and trains to gain ground) nearly forced *L'Auto* to call it off. By the 1920s, it was seen as the world's toughest bicycle race, in which manufacturers' teams battled it out. At that time the course was over 5500 km long and under severe rules, although, some felt, even then, that overt commercialism overshadowed the cycling.

In 1930 the competition amended its rules so that manufacturer teams were replaced by national squads (of eight riders, picked by the organizers and paid by the Tour itself); everyone rode identical bikes and a publicity caravan was introduced, to make up the cash shortfall from the manufacturers and their teams. For the first time, radio covered the race. It was first televised in 1952, television being new then.

During the 1960s national teams were once again replaced by sponsored teams. In 1978 riders went on strike over split stages and transfers. Concerns over drugs became an issue when Pedro Delgado won in 1988, having tested positively for a substance banned at the Olympic Games, but not by the Tour's organizers.

In 1998 it was thought that one third of France's entire population lined the route, but the event was remembered not for the immense public support and interest, but for another publicized scandal about drugs. The banned substance EPO had been found in one team car, days before the race, and the testing of staff and competitors led to various teams being withdrawn and a string of arrests, including riders, team officials and doctors, prompting sit-downs and go-slows among the riders. The Festina team suffered the worst publicity, but sponsors stayed loyal to the event. Despite the Festina team being at the centre of the media attack surrounding this race, the watch making firm has continued its sponsorship with confidence and remains a sponsor to the present day.

Since the days of the manufacturer teams, the Tour de France has been attractive to sponsors and they have stayed consistently loyal. For example, the US Postal Service began with a small team and a fairly low-key presence, but after 1997 replaced Motorola as the leading US team, expand-

ing into a multinational effort that included Nike within its family of sponsors and confirmed its continuing involvement, despite some domestic criticism in the USA of a public organization spending 'millions of dollars' abroad.

The Tour de France attracts many major national and international companies as sponsors: Nestlé, Champion, Credit Lyonnais and Ford formed the Club du Tour de France for the centenary event. While Astra, Coca-Cola, Festina, Nike, POMU, Sodexho and France Telecom were Official Partners. The sponsorship family extended to embrace a further 13 official suppliers. Each year the sponsoring organizations change a little and by 2009 the main sponsors had become Banque LCL and Cafe de Columbia, with Antargaz, Alden, Skoda, Nike and AG2R le Mondiale as partners.

Discussion Questions

1   How do cycling and the Tour de France compare, as sponsorship opportunities, with other sports and events?

2   How has the heritage of the race, including some of the negative aspects, affected the outlook for event, team and personal sponsorship?

3   What implications are there for ensuring that each of the several sponsoring companies gets an optimum return?

4   Why do sponsoring companies or organizations change and how might a long-running sponsorship relationship be maintained?

Websites

Related website for those interested in the Tour de France: http://www.letour.com/ and for some issues in sponsorship: **http://www.idealist.org/info/Nonprofits/Dev2/**.

Sponsors will be looking not only for hospitality opportunities, but also for events that raise their image (for example, as an organization that actively supports its local community) or supports some other marketing objective. In short, to get sponsorship an event organizer must fit (conveniently) into the sponsor's own plans, as well as matching the event's objectives. We must also be clear that sponsorship is, effectively, a commercial promotional technique, and not a method of obtaining donations. As such there are various mechanisms for seeking sponsorship, rather than just posting a letter and hoping for the best. Sponsorship agencies are now relatively common, and can be found by searching the web or the phone directory. These agencies, for a fee, will seek to match potential sponsors with causes requiring sponsorship (for an example, see: www.sponsorshiponline.co.uk). In addition, there are a number of trade and business related bodies with an interest in promoting relationships between commercial organizations and those seeking sponsorship, patronage or other support. In the UK, Arts and Business (formerly the Association for Business Sponsorship of the Arts) is one such example (www.artsandbusiness.org.uk). There are also bodies and trade associations that have an interest in corporate responsibility, take an active role in community activities and seek to promote an ethical and social approach to business, which may encompass sponsorship or patronage activities.

In cases where an event is sufficiently attractive to sponsors that it obtains one or more of them, the job is not over. An event organizer, having succeeded in getting the desired sponsorship, must then be able to service the sponsor, that is, to fulfil the sponsor's expectations of the event and its outcomes for the sponsor's business or brand. To do this a Sponsorship Agreement is needed (sometimes called a Sponsorship Business Plan). Quite simply, there are costs and benefits attached to servicing sponsors. Both the event organizer and the sponsor will wish to get the best from this arrangement, and to achieve this someone from the event organization will need to be responsible for liaison with sponsors, ensuring that the sponsorship agreement is fulfilled and that the objectives are achieved and measured. Elements of this plan would include:

- a Heads of Agreement, stating the objectives of the sponsorship on the parts of both the event organization and the sponsor, and the person in each organization who is ultimately responsible for ensuring the success of the sponsorship activities;

- a Marketing Statement, laying out the target audiences and stakeholders, and listing the methods by which the sponsor's name or brands will be placed in the public eye before the target audiences (target market);

- a Budget, dealing with how the funds received from the sponsorship would be allocated, e.g. on prizes, equipment, kit, gear, buildings, etc.; and also

- dealing with what supporting funding would be available for promotion (the sponsor would, no doubt, wish their name to appear on poster boards, publicity material, programmes, brochures, signs and any number of other items associated with the event).

Where there is more than one sponsor, respective areas of promotion are allocated in the sections of the agreement. An evaluation section will also be found here, dealing with how the impact of the sponsorship would be measured; for example, in the keeping of press cuttings, minutes of exposure obtained in TV or radio news or other media and whether participants' awareness of the sponsor had been raised.

In addition to this plan, the event organizer's liaison officer or team will need their own checklist to deal with those items needed to support the sponsor:

- liaison officer's time;
- allocation of corporate hospitality funds for sponsor's support;
- costs for publicity, printing, signage, VIP parking allocations, travel and other expenses; and
- ticketing arrangements for sponsors.

In fact, this type of checklist can also be used to work up an estimate of what costs are associated with servicing a sponsor and thus, how much money in terms of sponsorship is actually needed above and beyond operating costs for a sponsorship proposal to be worthwhile. Quite simply, if the costs of servicing a sponsor are going to be more than the sponsor is actually paying, then other sources of funding will be preferable.

Sponsorship is not the only potential alternative income source for an event (see Figure 6.13). The range of sources depends a great deal on the type of event. Local authorities or other funding agencies might be willing to put money into an event (e.g. a sporting or tourism event), if an appropriate and suitable case is made for it and if such a case complies with the objectives of the funding body. It might be that there is some kind of social regeneration, or other benefit to holding an event that could be of interest to the funding body. The event might, for example, attract large numbers of tourists, or have an arts impact for which arts trusts and foundations might consider grants. It should be noted, though, that funding from public bodies not only requires time and care in applying, but the response of many public funding bodies is notoriously slow. Let us repeat the word, 'slow'. Indeed, even after this slow process, your application for a grant may not succeed. Similarly, funding from philanthropic bodies has the disadvantage of being rather difficult to obtain as essentially you are seeking money from a patron or body that needs to have a personal or direct interest in your event. The short-lived nature of some events makes this a problem. There simply is not enough time to build up the relationships needed for philanthropic giving for many kinds of events. However, if we are dealing with repeat editions, this may change, and especially so with arts-related events,

---

Figure 6.13   Sources of patronage, grant funding and other income for events

- 'In-kind' arrangements, mutual benefit exchanges of goods or activities, volunteer work or donations
- Grants from local, regional or national governments or the European Union
- Grants from charitable bodies; development agencies; arts, leisure or heritage bodies
- Lottery grants or subsidiary (matching) funding
- Fundraising activities related to the event
- Commercial borrowing (from banks etc. – this will have to be repaid with interest)
- Funding from trusts or other philanthropic bodies, often listed in national directories of funding agencies and trusts
- The provision of funds or donations from a patron, commercial sponsership

which have a long tradition of attracting patrons through relationship marketing. Philanthropy can also be found in the strangest places, as even some of the most commercial companies have a strong awareness of their social responsibilities, resulting in company policies with very definite philanthropic outcomes. Indeed many companies maintain small grant or community funds for these purposes.

Any proposal for sponsorship, philanthropic (or other) funding would have to say much more than, 'This will attract a lot of participants who will spend money on your product after they attend the event'. Measurement and quantification of the benefits will have to be stated:

- Does the type of event being put on match the social or community objectives of the patron?
- Will there be a positive outcome in terms of public image?
- Will it result in, say, employment?

These are the types of questions which will have to be dealt with, very often, in order to get funding. In return, patrons should gain some personal or organizational benefits. Events patrons often gain preferential seats; admittance to VIP areas of the event; invitations to launch parties or to meet celebrities; attendance at a patron's lunch or VIP dinner, etc. In some cases patrons may wish their name on some aspect of the event, but this is by no means always the case; some patrons may wish to remain private supporters of an event, and to avoid the publicity associated with them.

SUMMARY

E ffective financial management of special events is increasingly complex. The financial implications of organizing even a relatively simple activity or celebration or a small personal event can be significant. The extent to which external funding, such as via sponsors, may be available could be more limited than organizers foresee. This makes careful budgeting for regular income sources and proposed expenditure extremely important. The careful monitoring, recording and control of these incomes and expenditures is a significant concern of clients, organizers, co-ordinators and finance officers of all kinds. The recording of the financial aspects, ranging from the purchase of items to the final budgeted accounts, is potentially important to the success of events, even those not intended to be profit-making. Therefore, even those new to event organization should regard good financial management as necessary and vital.

EVALUATION QUESTIONS

1 Identify some basic mistakes when first budgeting for events and for pricing of tickets.

2 What is the concept of 'Break Even' and why is this important even when planning non-profit events?

3 How does budgeting help the event planning process?

4 What funding methods might be available to an event manager or organizing committee apart from ticket sales?

REFERENCES

Bowdin, G., Allen, J., O'Toole, W., Harris, R. and McDonnell, I. (2011) *Events Management*, Oxford: Elsevier Butterworth Heinemann, p 315.

Garrison, R. H., Noreen, E., Brewer, P. C. (2009) *Managerial Accounting for Managers*, Maidenhead: McGraw-Hill (10 edn) pp 48–51.

Lucey, T. (2008) *Costing*, London: Continuum (7 edn) pp 27–38.

Jagels, M. E. and Ralston, C. E. (2010) *Hospitality Management Accounting*, Chichester: Wiley (10 edn).

Skinner, B. E. and Rukavina, V. (2003) *Event Sponsorship*, Hoboken: Wiley, pp 53–72.

Yeoman, I., Robertson, M., Ali-Knight, J., Drummond, S. and McMahon-Beattie, U. (2004) *Festival and Event Management: an international arts and cultural perspective.* Oxford: Butterworth Heinemann, pp 273–85.

CHAPTER 7
EVENT LOGISTICS AND SUPPLIES

AIMS

- To discuss the preparation for events including issues of venue finding

- To identify a range of logistics, supply issues and technical matters

- To consider some support functions for events including cleaning and catering

INTRODUCTION

The preparation and development phase for events is not necessarily separate from the planning phase and the two mostly run hand in hand. However, the business of getting an event ready involves considerable time, effort and hard work. At the point of implementation of the event, the workload will increase as will the number of staff and amount of resources required. The pace of preparation and development will also increase once the venue has been identified and orders begin to be placed for equipment, facilities and services. The logistics of ensuring that all these items arrive in time for the event, in their proper place, in good condition and in the style or format they were ordered, represent a considerable effort on the part of the event co-ordinator.

Support functions (such as food and drink, music and entertainment, technical services and related event activities) can be very complicated, depending on the size and importance of the event. If you consider the sheer complexity of the preparations for even a modest family wedding, it becomes evident how crucial careful logistical preparations are. Different types of events will require different support functions, which can be supplied directly by the organizers or contracted out. Where support functions are contracted out, the need for careful specifications of the service being purchased is particularly relevant.

FINDING THE VENUE

In the very early stages of planning an event we may not yet have identified the venue, let alone what other facilities and services we will need. Together with the planning there will be early exploration of issues such as, what the key requirements are, including those factors that will be critical to success. These might include the location of the event, the range of potential venues available, ease of access and the ability to ensure that all the necessary items of equipment, resources, personnel and visitors, can get to (and around) the venue easily. The preparation phase of the process will, therefore, consist not only of venue-finding, but also of assessment of the logistics process. In logistics terms, our supplies are not simply products and services; they also include the flow of visitors or participants and visitor or participant services. For example, when we choose a venue we must ensure that our potential visitors are able to get to it easily, using their typical mode of transport. There must also be suitable and adequate access for visitors, for goods and event supplies and in case of emergency. We can see from this that 'logistics' does not simply refer to on-site activities.

Venue-finding is probably one of the first important aspects of the development phase of an event. In some cases an event organizer might know exactly which venue to choose, in other cases the choice of venue may be extremely limited, especially in rural areas. In general, however, a reasonable choice of venue will be available. The first question an organizer will normally ask themselves will be, 'What location is required?' (bearing in mind the objectives of the event), and then, 'What are the available venues within that location?' (noting any criteria about the selection, that was brought to attention in the screening process). A number of questions have to be asked early on about the potential venue. What we know about the type of audience for the event and the event itself, will inform our judgement about the venue. For example, if our event were to be a national sales exhibition, then the venue would probably have to be large and central to the whole country. If it was to be a town carnival, then the venue might cover several locations in the town, as well as suitable areas for the assembly and dispersal of the carnival procession. Organizers themselves may have a good local knowledge, but if not, a visit to the area will be necessary to look around. Alternatively, a professional venue-finding agency can be used, which are quite common. Normally an agency or organizer will come up with a shortlist of three or four possible venues. These can be visited and a checklist made about the particular requirements of the event in terms of the venue. Whichever venue best matches the criteria should be chosen, bearing in mind price considerations and the professionalism of the venue management (see Figure 7.1).

Site visits are useful but the organizer needs to have a reasonable idea of the event requirements before visiting venues (if you go with a poor idea of what you need, you give yourself problems later). Visits should be arranged via venue managers or for larger sites, the venue sales team. Where a professional venue-finding agency has been used the agency may also be able to provide, for a small fee, an organizer with professional help to inspect venues. It is important for organizers to make out a list of questions to ask each venue before going, in addition to a checklist of criteria. Much depends on the event, for example, is a band required during the party? Is a stage needed? Will sound equipment be needed? Can the venue provide these?

First impressions are important. The first impression an organizer gets may well be the same that visitors and guests get. Organizers should pay attention to all their senses:

- What does the site look like?
- What are its surroundings?
- Is it attractive?
- What can be heard: is it quiet, noisy, under a flight path, does it have good acoustics (clap your hands to hear the echo, or listen for dead areas)?
- What does it smell like: is it neutral, does it smell of stale food?
- Does it have gardens?
- Are the toilets clean and fresh?
- Touch the furnishings and some of the equipment – do these feel clean?
- Do your shoes stick to the floor or carpets?

During your first visit you are probably not going to taste any sample menus. But if food is an element of your event, then once you have chosen the venue, you may wish to try samples of the food you have selected. This is especially the case if the event is large or involves VIP catering, so you can check if the kitchen or resident caterer is up to the job. On your visit, try to make sure you see all the areas your visitors will use, not only the main room, site, arena or hall, but also the entrances, corridors, car parks, toilets and food service areas:

- Are these places well kept?
- Is there evidence of activity, cleanliness, good maintenance?

All these are indicators of an active and capable management at the venue. The more capable they are, the easier your job will be.

Event: _____   **Date:** _____
Name of Venue: _____   Address: _____
Phone Number: _____   _____
Mobile Number: _____   _____
General Manager: _____   Event Contact: _____
GM's email: _____   Contact's email: _____

What are the objectives of the event in relation to the venue?
_____
_____

What factors are critical to the success of the event in relation to the venue? (What do you need?)
Factor 1 _____
Factor 2 _____
Factor 3 _____

Does this venue satisfy these factors?
Factor 1: Yes ☐ No ☐   Factor 2: Yes ☐ No ☐   Factor 3: Yes ☐ No ☐

Site Inspection–Venue Environment and Location:
General Environment: (e.g. leafy countryside, city centre) _____

Access:	Good	OK	Poor	Comment
By Road (Car and Taxi)	☐	☐	☐	_____
On Foot / Cycle	☐	☐	☐	_____
By Bus / Tram	☐	☐	☐	_____
By Rail	☐	☐	☐	_____

Nearest Station: _____

By Air	☐	☐	☐	_____

Nearest Airport: _____
Identify any access problems related to loading / unloading / mobility impaired visitors / limitations of parking:
_____
_____

Site Inspection–Venue facilities and services:
Capacity of main area: _____   Capacity of support areas: _____
Capacity of parking: _____   Capacity of kitchens: _____
Area (sq metres) main: _____   Area (sq metres) support: _____
Is internal access for entry and exit of visitors, loading and the mobility impaired adequate?
_____

Is a scale plan of the venue available? If so, obtain one. If not, measure main features.
State ceiling height: _____m   State access door height: _____m
State access door width: _____m
Does the venue have power? _____ How many power points? _____ Lighting / Dimmers _____
Does the venue have gas? _____ Air conditioning? _____ What sort of heating? _____
Attach a copy of the fire procedure to this checklist. In relation to the needs of your event, what other
specialist facilities / services are available: (e.g. sound system, presentation equipment, etc.)
or are missing?:
_____

Comment on your impression of the venue and the venue management:
_____
_____
_____
_____

Figure 7.1   Venue finding checklist

LOGISTICS

Logistics is the discipline of planning and organizing the flow of goods, equipment and people to their point of use. Logistics are important to events because of the need to concentrate resources on a particular location for a particular time (even if that event is multi-site and taking place over a fairly long period). Without careful planning of this activity, the supplies needed to undertake the event may not arrive correctly. Logistics is also sometimes regarded as those issues related to the 'supply chain' that is the flow of materials, goods and services into and through an event (and feedback from the event supply activity taking place to its suppliers) (Slack *et al.*, 2007).

Once given a venue, the event co-ordinator or logistics officer can address some of the major licensing and other official preparation activities, such as permits and insurance (see Figure 7.2). In logistics terms, services and supplies that have a long lead time must be considered early on. It is important to identify these issues and find suitable suppliers. Finding such suppliers and determining which supplier is preferable may be a significant and important task (Allen *et al.*, 2010). Once a suitable supplier has been found, purchasing arrangements or a contract will be needed (Goldblatt, 2008). The contract will determine the obligations involved in supplying a particular material, item or service and will be between the event organization as client, and its suppliers, which may range from caterers to entertainers (Silver, 2004). For example, the event may have special power requirements, it might need additional utilities laid on (e.g. telecoms, gas, water, sewerage, waste removal), all of which have typically long lead times to arrange, especially if groundwork has to be undertaken to put them in. The logistics officer has to be conscious of those event activities that have the longest lead times and that have to be dealt with first. A logistics plan showing the various needs and their prioritization may have to be prepared.

It is useful to recognize that the nearer the event deadline, the less able one is to make big changes without having to expend enormous amounts of money and effort. In short, there is a cut-off point at which the contractual arrangements have to stand (this varies, depending on what supplies or services are being provided and how long they take). Logistics officers will need to draw together a potentially wide range of support functions for an event to work properly (Westerbeek *et al.*, 2006). One of the challenges events co-ordinators face is that if materials, supplies or resources do not arrive properly for an event, there is rarely enough time to re-order or replace them. Whereas, in many other business activities if the wrong supply is delivered, there is probably not a time constraint in relation to its use and therefore it can be sent back and changed, without creating a major problem.

The key to the implementation phase of the event (i.e. running the event itself) is good communications. It is helpful to commit ideas and important issues to paper. With a large number of people to manage, it is impossible for one individual to communicate 'in person' with them all. Therefore, many forms of communication may be used to help ensure people know what to do: briefings about plans, the event programme, the emergency procedures, etc., must take place. A useful tool in the range of techniques available to an event organizer is the preparation of an event **production schedule** (see Figure 7.3). This is essentially a list of the activities that the event involves, in time order. This production schedule should be as detailed as possible for events where

production schedule
The scheme of work to be done, in time order, to ensure an event is set up properly.

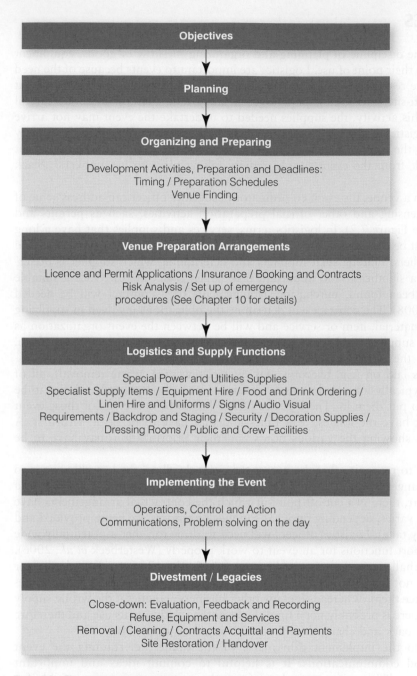

Figure 7.2   The events management process – organizational and logistical activities

timing issues are essential to a positive outcome. At this stage, the production schedule may go through several editions before the final one emerges and is agreed upon. In several cases the production schedule will also state who is responsible for the given timed activities and what methods are to be used to carry them out.

Figure 7.3 Example of a logistics production schedule

Middleburg Festival Production Schedule

Preparatory Work

Monday 27th August

Start at:	Production:	Finish by:
08.00	Co-ordinator's briefing at Park House, welcome volunteers, coffee	08.30
08.30	Site checks of Festival Park	09.00
09.00	Mark out parking, arena, market, marquee and tent sites	11.00
11.00	Hold meeting with emergency services, council representatives and others	12.00
12.00	Lunch on Park House terrace, delivered by Anna's Bakery (at 11.30)	13.00
13.00	Co-ordinators to assist afternoon deliveries of tents, utilities, Portacabins, etc.	17.00
17.00	Handover to night security man (and complete any outstanding set-ups)	17.30

Set up and Rehearsals

Tuesday 28th August

08.00	Co-ordinator's briefing at Park House, coffee	08.30
08.30	Co-ordinate arrival of supplies, check arriving items, direct to correct area	12.00
12.00	Lunch on Park House terrace, delivered by Anna's Bakery (at 11.30)	13.00
13.00	Organize volunteers to set-up arena, market, catering and entrance tents	16.00
16.00	Check completion of set-up, arrival of supplies, chase out-standing items	17.00
17.00	Volunteers tea on Park House terrace, delivered by Anna's Bakery (16.30)	18.00
17.00	Issue volunteers with T-shirts, badges, site maps and answer any questions	18.00
18.00	Test all services, list items not working for attention Wednesday AM	19.00
19.00	Middleburg Festival Orchestra rehearsal	22.00
22.00	Handover to night security	22.15

Festival Event

Wednesday 29th August

Start at:	Production:	Finish by:
08.00	Co-ordinator's briefing at Park House, coffee	08.30
08.30	Attend to out-standing problems, get volunteers to their posts, check signs	09.30
09.30	Check Festival market	10.00
10.00	Check Middleburg band is ready near Venetian Bridge	10.10
10.10	Welcome Mayor; provide coffee in Entrance Tent	10.25
10.25	Go with Mayor to Venetian Bridge for opening speech and tape cutting	10.45
10.45	Festival opens, band plays light music, festival market opens	10.45
12.00	Volunteers and band lunch (rotation) in Catering Tent	13.00
14.00	Afternoon concert by Middleburg band	16.00
16.00	Parade by Middleburg youth organizations	17.00
17.00	Various music soloists and small groups scheduled to play in Catering Tent	19.00
19.00	Guests arrival for main evening concert	19.30
19.30	Main evening concert in arena, seats and picnic places	22.00
19.30	Festival market closes down	20.00
20.00	Volunteers dinner on Park House Terrace (supplied by Catering Tent)	21.00
21.00	Catering Tent closes after concert intermission	21.10
22.30	Co-ordinator hands over to night security	22.45

Closedown

Thursday 30th August

Start at:	Production:	Finish by:
08.00	Co-ordinator's briefing at Park House, coffee	08.30
08.30	Suppliers arrive to remove utilities, tents, return equipment	13.00
12.00	Volunteers lunch on Park House terrace, delivered by Anna's Bakery	13.00
13.00	Volunteer litter pickers, site cleaners complete clearing	15.00
15.00	Hand-over site to park keeper, site repairs and lawns restoration begins	17.00

CASE STUDY 22

Event Logistics: DB Schenker

Courtesy of DB Schenker Logistics

DB Schenker – Germany and Europe

A DB Schenker Logistics support lorry delivers cargo to a freight aircraft

- DB Schenker Logistics
- Group established in 1872 – moving into global sports events in 1972
- Provides large-scale logistics support for major events
- It provided freight transport for 200 teams at the Beijing Olympics 2008 and for the German and other teams at the London Olympics and Paralympics 2012

Learning Objectives

The aim of this case study is to examine issues of logistics for events with the following objectives:
To consider the way in which logistics have become of major importance in large-scale events
To understand the way in which the issues of quality, cost and time interact in the organization and delivery of goods

One of the logistics groups that now has specialist Events Logistics subsidiaries is DB Schenker; in DB Schenker's case, there are teams for both trade-fairs and sports events. Originating from Deutsche Bahn Railways (Germany), DB Group is now a global inter-modal logistics provider and has been providing events logistics services for international sporting events since the 1972 Olympic Games in Munich.

At this scale, events logistics range from overall planning, scheduling and physical transportation to the smooth integration of all the documentation, customs clearance and knowledge of management issues. All of this will be thrown into sharp relief for certain large-scale events, such as the Grands Prix, where teams are knocked out of competitive rounds or sections as the tournament or event proceeds (where a team may leave during the event and the logistics of removal will take place then, almost spontaneously, rather than at the end, as well as when the overall event concludes; when everything has to be repacked and transported away in a planned effort and timescale).

For the Euro 2008 European football championships, co-hosted by Austria and Switzerland, DB Schenker provided logistics support for: the hospitality programme of major sponsor Coca Cola; for the press centre at Vienna, for the media subsidiary of UEFA (the European football governing body); plus for the transport arrangements of numerous other media groups. DB Schenker felt that its experience with the 2006 FIFA World Cup had enabled it to centre its logistics activities on three control points (in Vienna, Salzburg and Klagenfurt, Austria) and to schedule vehicles at specific times from these points for the movement of the supplies and equipment concerned. The group's global experience enabled it to address the customs clearance required since Switzerland is outside the European Union.

For the Beijing 2008 Olympic Games, DB Schenker's team had been planning for the 17-day event for almost two years; organizing transport, warehousing and storage capacity. As an official Olympic partner for freight and customs, it dealt with the freight requirements of some 200 national teams, involving some 1500 TEU containers (in shipping, container sizes are expressed in TEUs – 20-foot Equivalent Units that is to say the basic length of a container is 20 American feet: 6.1 metres) all of which had to begin returning almost as soon as the closing ceremony ended. Within Beijing, special 'Olympic Express Lanes' sought to

avoid the delays that the Atlanta Games were remembered for; while DB Schenker trucks carrying official Olympic equipment could take advantage of these express lanes, they required special stickers and accurate bureaucracy – moreover, the city's normal freight deliveries had to contend with significant bottlenecks.

The on-going tensions between quality and cost and time (QCT) that are ever present in events management were exemplified at the Beijing Games by DB Schenker having to transport some €550 million worth of media equipment for one US broadcaster, most of which was still being used in North America, just a few days before the Olympics started. Air-freight was the only option for this logistics requirement, as sea transport would have taken too long. The implication of this is that in order to provide for the quality of the service within the time required by the broadcaster, the cost would necessarily increase as air transport is more expensive but faster than sea or road transport.

Discussion Questions

1   How vital is it that your logistics provider fully understands the complexities of your event?

2   How might one best balance the overall blend of Quality Cost Time. For example if you are short of time for a delivery does this automatically mean the cost will be higher and the chances of a quality failure also higher?

3   What are the implications of having only a limited amount of money to spend on logistics in terms of time or the way it might be done?

Websites

For more information see: **http://www.dbschenker.com/site/logistics/dbschenker/com/en/about__ dbschenker/publications/customer__magazines/customer__-magazines.html** (especially issue 02/08) from published sources. For a more detailed consideration of event logistics, site planning and traffic issues related to both participants and audience see: **http://www.strc.ch/conferences/2002/liaudat.pdf**.

SUPPLIES, TRANSPORT AND DISTRIBUTION

We have said that logistics is the discipline of planning and organizing the flow of goods, equipment and people to their point of use. Therefore, logistics in events terms includes activities such as the supply of materials and services, equipment and provisions, arrival and departure of visitors, ticketing and enquiries (in co-operation with the marketing department), as well as the flow of people, artists and crew to and around the venue. Within this, the preparation, opening and running of an event (whether it is a wedding reception or a coronation) depends on getting all the elements to the right place in time for a range of deadlines (Tum *et al.*, 2006). This can be a complicated process and individual staff and departments will be expected to prepare their own order lists of requirements. Where events are being run by professional management companies, these organizations will keep on a computer database the general listings of supplies and suppliers used for previous events, which can be easily adapted according to the particular needs of the one currently being prepared. Supplies can be ordered and deliveries checked, usually at a central arrival point, and the supplies distributed as required to the parts of the site where they are needed.

At a small event such as a village fête, most supplies could be accommodated in a store once they have been delivered by the local suppliers. These can then be laid out or sent to the kitchen, service areas, stands, stalls or whichever department requires them (see Figure 7.4). For a large event such as an International Air Show, the logistics task is huge.

Many companies will be involved and the integration of the whole operation will be a significant task. A major air show may have 20 or 30 catering companies supplying visitor catering or hospitality pavilions which have to be set up, supplied regularly and wound down. Pre-planning may take nine months (perhaps following a previous year's event); detailed planning and ordering, another three months; site **set-up time**, three weeks, including pavilion erections and the provision of utilities. This would be followed by the public opening, three days of inputting goods and services, one day's breather, then three days of stripping out of goods and finally equipment. Lastly, a week of clearing up, followed by site restoration, all done to a carefully organized timetable.

There will also need to be clarity in the logistics officer's list of suppliers about who should be contacted at a supplier in case the wrong items turn up on delivery. The logistics officer should also have a list of alternative suppliers in key areas, in case of serious problems, and they should bring the local phone directory to an event: because they might not be able to get a Wi-Fi signal when trying to find something urgently (See Figure 7.5.).

set-up time
The time needed to arrange, or rearrange after a previous function, the necessary facilities for the next event.

TECHNICAL FACILITIES

The technical services that events co-ordinators and venues are expected to provide are becoming increasingly sophisticated, to the extent that events coordinators may choose to outsource the hi-tech needs of clients to production or multimedia companies. The larger and more important the event, the greater the likelihood of a need for specialists, although a contributory difficulty is that some venue managers may not be sufficiently knowledgeable about the capabilities of production companies and of the latest developments in contemporary technology.

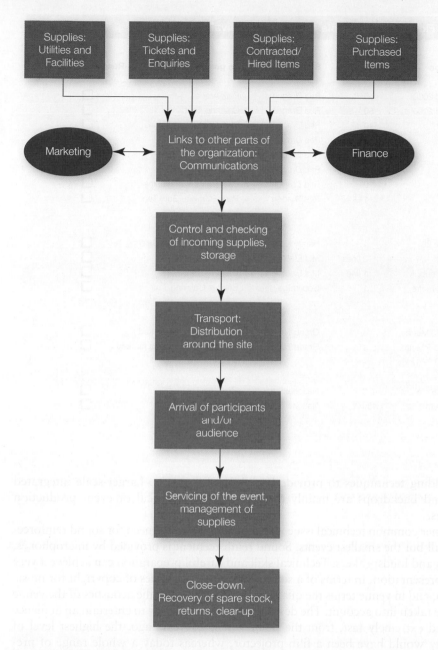

Figure 7.4   Logistic sequence for events

Multimedia can include video, computer-generated text and graphics, transfer of pictures from digital sources and the insertion of sound or video into presentations. Similarly, rapid development in communications has seen some use of video conferencing. At large-scale events, satellite links from one continent to another, enabling the presentation of a speaker in, say, Frankfurt, to be made on a video wall in Bilbao. There is also the issue of the image a client may wish to foster among the audience. Consequently, there has been a significant adoption of theatrical

Figure 7.5 Example equipment receival form

Item	Size/Type	No	Supplier	To go to	Received/Checked
Furniture					
Stacking Chairs Blue	Standard 2000	450	Red Dragon	Park Arena	☐
Stacking Chairs Blue	Standard 2000	50	Red Dragon	Catering Tent	☐
Office Chairs Blue	Operator	10	Red Dragon	Park Office Portacabins	☐
Round Tables	1 metre	6	Red Dragon	Catering Tent	☐
Square Tables	1 metre	6	Red Dragon	Catering Tent	☐
Trestle Tables	2 metre	2	Red Dragon	Catering Tent	☐
Trestle Tables	2 metre	2	Red Dragon	Park Office Portacabins	☐
Trestle Tables	2 metre	1	Red Dragon	Park Entrance Gate Tent	☐
Utilities					
Mobile Toilet Block	M/F Type 20	1	Handy Loo	100 metres west of Catering Tent	☐
Power	'3 phase'	2 lines	Mid Electric	Arena Stage	☐
Power	8 socket supply	1 line	Mid Electric	Catering Tent	☐
Mobile Chiller Room	32 cubic metre	1	Coolfridge Hire	Back of Catering Tent	☐
Tents and Shades					
Marquee White	Deluxe 50 Metre	1	Grand Tents	Catering Tent as marked	☐
Tent White	Standard 5 Metre	1	Grand Tents	Park Entrance Tent as marked	☐
Equipment					
Plates White	Dinner 25 cm	450	National Equip	Catering Tent	☐
Plates White	Side 10 cm	450	National Equip	Catering Tent	☐
Etc.	Etc.				

scene-building techniques to provide backdrops for events. Larger-scale integrated staging and backdrops are mainly the province of theatrical or event production companies.

The other common technical issue is that of sound and the need for sound reinforcement, at all but the smallest events. Sound reinforcement is provided by microphones, amplifiers and loudspeakers. Technical skill and careful preparation can achieve a very effective presentation. In terms of a soundtrack, there are issues of copyright for music and video, and in venue terms the quality of the facilities and the acoustics of the venue need to be taken into account. The development of technology to entertain an audience has moved extremely fast, from the point when, 25 years ago, the highest level of technology would have been a film projector, whereas today a whole range of presentation methods ranging from the laser projector to the laptop display are used.

If venues have suitable equipment available, venue management and technical staff may request that presenters come and test their material at least a week prior to the event. This applies particularly to computer-based presentations. Not all systems can be compatible and minor glitches such as cabling problems, or insufficient attention to text size for projections, are as much a problem as compatibility (or lack of compatibility) of the equipment and software itself. It is unreasonable to expect that hi-tech presentations will work first time unless the speaker and venue are regular partners. In addition, the level of technical skill required to solve the simplest of equipment problems is not always available on the spot. Increasing sophistication of communications is also permitting advances in how, and where, events can be held. However, the resources required to operate this equipment may have to be brought in specially.

BACKDROPS AND STAGING

The staging of events has become increasingly complicated as technology has become more sophisticated and the expectations of the public have become more used to complex sets and productions, this is particularly the case with music and theatrical events. Stage set design and construction has its origins in the theatre business but is now a highly professional activity needing experienced management and thorough planning. Considerations include how much money or funding can be put towards the staging, and what levels of expertise, equipment and supplies would be needed. The process, like many things in event management begins with planning and the first results of the planning process may be an equipment and technical specification, this might be followed by the modelling (either in virtual reality or physically) of the stage set being considered. From the model discussions of the full sized actual set may be discussed and issues such as the size, available space, back-stage area, access, **load-in** and **load-out** timings should be considered, as well as issues of safety and who the responsible persons are in the decision-making process. This information would be worked up into a production specification so that every-one knows what has to be done, by whom, when, where and how. Very often responsibilities for different parts of the set up lie with different members of a technical crew. So, for example, there would be someone in charge of Lighting and Effects, and someone else in charge of Sound and Stage, and this will be in addition to all the people involved in setting the staging up, rigging, carpentry, electrical work and so on. With large scale productions it often surprises unfamiliar people how long the stage set up and removal process takes, sometimes two or three days for a major music event. Examples can be found on You Tube of time-lapse work show-ing these things in progress (see http://www.youtube.com/watch?v=cjntOX1exts) or search for stage set up or **bump-in**). Naturally just watching the process doesn't give you the detail about what exactly is going on but you can research that using books or materials about stage sets.

While technical support may be thought to be essentially sound or visual reinfor-cement, it is also the case that event organizers (on behalf of a more sophisticated public) are perhaps looking for a standard that is extremely high and may be willing to pay for it. The backdrop, or staging, is of major concern. It not only provides the location of a screen, but is also the place where a corporate or marketing image is demonstrated. The backdrop may, of course, be simple: a contained screen with banner and a little special lighting. On the other hand, the backdrop may be a matter of considerable technical expertise incorporating stage design elements. These ele-ments may range from the preparation and construction of sets and stage flats to back projection and theatrical style lighting. Projected screen designs can be pro-vided from a range of prepared formats, such as cityscapes, star fields, etc. or be purpose-made with a logo or theme to use as a backdrop. Other technical features which might be included could be pyrotechnics (fireworks) and laser shows.

It is also more common for large-scale events to use video walls composed of a bank of monitors. This has been a feature of special events at concerts and gigs for some time, to enable very large (often outdoor) audiences to see the performers. Where

load-in
The arrival of equipment, stage crew, staging, materials, sound and lighting rigs and other various items of event set-up.

load-out
As load-in, but leaving.

bump-in
The arrival of equipment, stage crew, staging, materials, sound and lighting rigs and other various items of event set-up.

Sean Nel / Shutterstock.com

Setting up equipment backstage at the Orlando Stadium for the FIFA World Cup Concert, June 2010 in Soweto, South Africa

backdrops are constructed and set up by a production company, the company may work regularly with a particular venue (many large venues have links with local production companies), but where this is not the case, the production company will have to undertake preparatory site work to assess factors such as available space, power, structural capacities and access to the hall, arena or site in order to do the job properly. The company will also work closely with the event co-ordinator or logistics officer to ensure everything gets to the right place when it is needed. For this, a production schedule (shown above in Figure 7.3) will be drawn up. At music festivals, the staging issues are often complicated by the need to deal with several bands or performers during a day or evening. To make the transfer of bands faster, complicated parts of the band's equipment, such as the drum kits, are put on Drum Risers. These are low-level flat trolleys which can be wheeled onto the stage and connected to the power and amps by a single combined wired cord known as the umbilical, so that band changes can be done quickly.

The logistics officer, working with the marketing officer and the overall event coordinator, must also organize pre-event meetings and use tools such as site maps, bulletins and newsletters to help get across major issues to staff, crew, artists, volunteers and helpers, to achieve co-ordination of effort.

Here are some further web-based resources which relate to event logistics issues:

- An interactive graphic based on the staging at Glastonbury Festival on the BBC NEWS website demonstrates the complexities involved in getting one band off stage and the next band on at: http://news.bbc.co.uk/1/hi/in_depth/629/629/6231306.stm.

- Mark Fisher, architect of the stages used on a concert tour by the pop group U2, sought to find uses for them, as permanent venues, once the world tour concluded. Three steel structures (costing £20–£25 million) and each in the shape of a giant claw were used on different parts of the tour. The production credits, construction photographs, etc., on the Stufish website at: http://www.stufish.com, illustrate the planning issues and lead-times involved. The Stufish website also shows a whole range of staging designs for concerts and events.

- The virtual tours on the Keith Prowse corporate hospitality website show many of their event venues at: http://www.keithprowse.co.uk/KP/VirtualTours.aspx and enable one to appreciate all the other elements that have to brought to the event site and taken away again; from marquees, staff and IT systems, to the tickets/passes, food and drink.

Lighting

The lighting of venues has a number of purposes. In terms of function rooms themselves the main purposes are to provide ambient lighting, to highlight artists or speakers, to light backdrops and to enhance the atmosphere. In the other areas of venues the lighting has to provide adequate background illumination in both public and support areas, and some decorative illumination, particularly in VIP rooms, dining areas and foyers. The final lighting issue is one of provision for safety, and to help people feel secure, particularly in terms of exits and traffic routes in and around the venue or site.

Diffused illumination is necessary in the public areas of a building. Corridors, toilets, foyers and reception areas should be well-lit, although not harshly so. This is necessary to enable the proper functioning of these areas, to ensure safety and security, and to maintain a pleasant general ambience. Consideration must also be given to lighting control systems, dimmers and sensor switches. Typically, the scalar illumination of public rooms should be of the order of 150–200 lux and a modern approach to this is to weight the recommended level of lighting according to several factors such as the age of users, the reflectivity of surfaces and the legibility of reading or of performing the specific tasks which take place in a room. In addition, emergency lighting is essential, and a legal requirement, in public buildings. This is usually provided by secondary battery-powered lights lasting up to three hours, activated by the fire alarm system or a power failure. Exits should be clearly illuminated and the emergency lighting sufficient to allow adequate **means of escape**. In some modern buildings, floor lighting strips are provided along exit routes, similar to those provided on aircraft floors to direct people to emergency exits. Security lighting is also necessary for areas containing expensive equipment, such as computers. Externally, particularly in car parks and around the building, good lighting is needed to ensure visitors feel secure. Lighting should be provided throughout the venue from the various public areas to the place of **final exit**.

Sound and communications

Historically, the sound system at venues was, at best, a microphone and a couple of loudspeakers, and if you were lucky, an amplifier and a mixer. This tends to be inadequate for current needs. Consequently, provision of professional sound systems is often necessary. Not only is there the need for the audience to be able to hear the proceedings, there are also issues of sound reinforcement needed to go with visual tools and multimedia presentations, to accompany sets, to provide atmosphere, as well as provide the full range of aural stimulation for an audience at an event.

Notwithstanding copyright law (which imposes various requirements, including payments, and licensing for public entertainment and public performance), music may be played from whatever system is available. Major venues are usually equipped to provide modern sound equipment, but, while almost every home has a portable media player or computer to enable streaming, not enough small or municipal venues are so equipped. Organizers wishing to incorporate good quality sound often have to hire-in the equipment to provide it. Companies providing equipment are able to provide equipment packages that will include not only public address (PA) systems, but also complete music systems. Given the complexity of this technology, a package, including the hire of a technician (again an element that not all venues are able to provide) is often necessary.

means of escape
A structured way of providing a safe route for people to travel from any point in a building or site, to a place of safety, without assistance (such as a marked corridor, or pathway enclosed by rope).

final exit
The termination of an escape route from an event site in the case of an emergency, giving exit to a place of safety or dispersal to an open space (e.g. in case of fire).

A loudspeaker system may, in some cases, be built into a room such as an arena or large hall, but may also be in the form of quite large portable loudspeakers. These would normally be set up between presenters and audience, and would also usually be quite high up, at least head height for a seated event, to reduce the amount of sound absorbed by the audience. Most loudspeakers will be stand or floor mounted, but in purpose-built venues they can often be ceiling-hung from gantries designed for them. There are some issues of aesthetics to be borne in mind, and increasingly loudspeakers are screened by some means such as lightweight curtaining, floral displays, or careful illumination around them, so that the loudspeakers themselves are in relative seclusion.

Where an event is extremely large, and takes place in an arena-type venue, there may also be a need to allow communication between more than one technician and between co-ordinators. For this purpose it is preferable to provide a communication ring. While this can be done using radios or cell phones, there is a danger of these interfering with other systems and of failure in an emergency. In consequence, a communications ring should be a secure land line. Sufficient time must be allowed for crews to set up systems in the case of a large event, and to obtain frequencies for events radio communications, if these are needed. The logistics officer should, when planning the provision of communications, prepare a contact listing, both for internal and external contacts. This acts as a kind of event phone book and saves trying to track down contacts from bits of paper, and should be built up as the event is being created (see Figure 7.6).

POWER

In the case of indoor events there would normally be mains power, for an outdoor event electricity supplies can be taken from either a mains source or generator. Electricity is fed to a temporary distribution board, which then divides the power to separately protected circuits for lighting, heating or other uses (e.g. catering or a stage). Usually, the distribution board is placed in the catering tent, since this is to where most of the demand is likely to be drawn. In the event that the mains supply is not sufficiently powerful, or too far away, either a generator can be put in place, or the caterer may need to be limited in the amount of electricity they can use at any one time (for example, boilers use a lot of power). From the catering marquee, cables are discreetly laid to provide sockets for bands, lighting rigs, heating systems etc. Larger events will require twin-set generators (so that if the first generator fails the second one automatically starts) and multiple distribution panels to safely provide electrical power supplies over a wide area. All equipment must be fully waterproof and regularly tested for safety. An electrical technician should often be in attendance at larger events, not because equipment is unreliable, but because of any additional power needs that may occur.

AMENITIES AND CLEANING

Cleaning and clearing are issues sometimes neglected in the servicing of venues, sites and events. It is essential that when there is a break in the programme, or at any other convenient point, the opportunity is taken for minor rubbish clearing, bin emptying, replenishment of consumables and other stock. This should be planned to happen at regular intervals and can be regarded as 'preventative' action. Cleaning

Figure 7.6   Example communications contact list

Contact Listing

Add contacts to the list as you make them (in alphabetical order):

Telephones: **M** Mobile; **W**-Work; **H**-Home

Date / Time of this list: 24/03/2010 14.05

Internal Contact Network

Name	Job	Base Location	Phone	Radio
Jo Example	Event Co-ordinator	Site Office	07720 123456 (M)	Yes
			01234 234567 (H)	
Marc Sample	Volunteer Leader	Catering Tent	None	Yes
Mike Specimen	Stage Technician	Stage	01334 654321 (W)	No
Etc.				
Etc.				

External Contacts and Suppliers

Name	Address	Phone	Fax	Email
Catering Equipment:				
National Equipment	Arboretum Hall	01786 123456	01786 123457	Jock@necatering.com
	12 Castle Hill			
	Middleburg			
	Scotland			
	SG1 3PQ			
Furniture:				
Red Dragon Hire	Ty Gwyn	01792 123456	12792 12345	Rhys@reddragon.co.eu
	Fford Uwd			
	Abertawe			
	Wales			
	SA6 5RE			
Marquee Hire:				
Etc.				
Etc.				

equipment and materials must be available and accessible to the support staff. It may be a simple case of needing to clear up a broken glass. On the other hand, a guest may have over-indulged at dinner and in the bar and proceeded to vomit on the way to the toilets. Delay in responding to these crises, major and minor, is typically due to lack of correctly placed equipment, material and forethought.

In terms of the provision of amenities, the general rule is to provide one toilet for every 75 people (of each gender), which can be increased for VIP events. Portable toilets, for example, can be hired in blocks, different standards of facility can also be hired, such as shower blocks if required. It is essential to provide servicing for event toilets, and supervision to ensure that effective cleaning is done. Admittedly, there are difficulties in maintaining cleanliness of portable facilities that may not be used solely for ablutions. Nevertheless, a proper system for servicing and supervision is as much a necessity as any other support service. As with most other activities, this can be contracted out if necessary.

CATERING AND EVENT HOSPITALITY

It is not only the choice of a suitable venue that will certainly colour visitors' view of their experience but also the quality of food and drink provided. Event co-ordinators should bear this in mind and ensure there is sufficient time and space built into events for this important aspect, if catering is to be provided properly.

The organization of catering varies considerably according to the type of venue but as a generality there is a choice between in-house catering as practised by the banqueting departments of hotel-type venues, and contracted out catering as practised by the other types of venue, ranging from public halls to sports stadiums (Thomas, 2012). There are advantages and disadvantages to both methods and the method provided by venues to handle their catering may have as much to do with historical precedent in that venue as with matters of profitability, flexibility and convenience.

Having found a caterer, the basic questions and the starting points to determine what the visitor will have are the same. These are questions about the number of people, the refreshment times, the budget and the visitors themselves. It could be argued that one of the chief failings of catering at events is insensitivity towards the type of people attending. There is a tendency towards standardized and rather predictable menus which, while convenient for kitchens and sales co-ordinators, may be inappropriate for certain types of visitors. Increasingly, the public attending events is better educated in food and drink than at any other time in the past. The range of services on offer may be built around continuous provision throughout the event, rather than the traditional presentation of breakfast, lunch and dinner. The layout for café or buffet-type service also needs to be given careful thought. Bear in mind that people are inherently used to lining up in queues. In an unfamiliar situation (such as at a new event), they will naturally revert to this method. To plan catering outlets at events to be 'free flow' may, therefore, be counterproductive; people may be confused and irritated, especially if there is a log-jam at the cash desk (see Figure 7.7).

In cases where there will be a large number of people at an event, queues at catering outlets can be relieved by having smaller outlets that deal only in drinks and small food, to help take the weight of demand away from major food counters. The same kind of rules apply to cafeteria service as to buffet service – think carefully about how many

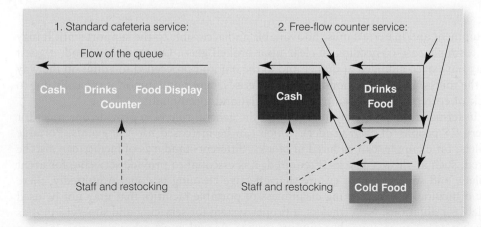

Figure 7.7   Alternative cafeteria flow services

people your counter can handle at once. Add more counters or small outlets to ease the crush.

Buffets are popular at events, and there are commonly two types: finger buffet or fork buffet. With the former, guests normally stand, with the latter, guests normally sit, and the buffet food may be hot or cold or both. Timing is an important issue. Many people will politely queue at a buffet, which naturally takes time and must be taken into account when laying out the buffet. More than one direction or side of a buffet table should be available. It will take the average diner 20 seconds to load his/her plate – multiply that up by the number of people and you will understand why more than one buffet flow is needed for a large event. It should also be borne in mind that buffets are often understaffed, which leads to chaos, inability to restock and inability to clear tables. The normal buffet service ratio is one member of catering staff to 30 diners. This can be raised to 35 if serving international delegates, as they are somewhat less likely to queue and this must be noted when laying out the buffet. For international delegates, it should not, generally, be laid out in a linear fashion but similar dishes can be laid out in various sections of a buffet table.

Buffet self service is a feature of event hospitality at many kinds of events

CandyBox Images / Alamy

Where events may feature a particular element, such as a gala dinner, organizers should ensure they have provided a seating layout for the event that will best suit the client (see Figure 7.8). For a full service meal, the typical service ratio is one catering staff member to between 10 and 15 diners, plus a member of drinks staff (for wine service) to every 30 diners.

Menu composition and the range of food provided is significant not only in terms of the menu, but also in terms of what is within a venue's capabilities. For example, a range of individually priced dishes may be suggested to the organizer, who then chooses a selection to suit the likely visitor profile. This is based on the view that organizers know something of the style, likes and dislikes of the public. However, not all do, and organizers often pick dishes they like, only to find that visitors criticize their poor judgement. Menu composition is, therefore, not simply a technical issue but also a serious question that organizers should ask themselves:

● What are our potential visitors like?
● What are their demographics?
● What are their most popular styles of eating?

The chief 'back of house' players in catering operations are the head chef and the bar manager, in the sense that they are responsible for food and drink costings, pre-planning, ordering and preparation of food and drink. Nevertheless, it must be remembered that the initial enquiry and first meeting between the venue and the organizer will probably take place with the venue sales manager or sales co-ordinator, although a

Theatre Style

Used for lectures or large groups that do not require writing

Banquet Style

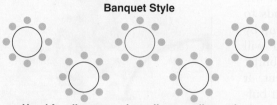

Used for dinners and small group discussions

Cabaret Style

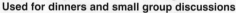
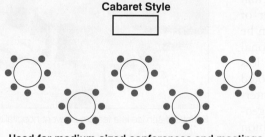

Used for medium-sized conferences and meetings

Hollow Square Style

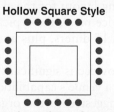

Used for dinners and meetings of groups fewer than 40

Classroom

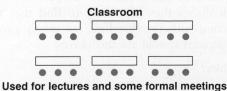

Used for lectures and some formal meetings

Figure 7.8   Examples of seated room layouts (*continued*)

U-Shape Style

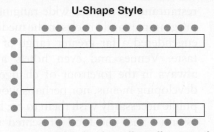

Used for some kinds of small-medium meetings

Boardroom Style

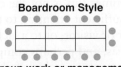

Used for small group work or management meetings and small private dinners

Figure 7.8   Examples of seated room layouts

number of organizers will ask for the chef to be present, to find out what the venue's caterers are able to produce.

The alternative is to contract out the catering to a specialist organization. These vary from large national operations with many contracts, to small individual caterers with only one contract or business. Catering of this kind is common in many venues. Contractual arrangements vary. Some venues may have one approved caterer who provides all the food, drink and related services for that venue. Alternatively, venues may have an 'approved' list of caterers whom they are happy to work with and who are familiar with the venue, its operation, management and typical requirements. Some venues, such as public halls, may allow any caterer including the event organizers themselves, to do the catering.

The advantage of contracting out is that the organizers do not need to concern themselves with the technicalities of food and drink provision. They simply make the best contractual arrangement possible and act as a link between the client (or visitor) and the caterers. The disadvantage is a certain loss of control: a contract caterer interested in cutting costs may have no incentive to provide a quality service. A related disadvantage is less well-known, but probably more serious – loss of flexibility. An in-house catering function is often highly flexible and can provide peripheral activities that contractors do not (e.g. an 'on the spot' VIP dinner for a key client). The chief problem is that contracts are often badly written, ignoring a wide range of needs, some of which may only occur occasionally but are nevertheless vital, and which a contractor will charge extra for ('variations to contract').

The number of visitors attending and expected to eat may not be the same. At some kinds of events visitors may bring in their own food, for example to a summer evening open-air concert. For the caterer it is also of importance to know approximate numbers up to two weeks before the event, and final numbers two days in advance. This is to enable accurate food, drink and equipment ordering. A deadline must be enforced for bookings where the event has elements such as sit-down gala dinners as opposed to continuous through-the-day catering. The time of refreshments should also be checked between the organizers and the caterers on the day.

Visitors and some sections of the public attending events may be traditional in their tastes, but they are no longer uneducated in food. Travel abroad, ethnic and specialist

Imagemore Co., Ltd./Corbis

Local foods may be a major element of creating local style and ambience for an event

restaurants at home, wide-ranging food programmes and articles in the media have engendered a far greater range of public taste. Venues and even hotels are not always in the forefront of change when developing menus, nor perhaps would the public necessarily wish them to be; but it is essential that the food presented is of a suitable standard, and appropriate to the type of people at the event (see Figure 7.9). Sometimes this is not the case, partly due to insufficient attention to the type of customer or visitor, or to a lack of competitor analysis, and perhaps complacency on the part of venues, which fail to do what in other industries, would be called 'benchmarking'. Older banqueting managers and caterers may recall the days when it was *de rigeur* to eat in competitor establishments or at similar events. This is now extremely rare among modern managers and the quality of event food sometimes suffers for lack of knowledge of what competitors are providing, or lack of awareness about how competitor's efforts might reasonably be exceeded.

There are other common weaknesses in event dining, some of which are training related. Event dining often relies on casual staff, even on volunteers, and this is a particular difficulty. Such staff may have limited food preparation knowledge, or poor hygiene training, or may have gleaned their meagre knowledge of food and drink service from other staff or from *ad hoc* demonstrations by the head waiter/waitress or head cook. Some considered effort needs to go into training, even if for waiting staff, this only amounts to a half-hour briefing before service about the food, the drink, whom to serve first, what colour the vegetarians' place cards are and how to look around for diners trying to attract staff attention. Nevertheless, where professional caterers are present, either in-house, or contracted, the standard of staff training is generally very good.

Meals are often intended as the highlight of an event, perhaps in the form of gala dinners or theme dinners. Regrettably, they can be badly done, with poorly cooked food, indifferent service and poorly presented staff. Style and content at many events are as important in this environment as in the fine restaurants of great hotels, and guests often expect the same standards of service at an outdoor event as they would receive in a fine restaurant (Lillicrap *et al.*, 2010). The problems of delivering this service for outdoor event caterers may be extremely severe: anything from having no main services, electricity, drainage, etc. to having to bring in fresh water in sealed containers, fresh food in chiller lorries, or even having no proper access to muddy fields where outdoor events are being held, except by farm tractor or golf buggy (see Figure 7.10).

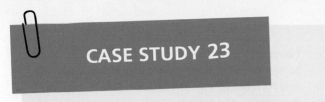

CASE STUDY 23

VIP Hospitality at the 2011 Alpine Ski World Championships

Garmisch-Partenkirchen, Germany

Christophe Pallot/Agence Zoom/Getty Images

Jean Baptiste Grange of France takes the gold medal during the FIS Alpine World Ski Championships February 20, 2011 in Garmisch-Partenkirchen, Germany

FACTBOX

- 2011 FIS Alpine Ski World Championships
- At Garmisch-Partenkirchen
- Large-scale temporary pavilion for 1000
- Containing cookery and service islands
- Also tabled, lounge and bar areas

Learning Objectives

The aim of this case study is to consider the complexity of large scale VIP hospitality service at a major event with the following objectives:

To consider the nature of the facility required

To highlight key issues in the hospitality provision

To understand the time sequence of set up

The International Ski Federation (FIS) have held world championship Alpine Ski events every two years since 1948, although there had been several championships at rather irregular intervals since the event was first held at Murren in the Bernese Oberland in Switzerland in 1931. These events are now extremely large and over the 14 days of the event, nearly 200000 visitors will attend.

Hospitality in and around the Garmisch Classic circuit, the Kandahar, which is within the three mountain area of the Hausberg, Kreuzeck und Alpspitze, was provided in a number of ways. The main permanent catering provision, open for regular skiers and visitors in the season is in the SonnAlpin Glacier Restaurant, the Glaciergarden restaurant, the Gipfelalm rustic summit lodge and the Panorama-Lounge 2962. The Gipfelalm is the highest restaurant in Germany.

For the championships however, it was also necessary to provide a far greater capacity and this was done by the use of temporary facilities including pavilions around the site and hospitality and catering services in the grandstands. One of the key elements of this temporary hospitality provision was the need for a VIP hospitality pavilion and this was undertaken by Arena One and its partners.

The VIP pavilion was a large-scale marquee pavilion structure put up and fitted out prior to the event, about the size of a soccer pitch and taken down following the event. A time lapse clip on You Tube: **http://www.youtube.com/watch?v=H5YBxBUE_h0** shows the pavilion from the point where it had been put up throughout its fitting out to its close-down. The time lapse shows the logistics of the interior layout being put in, the furniture being assembled and the service areas being constructed, then the facility being prepared with its equipment and stocked with its provisions, cleaned, dressed and then in use.

At any one service time up to 800 people could be served within the pavilion in the different areas for main meals and for general hospitality through the day, with almost 11000 people using the pavilion during the event. The facility required almost 100 staff of various kinds from chefs to waiters and baristas, as well as support staff, cleaners, amenity and hosting staff, maintenance staff and supervisory and management staff.

The VIP hospitality carried the theme of 'naturally Bavarian' (reflecting the German province in which Garmisch lies) and the layout of the pavilion included screened off lounge and bar areas, as well as dining seating areas by the windows, for groups, and central catering and service islands with individual stool seating where the guests could watch the food being prepared. The central islands had different roles such as the starter buffet, main and dessert areas as well as a culinary display area where the highlight of the pavilion, the Otto Koch Cooking Bar, was located. The theme was carried through using large scale graphics, that is pictures of the area and by dressing the service island and the pavilion with wood effect materials, planking and logs to give it a local feel, these being materials used in the area for buildings and structures.

Discussion Questions

1   Pick any given large scale sporting event, what are the different types or groups of customers which might have to be served, and how might the service styles differ to provide for these groups?

2   What is the sequence of set up and pre-opening preparation in a hospitality pavilion or marquee?

3   What is the sequence of hospitality activity once a facility is set up for operation?

4   Consider a large sporting event in your area – how is food and drink provided and to what range of customers or groups? Might corporate supporters have different arrangements from the general public for example, and what would these be?

5   If you have a "blank canvas" (in this case let us say an empty marquee) what can you do to give the structure some atmosphere or local feel?

Websites

For more information see: **http://www.zugspitze.de/en/winter/skigebiet/garmisch-classic/** and on YouTube: **http://www.youtube.com/watch?v=hevUkjyDzLs&feature=relmfu**.

Figure 7.9 Issues in determining menus and refreshments

- The number of visitors attending and expected to buy refreshments, and how many refreshment opportunities a visit to the event might represent.

- The number of staff or crew which have to be fed and at what times.

- Details about the visitor group themselves:

  - Who they are

  - Typical food interests and styles of eating

  - Age group

  - Male/female balance

  - Special dietary needs (e.g. vegetarians).

- Whether there is a budget for refreshments, or whether food is exclusive of the ticket price.

- The expertise and ability of the catering staff.

- The type of catering facilities, storage capacity and equipment available at the venue.

- Whether the food/drink is brought in from outside and how it is brought in.

- What utilities and mains services are available at the venue.

A further issue is the feeding of staff and crew, especially volunteers. This may be a charge supported as part of the budget. How many staff and crew need to be fed? With what? At what time and by whom? When will the staff dining room be open, if there is one? Do staff and crew pay for reasonable refreshments in such a dining room? If not, where and how are the staff and crew to be fed? Is food and drink for volunteers or staff entirely free, or subsidized, as part of the event, or as a contribution for their help?

On a final catering note, it is far better to plan activities (such as food restocking) as a matter of professional routine, than to allow something to go wrong and have to expend inordinate effort putting it right. This can be called the 'salt pot' syndrome – if a function is badly prepared and not checked, there will be things waiting to create maximum disruption: the missing salt pot will be discovered by a guest about to consume their main course, and who will, rightly, demand one at the busiest point of service, causing widespread disruption. Typically there will be no salt pots in the

Figure 7.10 Further considerations in food and drinks services

- Have licences for alcohol and food sales (e.g. from stalls) been applied for, and given?

- Is there sufficient space for food, drink and equipment storage, preparation and service?

- Are these areas easily accessible, do they have the necessary utilities and comply with hygiene regulations?

- What are the set-up, opening, closing, and departure times?

- What cleaning and clearing arrangements are there?

- Are there selection criteria for a mix of catering providers, and what arrangements are there for them to pay for their concession, pitch or stall area?

function area, and the staff will have to go to the wash-up area to get one – a location where, mysteriously, there will be no salt pots. This will necessitate the slowest washer-up in the entire site having to search for, wash, dry and fill a fresh salt pot, taking the maximum care, because it is now a 'special' salt pot, and thus taking the maximum possible time. The guest's food, now cold, will have to be returned to the kitchen, and the guest will have to wait for it to be heated up. In the meantime, the rhythm of service for the whole function will have been destroyed.

This kind of unprofessional shambles can often be seen in catering operations where staff have not been trained to maintain the flow of key supplies as they go along, or where there are a depressing number of staff behind a counter, none of whom are actually serving, to the considerable anger and distress of a large number of potential customers, who are watching them do anything and everything except serve. Poor managers and lazy staff may regard good preparation as a nuisance, but it is the bedrock on which all else is built.

Drinks services

Bars for events are essentially of two types: paid and cash. Paid (or account) bars are those where the client or organizer has arranged for some element of payment for guests; let us say for the VIPs, to have free drinks because the client or organization is paying. In some cases, organizers may specify that guests may cover their first drink by this method. However, such arrangements must be made clear. It is far better simply, to serve a pre-determined aperitif (e.g. juice, a spritzer or a fizz) than attempt to monitor who is 'just' having their first drink. The alternative method is to set a bar limit, which the organizer will pay for, and after which delegates pay for their own. Again, this method has severe limitations and could result in an undignified scrum at the bar to get as many free ones as possible before guests have to pay. It is far easier, and much more normal, to have a cash bar. Guests pay for what they drink.

Bars at events should normally have a ratio of one member of staff to every 75 drinkers (for example, at a pre-dinner reception). These ratios can be subject to variation. For instance, experience of a particular event may conclude that guests on previous visits have been particularly heavy drinkers, thus requiring a strengthening of the staff. The importance of this latter point is that the manager responsible for the food and drink service at an event meal must be flexible. It is far too easy to assume that a pre-set standard will do for all functions. This is an easy approach, but leads to a lack of attention to the detail of staffing and to potentially serious mistakes such as under- or over-staffing.

There is also the related issue of drinks served during a meal. The most common method is for organizers to include an allowance of one or two glasses of wine (or half a bottle) or juice with a meal for guests. Thereafter, diners may buy their own wine on payment to the sommelier (wine waiter/waitress); similarly, liqueurs are usually on a cash basis. One bottle of wine (70cl) will normally serve six persons; with a common ratio of three to one in favour of white to red in northern Europe, depending on the type of guest. Spirit service is of the order of 28 (25ml) measures to a bottle. In addition, jugged iced plain water should always be put on the table before the meal arrives. There is a belief that diners will not drink alcohol if water is put on the tables. This is fallacious, and it always results in tables asking for water and service being disrupted to get it. Such disruptions reflect an amateur approach.

SUMMARY

This chapter has sought to discuss the preparation and support activities for events, including logistics and the ordering and supply of goods, equipment and the other items needed to ensure everything is ready at the correct time and is in the correct place. All these elements have to be assembled in a way that will help the event co-ordinator create the right kind of event in terms of the efficiency of organization, so that visitors will regard the event as having been enjoyable to attend and well run.

EVALUATION QUESTIONS

1 How would a Logistics or Operations Manager find a suitable venue for an event?

2 What issues arise in terms of getting materials and equipment to an event in terms of quality of delivery, timing and cost of doing so?

3 Logistics isn't just a matter of the delivery of supplies. What other issues might a logistics provider have to deal with in addition to the core activities of staging, supply and support?

REFERENCES

Allen, J., OToole, W., Harris, R. and McDonnell, I. (2010) *Festival and Special Event Management*, Hoboken: Wiley, pp 344–53.

Goldblatt, J. J. (2008) *Special Events; the Root and wings of celebration*, Hoboken: Wiley, pp 172–205.

Lillicrap, D., and Cousins, J. (2010) *Food and Beverage Service*, London: Hodder and Stoughton (8 edn) pp 337–64.

Silver, J. R. (2004) *Professional Event Co-ordination*, Hoboken:Wiley, pp 282–84 and pp 299–302.

Slack, N., Chambers, S. and Johnston, R. (2007) *Operations Management*, Harlow: Pearson (5 edn) pp 400–34.

Thomas, C., (2012) *Off Premise Catering Management*, Hoboken: Wiley, pp 1–26.

Tum, J., Norton, P. and Nevan Wright, J. (2006) *Management of Event Operations*, Oxford: Butterworth-Heinemann, pp 116–29.

Westerbeek, H., Smith, A., Turner, P., Emery. P., Green, C. and van Leeuwen, L. (2006) *Managing Sport Facilities and Major Events*, Abingdon: Routledge, pp196–202.

CHAPTER 8

MARKETING AND PUBLIC RELATIONS FOR EVENTS

AIMS

- To explore some of the key marketing issues of events management including budgetary and timing issues

- To suggest appropriate marketing and public relations techniques which events organizers can use

- To consider some of the marketing needs for both new events and for further editions

INTRODUCTION

As with many aspects of events management, the breadth and range of types of special event make it hard to generalize about how to market events, when those events are intended to fulfil very different objectives and may be targeted at very different markets. The key to how an event will be marketed is the target market itself – knowing what kind of people will attend, where they live and how can they be influenced to attend. Marketing is not simply pushing out a few posters and hoping for the best. We need to know as much as possible about the target market, and be able to split it into convenient segments in order to best understand what techniques would make them aware of the event and attract them to it, as well as considering issues of differential pricing for the different segments of the target market. People have limited discretionary or disposable income, and limited time. This being the case, events compete for the public's attention, money and time, against all kinds of other activities and attractions, from eating out to engaging in sports and hobbies.

Careful marketing planning and effective marketing are required for activities that will help to ensure the success of what we are doing (Shukla and Nuntsu, 2005). As with other activities, there will be finite money, time and staff available for marketing and these resources need to be planned carefully and used effectively. At the initial stage, marketing was one of the filters, or screens, through which various event ideas could be put, in order to identify ideas that were appropriate. This filtering process should have given the events organizer a firm basis to work on, and a starting place to consider some of the more detailed aspects of marketing, beginning with research. Research may be required about the target market, as well as a thorough assessment of the competitive environment the event is operating in. Once this information is known and objectives have been set, work can begin on the budget and on the marketing schedule.

One of the key functions of the budget will be to obtain the most effective marketing impact for possibly limited money. Not all marketing is expensive. Indeed, some types of activities, such as public relations (PR), may have quite modest costs and be as effective as large-scale expensive advertising campaigns. The budget, therefore, has to relate to what needs to be done, and can either be calculated as a percentage of the overall budget, or built up from 'zero', based on what needs to be done and how much that will cost. Some commentators suggest that events should have quite a substantial marketing budget compared to normal kinds of products, perhaps as much as 10 per cent of the total event expenditure, as opposed to 3–4 per cent for most other goods and services, because of the short duration and unique profile of events, compared to other, longer-lived, types of goods and services. Of all the marketing planning activities, the marketing schedule is the one most likely to surprise people new to the job. The lead times for preparing some marketing activities can be shockingly long. It is not possible, for example, to bang out a brochure in a day or two, as you have to decide what you need to say in it, and find suitable pictures or graphics for it. The brochure also has to be laid out to look attractive, proofed, checked, returned, amended and checked again. This all takes time, if the end result is going to be professional.

This chapter also looks at events marketing in terms of the considerations needed for new or 'one-off' events, as these will need more detailed research and preparation work, due to the uncertainty of the target market and the questionability of the success of the event, if a new concept has not been tried before. This can be compared with the marketing of repeat editions of an event, where the event has run previously, perhaps for many years, and where a great deal of experience has been accumulated about it. In these cases the market, its participants or visitors, may be well known, although – especially where an event has been organized by volunteers – the information recorded might not be especially complete or particularly detailed. A case is, therefore, made for the kind of information that a marketing officer would find useful to record for the marketing of further editions.

THE TARGET MARKET

In our case, the term 'target market' refers, in the main, to the people who would be coming to a particular event. We should bear in mind, however, that for some events, a target market could be watching it on TV, or via the Internet, or follow it as a recreational interest (e.g. sports events). In the most general way, we can see that the target market for a rugby tournament would be very different from one for a heritage pageant or a motor show, since different people like different things. The issue for the events organizer is how much is known about the potential target market for a given event, and whether this can be used to marketing advantage. In addition, it might be wrong to think that an event could only have one target market, as this may not be the case (Stewart, 2006). Take the village fête. The main target market might be people who live in the village itself; a secondary market might be those who live in the surrounding area; and another secondary market might be tourists who happen to be visiting the village on the (hopefully) sunny summer day when the fête is being held.

In asking various questions about the potential market, the answer will help us decide what has to be done next (see Figure 8.1). For example, if the answer to the question: 'Is your event targeted at the general public?' is 'Yes', then the next step is to consider how this knowledge helps us. It provides some focus around which to work, indicates what techniques can be used and what marketing approach might be best for that particular target market, given the resources we have. Appreciating the limitations of the target market concept is also important. The larger an event, the more likely it is to attract a more diverse range of people, for which a more detailed market segmentation study might be needed. Also, there might be 'stakeholders' in the activity and opinion leaders who themselves could also be regarded as separate or discrete target markets, at least from the point of view of public relations.

Figure 8.1   Key questions to ask about the target market

WHO IS YOUR POTENTIAL MARKET?

Is your event targeted at the general public, or at a specific group?

What sort of age or lifestyle segment will your event attract?

Will your event appeal to special interest groups?

Can you identify different segments to attract?

Are the different segments likely to be responsive to different prices?

Source: adapted from Richards, 1992, *How to Market Tourist Attractions, Festivals and Special Events*, Harlow: Longman, pp 21–35

> ### Figure 8.2   Catchment and origin
>
> **WHERE IS YOUR CATCHMENT AREA?**
>
> Where does most of your target market live?
>
> From how far away will people come to your event?
>
> What is the most likely distance (or time) people would travel to your event?
>
> Can you say how many people in your various target markets are in each catchment?
>
> How will these various groups travel to your event?

Part of the process of identifying the target markets for an event involves knowing where your visitors will be coming from. This is easy if you are organizing a student ball, as the catchment area is the campus – students and their friends. Similarly, if you are organizing a wedding anniversary, catchment is not really an issue, because the target market is simply the friends and relations of the couple. However, for many events an understanding of the catchment area is useful for the marketing officer. The target market might have been determined, say, for a horticultural show, to consist of gardening enthusiasts and those in the general public in the 55-plus age group who are retired and enjoy gardening. In the case of a village show, the catchment might be quite small – people from the village and mainly those within walking distance. But for a larger show or event, a typical travel time of one hour might be seen as reasonable to define how far visitors might travel to visit the event, to be involved or entertained. As a ground rule the more important the event the larger its catchment area (see Figure 8.2).

Travel distances in the catchment are often influenced by the time it takes to get to and from the event from various population centres. An hour's travel time on a motorway may cover 100 km, but an hour's travel on a country road might cover only 30 km (see Figure 8.3). These limits in terms of time, rather than simply distance, are what will determine the outer limit of the catchment area for the event. It would then be possible to calculate the size of the catchment area in population terms from census information, or from other sources such as from local newspaper

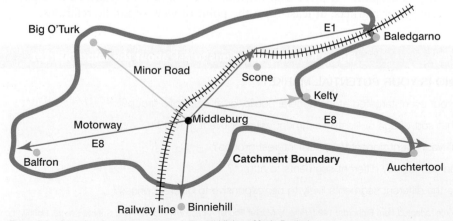

Figure 8.3   Example of a catchment area – The Middleburg Music Festival

'rate and data' information (local papers sometimes keep information on population structure and social groups in their area, in order to help sell advertising space), or from companies who provide market research assessments, or local council economic development departments. Combining this information about social group size and catchment area should give an idea of the potential size of, say, the working population, or that section of the population in a particular age group. Although not all information will have been collected in a way that makes it useful for event marketing officers. Nor will all the people in the selected target market attend your event. Attendance will be influenced by a whole range of things, from effective (or ineffective) marketing to personal preferences, the opinions of friends or something else going on at the same time.

More detail could be added to the catchment as a better picture is built up; for example, if the special event were, say an opera, a large-scale map could be drawn up showing areas of upmarket housing (given a presumption that opera goers would live in those districts, which is not necessarily correct, but serves to illustrate the point). Clearly, different towns and different areas within a town have different population compositions, and a thorough knowledge of the target market and the areas in which its members live would help focus the marketing effort on those areas.

HOW TO INFLUENCE THE TARGET MARKET

There are several reasons why a knowledge of the target market is important to the events organizer. The most important is that this knowledge enables some thought to be given to how to promote the event to a particular group, as well as knowing what kind of activities they would enjoy, or what publicity material they might respond to. For example:

- what they read;
- what they watch on TV (If they watch TV at all).
- what websites they like; or
- what type of lifestyle do they have?

There are probably aspects of their lifestyle that the marketing officer could use as a marketing mechanism (see Figure 8.4). This also helps us understand the likelihood of their coming to our event. In all probability, our marketing plan will have to contain a range of activities both to raise awareness of the event and to convert possible visitors into definite visitors.

A word of caution for the marketing officer who might feel that once you know who your target market is, and what their media habits and buying habits are, all you have to do is to get the promotion or advertising right for them: there are a range of influences on why a target audience might or might not attend an event. Sometimes such reasons are straightforward, like the weather. On the other hand, for an event to be popular it might be necessary to have a critical mass of people showing an interest in attending. This critical mass might only develop through word-of-mouth via a reference group (that is to say, the people we know). For example, suppose the event is a student summer ball. Ticket sales might not have reached the break-even point needed by the break-even deadline, in spite of advertising in the student magazine, posters, Facebook invites, or other sales efforts. The

CASE STUDY 24

Marketing catchment areas: Lake Vyrnwy Marathon

Lake Vyrnwy, Wales

Janet Roberts/ lakevrnwyhalfmarathon.com

Lake Vyrnwy, a view across the lake to the Straining Tower

FACTBOX

- Lake Vyrnwy Marathon, Powys, Wales
- Attracts some 1200 runners
- Runners from over 200 clubs take part
- Entry is about €12
- Takes place on the third Sunday in September
- Involves runners, friends, race-watchers and marathon staff and stewards

Learning Objectives

The aim of this case study is to examine the target market area for the marathon in terms of both participants and observers with the following objectives:

To consider the geographical extent of the target market

To highlight comparisons between the size of a target market in a rural area and in larger urban areas

To understand why splitting the target market for an event might be useful in planning the marketing strategy of the event

Running is a very popular sport, with large numbers of road races, marathons, multi-terrain races and related activities such as triathlons taking place throughout Europe. There are a very large number of clubs associated with the sport, which also has quite a lot of sponsorship activity attached to it. The 'Severn Trent' Lake Vyrnwy Marathon is an extremely popular event attended by some of the best runners in Wales, around a good course known for its fast scenic route.

The race takes place during the afternoon, starting at 13.00, with the fastest runners able to get around the course in about one hour and ten minutes, and an average time of one and a half to two hours. The race has over 12 classes, depending on the age and sex of the runners, with a number of awards for the various classes and overall winners. The race is organized by the Oswestry Olympians, who also organize various other races and competitions in north and mid-Wales, for example:

Race	Location	Type of Race	Type of Participant	Date
Park relays and 10k run	Oswestry	Relay race	School years 5 and 6	1 July
Mynydd Hill run	Trefonen	Recreational run	Under-18s short run Over-18s long run	29 May
Gobowen pentathlon	Gobowen	Pentathlon	Club members Individuals	4 August

The target markets for this type of activity are:

- Amateur and professional runners
- Members of running clubs
- Recreational (occasional) runners
- Individuals interested in trying the sport, but not wishing to do a whole marathon
- Race watchers and sightseers
- Friends and family of the runners

The catchment area for this race is quite large. It is a well-known race, through popular scenery. It attracts runners from a catchment area covering the whole of Wales, the Midlands and the north of England, from where the drive time is about two hours

to Lake Vyrnwy, which is about 20 km west of Oswestry and Welshpool. Consequently, the race is marketed locally and regionally in newspapers and by poster promotions, as well as in national running magazines and by flyers to running clubs and other relevant locations (such as leisure centres) in the area.

The catchment area for those watching the race is rather less than the catchment for runners. Apart from friends and family of the participants, running is not a huge spectator sport on the scale of soccer, but nevertheless, people interested in running as a recreational activity do go to watch the race. Because of its scenic location, there is perhaps a one hour travel time for spectators. There is no separate marketing programme for spectators.

The issue of catchment and travel time must also be seen in the light of accessibility. If we were to say that catchment was an hour on motorways, this would cover a far larger area, because you can drive further and faster on a motorway than on minor roads. This means that catchment areas are unlikely to be circular, but will vary according to the quality of roads and access to the event location. (This can be seen from the shape of the example catchment pattern shown in Figure 8.3 above.)

Discussion Questions

1   Take a map of Wales and the surrounding area. Consider the road network around Lake Vyrnwy. How does this affect the potential catchment for runners?

2   If this race was held in central Birmingham or central Frankfurt, how would the catchment compare, and why?

3   Consider an event you have recently attended, what different types of people were there and how could they be classed into various target markets? How would this information be useful?

Websites

For more information see the related websites: **www.oswestryolympians.co.uk** and **www.lake-vyrnwy.com**

For some thoughts on runs as charitable activities see: **http://www.activenetwork.co.uk/event-management-resources/articles/how-to-plan-a-charity-walk-or-run.htm**

Figure 8.4   Influencing the market
HOW CAN YOU INFLUENCE PEOPLE TO ATTEND?
What are their media habits, what newspapers, magazines, websites, etc. do they read?
Can you use direct mail or newspaper inserts to influence them?
Do they watch TV, go the cinema or listen to local radio?
How can you influence them if they are not engaged by the media? (Not everyone is.)
What public relations activities could you use for these groups?
Who are the opinion leaders and how might they be influenced?

reason for this could be that the reference group (other students) might not have shown a wish to go, perhaps because of other events planned on the same night, or of a lack of immediate interest, or other reasons.

In general, the determinants of why or whether a visitor would come to an event are very varied (and not just about whether we can advertize or promote our event in front of their noses), and some understanding of this process (the buying process) can help us in deciding how best to promote our particular event. In general, these motives can be seen as relevant to the marketing of other activities and products, not just events (Funk, 2008). It is also useful to remember the points made in Chapter 2, about some of these motives being more important than others – primary and secondary motives – because we need to know how best to promote the event given what we know about why people will come to it. For example, a primary motive may be social, because the person knows that many of their friends will go. A secondary motive might be to be entertained. This process is also influenced by other determinants, such as whether the event will be repeated, whether it is easy to get to, whether it is adequately sign-posted, etc.

It can be seen that there are some differences in the 'buying process' between, say, the purchase of the weekly shopping or of new clothes, and the purchase of a ticket for a special event. In the case of certain types of event, no purchase may be taking place. If you have been invited to a dinner party, you are not 'purchasing' the event – you don't buy a ticket, you go because you enjoy the company of your friends. This is true of many types of event: no buying decision is involved, only a social decision (although there is the hidden cost of time and effort, which might be interpreted as buying factors). On the other hand, many special events, particularly in the sporting, cultural and organizational categories, will involve a buying decision: whether to buy the ticket; whether it will be value for money; whether the event will be enjoyable or productive; and these issues might all be part of the decision in such a case (see Figure 8.5).

A number of determinants can be seen as being specific to an 'events buyer'. This is rather a tricky term to use, as the 'buyer' may be a whole family having a day out; a group of people in a minibus going to a sports competition; or one person buying a ticket for a beer festival. If you were the marketing officer for an event, it would be important to have an understanding of who was doing the buying, of who gets the ticket and how you might influence them to do it. What places would you advertize in? What are the benefits of the event you are promoting, to the attendees, visitors, guests or participants? What price would be charged for tickets? Where could people actually buy the tickets?

Figure 8.5   Determinants for participation in an event ('buying process')

- Whether your friends might go (cultural, personal or other reference groups)

- What decision-making time is available, or what the lead times are before you have to buy a ticket

- Whether the price is a major concern ('price sensitivity' – high cost, low cost, total package, and value for money)

- Whether the event will be good enough – the perceived quality of the event

- Access factors – e.g. local, regional, national and international; do people in your area go to this type of event? How easy is it to get to?

- One-off or repeat sales opportunities – is this annual, biannual or occasional; will the event happen again, or is this the only opportunity to go?

- Familiarity – people's knowledge and awareness: Have they been to one before, or something similar?

- Propensity to join in community activities (high, low)

- Inclination to join in the activity due to personal interest, education, entertainment, relaxation, status, etc.

- Considerations of personal enjoyment, arousal or other satisfaction from the event

For the marketing officer, perhaps a significant issue is the benefit that a visitor or attendee gets from the event. This may also be related to the question of expectations. If the visitor expects an excellent, well-organized, enjoyable and good value event, then the level of satisfaction he/she would have would be very high. On the other hand, if the visitor is led to expect these things, but gets none of them, then the outcome will be not only dissatisfaction, but possibly bad publicity for the organizers. Marketing, then, is not just about getting people in through the door. It is, at least in part, about ensuring they get the kind of satisfaction they have been led to expect from the event (see Figure 8.6).

Figure 8.6   Individual's expectations of an event

- What are the benefits of attending the event – will it be enjoyable, entertaining, diverting, educational, stimulating or exciting?

- What will be the style and standard of the venue; distance from home; closeness to transport; convenience of getting there, ease of parking, arrival and departure and other facilities?

- What will be the likely standard of the event – will it be professionally done – even by amateurs or volunteers, will it be well organized, will it be value for money, or will it just be a jolly, convivial, if moderately disorganized shambles? (This latter may be a *normal* expectation held by a potential visitor...)

- What will the people be like – can we expect excellence, commitment, enthusiasm, knowledge (or otherwise) from staff, volunteers or other participants?

- What is the price (or value) in comparison to other uses for the money – other possible events, other days out, meals or other leisure or social activities?

- What range of activities is available, interaction, sights and sounds, inclusiveness?

- What is the reputation of the event if it has been held before?

- How easy is it to get information, get tickets or have questions answered?

Leading on from the issue of what motivates and influences people to attend or participate in an event, we have to recognize the difficulty of marketing what are essentially unique, one-off occasions to a diverse market – and very possibly, a diverse market of people who do not know they want to attend or participate. In terms of personal events, there are no conventional marketing issues in getting people to a private party. These events are 'invited', not marketed; in fact, in some cases, the problem is to stop people coming to events where they might not be wanted. Gate-crashers are an example of this. We can organize a party for friends, only to find that they turn up with people we might not expect, perhaps even do not like, or that word has got around to people whom we would not want at our party. This happens not only at some types of personal event, but also at high profile public events, which involve celebrities or film stars. Various people might try to **blag** their way into an event by all kinds of unscrupulous means, such as emailing the organizers to say they have not received the tickets they were promised (when no one said they could have tickets); trying to get in by hanging around, in the hope someone will recognize them and take them in; trying to buy tickets from **ticket touts** and so on.

For most events in the leisure, cultural or organizational categories, the issue is not how to stop people getting in, but how to encourage people to come. For a local charity fundraising event, the issue will be both how to get a good crowd in and to make some money for the charity concerned. For organizations selling products, there may well be a clear need to market the event, so that a lot of people come to see the product and hopefully some of them will buy it. This is especially the case with events such as trade shows and exhibitions, but the need to market an event applies to a large range of activities. An example of the decision-making process is shown in Figure 8.7.

There are some key marketing issues in this scenario. In promoting an event, it is necessary to create an awareness of it among the target market. In this example the method is posters, and the market is students. The interest phase is about stimulating

blag

To attempt to get into an event by gate-crashing, or get tickets under false pretences.

ticket touts

A person who resells a ticket for an event at greater than the price of the face value of the ticket, also sometimes called a **Scalper**.

Figure 8.7   Event decision-making process for a university ball

ATTENTION

Saw poster at university for the summer prom
Instinctive consideration of whether the date and the cost would be OK

INTEREST

Talked to friends in the class (or other reference group) to see if anyone else was interested
If lots of people interested, do the benefits outweigh the cost, (being a student
with limited money)?
Is there anything else going on?
If not, why should I go?

DESIRE

Primary motives for going: Have a good time, have some drinks, dance all night
Secondary motives for going: Don't have to watch awful television in study bedroom; food is free
Reasons for not going: Maybe too difficult to get a ticket

ACTION

Ticket seller knocked on the door, so bought a ticket

the interest of the target market. In any target market, people who are considering attending the event will be seeking a reference mechanism for confirming that the event is what they want.

For many people, the reference mechanism is from people they know, either directly in person or from social media exchanges, whether they are having a chat on Facebook, on Skype or whatever their favourite way of talking to their friends about the event is (Preston, 2012). One of the biggest difficulties facing the marketers of events is that for new or unusual one-off occasional events, the word-of-mouth support may not exist, as no-one has been to the event before, or been able get a view of how good or bad it is. They then have to rely on external referents, such as the quality of the advertising material, or the views of critics (as with a new play or film). In some respects, events marketers can try to generate word-of-mouth support by targeting opinion formers, (such as by offering pre-meetings, advance 'tasters' or familiarization visits to the event site), but this is problematic because not everyone may attend these warm up events and they are only suitable for certain types of events. What we are seeking to create is desire for the product, through encouraging people to feel that the event will fulfil their particular needs and by generating a positive 'buzz' about it. From here onwards it should be easy. The prospective attendee simply takes 'action' and buys the ticket, and the event, of course, goes wonderfully well.

THE MARKETING PLAN

The marketing plan, like the operational plan and the financial budget, will be developed from the event objective, in a number of stages (see Figure 8.8). Marketing techniques employed by destination managers and events organizers vary, and the range of approaches is extremely wide, because of differences in the types of events being put on and the different characteristics of target markets. Nevertheless, the nature of the event buying decision and the influencing factors make targeting potential visitors relatively complicated for certain types of event (although not all – a village fête would have a relatively simple target market in the catchment area of the village and its immediate surroundings).

The event marketing officer's expertise and resources in selling the event may not always be large, perhaps depending on volunteer effort and small budgets, perhaps tending to rely on general awareness and word-of-mouth, or responses to enquiries, rather than expensive advertising. For this reason, public relations (PR) may play a greater role in promoting some events than paid advertising. However, this should not prevent careful thought and planning about marketing as a whole activity, nor should it prevent due consideration of the need for public relations to address both external and internal audiences.

MARKETING FOR A NEW EVENT

Objectives and analysis of the environment

If the marketing of an event has to be started from a blank sheet of paper, then the marketing plan will have to be written to cover six main elements (see Figure 8.9). Some of these should have been identified early on in the event planning process, and should be easy to summarize in the first few sections of the marketing plan. These are

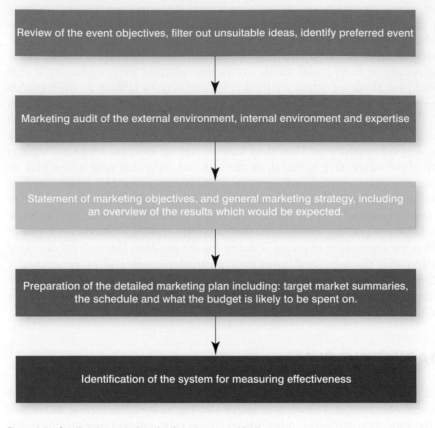

Figure 8.8   Creating the marketing plan from the event objectives

the sections dealing with the purpose of the event, which might be written as one line or sentence, and can then be broken down into several smaller objectives. To make this as simple as possible there should be no more than about five aims for the event (there might be only one, remember), because the more aims you have, the more difficult it will be to achieve them all adequately. In addition, either too much complication, or too much vagueness, about objectives can render marketing, promotion and public relations efforts meaningless. This is followed by the analysis of the environment in which the event will operate, what competition there might be, what other things are going on at the same time that might take some of the potential target market away and whether there have been, or are, similar events that could be seen not so much as competitors, but as complementary to your event.

Event components mix and target markets

The summary of the component products and services of the event is a list of its respective parts (which might also be called the product/service mix), that might attract different parts of the target market. In the case of a garden show, this mix might comprise the main garden exhibition itself; seminars on gardening given by experts to visitors; the prize-giving ceremony for the best flowers; the catering tent; the sales and retail stands; the prize draw competition to win a garden makeover from an expert; and the children's crèche.

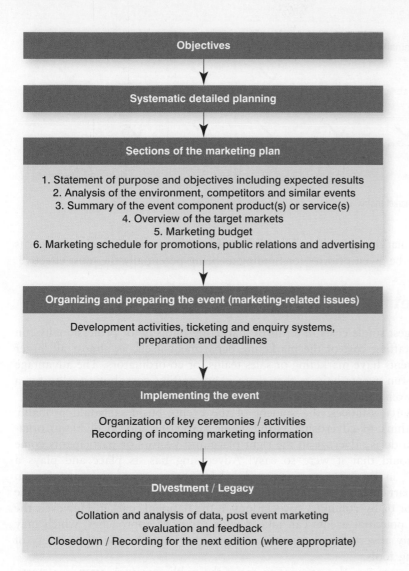

Figure 8.9 Elements of the events marketing plan

When preparing the summary of the event's components, the ability to cross-reference the products and services being offered against the likely target markets, will help to identify which parts of the event might turn out to be the busiest. It will also indicate how the marketing and promotion effort might be targeted at individual markets (rather than the general whole), by showing which elements of the event's components mix could be highlighted in specific literature or other promotional material for a given market segment or target (see Figure 8.10). At this point in the marketing plan, the target markets can be isolated and described in some detail, together with information about the catchment; the kind of marketing tools that will be used to influence each target market segment to come to the event; what media habits each target market has: and what other promotions or public relations activities might also have an impact on the decision to attend. From this list, the

	Exhibition	Seminars	Prize-giving	Catering	Sales	Prize draw	Crèche
❶ Families	✓			✓	✓		✓
❷ Pensioners	✓		✓	✓		✓	
❸ Hobbyists	✓	✓	✓	✓	✓	✓	
❹ Tour Groups	✓			✓	✓		

Figure 8.10   Event components and target market matrix

most effective marketing tools can be identified, which as the marketing budget is assembled, can be given priority for funding as being potentially the most effective.

The marketing budget

One of the largest single costs in terms of marketing budgets for professionally run events is the staffing cost of the marketing department itself, as almost all larger professional events have marketing or sales teams, or co-ordinators. The advantage that volunteer-run events have is that there is no staffing cost, but equally, for a volunteer-run event, the marketing budget might be very small.

In normal circumstances, the student of the events business would probably automatically think of advertising as the major marketing tool available to organizers – all you do is advertize in the right place and visitors or participants come flocking in; would that it were so easy! Advertising has its place and plays a significant role in raising awareness and helping to support an image for an activity. It is particularly relevant on a national scale for events organized in the corporate sector or by voluntary associations in the national market. However, the wide range of potential events can take a wide range of approaches, which may include not only advertising and public relations, but also the use of a variety of other marketing tools.

Individual events can also attempt to entice the public, visitors, attendees, participants and even potential staff by providing pre-event activities, or a series of awareness-raising promotions to help familiarize people with the main event. It is also important to keep the target market 'warm', i.e. to call and talk to opinion leaders, or invite them to familiarization or hospitality events. In this way, some of the target market or 'buyers' for an event can be influenced or at least informed of the planned activities.

It is difficult to ascertain the effectiveness of the various methods, but personal contacts are often significantly important to marketing an event and do not show as a cost in a marketing budget, except perhaps as travel or hospitality expenses. In addition to the paid advertising, which an event manager or organizing committee might or might not be able to afford, many events rely significantly on good public and media relations, anything from word-of-mouth to imaginatively written press releases (see Figure 8.11).

The marketing budget should be carefully prepared and costed. All the items that are needed should be included, how many are required, and their size or type. In

Figure 8.11 Examples of marketing expenditure items
1. Print items: tickets, posters, brochures, leaflets, visitor maps (design costs, display costs)
2. Direct marketing: sales visits to opinion leaders / event organizers / agencies / mailings.
3. 'Advertorials': journal/magazine inserts or advertising copy pieces
4. Hospitality: familiarization visits, pre-event days
5. Exhibition material for local promotions, stands, site models
6. Paid advertising: newspapers, magazines, radio, TV
7. Websites, Facebook or Twitter page creation and moderation
8. Payments for celebrity guests
9. Press kits, photography and artwork activities
10. Banners, signs, etc.

addition, for items such as brochures or leaflets, the cost per thousand (if this kind of number is needed) should be compared to see which type is the most cost-effective. Wherever possible in the costing process, more than one estimate or cost quote should be obtained (see Figure 8.12).

The marketing schedule

In order for a special event to be marketed properly, not only must the planning and budgeting of the marketing programme have taken place, but a schedule of activities should have been prepared. This schedule is intended to give the organizers an idea of the lead times for various marketing activities in order to plan what needs to be done and when, to get the most benefit from the marketing effort (see Figure 8.13).

In preparing a marketing schedule, it is important to understand that many activities have long lead times. Brochures, for example, may take several weeks: the text has to be written, photographs provided, a draft assembled by the graphic designer or printer, checked for errors, corrected and then checked again before being printed. Similarly, for those particular media that a marketing manager may wish to use, it will be important to check the lead times. National monthly trade magazines might need two to four months notification of an event to get an advertizement in, with editorial. TV and radio shows require up to six weeks notice. Even a website might need several weeks' intensive design work, and will itself require follow-up advertising. Local media can work on shorter lead times, but it is best to find out whether their deadlines for stories are a certain day and time of the week. A media kit or press pack can be prepared at an early stage of the activities, and could include various fact sheets about the event, an artist's impressions (or suitable photographs), a media contact list, information about sponsors, beneficiaries and key people involved (Goldblatt, 2010). However, the first version of the press kit should not include admission prices, as the media might focus too strongly on these at too early a stage in the development process.

MARKETING BUDGET PROPOSALS

Event: _____

Date of Event: _____   Date of this budget: _____

Target Market Segments:	Target Numbers:	Ticket Price:
Individuals	_____	€_____cent
Families	_____	€_____c
Children	_____	€_____c
Concessions/Students/Elders	_____	€_____c
Groups	_____	€_____c
Complimentary/Hospitality/VIPs	_____	Nil
Press	_____	Nil

Examples of expenditure:	Budget €:	Actual €:	Number/Size
Research			
Staff: Marketing Office	_____	_____	_____
Staff: Booking and Enquiry office	_____	_____	_____
Volunteers: Custom T-Shirts, Leaving Gift	_____	_____	_____
Advertising: Newspaper/Magazine	_____	_____	_____
Advertising: Radio	_____	_____	_____
Advertising: Posters	_____	_____	_____
Advertising: Other: Specify_____	_____	_____	_____
Direction Signs	_____	_____	
Internal Signs	_____		
Printing: Tickets	_____	_____	_____
Printing: Brochures	_____	_____	_____
Printing: Posters	_____	_____	_____
Printing: Programmes, Site maps	_____	_____	_____
Printing: Menus, Place Cards	_____	_____	_____
Printing: Other: Specify_____	_____	_____	_____
Uniforms/sashes	_____	_____	
Badges	_____	_____	
Celebrity costs	_____	_____	
Prizes	_____	_____	
Complimentary Items/Giveaways	_____	_____	
Marketing Office Hospitality	_____	_____	
Marketing Office Travel Expenses	_____	_____	
Display Stands	_____	_____	
Photography	_____	_____	
Video Company	_____	_____	
Press Kit	_____	_____	
Ticket Distribution	_____	_____	
Postage/Mail Out Costs	_____	_____	
Stationery	_____	_____	
Other items e.g. website	_____	_____	
Total Costs	€_____	€_____	

Figure 8.12   Event marketing budget form (adapt as required)

Figure 8.13   Example of a marketing schedule

MARKETING SCHEDULE: MIDDLEBURG GARDEN FESTIVAL

5–6 months before opening

1. Hold meeting to define objectives and to ensure co-ordination of various public relations activities with paid advertising. Establish timetable to match scheduled deadline opening date. Identify target market at a meeting with the organizing committee.
2. Prepare a media kit (information pack, contacts, etc.)
3. Order photographs / artists impressions / logo or design drafts, begin website design.
4. Begin preparation of mailings and media lists.
5. Contact all prospective beneficiaries of the events and start listing VIPs and opinion leaders.
6. Book dates for press conferences at suitable venues (probably off site to begin with).

4–5 months before opening

1. Send out initial press releases with suitable pictures to all media (local, regional, etc.).
2. Write a 'progress bulletin' or newsletter, for agents, media, VIPs and opinion leaders. This can also be used or adapted for internal marketing i.e. to keep site and event staff and volunteers up to date.
3. Begin production of adverts, posters and promotional brochures.
4. Set up enquiry desk and advance ticket office.
5. Test and set up website.
6. Make final plans for the opening ceremony and associated events, including arrangements and invitations for VIPs and other invited guests.

3–4 months before opening

1. Launch publicity campaign to national media
2. Send out mailings to all media
3. Send second progress bulletin
4. Arrange interviews with local media, also trade media, gardening, design and leisure publications (not at the site, as it will not be ready or well presented).
5. Begin awareness raising advertising, e.g. posters.

2–3 months before opening

1. Launch campaign to local and other media with a short lead time, emphasising the event's contribution to the community, local business, etc. Highlight the contribution of volunteers, sponsors and benefactors.
2. Send out a further progress bulletin together with a brochure to the completed mailing lists and to people who have booked advance tickets already.
3. Provide a site model and publicity displays for the enquiry area or for use in local public places such as libraries and shopping centres.
4. Begin 'behind the scenes' public tours. (Only if the site is nearly ready).
5. Hold 'hard hat' lunches for invited guests such as media writers.

1–2 months before opening

1. Send out further progress bulletins, including useful comments from people who have had previews.
2. Undertake a 'mystery guest' enquiry and ticket booking to test the system. Deal with any problems which arise.
3. Establish final plans for the opening ceremony, send out appropriate invitations.
4. Hold the 'soft opening' (an event where you use staff and their families to test the systems, such as catering, toilets, parking and queuing arrangements, etc.)

The opening month

1. Begin final mailings
2. Check invited guests' attendance at opening
3. Hold orientation press/media visits
4. Hold the opening ceremony
5. Get pictures of opening ceremony to media, same day.

Post event

1. Send out a further progress bulletin, highlighting the success of the opening and especially thanking volunteers, sponsors and beneficiaries.
2. Final media coverage, more photos, success of event, handover ceremony or publish date of next event.
3. Thank you letters.

MARKETING FOR REPEAT EVENTS AND NEW EDITIONS

Up to now, we have tended to stress that many events are one-off, unique activities. In some ways this is true, but all kinds of events are repeated, perhaps annually or biannually, or on some other timescale (e.g. the Olympics every four years). Even events that happen annually, in the same place and at the same time of year, may not be exact replicas of what has gone on before, perhaps because of a different organizing committee, different participants, different visitors or any number of changes in the operations and activities taking place. For this reason they are often called 'new editions'. Consequently, these types of events are based on existing knowledge and techniques, but, as with a book, some changes are made each time, perhaps some things removed, or some new things added.

Admittedly, new business often presents a more exciting challenge to event marketers and salespeople than the routine of carefully recording, monitoring and caring for an existing target market. Yet it is this attention to the detail of maintaining, and enhancing, an existing business base that is probably the acid test of a good marketing officer. The development of the existing visitor base into repeat business and also as a lead to further new visitors may be very useful indeed. Careful recording of attendance information about visitors and participants is the first stage in making sure they can be encouraged to return to the next event. It is also important to collect the same information each year, for the sake of consistency and to be able to make accurate comparisons. The basic information that we should be attempting to collect is detailed in the following subsections.

Records of visitor numbers

In assessing total visitor or participant numbers, how many and where from, the 'where from' can be done by sampling surveys or by getting people to fill in some details as part of the booking process – it depends on how big your event is, and what resources you can put into recording. With limited resources, such as volunteer staffing, you have no need to collect details from every single visitor. You will know how many tickets you sold, and of what types. If the event is free, volunteers can still be put on the entrances or gates to give a rough count of people coming in, and if it is in an open area estimates can still be made (see also the Deventer Book Market Case Study 34). More detailed information such as place of origin, mode of travel, etc. can be put on a simple questionnaire and attached to the ticket, to be filled in if the visitor wishes and placed in a box near the exit(s). Large numbers of questionnaire replies are not needed to gather this kind of information: if only 100 questionnaires were returned (note the limitations of doing this without a representative control sample that preferably includes some non-attendees to find out why they didn't come), this would still be enough for a modest analysis of the information, and is not too much to collate and write up in a short Visitor Attendance Report. Gathering this information will help you promote the event in the right places next time.

Details of spending and use patterns

How much was spent, and what on? How many people did what, and when? This kind of information helps you find out what aspects were most popular. Your event might have included several different components or activities (the product service mix), and in the next edition you might want to add or remove some of them, or make some of them better, or try out new layouts or locations. To do this you need information on what components of the event people are using and what is popular. This information can be obtained from spot checks and from sampling elements such as queue lengths at given times. More detailed information can be found from ticket sales, and from sales records of catering or other activities. Even where no money changes hands, volunteers can count the number of people using parts of the event, or visitors can be given tokens or ticket strips (carnet strips) to hand in at the various locations, activities or stands as they use them. These can be counted, or just weighed. Gathering this information will help you decide what parts of your event are most popular, and which should be kept or changed next time.

Marketing effectiveness

What parts of the marketing, publicity and public relations effort were successful? It is quite common for people to be asked on a questionnaire, 'How did you find out about us?' You can ask this by getting people to tick boxes on a questionnaire ('Advert in the newspaper; Advert on the radio', etc.), – but, bearing mind what has just been discussed about how people decide and what influences them, it would better to do this through informal chats with visitors. These can, in fact, be loosely structured by writing down a few short questions and using them as a guide during each chat. Following the chat, write out the responses on a summary sheet (just a list – chat 1, chat 2, etc.). You will be surprised what you learn and, most importantly, this gives people the opportunity to tell you more about what they did and how they found out about you, than if you had given them a list (provided you use open-ended questions, such as 'How did you get here?', rather than 'yes/no' questions, 'Did you come by car?'). Gathering this information will help you find out what part of your marketing effort was the most useful, and how you could improve it.

Expectations and satisfaction

What did your visitors expect and were they were happy with their experience, i.e. did your event fulfil their expectations? Like the effectiveness assessment of marketing, checking expectations and satisfaction is probably best done by talking to people. This helps to explore their expectations in a way that would probably not be expressed in a questionnaire. Be careful how you formulate questions. For example, it is very common in a restaurant to be asked, 'Is everything all right?' Remember what we said about asking open-ended questions, as the response to this is almost certainly 'Yes, it's fine'. This is, first, because the question is framed in a yes/no way, and second, because it is socially difficult for people to respond to such a question by

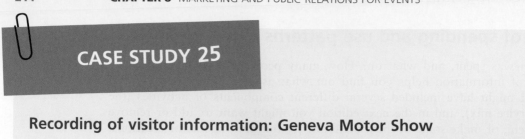

CASE STUDY 25

Recording of visitor information: Geneva Motor Show

Geneva, Switzerland

Visitors gather at the Geneva Motor Show Palexpo 2009

Fedor Selivanov/Shutterstock.com

FACTBOX

- Geneva International Motor Show
- Attracts over 714 000 visitors from 87 different countries
- 4700 journalists attended
- There were 275 stands showing 900 models of cars, covering 90 000 square metres of exhibition space.

Learning Objectives

The aim of this case study is to consider the usefulness of information collected during and event about its visitors with the following objectives:

To consider the break-down of some basic information collected at an event about its visitors

To apply the understanding of the need to collect marketing information which might then be used to market future editions

To examine whether all events should collect information

The Geneva International Motor Show, with its 82nd edition in March 2012, attracts a huge number of exhibitors and visitors to the Palexpo halls in Geneva. The show lasts for 11 days and includes not only car exhibits, but equipment and components, events and interactive displays. It is one of a series of motor shows throughout Europe, each country being allowed one International Motor show, as well as domestic shows and dealer exhibitions. Past Geneva shows have been of such importance that they have been opened by the President of Switzerland and the President of the Council of State, with attendance by other major political figures and celebrities at the opening ceremonies.

The 11-day event takes more than two weeks to set up inside the exhibition hall from the initial layout of where the respective stands will be, through the construction of the stand shells (exhibition booths), the delivery of exhibitors' stand equipment, the fitting of power and lighting, the arrival of major exhibits – including the cars, which are covered with tarpaulins – to the final fitting-out of the stands with furniture and promotional materials ready for the opening day. This sequence of construction can be seen in a series of development pictures on the motor show website.

For marketing purposes, the motor show organization, in conjunction with Palexpo, records and publishes admissions information and also breaks this down into various segments:

Total number of visitors	714 000	
Total number of Swiss visitors	421 000	59%
Total number of external visitors	293 000	41%
Number of countries of visitor origin	87	
Other main countries of origin		
France	228 500	32%
Germany	14 250	2%
Italy	14 250	2%

All others	37 750	5%
Total number of visitors in age group 18–54	628 000	88%
Total number of visitors in other age groups	86 000	12%
Total number of male visitors	52 1000	73%
Total number of female visitors	19 3000	27%

Discussion Questions

1 Identify how the break-down of visitor information can be useful in marketing terms.

2 Examine an event for which you can obtain visitor information: How can this information be used for marketing purposes? What kind of details would it be especially useful to know about the visitors at the event, if you had a further edition to prepare for a coming year?

3 Clearly, large scale events collect visitor information in various ways, (in what ways?) but do all events do this and if not, why not? Do you need to collect marketing data at: A. a private dinner party; B. a single one time only music event; C. an annual village flower show?

Websites

Related websites include: **www.salonauto.ch/ and the Palexpo Halls: www.palexpo.ch**
For some thoughts on interviewing participants to obtain market research information You Tube has some videos, for example: **http://www.youtube.com/watch?v=ECAR871eano**.

saying, 'No. The food is terrible, the service is slow, the carpet is sticky and the toilets smell' (or whatever). Therefore, in exploring whether your visitors are satisfied you need to think carefully about what you will ask them and how, and also what opportunities there are during your event when visitors will be socially comfortable to answer questions. Although we may not use questionnaires during the event itself, it is probably a useful exercise to give people some to take away, or mail some out a day or two later, in order to obtain opinions after the event or after people have had time to reflect. Clearly, the most useful purpose in getting satisfaction information is to help identify strengths and weaknesses and to help grow the potential number of visitors attending by knowing what went well and what didn't.

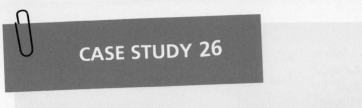

CASE STUDY 26

Social Media: Epica

Imagebroker / Alamy

The Netherlands and Reuver

Epica performing live at Norway Rock Festival in July 2010

● Epica is a Dutch gothic metal band
● The band was founded by Mark Jansen
● Known for their symphonic sound
● The band plays throughout Europe

Learning Objectives

The aim of this case study is to examine the usefulness of social media in marketing terms with the following objectives:

To consider the way in which social media may support the more traditional marketing methods
To highlight how this type of media is used
To understand issues about social media which might result in an organization getting unusual publicity or unexpected public relations outcomes

Epica, a Dutch gothic metal band, originating in Reuver in Limburg, has six members who perform in a style which might be described as a blend of progressive, gothic and symphonic metal. Their music is aggressive, bombastic and excessive with some songs being described as epic, grand and majestic and others being described as more subdued and introspective. The band also uses larger forces in outdoor concerts (as opposed to studio music) including choirs and orchestras, they were founded in 2002–2003 by Mark Jansen.

Epica uses a range of traditional marketing techniques and social media to promote their work, both in terms of live performances and recorded music. Their website demonstrates this mix of techniques with links to venues for gig dates, tickets and for information about the performances and the venues. Social media plays a major role in terms of their fan base and spreading the word about Epica. The website enables fans and supporters feedback what they think, to raise issues and be positive (or otherwise) about what Epica are doing. The chat room enables fans and others to engage with each other and learn what is going on or what might be happening.

Social networks such as MySpace and Twitter have official Epica pages, as does Facebook and other networks. Taking Facebook as the example, Epica can be seen and liked by huge numbers of people (1.3 million likes, rather more than 'liked' the last thing most of the rest of us posted!). As with all things Facebook, there is a tendency for most users to be supportive of what's going on, but as Facebook users know themselves, posting a status sometimes generates strange or obscure responses.

In terms of public relations, any organization using social media, and most now do so, involves just as much time, effort and care as any other form of activity. Social media can be very supportive of an organization, but can also be very critical and it is essential that an organization has a member of staff with a management responsibility for engagement and oversight. Sometimes the use of social media can result in big, and occasionally, quite unpleasant surprises for organizations, notably where the management of such organizations has lost contact with the reality of the world as seen through the eyes of its supporters and perhaps the public, and there are examples where this has had a big impact on what an organization chose to do.

Discussion Questions

1   How does Epica use social media?

2   Is social media a generally positive activity and why is this?

3   How do organizations gauge whether social media feedback is of major importance and how should organizations provide oversight of what is happening in the virtual world?

4   Are there costs attached to running or overseeing social media activities?

Websites

For Epica's website see: **http://www.epica.nl/**.

SUMMARY

Marketing is attractive to many people as an interesting and stimulating activity, one that they enjoy doing. However, as with the other components of events management, from logistics to finance, it requires a high level of skills to undertake it properly. Sound knowledge of the kind of people who will attend an event, whether as participants, visitors or guests, is essential to promoting it and ensuring its success. This knowledge helps the event marketer understand how to raise awareness, advertize, promote, improve an image or maintain the event's impact in the media. Part of the marketing function is also to evaluate how an event is received. Sometimes this is done as an event is progressing, sometimes by feedback at the end. In those cases where there will be a further edition, the knowledge gained from evaluation should enable improvements or changes to be made for the future.

EVALUATION QUESTIONS

1 Identify some of the key marketing issues of events management.

2 Suggest appropriate marketing and public relations techniques which events organizers can use for one or two example events. For example, a large outdoor music concert or festival, and a small town carnival.

3 What differences exist between the marketing of new events and further editions?

4 Identify four traditional or conventional ways of marketing an event and four social media methods of marketing an event.

REFERENCES

Funk, D. (2008) *Consumer Behaviour in Sport and Events*, Oxford: Butterworth-Heinemann, pp 15–28.

Goldblatt, J. J. (2010) *Special Events: A new generation and the next frontier*, Hoboken:Wiley, pp 324–58.

Preston, C. A. (2012) *Event Marketing: How to successfully promote events, festivals, conventions and expositions*, Hoboken: Wiley, pp 113–15.

Rogers, T. and Davidson, R. (2006) *Marketing Destinations and Venues for Conferences, Conventions and Business Events*, Oxford:Butterworth-Heinemann, pp 74–101.

Stewart, M. in Ali-Knight, J. and Chambers, D. (eds), (2006) *Case Studies in Festival and Event Marketing and Cultural Tourism*, Brighton: Leisure Studies Association, pp 1–24 .

Shukla, N. and Nuntsu, N. in Tassiopoulos, D. (eds), (2005) *Event Management: A Professional and Developmental Approach*, Lansdowne: Juta Academic, pp 252–93.

CHAPTER 9

RISK MANAGEMENT AND LEGALITIES

AIMS

- To appreciate issues of risk management in terms of event planning and operations

- To identify those licensing, health and safety, and insurance requirements which are the key to secure operations

INTRODUCTION

This chapter considers some of the issues which an event co-ordinator, managing committee or other responsible person must take into consideration in order to ensure, as far as possible, safe event activities for all those involved. The planning process for an event must take into account all the aspects of management which bear upon our legal duties and these aspects include risk management, official licenses and permissions, general and specific health and safety issues and insurance matters.

Although risk management tends to be regarded as the mechanism by which we attempt to be aware of those things which could go wrong at an event or venue and for which we should make plans or take steps to prevent or mitigate those risks, 'Risks' are really things that don't turn out as one expected them to. Attracting more visitors than you expected can be just as damaging as attracting too few.

Risk tend to fall more or less into four groups:

1 Economic Risks – such as financial losses or lack of sponsorship or grant support.

2 Performance Risks – such as the failure of an event to take place due to, say, booked entertainers or competitors not turning up.

3 Psychological Risks – such as a location, venue or previous similar event having a poor reputation.

4 Physical Risks – that is danger to the public or participants; health and safety problems; or crime and security difficulties.

In terms of legalities, while there are some aspects of law and legislation that are Europe-wide, many issues in terms of the legalities of an event may vary from country to country and region to region, so events managers need to have an understanding of their national and local legal requirements. These requirements are likely to cover licensing issues, such as the licenses needed for the sale of alcohol or the sale of food; also performance licenses, perhaps for music or other entertainment; matters of copyright (especially for music); legal requirements for a wide range of health and safety issues ranging from Food Hygiene to Crowd Safety; contractual arrangements between the organizers, promoter, client or venue and their suppliers, local authorities, broadcasters and so on; as well as insurance requirements for a whole range of issues from employer's liabilities to public safety.

RISK MANAGEMENT

Although the media tends to be dominated by recent events, the scale and scope of risk have not changed (Swiss Re, 2010), indeed the Centre for the Study of Financial Innovation (2012, p 4) reminds us, that the risks people look for seem to be driven as much by recent concerns as by any realistic appraisal of coming challenges. Hence, the tragedy at the 2010 *Love Parade* (BBC 2010) echoes the 1883 tragedy at Victoria Hall, Sunderland (SPLS, 2012), the 1896 *Khodynka Field* tragedy (*Time-lines*, 2012) or any number of similar tragedies, since Event Managers need to adopt realistic approaches. More than ever, the events co-ordinator must address the possibility that something might go wrong at an event; seeking to identify potential risks and taking steps to reduce or mitigate them; as a starting point for producing contingency plans and emergency procedures (Tarlow, 2002). Although we will concentrate on risk as a threat to safety, it is important to recognize that the more general approach of risk management (Parry, 2004) is to look at any aspect of a project or activity to identify its risks. In this more holistic approach, the risk inherent in putting up a marquee is that, as well as the chance it might fall down on top of 200 guests, it might not arrive at all. Perhaps the marquee company went bankrupt and forgot to tell you – so, what contingency is available in the event of that type of risk? (A contact name and number for another marquee company and event insurance.)

Event organizers need to balance offering the best achievable duty of care to visitors and staff with maintaining a sense of proportion. This tension cannot be overstated and it is critical that you as an organizer wrestle with it early on, or it will prevent you doing your job effectively. The first meeting about risks that an event co-ordinator might hold with an organizing committee might raise a long list of potentially dire consequences for a simple activity (think of the potential dangers of boiling a kettle); but there are established ways of putting such risks into some kind of context and evaluating them. The media can be seen, increasingly, as taking an unpleasant delight in highlighting the downside of issues and exaggerating worst-case scenarios, so that an appropriate response is required (Hall, 2002). The purpose of risk management is, therefore, to help us lead our event through this minefield, by means of a policy of heightened awareness, assessment, evaluation, moderation and recording. Parry (2004), Laybourn (2003), Tarlow (2002) and Jennings (2010) deal with the detail of these issues.

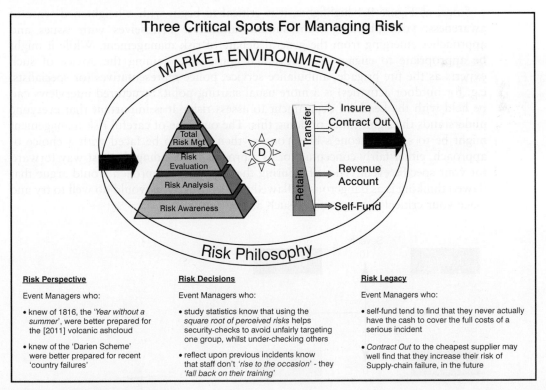

Figure 9.1   Hollistic understanding of risk
Parry (2004)

Figure 9.2   Various risk categories

- Risks to staff and others, due to confused organization, poor health and safety practice or the presence of chemicals or other potentially dangerous substances and items.

- Risks in marketing an event, perhaps due to (natural) enthusiasm or optimism about what the event will do, therefore the risk of expectations not being fulfilled, but also the risk of the media finding a negative story about an event and making a big performance of it.

- Risks in health and safety, especially for the public, and especially at outdoor events which are large and complicated, or involve some inherently risky activity.

- Risks in catering provision, especially for concessions and food stalls, in hygiene and sanitation provision

- Risks in crowd management, overcrowding, potential crush points, the positioning and availability of emergency exits, alcohol provision, noise control and rowdy or violent behaviour.

- Risks in security, particularly at large events or where VIPs are present.

- Risks in transport of items to and from the venue, deliveries and movement at the site of unusual or large items.

Based on McDonnell *et al.*, 2001. Events Management, Butterworth Heinemann, Oxford, p.123

Since, as Figure 9.1 highlights, it is critical to begin with a heightened sense of awareness, your planning team should familiarize themselves with issues and approaches emerging from the general debate of risk management. While it might be appropriate to engage a professional consultant, gaining the advice of such experts as the fire brigade, ambulance service, police representatives (or specialists, e.g. for outdoor activities) is a more usual starting point. Structured interviews can be held with the heads of department to assess risks. It is important that everyone understands the significance of doing this. The outcome of careful risk management might be to save someone's life. You are then likely to be faced with a choice of approach, either fairly conceptual or as a process, in deciding the best way forward for your specific event. Those favouring the conceptual approach would argue that flawed thinking is as dangerous as flawed policy; hence you would do well to try and place your critical risks in a table such as Figure 9.2.

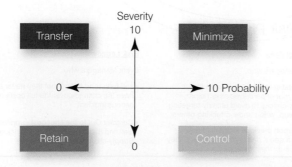

Figure 9.3   Risk Analysis Quadrant

The advantages of such an approach are that it is less likely to downplay such unlikely but high-profile risks as a crime outrage and that it groups risks by their most likely management response, e.g. transferring the risk to an insurance company or outsourcing its management. The disadvantages are that it requires a fair amount of management focus and still requires decisions as to practical processes. When judging Severity and Probability (as in Figure 9.3), you will find it a lot easier if you use a logarithmic scale, much like the Richter Scale for earthquakes, in which each whole number on the scale represents a tenfold increase in the earthquake's severity. In 2011 a volcanic ash cloud grounded European flights (BBC, 2011); fitting these on the same scale as guests at a dinner receiving a cold meal when it should have been hot will prove tricky, unless you use the Richter Scale approach, in which case you can easily fit all types of potential risk onto a single sheet of paper.

Take a moment to see if you can fit the full range of risks likely to face your event into the framework in Figure 9.3. For example, did you remember to include fraud? If so, are you sure that it will be as frequent, or as severe as you think? Look at the largest risk that you intend to insure: will the insurance company pay as much (or as quickly) as you think? If not, could you still host the event? Which risks are the most difficult to position? Would more information help or does the severity/probability of these risks actually vary over time?

Figure 9.4   Example of a Risk Assessment Form

Event: Eastern Regional Kite Flying Championships
Location: Long Road Recreation Ground
Date of this assessment: 20 March 2xxx

Date of event: 10 and 11 June 2xxx
Assessed by: A Dangerfield

	Hazard	People at risk			A - Worst case outcome			B - Likelihood			Rating
		Staff	Contractors	Public others	Slight 1	Serious 2	Major 3	Rare 1	Possible 2	Likely 3	AxB
1	Spectator being hit by cricket ball	✓	✓	✓		✓		✓			2
2	Cricket player being hit by kite			✓		✓		✓			2
3	Spectator being hit by kite	✓	✓	✓		✓			✓		4
4	Overcrowding in event arena	✓	✓	✓	✓			✓			1
5	Overcrowding in catering tent	✓	✓	✓		✓		✓			2
6	Member of the public being hit by fly-away kite in the area.			✓		✓		✓			2

Security help a fan from the crowd in to the pit at T in the Park music festival

Those preferring a more process-driven approach may well favour the widely used practice of multiplying a risk's probability 'score' with its severity 'score', to derive a ranking for that risk. This seems a sound approach but, for the reasons given already, needs great care if the results are not to become hopelessly flawed. Greater interpretation might be required and issues such as 'Time Impact' and 'Cost Impact' considered which require a mitigation strategy – so that you might be able to quantify 'Quality Impact' for your own event and enhance the approach still further.

Having dealt with the criticality of addressing the appropriate scope and detail of the likely risks facing your event, we propose a very simplistic risk management table, in Figure 9.4, to help you address the mechanics of working through a Risk Assessment.

In either case, this process should also be seen as on-going, as anyone who feels they have identified a risk, perhaps while some activity is taking place, must be able to flag that risk and have it dealt with immediately. For this reason, all events must have an appointed Safety Officer, who has the power to stop an activity on the spot,

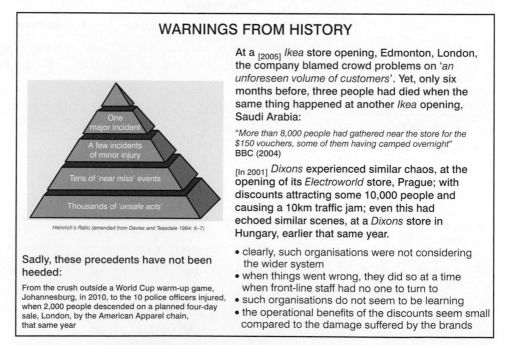

WARNINGS FROM HISTORY

At a [2005] *Ikea* store opening, Edmonton, London, the company blamed crowd problems on '*an unforeseen volume of customers*'. Yet, only six months before, three people had died when the same thing happened at another *Ikea* opening, Saudi Arabia:

"*More than 8,000 people had gathered near the store for the $150 vouchers, some of them having camped overnight*" BBC (2004)

[In 2001] *Dixons* experienced similar chaos, at the opening of its *Electroworld* store, Prague; with discounts attracting some 10,000 people and causing a 10km traffic jam; even this had echoed similar scenes, at a *Dixons* store in Hungary, earlier that same year.

Heinrich's Ratio (amended from Davies and Teasdale 1994: 6–7)

Sadly, these precedents have not been heeded:

From the crush outside a World Cup warm-up game, Johannesburg, in 2010, to the 10 police officers injured, when 2,000 people descended on a planned four-day sale, London, by the American Apparel chain, that same year

- clearly, such organisations were not considering the wider system
- when things went wrong, they did so at a time when front-line staff had no one to turn to
- such organisations do not seem to be learning
- the operational benefits of the discounts seem small compared to the damage suffered by the brands

Figure 9.5   Lack of attention to precedents
amended from Davies & Teasdale (1994: 6-7)

| | Figure 9.6 Example of a Risk Control Plan | | | | | | |

Event: Eastern Regional Kite Flying Championships
Location: Low Road Recreation Ground
Date of event: 10 and 11 June 2xxx
Date of first assessment: 20 March 2xxx
Assessed by: A Dangerfield
Date of this review: _____
Reviewed by: _____

Risk Control Plan

Hazard Found	Existing Control Measures	Additional Control Measures Required	Priority	Person responsible for measure	Complete By:	Action Taken	Review Date
1	None	Temporary cordon fence installed 20 metres beyond cricket boundary line		A Dangerfield	8/6/12	Fencing instructions sent to T Sutton and Company	9/6/12
2	None	All kite flying will be sectioned off in areas away from the cricket pitch		A Dangerfield and stewards	10/6/12		
3	None	All kite flying will be sectioned off from the public within a 100 metre arena		A Dangerfield and stewards	10/6/12		
4	None	Stewards and police to take appropriate action		A Dangerfield, stewards and police	10/6/12		
5	Catering Manager makes people queue outside	None, action adequate		Catering manager	10/6/12		
6	None	Stewards to ensure only competent people to fly properly constructed kites		A Dangerfield and stewards	10/6/12		

or to order the necessary resources to sort it out, and has contact lists for the events team and for the emergency and back-up services.

In the examples shown in Figures 9.4 and 9.6 (provided courtesy of Tendring District Council, with some details and names amended for publication), the event taking place is a small regional kite-flying championship, which happens to be taking place next to a cricket ground on the same day as a cricket match. Hence, there are some limited risks attached to objects flying through the air. The event does not attract large numbers of spectators, so overcrowding in the arena area of the championship is not thought a major risk. The catering tent is small, and in bad weather could get quite crowded, and with many people in it, as well as quite a lot of catering equipment, in this particular event it has a somewhat higher risk associated with overcrowding than the main arena. Naturally, each event is different, and the impact must be assessed individually.

The risk management of an event takes place in several linked stages: first, the assessment; second, the evaluation, which results in the preparation of the risk moderation form; third, the control measures, which also stem from the risk moderation form, but which may lead either to special preparations before the event, or to special measures during it; finally, a recording activity, particularly important where a further edition might take place, and especially so if other risks were identified during the event itself. These need particularly careful recording and review, as they are often surprisingly important and are learned from experience rather than foresight.

The implication of this last issue is that we cannot foresee everything that might happen at an event. In the end, although we may have taken every reasonable effort to manage risk, we must always be watchful for something that might still catch us out. It is the tendency of such minor things to trigger a cascade of events that can lead to disaster or unexpected and serious safety problems (see Figure 9.5).

In assessing the risk at events, our initial judgement of what is involved can be based, at least in part, on existing practice and on an awareness of what constitutes the routine and predictable and what does not. For example, we might consider the level of risk varies according to the type of event and the activities that will take place:

- 'Low risk' events – Typically, these are indoor events, which, while not completely regular or routine, are nearly so, and involve no unusual or specialist activities. The people involved (both organizers and participants or attendees) are well within their range of experience, and there is already considerable expertise and experience among management and staff. Examples might be banquets and dinners, either indoor or in marquees.

- 'Medium risk' events – These might be very large indoor events, in locations that the public might not attend regularly, or that are rather outside their range of experiences (but that a significant number of the attendees, management and staff have experienced in similar circumstances), where the activities are more complicated than normal. Alternatively, they may be outdoor, involving large numbers of people, but with no obvious or perceived dangerous activities. Examples might be large-scale sporting competitions, public shows and street festivals.

- 'High risk' events – These are events involving significantly large numbers of people in activities and locations they are unfamiliar with, or have never been to before, where there is little or no existing knowledge or experience of the event or of the environment among management, staff or emergency services. In addition, there are visible, clear and evident dangers of undertaking the event or participating in it, if the safety features are ignored or are inadequate. Examples might be high speed racing events, large-scale complicated open air events taking place for the first time (hence public and staff unfamiliarity), and small-scale events such as corporate outdoor team-building activities, where the safety rules and the knowledge of experienced staff are the key to safety, but risky for those without experience, expertise or qualifications.

Event managers and co-ordinators should strive to ensure that they not only provide a safe event and a safe environment for all concerned, but also that the

CASE STUDY 27

Crowd safety: the Moshpit at Roskilde

Roskilde, Denmark

Ben Mount of the Australian electronic rock band 'Pendulum' performs on stage on day 3 at the Roskilde Festival on July 3, 2010 in Roskilde, Denmark

FACTBOX

- Roskilde Music Festival, Roskilde, Denmark
- Major international rock festival
- Attracts 90 000 people
- Features around 170 performers
- First held in 1971
- Takes place over four days around seven stages

Learning Objectives

The aim of this case study is to examine the media reaction to accidents with the following objectives:
To consider the way in which the media makes 'news' by being under pressure to provide information instantly, especially in rolling 24 hour news programmes, which often distort or ignore facts because of lack of patience with necessary and proper investigation.
To highlight how this media distortion leads to criticism of otherwise rational decisions made by event managers
To understand the need for risk assessment in crowd and general safety

The Roskilde Festival, some 25 km west of Copenhagen, is one of the longest running rock festivals in the European calendar and attracts almost 90 000 people each year. One of the pleasures of going to rock gigs and festivals is throwing yourself around the **moshpit**, the area of the crowd nearest the stage, where the most physical activity is going on, with fans dancing and body-surfing along with the music. In the natural way of things this area is crowded, and the physicality is part of the attraction of being there. These activities are part of the cultural behaviour of rock festivals and are regarded by the crowd as perfectly normal.

Approaching midnight on Friday 30 June 2000, after a day of steady rain, the moshpit under the Orange Stage at Roskilde was throbbing with young people enjoying the music of the American rock group, Pearl Jam. There were about 70 000 fans at the festival, a large number of them around the Orange Stage and in particular in the natural crush of the moshpit. As Pearl Jam's **set** continued it became obvious that the crush was significantly worse than normal, and Pearl Jam's singer, Eddie Vedder, asked the crowd to move back. In the sliding mud, in the overcrowding near the stage, nine fans died of suffocation. Three were from Sweden, one was from Holland, one from Germany, one from Australia and three from Denmark itself.

In the following days, television and newspapers, with a lack of facts and an excess of speculation, alleged that several factors, from faulty sound equipment to drug taking, people being crushed against the stage or scuffles in the crowd, had caused the accident. None of these has been proved correct. Tests of the equipment that found it to be in perfect working order were barely reported in the media the following week. The causal reason was essentially the cultural behaviour itself being more than normally concentrated, the effect being to focus the dynamic or lateral surging of the crowd, causing a crowd collapse. In so far as there have been a number of similar crush collapse moments at rock festivals, whose causes are now better understood, steps can be taken to mitigate them and a useful reference book on crowd safety is the HSE book '*Managing Crowds Safely*', now updated with a comprehensive website.

The Roskilde Festival has a significant reputation for safety, and a measure of this was that first aid staff and police were on the scene immediately, and there were few injuries of any kind beyond those who died. The tragedy also stimulated much moralizing about youth culture, with politicians and public officials calling for all kinds of restrictions on what people do at festivals and events, without first identifying the real reasons for the accident.

For the organizers of the Roskilde Festival, the media reaction came as something of a shock, and is an issue in contingency planning that those members of an events organizing team who have media contacts and who are involved in the public relations activities surrounding events should bear in mind. The festival was especially criticized for continuing after the accident, but the decision to do so was taken in good faith, and to allow festival-goers to keep to their original travel plans, rather than have 90 000 people spill into the street in one massive and unplanned departure, which itself would have carried inherent further risk.

Discussion Questions

1 Is the media reaction to disasters normally measured and reasonable, or is it intended to be hysterical and critical?

2 Why should this be the case, and what effects does the lack of a knowledgeable commentary have on efforts to identify the genuine reasons for accidents?

3 Does this impact on the ability of those involved and those in authority to react to accidents in a way that will make future events safer not less?

4 What steps can and should be taken by organizers to ensure crowd safety at events?

Websites

For further information about the Roskilde Festival see: **www.roskilde-festival.dk**
See also reports regarding the Loveparade disaster in Duisberg at:
http://www.spiegel.de/international/germany/the-world-from-berlin-love-parade-stampede-was-a-tragedy-waiting-to-happen-a-708474.html

Figure 9.7   Event Site Map coverage

Site overview

Access and transport: road, bus, railway, foot, cycle and waterway links
Parking: public and disabled
Entrances and exits: emergency access
Ticket stands and toilets
Main arena, focal points, stages or competition viewing areas
Catering area, food court, food stalls and catering van sites
Hospitality, corporate or VIP areas*
Service area: toilets, baby changing, waste disposal, recycling, shower or bathing blocks
Children's area, lost children's point, first aid
Organizer's office and/or emergency control point*
Public zoned areas, restricted access areas*, private or secure areas*
Service roads*, assembly areas* and the event trailer park*
Fire assembly points, emergency crowd overflow areas*

* These areas may not necessarily be shown on public maps

systems and emergency procedures are in place in case of an accident or other problem arising. In all events, but especially high risk events, the need for adequate and sufficient staff training, especially of volunteers, is absolutely vital.

PLANS AND MAPS

Part of the process of providing information for the public for a large or outdoor event will probably be the preparation of a scale or sketch map or plan of the site, such plans can have a number of uses, one of which may be to assist the risk assessment process.

Maps have several advantages, they are a useful tool for the management and planning of an event in so far as they can be used in the first case to assess the site, its advantages and disadvantages, as well as plan where the various attractions or focal points may be and where the associated facilities and services can be located. See Figure 9.7 and 'Wirksworth Wapentake' case study plan.

The risk assessment use of these maps takes into consideration the general and emergency access arrangements; parking, footway routes, disabled access; emergency or help points; fire and first aid points; and location of the control point or organizers' office in terms of the site in general, as well as dealing with any specific risk issues which might arise from sitting down and look at the plan as a whole.

For small events plans can be done by hand and these will still act as a helpful tool. For larger, more professional events, plans can be prepared by computer aided design (CAD) or similar techniques. In all cases it will be necessary to have correct measurements for the site and, if it has never been used before or measurements are not already available, then the event co-ordinator will need to go out with a colleague and take careful measurements.

In the case of those events which are major in some way, this process may have to be done by professional surveyors in case blueprint plans are needed (say if a new

moshpit
The place at the front of a gig audience where the liveliest activity takes place.

set
The performance given by one individual or group at a concert or gig.

CASE STUDY 28

Emergency service arrangements at events: Clacton air show

Clacton, England

Peter Barrett/Shutterstock.com

RAF Hawks in a Red Arrows display team, executing a bankng turn with smoke

FACTBOX

- The event is run by Tendring District Council
- It consists of two days of air displays, including the Red Arrows RAF display team, parachutists, historic and modern aircraft and aerobatics
- It attracts 65 000 day trippers
- Comprehensive risk assessment and procedures

Learning Objectives

The aim of this case study is to consider the nature of risk management and emergency procedures with the following objectives:

To consider how risks might be judged in terms of different types of events, for example, major outdoor events might be considered more risky than small indoor ones, but it depends on the type of event, so an outdoor air show might have a greater risk than an outdoor golf tournament (the risk outcome of being hit by a falling aircraft being perhaps rather greater than being hit by a falling golf ball)

To highlight who and what organizations might be involved in emergency planning for an event

To understand that even the best planning for emergencies cannot cover all possibilities: some are unforeseen and unexpected

The small English seaside resort of Clacton-on-Sea hosts a number of annual events intended to attract tourists. These include an annual carnival, a classic vehicle show, a jazz festival, a real ale festival, a sci-fi convention and its largest annual event, the Clacton Air Show. Such a range helps to stimulate tourism in a resort that relies on its family image, its beaches and its good weather to attract tourists from towns and cities in the east of England and from north London.

The air show is estimated to attract some 65 000 day trippers to the town, in addition to the normal level of tourists. This number is very creditable when compared with some national events, such as the Henley Boating Regatta, which attracts 95 000 people and the Royal Windsor Horse Show which attracts some 80 000 people (source: English Tourist Board). The economic impact of the air show is quite significant. It is a two-day event contributing about €500 000 (an average of €14.50 a visitor) to the local economy. Visitors to the air show spend money not only at the show ground, but also in local pubs and restaurants, shops and other retail outlets, and at a range of local facilities and services including the pier, gift shops and other local attractions.

Many of the events that take place in the resort, like the air show, are organized by the local council's Economic Development Department. The tourism section of this department is responsible for three main areas of activity:

- The promotion of the resort and the surrounding area
- The running of the town's tourist information centre and other information centres in the district
- The organization and management of a number of larger special events, including the air show.

The air show requires careful organization, especially in terms of risk management, crowd management, emergency services, transport and access and co-ordination between various public service departments including the coastguard, the fire brigade, the police, the ambulance service and air traffic control. These are crucial, because of the large number of people attending and the potential dangers associated with air displays, aerobatics, parachuting and similar activities. In addition to full risk analysis, the planning phase includes a series of briefings between the public service departments, the tourism officer and other council departments, including the Department of Emergency Planning, the Department of Highways and the Environmental Department. This is followed up by briefings to staff and volunteers for the event.

For each air show, a set of emergency service briefing notes is prepared which state the allocation of resources and manpower for various kinds of emergencies. These include back-up plans for dealing with emergencies ranging from an air crash to a bomb alert, or other types of accident, in order to ensure that the public is as safe as reasonably possible while at the show. This liaison process also includes co-ordination with the council's own staff, who man information points and act as guides, together with a range of voluntary organizations such as the St John's Ambulance Service, which assists the main emergency services.

Discussion questions

1   Does your local council have a department or unit that deals with tourism in general and special events in particular, if so, how is it organized and what does it do?

2   What other types of events might require a major input from emergency services?

3   Do even small events require a risk analysis and should thought be given to emergency procedures?

4   What training should take place to ensure the safety of the public at an event?

Websites

For more information see the related website at: **www.essex-sunshine-coast.org.uk**.
For event safety guidance, the European code is *The Event Safety Guide*, which can be obtained from: **http://books.hse.gov.uk**.
An example of the way in which a developing emergency could be addressed can be found at: **http://www. hse.gov.uk/event-safety/developing-emergency-case-study.htm**.

Figure 9.8 Permits, Licences and Legalities	
Permit	**Suggested place of enquiry**
Alcohol	Licensing Justices / Local Council Licensing Committee
Bingo, Lottery or Gaming	Local Council Licensing Department / Licensing Justices
Fireworks	Fire Brigade
Food Handling	Local Council Environmental Health Department
Marches and Parades	Police / Local Council Highways and Transport Department
Music	Copyright Owners / Broadcast Authority
Occupancy (maximum numbers)	Fire Brigade / Local Council Licensing Department
Parking	Local Council Highways and Transport Department / Police
Parks (use)	Local Council Parks Department / Park Owners
Public Assembly/ Entertainment	Local Council Licensing Department
Sea or Beach Use	Coastguard / Local Authority Tourism Department
Signs and Banners	County Council Highways and Transport Department
Street Closure	Local Council Highways and Transport Department / Police
VAT	Department of Revenue and Customs

building or facility is to be put up) or if a model of the site is required. Detailed plans of this kind may be needed not only by the event team but also by the contractors and suppliers – lots of people may need them – electricians and technicians, the emergency services and stewards, hosts and guides, coach party leaders, participants and exhibitors and, of course, the visitors or audience.

LEGALITIES AND INSURANCE

The difficulties that organizers of events have faced over insurance cover (OFT, 2004;) and the tragedy at the 2010 Africa Cup of Nations football tournament (Harris, 2010) have provided a stark reminder of the need to bear in mind the large number of legalities and similar issues associated with undertaking an event. These include licensing, health, safety and insurance requirements, which are the key to secure operations. Practice about how these are dealt with varies considerably across the European Union countries, making it difficult to generalize. However, permits and licences are generally dealt with at a local level (town, city or district), although a few may be dealt with at regional or provincial level, within a framework of national and European Union legislation. It will be necessary for events organizers to check locally to identify what legal requirements prevail for aspects such as staffing, permits, licences and other regulatory issues (UK: Croner, 2012). Figure 9.8 above provides some possibilities, but is by no means definitive.

The applications procedures for these vary from country to country, so that local documentation should be checked for whom to apply to for permits, and what kinds of permits are needed (licences for the sale of alcohol are obvious, but even the placing of a waste **skip** on a public road may need the permission of the local authority). In addition to permits and licences, requirements for insurance need sufficient time to be investigated with a reputable insurance broker, or with

skip
A large waste or rubbish container that is moved by lorry.

CASE STUDY 29

Insurance and event contractual issues: Regia Anglorum historical re-enactment

European historical societies

wirksworthwapentake.org.uk

Wirksworth Wapentake re-enactment 29 March 08

FACTBOX

- A historical re-enactment society
- Presents historical pageants, shows and battle re-creations
- Volunteers and members of the society are involved
- Various legal and contractual requirements are needed

Learning Objectives

The aim of this case study is to consider issues of risk in terms of some legalities and insurance issues with the following objectives:

To consider what legal and insurance issues might emerge when planning an event

To highlight why certain types of event might have greater insurance implications than others

Events activities range from the inherently safe to the rather dangerous. Certainly in terms of public perceptions, you might feel safer at a family dinner party than you would be as a participant in the Annual International Parascending Competition, even though you could get run over by a bus the moment you left the dinner party, but might not so much as receive a bruise while parascending. But the nature of risk, and why an event might run or be cancelled, could be more complicated. Suppose you were the organizers of the historic battle recreation day, what risks might you want your event to be insured against?

Regia Anglorum is one of a large number of the popular history or battle recreation and hobby societies which exist throughout Europe dealing with living history and costumed historical re-enactment and entertainment ranging from Viking Societies in Scandinavia to Guard's Parade Societies in Germany. There are many of these, such as the 'Sealed Knott' an English civil war re-enactment society; 'Legio X Gemina' a Dutch Roman army re-enactment society or the Magnus Kompanie dealing with medieval combat re-enactment based in Hessen-Kassell in Germany. There are perhaps over 500 such societies which feature a wide range of historical periods, locations and individual historic events. Regia Anglorum covers the predominantly Saxon period in England and it undertakes historic recreation shows and pageants of all kinds including battles, living history exhibitions, ship burning ceremonies, torchlight parades and so on.

The insurance arrangements for a battle recreation event are:

- Public liability cover up to €5 million
- Employer's liability cover for staff, including casual and volunteer staff
- Cover for equipment loss or damage
- Cancellation or abandonment cover (including severe adverse weather conditions).

Cover for events may also include 'financial cause insurance' (e.g. exhibitor or re-enactment society going broke) and insurance for damage to the venue. It is also possible to cover for the non-appearance of key speakers or entertainers, and failure to leave the venue at the prescribed time (e.g. snow blocks the venue). Exclusions for event insurance typically include small items damage (up to the first €400) and in some cases, damage to ground/grass surface.

The contractual arrangements for events of this kind usually cover a number of headings such as:

Execution – that is how the re-enactment will be done and what main features it would comprise.

Fees and expenses – what costs accrue to the client or organizing committee for staging the pageant and what liabilities or insurances are covered.

The duties of the Society or the company performing – that is issues of copyrights, provisional of personnel, arrangements for security, clear up, access, timings, water and service supplies, general goods and equipment supplies, camping (often re-enactment groups are encamped at a pageant site), publishing and promotional arrangements, programme and theatrical arrangements and all related contractual matters.

An outline schedule – that is what arrives and when, what the basic programme is and what leaves and when, also any specific requirements which have to be fitted into the timing, for example Regia Anglorum require a tonne of wood per day to be delivered to maintain the open fires used for historical enactments such as for cookery, ironwork forges and camp fires of various kinds.

Terms of business – this section will deal with all associated legal issues that would be found in a contract such as cancellation and payment terms.

Discussion Questions

1   Are the risks for this particular event unusual?

2   If you were the organizer of a public carnival or street festival, what might the most risky activities be, and would these be considered high, medium or low risk?

3   Is this classification of risk linked in any way to the nature of the insurance provision for events?

4   What activities might constitute high risk for participants and spectators?

5   If you have identified a need for insurance of your event, have you allowed for the cost of it in your budgets?

Websites

For more information on historic re-enactment events see: **www.histrenact.co.uk/histrenact/societies/mainpage.php**, and for various safety issues: **http://www.hse.gov.uk/event-safety/getting-started.htm**.

insurance companies specializing in the events field. Insurance, however, does have some commonality of approach, and various insurance companies have experience of dealing with cross-European events. Normal events insurance would cover items such as:

- cancellation;
- venue operator's bankruptcy;
- non-appearance of celebrities;
- failure to vacate the venue;
- damage to property or premises;
- legal liabilities;
- damage to equipment; and
- public liabilities.

Apart from permits and insurance, various kinds of contracts will be needed if the event provides entertainers, musicians, pyro technologists (fireworks showmen), guest speakers or celebrities, in order to ensure the arrangements are correctly made. Contracting of this kind needs to be undertaken carefully, bearing in mind that bookings for specialists have to be made long in advance, together with some form of prepayment, and arrangements in the event of cancellation of either party to the contract. Where such a contract is likely to be used, some legal advice should be taken, especially if the contract is out of the ordinary or non-standard in some way.

SUMMARY

We have attempted to provide an overview of some of the more serious issues regarding the risk management and key aspects of insurance, as well as of legal, health, safety and licensing requirements for events, or at least where to look for further information about them. The HSE website is especially recommended when dealing with health and safety issues. We have also sought to provide an overview of the operational activities that take place immediately prior to, and during, an event, noting that efficient preparation and due thought to operational issues will reduce the risk of something going wrong. These things said, in no way can every risk or potential danger be completely eliminated: the world is complicated and often haphazard, as is human behaviour. The best that can be done is to take every reasonable precaution. No one can ask for more if this has itself been done with proper care and concern.

EVALUATION QUESTIONS

1 What might be the major or principal issues and considerations for risk management in terms of event planning and operations?

2 What licensing, health and safety, and insurance requirements should be taken into account when planning and operating events?

3 Do all events have a heavy burden of health, safety and risk requirements? For example: compare the difference between those for an outdoor music festival and a village fair.

REFERENCES

BBC (2010) *Stampede at German Love Parade Festival kills 19*, London: BBC (http://www.bbc.co.uk/news/world-europe-10751899) (Accessed 10 May 2012).

BBC (2011) *Flights cancelled as ash cloud heads towards UK*, London: BBC (http://www.bbc.co.uk/news/uk-13498477) (Accessed 10 May 2012).

Croner (2012) *(http://www.cronersolutions.co.uk/index.html)* (Accessed 10 May 2012).

CSFI (2012) *Banking Banana Skins*, 2012, London,: Centre for the Study of Financial Innovation.

Hall, C. M. (2002) 'Travel Safety, Terrorism and the Media: The Significance of the Issue-Attention Cycle', *Current Issues in Tourism* 5(5):458–66.

Harris, N. (2010) 'Most players have no insurance', *Sunday Times*, 10 January.

HSE (2012) *Guidance on running events safely* (up to date information replacing the '*Event Safety Guide*' and '*Managing Crowds Safely*') see: http://www.hse.gov.uk/event-safety/index.htm (Accessed 28 June 2012).

Jennings, W. (2010) Going For Gold: the Olympics Risk and Risk Management, London: ESRC (http://www.esrc.ac.uk/my-esrc/grants/RES-063-27-0205/read) (Accessed 10 May 2012).

Laybourn, P. (2003) 'Risk and decision making in Event Management', in Yeoman, I. *et al.*, *Festival and Events Management*, Oxford: Elsevier, pp 286–307.

OFT (2004) *Competition Act exemption for terrorism insurance by Pool Re* (http://www.oft.gov.uk/news-and-updates/press/2004/68-04) (Accessed 10 May 2012).

Parry, B., in MacMahon-Beattie, U. and Yeoman, I. (eds) (2004) *Sport & Leisure Operations Management: A Textbook for Courses and Modules*, London: Thomson Learning.

SPLS (2012) Local Studies Fact Sheet Number 5: The Victoria Hall Disaster 1883, Sunderland: Sunderland Public Library Service.

Swiss Re (2010) Sigma No.1: natural catastrophes and man-made disasters in 2009 Zurich: Swiss Re – Figure2 (Available: http://media.swissre.com/documents/sigma1_2010_en.pdf) (Accessed 10 May 2012).

Tarlow, P. E. (2002) *Event Risk Management and Safety*, Chichester:Wiley.

Timelines (2012) *Khodynka Tragedy*, Timelines (http://timelines.com/1896/5/18/khodynka-tragedy) (Accessed 10 May 2012).

CHAPTER 10

EVENT PROJECT MANAGEMENT AND SET UP ISSUES

AIMS

- To provide a framework for managing event projects

- To consider issues relating to setting up events

- To provide an overview of the preparation activities that may take place prior to an event

INTRODUCTION

The purpose of this chapter is to look at events from the operational viewpoint – how to operate the event as a project and as an experience and how to address some of the planning and organizational complexities which, while critical, often receive insufficient attention. (Berridge, 2012; O'Toole and Mikolaitis, 2002).

In setting up events, organizing committees or individual event co-ordinators may be faced with a number of set-up challenges. These challenges could be viewed in terms of their varying levels of complexity. For a simple indoor event such as a flower show in a village hall, we can understand this would be fairly simple to set up: all the services are available, the venue is indoors and the event itself is in no way complicated or unsafe in any way, or beyond the abilities of relatively untrained people to undertake or enjoy. On the other hand, to stage an event in a field, or on an island, or in any location where services, equipment or supplies have to be brought in, will require close attention and planning for its effective management and operation (Ferdinand and Williams, 2012).

This chapter also considers how to make the final preparations, those things that need to be done immediately before an event opens. These should be taken in conjunction with the sections about logistics and about how to run events on the day. The various sections overlap somewhat depending on how an event is timed and organized. In some cases the preparations will happen all in one day, in others the groundwork may take several days or even weeks and have to be ready well before the public arrives.

THE EVENT AS A PROJECT

There are considerable similarities between the management of projects and of events, so much so that many of the techniques developed in the management of large-scale building, logistical or public projects can be used to bring organizational discipline to many kinds of events (see Figure 10.1). Both are unique, time-limited operations. The application of project management techniques to events may therefore provide a vehicle for ensuring the modest success of an event, as opposed to a spectacular failure. Why only a modest success? Well, events management, rather like project management, can be a somewhat thankless task. The outside world does not see the event co-ordinator toiling away for weeks, coping with late nights, wrestling with tricky problems and recalcitrant suppliers to make the event a success, but the first time that the most minor thing goes wrong ('Oh dear, the flowers are red, they should be pink …') the event co-ordinator will get the blame. Reiss (2007), in a usefully chatty book about project management, makes these points very well, and also highlights the opportunities a project manager may have to show how much work is going on behind the scenes.

The management process involves very similar approaches, which the event co-ordinator or organizing committee can seek to use. In setting objectives for an event, these can be tested using the SMART formula:

Specific
Measurable
Achievable
Realistic
Timely

Event Management Activities	Project Management Activities
Objectives and getting started	Conception
↓	↓
Planning	Definition
↓	↓
Organizing and preparing the Event	Production
↓	↓
Implementing: running the Event	Operations
↓	↓
Divestment/Legacies	Handover or divestment

Figure 10.1   Event and project management activities

If the objectives are framed or worded badly, or are confusing (rather than specific and precise), then we will have difficulty creating the event from them. The objectives must be measurable, in terms of being able to know whether they are being achieved, or whether progress is being made towards them. This highlights the need for progress meetings and schedule deadlines. The objectives must be achievable; it must be genuinely possible to put on the event, especially given the limitations of money, staff, management or volunteer expertise that the event co-ordinator might have to contend with. Similarly, the objectives must be realistic, irrespective of whatever flights of fancy (or fantasy) the clients may want you to achieve. Finally, the objectives must be timely, taking into account what can be done in the time available, what the deadlines are and the natural tendency for timescales to slip. We can plan to put on a party in a tent a week from now, but are we being realistic? Is the timing possible? On the computer plan we have prepared it may seem so, but in reality, the weather may be bad, the tenters may take frequent coffee breaks, there may be a missing piece, the ground may be wet, the tent may be dirty and need scrubbing, the lorry delivering the poles may get stuck in the mud ... who would want to be an event co-ordinator?

Having tested the objectives, techniques that can be adapted from project management include:

- The use of **work break-down structures**.
- Project planning, including identification of **critical tasks** and **external dependencies**.
- **Gantt charting** (related to Critical Path Analysis).
- Risk assessment.

These are only a few of the possible techniques that an event organizer can adopt. In addition readily available software can be obtained to assist the event organizer. If

work break-down structures
A schedule of the various jobs that have to be done to complete an event.

critical tasks
Those tasks or jobs that must be completed in a sequence, before any other, or all other tasks, can be done.

external dependencies
A task performed by a person or an organization outside the direct control of the event organizer, perhaps by a contractor or supplier.

the event is going to be huge, then hire a project manager and get in all the computer software and gizmos you need.

Gantt charting
A project planning chart that resembles a horizontal bar diagram.

Work break-down structures

A work break-down is just what it says it is: the job broken down into its rough component parts. At this stage detail is not needed or expected, as the work break-down is simply the first stage in looking at what has to be done, identified in its respective component parts by the work that one person or a related team of people can do. It looks rather like an organization chart, in so far as it is hierarchical. It starts at the top, with the event, or major event activity, and flows down the chart to the point where the one person or team has been arrived at (see Figure 10.2).

Project planning techniques

There are various project planning techniques which an event co-ordinator could usefully adopt, including the identification of critical tasks and external dependencies. Once a work break-down structure has been drawn up, it should be possible to identify those activities that are critical to the event's success. Critical tasks are essentially those functions that must be completed first, in any sequence of activities, for the activity to proceed. This not only helps to concentrate attention on the jobs within the event that are central to the task, but also provides the framework for setting deadlines for checking progress on event preparations, because the critical tasks must be completed on time for the following activities to be carried out. In the example of the wedding marquee, two critical tasks might be identification of the venue, followed by the construction of the tent. The key aspects of the construction are the setting up of the framework and the fitting of the external covers. Once these things are achieved other activities can take place. For example, once the marquee is weatherproof, the electrician could start installing the lighting at the same time as the tenters are still fitting the internal canvasses and curtaining. These follow-on tasks

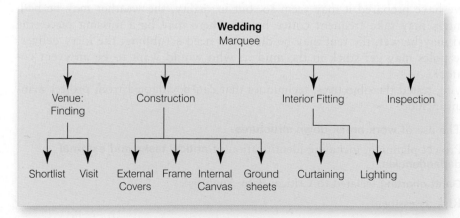

Figure 10.2   Work Breakdown Structure for a Wedding Marquee
Source: adapted from Nickson and Siddons, 1997, *Managing Projects*, Oxford: Butterworth Heinemann, pp 17–18.

are called dependencies. External dependencies are those issues that are outside the event co-ordinator's direct control (Starr *et al.*, 2003). Having to hire furniture for an event is an external dependency, as it relies on the furniture hire company turning up with the correct items at the time and place they were ordered for. Without the furniture, there will be no event. Arguably, the more external dependencies a project has, and the more unusual they are, the more risk there is of failure.

It is therefore necessary to turn an initial work break-down sheet into something that is not only more detailed, but which also shows the exact sequence of activities and how long each will take. This can be done on computer (using software such as Microsoft Project), or, if you had a very small event, can be done by hand using graph paper, but doing it by hand has the limitation that whenever you wish to add something while you are doing the planning, you have to redraw the chart. You need to identify tasks clearly enough so that you know what is going on, but not to over-specify them in such detail that you prevent the free thinking and association needed for creativity. 'Decorate venue' (with due regard to safety) may be a perfectly adequate statement of a task, but 'Put green balloons one metre above the doors' is probably over-specification.

Gantt charting

There are a range of ways in which task sequences can be shown visually. These include charts that show resource charting, Critical Path Analysis using **PERT** charts (suitable for the experienced, see Slack *et al.*, 2012), but the easiest and most applicable kind of chart that event organizers can adopt from the project management sphere is the Gantt chart. This simply shows the various tasks that have to be done in a time-sequence order, so that is easy to see what the various tasks are and, most importantly, how long they should take, when they should be completed and what happens if a task, especially a critical task, is delayed. Figure 10.3 is quite a simple Gantt chart.

The filled boxes: ■ indicate the tasks which have been completed so far, the open boxes: ☐ show those still to be done, so that it is easy to see how preparations are progressing, what is still outstanding and if any problems are emerging.

The project started on the 1 May, and the Gantt chart example, gives a snapshot of the work as 14 June. Various things were ordered and arranged at the beginning of the process, including the venue, marquee, furniture and caterers. Only one item is shown as having been ordered during the snapshot period – the flowers, which have a shorter lead time than, say, obtaining a marquee.

There are some limitations to the Gantt chart. It does not show, in our example, the resources available to do the job or if you have given someone too much work to do in the time available, nor is it really suitable for large projects, as it would be too cumbersome. However, for the modest help it gives to planning events, it can be very useful, not least in that it makes the organizer(s) sit down and think through the steps needed to do the work. In some cases, this planning technique might be best applied backwards, that is to say, starting at the deadline (the end) and working back in order to find out how long doing something will really take. Do not come along and say, 'Hey, we've got three days to get the tent up and sorted, just cram it onto the chart …'. The other important activity that Gantt charting will compel you to do is to find out how long things genuinely take to do. Without this accurate information, the chart will be useless. For example, will it really take two days to get

PERT
Programme Evaluation and Review Technique. A project management planning technique for plotting work to be done in a given timescale, generally in a computer programme.

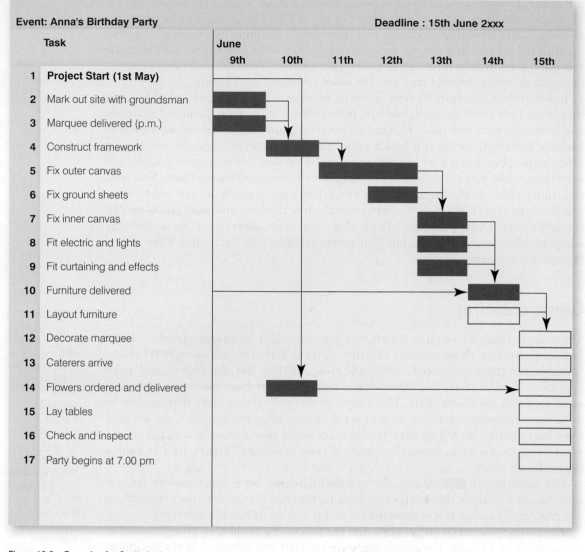

Figure 10.3   Example of a Gantt chart

the outer canvas on the marquee? In our example, it does. If you have ordered a marquee, ask the tenters how long it really will take them.

TICKETING AND PRE-BOOKING ISSUES

When setting up an event, it is very easy to become deeply involved in the weight of effort and detail needed to get it off the ground, and for public events, the effort and the excitement of promoting it. The marketing activity, according to received wisdom is about ascertaining customer needs, tailoring the product or service as closely as possible to meet those needs, persuading the customer to satisfy his or her needs, and, finally, ensuring the product or service is easily accessible when the customer wishes to purchase it. The organizer of special events should take careful note of the last point. If there is a common failing in events organization, it is often at the beginning of the delivery stage, and that delivery stage starts with enquiries and the issue of tickets.

For all its modern complexity, the final piece of the events jigsaw, the buying, that is, the purchase of tickets, still depends on one element – the visitor picking up the phone and wanting a ticket, or walking in and paying for it. It is true that 'picking up the phone' may mean texting you, emailing you, using the Internet or sending someone along with a wad of cash on the bus, buying the ticket on-line, but it is still down to someone showing an interest in the event, and that display of interest has to be responded to efficiently and effectively.

Setting up a system to deal with enquiries and sell tickets might be as simple as putting your phone number on the posters for the village fête and getting the barman to sell them from the village pub. In all probability, though, for those events for which the public can buy tickets, you need to give some careful thought to making it easy for them. Do not exclude part of your potential target market by making it difficult, or impossible, for them to get the tickets or make the booking they want to. Ideally, you should have as many ways of selling tickets and as many outlets (besides the central enquiry and ticket office) as you can imaginatively think of and can reasonably service. That is to say, you have to be able to supply outlets with tickets, to monitor what is being sold, and to react to increased sales at any one point by being able to increase the allocation, if that is reasonable given the number of people you can admit (or have seats for, within the capacity of the venue). A central computer at your main office, with a software programme such as 'Ticket Pro', should be able to cope with these demands easily and perhaps also, if a system has been set up, to report daily sales.

In setting up your advance ticket sales, there is no reason not to use various methods and channels. If your main method is from your own central ticket office, then think about how the weight of demand can be reduced if you have other sales channels, such as selling tickets online. On the other hand, you might decide you have a big event to prepare and only modest expertise, in which case the activity could be contracted to a ticketing agency, which will earn a small commission from each ticket they sell, but relieve you of the whole activity. Finally, you might have an event where the number of tickets is strictly limited for genuine reasons, and in such a case, one central office, with carefully considered limitations, might have to be your solution.

Taking tickets 'on the door' also requires a little forethought. The most important issue is whether your 'door' will be able to cope with the demand. If only 20 people turn up, no problem. But what if 2000 come? What do we know about selling tickets 'on the door'? What we do know, from research done in cinemas (which have to have quite good 'on the door' systems) is that the average time taken to process a ticket request from a member of the public is about 20 seconds. A little simple maths shows that 2000 members of the public waiting at your (narrow) gate for tickets for your evening extravaganza would progress at three a minute, totalling almost 670 minutes – 11 hours. You need more gates, more ticket sellers and more people to deal with the odd enquiries that block up the system.

It should be remembered that tickets not only act as evidence of payment or permission to enter an event, but are also a means of security. Tickets should be checked as visitors arrive for various reasons: to ensure that they are properly directed to their seat; to ensure that the ticket itself is genuine; perhaps to exchange the ticket for some other evidence of entry or means of obtaining services, such as wristbands (different colours of which may represent entitlement to entry or use of, say, VIP or media areas). However, once again, remember that a ticket and wristband may effectively perform the same function: do not duplicate it unnecessarily. If you issue tickets and then issue wristbands as well you are probably doubling the check-in time – this time wasting may result in huge queues or slow public entry down so much that you cannot get enough people through the doors fast enough – an issue which has nearly resulted in the collapse of several big events. Collecting tickets is also a means of confirming the number of people who actually attended and can be used to check attendance against revenue.

In effect, ticketing is a control mechanism. It not only tells you how many people have attended (or will attend), it is a means of visitor management, because it enables you to control capacity; thus enabling you to ensure the safety of the public and participants and stay within the carrying limits of the venue, either because of the finite maximum number of seats or places available, or simply the venue size, limitations of the permitted licence or possibly because the venue itself might need to be protected (such as a historic building or conservation area). Tickets may be colour coded (we have noted) to limit or enable access to various parts of a site or venue, and time specific tickets may enable you to control numbers and throughput of visitors during the day or during times of high demand, so managing queuing, access pinch points or enabling you to spread arrivals or departures of large numbers of people. Advance booked tickets crucially may provide your event with the income it needs to take place and also help you deal with issues such as group bookings or people who wish to be seated together or who have some other seating or locational need, such as to be near disabled facilities or access. In addition, pre-booked and some other forms of tickets may provide useful marketing information in terms of data capture (that is, for example, people providing address information which may be used for later relationship marketing activities) (see Figure 10.4). A useful overview of event ticketing is provided by Beavan and Laws (2004).

The process of booking for events varies depending on the type of event and the target market. Online booking or reservation systems are a feature of many types of event, especially for organizational events, conferences, seminars, etc. Online ticketing systems are a feature of all kinds of public events, sporting and cultural events, festivals, concerts and performance events. Booking or ticketing can be achieved in two ways:

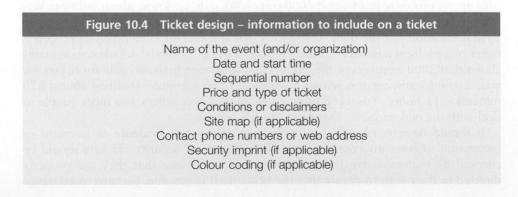

Figure 10.4   Ticket design – information to include on a ticket

Name of the event (and/or organization)
Date and start time
Sequential number
Price and type of ticket
Conditions or disclaimers
Site map (if applicable)
Contact phone numbers or web address
Security imprint (if applicable)
Colour coding (if applicable)

1 By personal visit, telephone, post, text or email to the organizer's booking or ticket office itself or to an agent's office.

2 By booking through the on-line booking or ticket section of the event website or through an agent's website dealing with the ticketing of that event.

With conferences, seminars or organizational events, potential delegates are informed what the preferred method of booking is, and they are encouraged do this in preference to any other method. Clearly, if this is a conference, not a public event, there is no 'booking' on the day at the entrance, because final numbers are needed for room lay-outs, meal ordering, etc. beforehand. This approach to booking has the advantage of administrative efficiency, since all bookings go to one central location where they can be co-ordinated and confirmed online, allowing organizers to check the status of bookings in real time, on a common system, without having to check through and count individual correspondence. The system has the further advantage of saving staff time, as the potential delegate fills in their requirements on a standard online form. It is typically used where no money changes hands at the start of the event from individuals (that is to say the individual's organization or employer might be paying for their place at the conference and the payment for that place might be invoiced to the employer before or after the event, so the system in this case is affectively for the registration of a place, not for the buying of a ticket.

The concept of 'pre-booking' is not suitable for every potential visitor. It cannot be used on its own for the full range of sporting or festival type events, as some people will always make a decision about attending shortly before the event and will buy a ticket on the gate (reasons for just turning up vary: but the 'just turn up' approach has the major and important personal advantage that it is flexible in terms of people's changing short term plans and their view of what they might want to do on any given day, depending on their likes or dislikes, their mood or the weather). So, too, with many voluntary and charitable events, public open events and so on, where the equipment and systems may not exist to deal with any kind of pre-booking, nor might the potential target market have access to online systems or even be computer literate. On the other hand small events such as birthday parties can be 'pre-booked' in the strict sense of the word by those using social media, to confirm their attendence. For example Facebook allows you to invite your friends to an event you have organized. This comes with a caveat though! Not everyone uses the same kinds of social media even among one's direct friends – there will always be someone you have to text or call.

For these reasons, event organizers must think carefully about the ticketing and booking systems they wish to set up in relation to their target markets and the usual way in which those target markets might buy a ticket or pay the entrance fee for an event. Equally, systems must be set up to support the booking process, by way of recording, dealing with enquiries, controlling total numbers, monitoring demand and gathering market research data.

OPERATIONAL ACTIVITIES

The big day is almost upon us, we have done as much planning as was needed, we have organized all the various people, parts, organizations, supplies and equipment that we planned for, it's six in the morning and time to throw ourselves out of bed

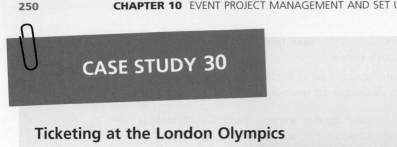

CASE STUDY 30

Ticketing at the London Olympics

London, England

Paul Kitagaki Jr. /ZUMAPRESS. Com/Alamy

The Olympic Torch is carried during the Olympics 2012 Opening Ceremony at the Olympic Stadium on July 28, 2012 in London

FACTBOX

- London Olympics 2012
- Ticket sales made on-line in three phases
- Tickets covered attendance both at events and for visitors to the Olympic Park
- In the final phase of ticket selling just under one million tickets were available

Learning Objectives

The aim of this case study is to consider the difficulties of very large scale ticket sales operations at the London Olympics 2012 with the following objectives:
To consider the way in which the event and associated ticket sales were made
To highlight how heavy demand affected the ticketing system
To understand issues of ticketing and to apply them to smaller scale events

The London Olympics of 2012 was the largest sporting 'event' held in the UK that year. although it was one of the series of Olympic events now held every four years around the world. In the UK prior experience of large scale sporting event existed, notably from the Manchester Commonwealth Games, but the scale of the Olympics required an almost entirely new infrastructure. One of the elements of this infrastructure was the mechanism for selling tickets.

Ticket sales had been placed in the hands of outsourced operator 'Ticketmaster' and this approach was no doubt based on the need to use systems and staff which were effectively already tested, at least in part, through frequent use at other events, not just sporting events but also fairs and festivals. Tickets were sold in three phases for different elements of the Games, the final phase operated as follows. The spreading of ticket sales over several days was an attempt to overcome the problem of the rush for tickets overwhelming the booking system, so that spreading the ticket sales also spread the load on the system to attempt to stop it crashing due to weight of demand.

- May 11 and 12, 2012: tickets on sale for that group of 20 000 people who had not been able to obtain tickets before due to failures of the ticketing system in the previous phases. There were tickets for all events apart from the Olympic Park tickets. Limited tickets for opening and closing Ceremonies were included.

- May 13, 2012: hockey, tennis, wrestling (freestyle), wrestling (Greco-Roman), beach volleyball and football tickets.

- May 14, 2012: athletics (race walk), athletics (marathon), canoe slalom, canoe sprint, shooting, swimming, volleyball, weightlifting and cycling (track) tickets.

- May 15, 2012 equestrian (dressage), equestrian (eventing), equestrian (jumping), diving, synchronized swimming, handball, table tennis, swimming (marathon) and water polo tickets.

- May 16, 2012: basketball (North Greenwich Arena sessions), badminton, sailing, gymnastics (artistic), gymnastics (rhythmic),

gymnastics (trampoline), judo, taekwondo, boxing and fencing tickets.

- May 17, 2012: archery, basketball (Basketball Arena sessions), cycling (BMX), cycling (mountain bike), cycling (road), modern pentathlon, rowing, triathlon tickets.

- May 17, 2012: Olympic Park tickets.

Applicants for tickets were only permitted to buy tickets for one session and a maximum of four people, in order to spread the limited availability of tickets to as many people as possible.

Discussion Questions

1 Can the Olympic ticketing system be regarded as representative of events ticketing systems in general and if not, why not?

2 If you are managing an event where the demand for tickets is likely to exceed the supply (that is the number of seats or places, for example), what steps can you take to make the distribution of tickets fair and equitable or is it sufficient to operate ticket sales on a 'first come, first served' basis?

3 For smaller scale and more local events, such as a village carnival, is on-line ticketing realistically the only way to sell tickets or are more conventional ways just as suitable – what are the costs, technology and management implications of ticket sales and do these affect the type of approach or method being used?

Websites

For more information of the 2012 London Olympics: Input London 2012 into your search engine, or see http://www.guardian.co.uk/sport/olympic-tickets.

with enthusiasm and get the tea or coffee on. This is not a joke. You are going to be awfully busy on the big day, and you might have little or no chance to eat and drink; if that happens you become dehydrated and you become tired, and so you also become poor at decision-making, and you won't notice problems quickly enough. So make the time, have a decent breakfast or other meal before the event and drink a lot during it. It will help to ensure you are competent. And while you're having your breakfast, check the weather report and local travel news.

Correspondence and schedules check

To help prioritize your activities, check for any last minute changes, notes left for you, correspondence, phone messages or emails. Once you've done this, re-read your planned schedule for the set-up and make any amendments or notes. Carry a notebook and any checklist you have around with you: people have a habit of mentioning things as you go round that you may need to deal with. It will be a busy day, and you will forget otherwise. Whenever you sit down to rehydrate (have a drink), check your notebook. As the event co-ordinator or floor manager, you would normally expect the arrival of other staff, volunteers and helpers early on the day, or, in the case of large events, possibly before (particularly if staging, rehearsals or complex setting-up is required). A check can then be made of arrangements between co-ordinator and staff to deal with any final requests or changes to the booked details. Experienced clients can be expected to phone or call in, up to a week beforehand or the day before, in order to make general checks. This is to be encouraged, as is a 'pre-con' meeting between the venue, yourself and the other organizers to iron out any last minute problems (see Figure 10.5).

The organizer's office

In order to reduce stress on organizers, helpers, staff and visitors, ensure that there is a central point of enquiry for an event, also to act as a control location in the case of

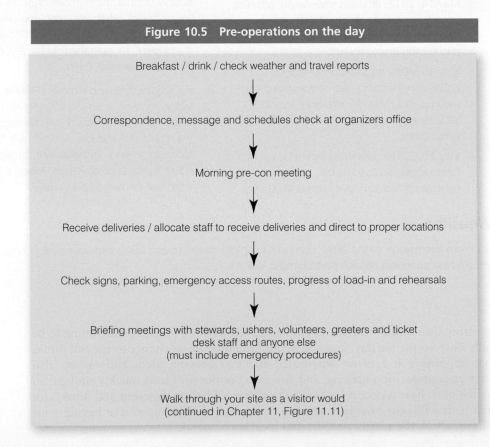

Figure 10.5   Pre-operations on the day

Breakfast / drink / check weather and travel reports

↓

Correspondence, message and schedules check at organizers office

↓

Morning pre-con meeting

↓

Receive deliveries / allocate staff to receive deliveries and direct to proper locations

↓

Check signs, parking, emergency access routes, progress of load-in and rehearsals

↓

Briefing meetings with stewards, ushers, volunteers, greeters and ticket
desk staff and anyone else
(must include emergency procedures)

↓

Walk through your site as a visitor would
(continued in Chapter 11, Figure 11.11)

an emergency. An organizer's office should be provided whenever an event is going to be large, long-running or VIP in nature. Where possible, offices should be in a convenient location (preferably not a hotel bedroom) and can be anything from a Portacabin to a desk in the Park Keeper's potting shed (however, also see security issues noted below about the location of a control point at major events). As a minimum, everyone should know where it is, and it should be supplied with a landline phone and if possible Wi-Fi. Without it, the venue itself (in the case of a hotel or public hall) will become the clearing house for any activity relating to the event, or people will simply stop and ask the first person they find. Before the event, the arrival of the staging, lighting and PA equipment, suppliers and speakers with queries, the sponsor's chief executive wanting somewhere for a 'quiet meeting' will have to be dealt with. Providing a room is not so much a matter of politeness, but of good planning. Without this, staff can be inundated with enquiries that they may not be able to deal with directly, or find the organizer in time to deal with them. If you, as an event organizer, are out and about around the venue, arrange for a mobile phone or 'walkie-talkie' radio, and if it stops ringing, that's because it's broken, not because no-one wants you. Make sure you go back to the office at some specified times to check that things are going satisfactorily and to deal with anything that can't follow you around.

Receiving supplies

Various items will be delivered as preparations progress, and make sure these are carefully checked against the purchase orders by the designated person. One of the difficulties faced by events organizers is that an event is at the end of a supply chain which is very time-specific. To illustrate this, if you had 300 best porcelain plates delivered to a hotel as new stock, and they were the wrong size, the wrong colour or the wrong design, the hotel could send them back and continue to operate using its older, existing plates. However, because events are unique and one-off, perhaps limited to a few hours of high-pitched activity, and 300 best porcelain plates are delivered that are the wrong size, what do you do? First, you don't send them back, as they might be the only ones you can get in time, and you can't serve 300 chicken dinners on the tablecloth. You accept them, writing on the delivery note that they do not comply with the purchase order number and you then phone the supplier to see if they can get you the right ones in time. Be careful to set up a controlled delivery acceptance system. It might have to be a volunteer helper standing next to the main gate with a list, whose job is to check what is coming in, sign for it and direct it to the place where it needs to go, but better this than having to chase around every time a surprise in a lorry turns up.

Transport and parking

With some major events, particularly international ones, there may be a need to make suitable arrangements to transport participants to and around the event, to deal with baggage and to make arrangements for materials and equipment both in advance and afterwards. Various companies specialize in ground handling, that is, the movement of transport, baggage and goods. Related to this are activities such as venue/terminal and venue/hotel transfers. In the case of venue/terminal and venue/hotel transfers the nature of transport varies, depending on distance and ease of finding the venue. Participants and visitors may be able to walk; there may be public transport laid on; or taxi services may be appropriate and may be provided formally or informally. There are many events, in all categories, where transport and transfer of people are significant. At the top end of the scale would be the provision of chauffeur-driven executive cars to deal with VIPs and dignitaries, but coaches may also be hired, and typically range from 18 to 52 seats, including luxury vehicles with on-board toilets, drinks, video facilities and host/hostess guides. Coach hire of this kind is particularly useful for both executive travel and transfers of large numbers of people to remote venues. On the other hand, for many kinds of events, people will simply arrive on foot, use their own car or come by public transport. Adequate and convenient car parking arrangements will need to be made, including arrangements for mobility-impaired visitors, for which close liaison with the local authority and the police, who have a role in traffic flow and control, will be necessary in advance. You may also need to provide volunteer or staff car park stewards on the day.

Load-in

The most likely item to arrive after the organizer at a major event is large scale equipment or large staging (some may take several days to construct and this should be foreseen in the scheduling and booking of the venue). A ground plan should be made by the co-ordinator, and a copy left with the venue to enable work to proceed if the organizer is not yet present or has been held up. Parking for trucks bringing this type of equipment or for support trucks and trailers may also be needed, especially at certain types of sporting events and music festivals.

A stage set will often be followed by the technical equipment (lighting, sound rig, etc.) a part of the set-up that is sometimes referred to as 'Load-in or Bump-in'. Doing this properly, with stage and layout plans and with the area clearly marked out (having been carefully measured for the original plans) should help ensure that getting a set and its technical equipment up and running is done quickly and efficiently, in time to be tested or used for rehearsal.

Jay Drowns/Sporting News via Getty Images

Trailers and crews during the Nextel Cup 3M Performance 400 at the Michigan International Speedway in Brooklyn, Mich., June 2006

At this point, once all the equipment is in place, cleaning can be done, message boards put up, together with signing and other support activities, such as the layout of arrangements for visitors' arrival.

Signing the site or venue

It is important that the event is properly signed, and signs are needed for two main purposes:

- information; and
- emergencies.

Information signs deal with aspects like normal entry and exits, the location of services and activities, where to queue from, and how to do particular things. Emergency signs deal with emergency procedures, emergency exits and escape routes, how to operate emergency equipment and how to call for help. The design of these two types of sign must be distinctly different. In general, emergency signs of various kinds can be obtained from specialist suppliers, from office or workplace suppliers or from suppliers listed in the phone book. Most indoor venues will already be properly signed for emergencies, as this is a legal requirement. This can be checked during the risk assessment process. For events that are in an unusual venue, or are outside, careful thought needs to be given to emergency signposting. As part of the planning stage, a ground plan of the site should have been drawn up, including the layout of emergency exits, access for emergency vehicles such as ambulances or fire engines, and plans for emergency routes. These can then be signposted and roped off; with stewards allocated to keep them clear during the event.

The design of the information signs depends on what sort of event you have. If this is going to be a large-scale professional event, then you can employ a professional sign-making company. If this is a modest volunteer event, then the design of the signs depends on your skill with a computer. You will not even need any fancy software. Keep your design simple so the signs can be seen from a distance, and if you draft them up on A4 paper using the largest font you can fit on it, you can always get them enlarged and laminated at a print shop to A3 so they are easier to see from a distance. They do need to be all the same design and font. This is not just a matter of how professional your signs will look, but that visitors should be able to recognize information or emergency signs from the mass of background material they will encounter when visiting your event.

SECURITY: ISSUES, PERSONNEL AND A CONTROL POINT

Only certain types of event will involve security issues. For VIP or political events a security check may take place at some point prior to the start of the event, usually between set-up and public arrival (in these cases, the set-up will have to be completed at least a day before the event). Police or Interior Ministry security (in England called the 'Home Office') may want to physically check the venue site and may well use sniffer dogs and metal detectors to do so. In some cases, visitors or the audience may be required to pass through metal detectors of the kind found at airports, with specialist security staff on duty, video surveillance and security checks of staff. At this level it is also likely that staff may be required to hold special passes, although it is common for all staff to be badged in some way, not only as a courtesy to delegates, guests and visitors, but for routine security.

Advice on security can be sought from the local police for smaller events, and from security companies, some of whom specialize in security at events such as rock festivals. Security is a serious matter, but a note of caution – do not make a big performance out of it. Making security into a major issue can be counter-productive to people's sense of feeling secure. If security is too obvious people will wonder why it is there, possibly leading to them feeling more fearful, not less. Second, remember media reactions: if your marketing department organizes a press call, or gets a TV crew to your event, the media will almost naturally look for the bad news. You will watch the TV later to see what great pictures of your event are shown across the national network, to find that the TV presenter stood in front of the largest security guard on the entire site (usually holding an enormous dog on a leash), made one positive comment about your event and then talked on national TV for five minutes about the heavy security, a non-existent 'terrorist threat' and all manner of crimes you don't have (Bladon *et al.*, 2012).

Most events do not require security of any kind – personal events and most internal events, external events, or private corporate events do not require it and only a very small number of leisure and large cultural events may involve it. In many cases the venue itself will provide any security that is needed, for example large hotels and conferences centres generally have their own Security Officer or Manager. Where 'external' or additional security is required, this is often a matter of the sheer size of an event – for example big rock festivals, big sporting events, events with large crowds and so on, and the identification of whether an event needs security can be part of the risk assessment process, or by seeking advice from the local police. While it might be thought that asking a security company for advice in the very first case is advisable, remember that they will want to sell you security and you may not need it. Only if there is a genuine security or safety risk, should the need for security or security personnel be an issue, very often your own stewards and a few local police on routine patrol might be the very most you need.

Where required, security personnel should in all cases be properly accredited and be properly identifiable by uniform or by badges. Their primary purposes are to ensure responsible action in an accident or emergency; to ensure controlled access to limited or secure areas; to assist in the case of crowd distress or deal with minor disturbances. On rare occasions they may be needed to eject the unruly, this is usually in conjunction with the local police. In employing a security firm it is necessary to check they are properly licensed and that they carry the appropriate insurance for their role (Swart, 2005). Where security is required it will be necessary to discuss with the firm the number of its staff required in relation to whatever risk is assessed or perceived and in relation to the size of the venue or site; the number of entrances; the areas requiring access control and the number of attendees, and the public and any VIP or guests who may have a specific security need (e.g. major celebrities or high level ministers). Security officers or trained security stewards are likely to cover the following roles:

- The general patrolling of large venue areas or sites.
- The understanding of emergency and/or evacuation arrangements.

- The oversight of crowded areas: reassurance of a crowd; assistance, persuasion and deterrence.
- Counting at entry points so as not to exceed the maximum load or numbers which the venue or site can cope with or is licensed for.
- The protection of persons, premises or equipment at the event.
- The installation, maintenance and use of security devices (such as CCTV cameras).
- The provision of advice or training for general site stewards or hosts in security concerns.

In terms of control in the case of an emergency, the senior security officer must have access to the designated control point or organizers' office and be able to liaise directly with the senior event co-ordinator, the senior venue manager and senior health and safety officer. In locating the control point, in those cases where security or crowd control are an issue, it should best be located in a place where visual oversight of a large area can be achieved or at the central place where CCTV is monitored. Access to the PA system or the big screens for safety, control and reassurance announcements should be possible from that same location, which should also be in proximity to any medical service area or a first aid point.

In an emergency or crisis, where you need to deal with an urgent response, you should already have an emergency plan or manual, part of this would be a section about media issues: the event background, statistics, emergency procedures and planned responses, expertise to call in, resources available in terms of the location of the control point, the staff, stewards, first aid, fire and security crews available to you; planned emergency messages, how the PA and screen systems are operated; checklists about preparing for interviews and how to gather information and who from.

MEDIA HANDLING

Most events may have next to no media handling issues: it might only be necessary to meet one or two local journalists or photographers and show them round. If, however, an advanced press viewing or familiarization visit is being organized, it must be competently done and careful thought given to it beforehand, especially in terms of what the event team want out of it. Plan what you want to show and how it is shown, where to take breaks on your tour round so people get a good view and they can hear what's going on and ask questions. Plan the refreshments for yourself and your media guests, as well as a place to sit and chat informally and quietly about the event without being interrupted. Deal with any questions politely and graciously, and make sure everyone can see and hear properly; be patient and positive. Don't let the media wander round aimlessly on their own. Always bear in mind that the media is supposedly interested in what the public wants, not necessarily in what you want to tell them. So you must give due consideration to what you may want to show them on a site visit, what the philosophy and highlights of the event would be for the public, as well as being able to provide some statistical information, suitable photographs or photographic opportunities and what the background to the event is and who the key people and/or sponsor are. This might be done in the form of a press kit or press release which you can give out, this way you have a better chance of the information being provided in the way you want it rather than journalists collecting it, 'on the hoof' and writing it down haphazardly.

For a very large event with a major media presence, appropriate care should be taken, and proper facilities provided. This might even include a media centre, tent, etc., equipped with its own power and phone lines, Wi-Fi and computer workstation(s); perhaps a lounge area, small interview rooms and a room large enough for a press conference; as well as adequate and sufficient refreshment (keep provision of light refreshment moderate in order to avoid press criticism of extravagance and wasteful expenditure on the part of the event organizers).

The media's tendency to latch on to the smallest whisper of bad news can give your marketing and public relations team nightmares. Reporter: 'Did the ceremony go well?' Your press officer: 'Yes, we had an excellent day, with 30000 people attending, although there was a bit of an argument between two blokes in the catering tent over a cream bun'. Later, the local newspaper's website has the headline: 'Public brawl ruins opening ceremony'. In case you think this cannot really happen in real life, the headline from the opening ceremony of the Welsh Highland Railway in 2000 was that a Tractor protest had marred the Welsh Highland opening. During the culmination of a ten-year, €5 million effort by volunteers, a farmer left his tractor across the track and 'the police were called'. This is rural Wales: when someone leaves a tractor on your railway and you have to ring the police, the nearest policeman is probably 20 km away, but the impression given in the media was of a major incident.

In an unexpected crisis, you may find that you are telephoned or called on for an 'immediate' interview. In no instance must you do that there and then. Take the name and contact number of the journalist and find out what they most want to ask and call them back in 10 or 20 minutes to give yourself time to compose yourself and check your information in response to what they want. Or hand them over to the proper person who is responsible for public relations and the media. Remember the over-riding need in a crisis is to be reassuring to the public, not to spout on about what a disastrous day you have had since you got out of the bath that morning.

REHEARSAL AND BRIEFINGS

A rehearsal may take place for technical reasons, particularly of the sound and presentation systems for many kinds of events. While a rehearsal may be a purely practice activity for certain types of high profile organizational events, product launches or public relations events, it is possible that it may be of the 'full dress' kind, including practice by actors, musicians, entertainers or other artists, including timing arrangements, acoustics and so on. Ushers or stewards, if required, can be briefed at this point, together with any meeters/greeters the organizer may have arranged.

Briefings (see Figure 10.6) for casual and specialist staff should include elementary issues such as what the event is for, who is coming and the opening and closing times: also details such as the location of toilets, cloakrooms, organizers' office, refreshment areas, check-in areas and what to do with the VIPs (such as direct them to a VIP hospitality room). How to assist mobility-impaired visitors into the event, and what action is required in an emergency, including the nature of the alarm system, emergency exits, assembly points, location of the medical centre if there is one, or how to get a first aider quickly if there is not. All staff at the event must be given a copy of the site map, information sheet, emergency contact list and emergency procedures. The site map and information page should be one sheet of A4, the

> ### Figure 10.6 Pre-event briefing meeting for all staff
>
> **Agenda: (Give out staff briefing and emergency sheets)**
>
> 1. The purpose of the event, type of visitors, likely numbers
>
> 2. Opening and closedown times, the programme, facilities and services, time check
>
> 3. Parking and access, facilities for the mobility impaired
>
> 4. Who you report to and arrangements for staff refreshment
>
> 5. Emergency contacts, systems and procedures, checking emergency routes and exits are clear, and knowing who is in charge.
>
> 6. Who to direct the media to
>
> 7. Questions and answers

emergency contact list and procedures should be on another sheet of A4. Any more than this, and staff will not read it. Clarity is essential.

LAYOUT OF ENTRANCES AND VISITOR RECEPTION

The entrance areas or visitor reception area should be ready for use prior to the start time; even in the case of a small informal event, this amounts to no more than a table with programmes for people to pick up as they arrive. At large events, for convenience of organization, the layout of the arrival area might be alphabetical (in the case of a conference) or might have several ticket desks. It may also be necessary to provide greeters or an information desk, or both, as minor queries from incoming arrivals can slow down the entry process. Queries can be dealt with by the greeter moving along the queues.

The greeters have the additional function of helping to direct visitors; while signage is necessary and important, people arriving in unfamiliar locations will look first for someone to ask, and only secondly for (inanimate) directions. Toilets should also be located near the entrance areas: the first request, especially if your event attracts the public, and particularly families, will be for the toilets.

Where it would help, packs, site maps, entry badges and tickets (such as refreshment tickets) and programmes should be laid out in boxes to ensure the arrival process goes quickly. It is preferable that in this layout process all items (programme, site map, badges, tickets and pack) are put into large envelopes or 'goody bags' and stacked (for those events or occasions where the visitor is going to receive a pack). Not only does this increase the speed of entry, but it saves a great deal of stretching across a vast array of material spread on a table. Any urgent messages can be displayed on a board at the arrival point, or even mounted on stage screens during refreshment breaks. It is preferable to have your most experienced staff available at the entrances, as first impressions count, and an impression of confusion given by inexperienced staff at the doors will reflect badly on the event as a whole. In planning the arrival areas, thought should also be given to providing power, and phone points for tills (both for enquiries and if automated transactions are to take place), and to the way in which the tills will be supervised, supplied with cash and change, emptied and the income recorded and banked.

CASE STUDY 31

Site layout issues: the Wirksworth Wapentake

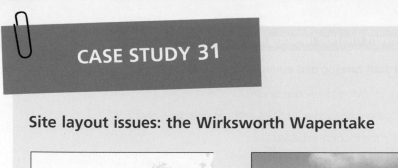

Wirksworth, England

wirksworthwapentake.org.uk

Re-enactors at the Wirksworth Wapentake, Yorkshire, England

FACTBOX

- Wirksworth Wapentake: Wirksworth, The Peak District of Derbyshire, England
- A Wapentake – an ancient gathering of armed men
- Re-enacted in 2008
- A range of site planning issues

Learning Objectives

The aim of this case study is to examine some issues of site selection and set up criteria with the following objectives:
To consider the way in which the site for a particular type of event was selected
To highlight what main issues might arise in the selection
To understand that many issues overlap in the determination of site layouts

In olden times, the administrative divisions of England were not called Boroughs or Districts; they were called Hundreds or Wapentakes. The Wapentakes were mainly in the north of England in those areas of the country which had been invaded by the Vikings from Denmark and Norway in the years between 875 and 900 AD, that is in two of the component kingdoms of England: Northumbria and Mercia (the third component kingdom of England was Wessex, in the south). It had long been remembered that the small historic town of Wirksworth had been the chief town of its Wapentake: The Wirksworth Wapentake in the Kingdom of Mercia.

The Wapentake was both an administrative district and an actual meeting of the local inhabitants acting in government. This meeting, the 'Wapentake' itself, was an annual event, where a jury was elected to serve for the year and votes taken on important issues. Those persons who owned their own weapon, such as a spear or sword, were entitled to vote.

In 2008 it was decided to hold a Wapentake to celebrate the history and community spirit of the Wirksworth area, and this was probably the first time a Wapentake had been held for perhaps 1000 years. The organizing committee and the re-enacting group had several challenges to overcome, including funding (mainly via a grant and ticket sales) and most significantly where to hold the main event, as no-one then remembered or knew where the original Wapentakes had been held.

There were several site selection criteria:

- The size of the site needed – in essence a site the size of a large cricket pitch or several football pitches was needed.
- There needed to be good access and parking either on-site or nearby.
- The site needed to be largely level.

In consequence, four possible sites were viewed in different locations in and around the town. The site selected was a former quarry, now filled in as a field, at the National Stone Centre near the town. The site was completely overgrown, but had been used up to five years previously for car boot sales.

This site (see sketch plan) had some advantages and some disadvantages:

Advantages:	Disadvantages:
Adequate size at about 16 hectares	No mains services at all
Relatively level and well drained	Entirely overgrown
Close to parking and a main road	No on-site buildings or facilities
Sheltered by surrounding woods	

The key issue regarding this site was that the central area was to be used for an arena for a battle and a boat burning ceremony. It was initially thought that the field was level and that it only needed the turf cutting, but once a local farmer had cut it, the organizers found that the underlying surface was entirely covered in loose stone, both hazardous to walk on and impossible to conduct a battle re-enactment on. Consequently, the field had to be cleared of stone. There was no money in the budget for this to be done mechanically so it was done by the ground staff of the centre, assisted by volunteers using rakes and wheelbarrows to pick up the stones over a period of six weeks. Once cleared of stones, the surface had to be sown with grass seed, which had to be allowed to grow for a further six weeks before being cut prior to the event. (This timescale gives a hint about how long some matters take when dealing with fields!). When finished the field was named 'The Great Moot Field'.

The site had no mains services. Water was therefore piped through a garden hose from the nearest supply in a building 400 metres away to a stand pipe and tap. There was no sewage or drainage system so portable toilet and washroom facilities had to be brought in. Food and drink were provided from mobile catering suppliers in vans with their own bottled gas and bottled water. The re-enactors camped in tents around the site and prepared camp fires using a wood supply pre-ordered and delivered to the site before the event and by cutting down selected small trees with their battle axes (only certain re-enactors were trained how to do this). First aid facilities were provided by the St John's Ambulance Service volunteers for a small fee who brought a caravan to act as their first aid room. A control point was set up in the entrance marquee where tickets were also sold. This was a family event so there was no security, though the local police had been kept informed and attended on a casual 'look in' basis. In the case of security, many of the re-enactors were in full armour with huge axes: you don't argue with a bloke in full armour. In the case of fire prevention, because camp fires and a boat burning were a necessary part of the re-enactment, sand was supplied to extinguish fires, as well as filled water buckets, and fire extinguishers were provided at four locations around the site.

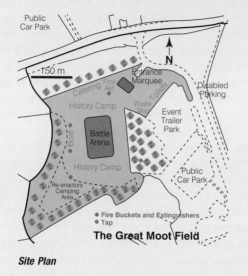

Site Plan

In terms of the '**load-in**' everything had to be brought in, starting with the marquee two days before the event. At the same time the arena had been demarcated by two lines of rope fencing, an internal one and a perimeter one as well as hay bales outside this for people to sit on while watching the battle in the arena area. The toilets arrived the day before, when everything else, from the living history camp to the litter bins arrived, including portable electric generators for the caterers; battery lighting to illuminate the exits during the boat burning (which was held after dark), to tables and chairs for the entrance marquee.

The 2008 Wirksworth Wapentake provided an enjoyable historic re-enactment with a battle, a boat burning ceremony, a Saxon-Viking living history encampment and displays of how a warrior was armed, how things were made in ancient times and the styles of dress the people wore. Parts of the event were also held in the town and in the parish church, itself of Saxon origins. The event took place over two days in July 2008 on what transpired to be the hottest weekend of the whole year – one of the things which had not been foreseen was the need for sunscreen lotion, but supplies of this were obtained from the town. There were no injuries of any kind to the battle re-enactors or to the public, and the event took place in an entirely safe and enjoyable way.

Discussion Questions

1   What site selection criteria might be used if you were looking for an outdoor wedding site rather than a battle re-enactment site?

2   When choosing a site for a unique or unusual event, what impact would the lack of basic services (water, electricity, gas, sewage, toilets, washrooms, changing or store rooms) have in terms of the difficulty level of putting an event on, and how might these matters be overcome?

3   Could the site set-up issues identified in this case be put into a time schedule or work break-down plan?

Websites

For further information on the Wirksworth Wapentake see: **www.wirksworthwapentake.org.uk**
For some consideration of site issues for large scale events see: **http://www.strc.ch/conferences/2002/liaudat.pdf**.

If the event is a conference or VIP invitation-only event, a list of delegates or guests expected, plus badges (for conferences) or some suitable small gift (for invited events, such as corsages or chocolates), should have been made up prior to the event. (Where security is an issue, guests must be politely required to wear their badges, although normally most guests are happy to do so; at informal events, or where there is no security issue, not everyone may wish to wear a badge and should not be compelled to if they are unwilling.) But it is important that guests are checked against the guest list, as this will provide accurate final numbers of the people attending and can be passed on to catering staff for any last minute amendments to seating or refreshment arrangements. This also acts as a key security check, which should not be overlooked in case of gate-crashers.

In addition, it is also common at conference-type check-ins to issue information packs, including agendas; working papers; delegate lists and a little information about the venue for delegates to take away with them. This latter should be provided by the venue marketing department to the client, if the organizer is making up their own packs to ensure that a selling opportunity for the venue is not missed. For this kind of event, co-ordinators would be supported by check-in staff, normally one to every 50 delegates, either provided by the organization itself or by the venue, to ensure delegates find the right conference and do not get mixed up with any other activities taking place. Normally, the co-ordinator would be on hand at least half an hour before the published start time to deal with supervising the arrival area.

load-in

The arrival of equipment, stage crew, staging, materials, sound and lighting rigs and other various items of event set-up.

THE EVENT EXPERIENCE

Getting everything in place for an event is not only a matter of the behind-the-scenes efforts in terms of logistics, organization, preparation, layout and design; it is also crucial to the ambience and atmosphere that will be created and experienced by the participants, visitors or guests. Events may be simple or complicated; in the modern world it is more difficult to impress an audience with an event because the public is much more used to seeing events in the media and to attending events. This means that the efforts that may have to be put into creating a pleasant experience at an event, in circumstances that might make its staging quite difficult, may have to be quite considerable.

This design part of the process may have to take into account the venue, its layout, its environment, decor, lighting, music, colour scheme and a whole range of other incidental factors. Nevertheless, we must also bear in mind that at a vast majority of events it is the guests or visitors themselves who will help create the atmosphere and ambience of the event, simply by their presence or by their participation and involvement, as well as their enjoyment, or otherwise, of it.

Ambience is often significant to the creation of a good event. An event with the right ambience can be a huge success. An event with the wrong ambience can be a huge failure. At a personal event, such as a birthday party, the ambience may be created simply by the people who are there, without the need for anything else – good company among friends can make an excellent event.

Some events, however, may need a little help to go well. As at a birthday party, there might be the need for decorations, music and games, as well as food and drink. But it is important to understand that the presence of these elements does not in any way guarantee that things will go well. There can be a wonderful environment, expensive themed decor, large amounts of excellent food and drink, yet the event might still not be quite the success that the organizers intended. However, one of the roles of an events co-ordinator is to try and ensure the event succeeds by careful attention to detail and by trying to make sure that the experience which guests receive is a good one.

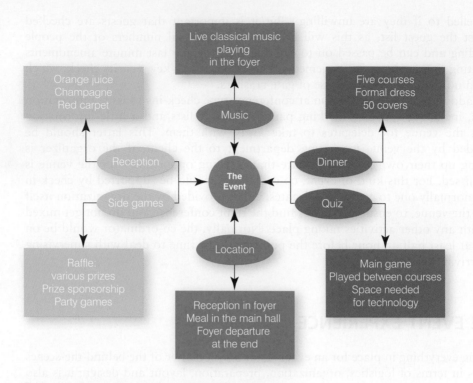

Figure 10.7   Example of the component elements at a quiz dinner

In simple terms we can regard the staging and ambience of an event as comprising a number of interlinked features (see Figure 10.7). The physical setting of an event, which deals with various design and staging activities, is primarily intended to look after the event's surroundings and the visitor's responses to them. Visitors respond to stimulus of their senses of smell, sight, touch, hearing and taste. The physical responses to a pleasant meal environment are well understood, and much the same applies to an event environment and to the experience a visitor receives while attending (Berridge, 2006).

An event environment can probably be quite complicated in certain situations. Suppose we are organizing a medieval themed night. In order for the night to be successful, its planning and execution will have to appeal to all the senses and you will need to provide a themed environment that would be convincing or satisfying to the guests. This might require the careful selection of a venue, as it would be easier to adapt a suitable building than to create a total medieval experience in a marquee (although this could be done, with enough time and resources). After this, all the elements of the theme could be prepared, from the decor to the costumes, and care would have to be taken that this is done well in order for the best possible experience to be received. For example, how should the event smell? For a medieval theme, the answer to this question may be based on how a wood fire smells, so there might have to be one, and bearing in mind different kinds of wood smell of different things. The answer is less likely to be based on what a medieval cow smells like – we are not, after all, attempting to recreate the medieval world at a theme night – only to give a feel for it, but this recreation might be the case at a historical re-enactment, where something approaching accuracy may be an issue for the re-enactors.

CHAPTER 10

CASE STUDY 32

The atmosphere of events: Glastonbury Festival

Glastonbury, England

The audience looks toward the pyramid Stage during an event at the Glastonbury Festival

Getty Images/Jon Super/Redferns

- Glastonbury Festival, England
- 134 000 'weekend tickets' for the three-day event, capacity is set at 150 000
- Employs some 1700 during the event (excluding volunteers and pre-event contractors)
- 37 500 passes for performers, stewards, traders, crew, etc.
- Admission price in 2012 was €257
- Famous for its informality

Learning Objectives

The aim of this case study is to consider some issues relating to the atmosphere at events with the following objectives:

To consider the way in which the environment and festival attendees at Glastonbury contribute to the atmosphere

To examine whether the event 'experience' is simply determined by physical factors or by the inherent success of the core activity and the interaction of participants

In a number of large fields on Worthy Farm in Somerset, nestling in the rolling green English countryside, over 100 000 people gather to listen to bands playing anything from hip hop to jazz. This is Glastonbury, put on almost every year at the summer solstice by Michael Eavis, a large number of volunteers and some paid staff. Not quite every year, because sometimes the land needs to be given a rest. This is a farm and it has real cows. In fact, at the first festival, the admission price included free milk for the 1500 people who attended it then, in 1971.

Glastonbury has, over the 40 or so years of its existence, become internationally famous. It has played host to hundreds of bands and individuals. It is 'peculiarly British' in the type of people it attracts, a cross-section of the music-loving public, and is relaxed in a hippy, New Age kind of way. It is well known for the nature of its portable toilets and, in rainy summers (this is England), its sea of mud. Although there are headline bands each year, the programme is not especially fixed but might contain over 50 bands or acts over the three days who play on several stages throughout the farm area. There is a tendency for much of what goes on to be impromptu and because of its rural situation it plays all night (to the annoyance of a few local residents).

The general theme has tended to be dance music which makes for an enjoyable environment. The social inclusiveness of the festival also means that considerable charitable funds are raised for Greenpeace, Oxfam, Campaign for Nuclear Disarmament and other local and national charities.

The audience is catered for by facilities such as the festival markets, which include over 700 stalls in five or so main market areas, laid out in pre-sold pitches (in effect, a way of licensing stalls). These markets are grouped together around key services such as water, electricity and toilets. Camping, in the open, in tents, vans, motor caravans, caravans and big motor homes is a feature of Glastonbury and the campsite fields have various facilities including cafés. In the evenings, the warm glow of campfires in the summer dusk contributes to much of the festival's atmosphere, also created by its location in a beautiful valley extending towards the Tor (rocky hill) at Glastonbury itself. The music also impacts on the festival atmosphere, depending on which bands, players and sets are performing and when. The mood can be raucous or peaceful. For example, it was reported by Dorian Lynskey (of *The Guardian* newspaper) that the 2002 event did not have one of the great line-ups of the festival in terms of range of bands but that the massed singing during the Coldplay set of their piece '*Trouble*' was some of the gentlest mass singing ever heard.

The festival has also had a number of impacts. Its informality (as well as sound) did not go down well with some locals, to the extent that in 1981 the local Conservative Member of Parliament tried to stop the festival by creating a law (via the British Parliament) requiring all festivals in Britain to be licensed by a local authority (council). The intention was to stop the Glastonbury Festival but the local Mendip Council approved the licence. The festival attracts a large number of visitors and participants and injects a significant amount of money into the area and into local businesses associated with it; these are also significant considerations.

Discussion Questions

1   In what way does the setting of Glastonbury have an impact on the atmosphere and style of the festival?

2   Identify the major features of the surroundings and of the communal lifestyle that predominates at Glastonbury. Is the atmosphere due solely to the type of music or are a range of other factors in place?

3   Can these factors be successfully transferred to other festivals?

4   Which features make the Glastonbury Festival unusual in organizational terms?

Websites

For further information on the Glastonbury Festival see the related website at: **www.glastonburyfestivals. co.uk**; for media material, search the websites of the news media. In terms of successful festivals from the point of view of the audience, this is of interest: **http://www.gooutdoors.co.uk/expert-advice/guide-to-a-successful-festival.**

Figure 10.8   The event service experience

1. Chilly reception: A bad day in the catering tent

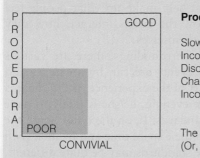

Procedural	Convivial
Slow	Insensitive
Inconsistent	Cold
Disorganized	Apathetic
Chaotic	Uninterested
Inconvenient	Bored

The guest thinks: 'Why is this a shambles? I waited for ages'.
(Or, 'Where is the damn salt pot?')

2. Get them in and ship 'em out: The production line at the burger stall

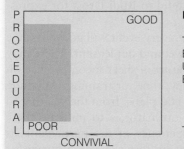

Procedural	Convivial
Timely	Insensitive
Efficient	Cold
Uniform	Apathetic
By the book	Uninterested

The guest thinks: 'That was quick, but I didn't enjoy it much'.

3. An amateur production: A funny day at the fete, happy people and cold coffee

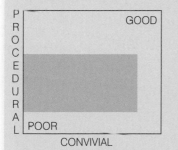

Procedural	Convivial
Slow	Friendly
Disorganized	Personable
Inconsistent	Interested
Chaotic	Tactful
Inconvenient	

The guest thinks: 'They're trying hard, but it's a bit of a mess'.

4. Satisfaction guaranteed: A professional event

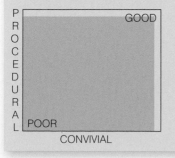

Procedural	Convivial
Timely	Friendly
Efficient	Personable
Uniform	Interested
Adaptable	Tactful
Visible Management	

The guest thinks: 'I enjoyed that, they were on the ball'.

The physical elements of surroundings, props, layout, equipment, personal arte-facts, etc., go towards making up the whole environment. This environment, together with the cognitive, emotional and physiological responses of the guests (as well as of the staff, crew, artists and entertainers) help make up what people feel about the event and will also help determine how the guests interact, how they respond to staff and whether they stay and enjoy themselves.

In addition to the setting of the event and its surroundings, there are various service factors as perceived by the guests. Many events are run by amateurs and volunteers, and this may (or may not) be a key part of the experience. If the client is paying a professional to put on a medieval theme evening, he/she is likely to have certain expectations of the event and its service standards. If, on the other hand, the event is a co-operative one, put on by volunteers in their spare time and by their own efforts, the expectations of the event and its service standards may be quite different. Service at events might be thought of more in terms of procedural and conviviality characteristics, as shown in Figure 10.8. (We are grateful to Rudi Drost for expressing this concept in terms of events).

We can see from this that it cannot be assumed that every event will go well, some events are disastrous, shambolic, disorganized, cold, wet and unpleasant. There may be many reasons for such unhappy outcomes, ranging from sheer incompetence on the part of the organizers, to lack of resources, money, time, or training. Anything and everything can conspire against some of the best laid plans, from the weather to blocked drains. The art of being a good events co-ordinator is to mitigate these problems where they occur, so that the overall experience of the participants is positive. We can be forgiven if it rains. We will not be forgiven if the queue for the toilets is 30 minutes or it takes two hours just to get out of the car park.

SUMMARY

We have attempted to provide an overview of some of the more serious issues regarding the project management of events so that, particularly in the case of large or complicated events, these techniques can be used to formalize the approach of the event co-ordinator to the requirements of the occasion.

We have also sought to provide an overview of the set-up and preparation activities that take place immediately prior to, and during the start of an event, noting that efficient preparation and due thought will reduce the risk of something going wrong or some important matter being overlooked.

The set-up process should not be seen as separate from the activities of running the event on the day, as this is often a continuous process, and the reader should also look at 'Running the event on the day', for more information.

EVALUATION QUESTIONS

1 What kinds of management techniques are available for planning an event project in terms, for example, of time and sequencing of pre-event activities?

2 What security issues may relate to setting up events, and why do such issues not apply to all events?

3 Is it always certain that an event will be a success if the management of it is 'good'?

REFERENCES

Beavan, Z. and Laws, C. in Yeoman, I. and Robertson, M. (2004) *Festival and events management: an international arts and culture perspective*, Oxford: Butterworth Heinemann, pp 183–93.

Berridge, G. in Page, S. J. and Connell, J. (2012) The *Routledge Handbook of Events*, New York: Routledge, pp 273–88.

Berridge, G. (2006) *Events Design and Experience*, Oxford: Butterworth Heinemann.

Bladon, C., Kennel, J., Abson, E. and Wilde, N, (2012) *Event Management: An Introduction*, Abingdon: Routledge, pp 386–406.

Ferdinand, N. and Williams, N. in Page, S. J. and Connell, J. (2012) *The Routledge Handbook of Events*, New York: Routledge, pp 234–46.

HSE (2012) Guidance on running events safely (up to date information replacing the HSE Event Safety Guide) see http://www.hse.gov.uk/event-safety/index.htm.

O'Toole, W. and Mikolaitis, P. (2002) *Corporate Event Project Management*, Chichester: Wiley, pp 15–40.

Reiss, G. (2007) *Project Management Demystified*, Oxford: Taylor and Francis (3 edn) pp 1–4.

Slack, N., Brandon-Jones, A., Johnstone, R. and Betts, A., (2012), *Operations and Process Management*, Harlow: Pearson, 3edn, pp 495–528.

Starr, R., Newfrock, J. and Delurey, M. (2003) 'Enterprise Resilience: Managing Risk in the Networked Economy', *Strategy & Business*, Spring.

Swart, K. in Tassiopoulos, D. (ed) (2005) *Event Management: A Professional and Developmental Approach*, Lansdowne: Juta Academic (2 edn) pp 424–25.

CHAPTER 11

THE ORGANIZATION MANAGER AND THE TEAM: DURING THE EVENT

AIMS

- To identify the kinds of organizations found at events

- To explore organizational effectiveness

- To discuss recruitment issues for paid, voluntary and permanent staff

- To consider issues about event management 'on the day'

INTRODUCTION

The organization and staffing of special events vary considerably. Personal events, for example, often involve friends and family and volunteers. Organizational events may employ events management companies or professional events organizers. Both paid and volunteer helpers are common at a large number of events, notably those involving community activities, sports and so on. Professional organization is common but expensive for some kinds of event. As a typical example, weddings could be undertaken entirely by volunteer help, or entirely by professional help, or by a mixture of both – it may simply depend on the budget. The event organizer must be aware, though, that this is not the only criterion: the issue is partly one of knowing what volunteer help can accomplish, or when to bring in professionals for reasons of size, safety, standards or other reasons.

As with many other labour-intensive service industries, the events business has a considerable need for staff. This is satisfied by on-the-job training and by the recruitment of staff from outside, whether direct from the labour pool or by recruiting from colleges and universities. Unlike other service industries, however, there are a limited number of events-specific courses in the current academic world. This means that the events business has to rely on adapting its staff from other sources, such as the hospitality or tourism industries, and from courses in these fields, as well as from marketing, business and leisure programmes.

For all the considerable effort that goes into preparing an event, running it on the day can still prove a challenge. The co-ordination of a wide range of disparate and even unusual activities, facilities and services can be overwhelming. Events management has to be effective and events managers must be effective in situations that may be constantly changing. The importance of good planning and preparation is that it reduces the variability and uncertainty of what is taking place during the event and allows the event co-ordinator to concentrate on those matters that require immediate or frequent attention.

ORGANIZATION

One of the themes that has emerged in the preceding chapters is the diversity of events. The organizational issues mirror this diversity. It is extremely unlikely that any two events would have exactly the same organizational structure or staffing. This said, there are some similarities, and we would expect core services to be organized in broadly similar ways. There is a probability that event organizational structures would include five main functions:

- visitor services operations;
- support services operations;
- marketing;
- administration; and
- finance.

These five functions can be further sub-divided depending on the nature and size of the event, but a survey of the organization charts of a number of events would probably show that all five functions are likely to be present in some form.

The organizational structure for an event forms the framework around which the various activities and services operate (Van der Wagen, 2005). It has been previously noted that events provide a mix of products and services, for example: ceremony and celebration; food and drink services; presentation and technical services; support and ancillary services. These activities will probably come under an operations department, which might itself be subdivided into visitor services and support operations (as in Figure 11.1, the former for parts of the event that have public contact, the latter for those that do not). In addition to the operations department which will be specific to any given public event, the organizational structure will typically have a marketing department whose role may be to cover sales activities, and perhaps enquiries and ticketing, depending on the type of operation. There is also likely to be an accounts and control function, to deal both with outgoing and incoming invoices and financial business, and which may also include a purchasing role, particularly in larger events. Underpinning the support activities will be an administration department, covering not only general administration but also personnel issues, recruitment and induction, payment of wages, etc.

In this kind of organizational structure, the key members of staff, or key managers, might be the only paid staff at the event, and the actual staff doing the work might otherwise be volunteers. Similarly, if the event is being run by a club or society, the key staff might simply be the members of that organization's normal committee. Committees are extremely common in events. In consequence, in many events organizations it is common to find a core body of officers, managers or co-ordinators that have the job of organizing the activities and of supervising either volunteers or paid casual and part-time staff. This body is the skeleton and framework of the organization and is sometimes called a cadre.

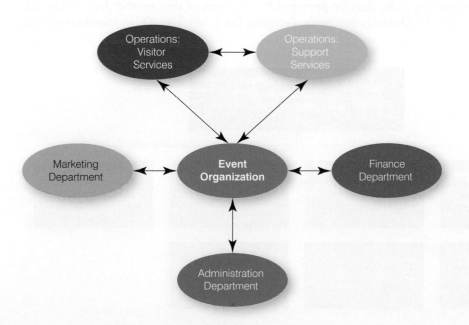

Figure 11.1 Simplified events organization structure

The organizational structure for an event may simply consist of the cadre and their helpers. At a small village flower show, the total number of people organizing and helping to organize and run the event might be fewer than 20, with only six of them being the cadre, or key organizers, perhaps because they form the village horticultural club's regular committee. On the other hand, the organizational structure of an event may become enormously complex, with a mixture of key organizers, volunteer helpers, paid full-time, part-time and casual staff. The organization might also include some outsourced activities such as catering or concessions, resulting in something that is well suited to the event taking place, but which would be regarded as extremely odd if it were a conventional organization.

The organizational structure (see example in Figure 11.2) may appear very conventional. This is because there is a need in an organization, where unfamiliar people are working together, to know exactly who is in charge. There must be no ambiguity over the safety of the public and the efficiency of the organization (which, having been created to run an event may be a relatively short-lived entity). The lines of communication, in events organizations, not only pass up and down the hierarchy but also run from side to side. This is essential to ensure that information gets passed around the organization quickly, and does not get bogged down by having to be transferred up to line managers and back down again. For example, if there is a change in the music programme, the Music Officer needs to tell the Visitor Services Officer, but also needs to be able to speak directly to the information and ticket office without waiting for other managers or officers to turn up, these being staff who might be part-time or only at the venue at certain times. The one person who is slightly detached in this example system is the Catering Officer, whose own organization tends to be self-contained.

In this type of organization, we can also see a mix between paid and volunteer staff, and that staff might originate from a number of sources. Suppose a festival is being organized by a city tourist department, rather than by a voluntary committee; in this case the cadre may be provided by members of that tourist department (see Case Study 34: Organization at the Deventer Book Market). Other members of staff

Figure 11.2   Visitor Services Department at the Middleburg Music Festival

might come from other organizations involved in the festival, including performers, contractors, sponsors or volunteers.

ORGANIZATIONAL EFFECTIVENESS

The culture of an organization is thought to impact on an organization's efficiency and ability to do its job. Perhaps it can be said that events are about creating wealth: wealth of experiences; wealth in socialization; wealth in community spirit. 'Profit' alone is too limited a concept. In our analysis of events so far, we have repeatedly made the point that it is the purpose of only certain types of events to make a profit. For the family and friends organizing a wedding the objective is not to make a profit, but to celebrate the wedding; for the athletics club running its annual sporting competition, the primary objective is not to make a profit, but to showcase the best performers in the sport, to encourage supporters and athletes and to test these athletes in competition. If a little money is taken on the gate, well and good, but this is secondary to the sport. Therefore, in considering organizational effectiveness at an event we must take into account the kind of organization culture which is present, and this may be co-operative and social rather than focussed on commercial or bureaucratic aims (Tum, 2006) (see Figure 11.3).

The issue for event managers, then, is about how to organize an effective event, possibly with a disparate range of people, whose reasons for being there may be social rather than commercial, and who will work towards an objective over a relatively short period of time without too much concern about the style of

Figure 11.3 The culture of an event organization

Source: adapted from Johnson, G. and Scholes, K. 2002, *Exploring Corporate Strategy*, London: Prentice Hall (6 edn) pp 74–75

CASE STUDY 33

Volunteer staffing at the Mainz Carnival

Mainz, Germany

Patrick Poendl/Shutterstock.com

The Rose Monday Parade in Mainz, Germany. It marks the culmination of the annual carnival season

- Mainz Carnival
- Known as 'The Fifth Season of the Year'
- Comprises: Saturday Youth Carnival, Sunday Carnival Guards Parade, Rose Monday – Carnival Procession and three days of costume balls
- Admission ticket, with grandstand seats, a costume ball and a carnival show: €70

Learning Objectives

The aim of this case study is to examine a cultural event and how voluntary effort is important to its organization an operation with the following objectives:

To consider what role volunteer support has at the Mainz Carnival

To highlight how different types of stakeholders interact to support the Carnival

Volunteer support co-ordinated by a central carnival office is a key feature of the three-day Mainz Carnival. Local people are intensively involved in the carnival preparations, which take many months and include special preparations by a large number of carnival clubs, made up of volunteer members who wish to contribute in some way to the success of the event. The carnival has a long history associated with the traditional German festival of 'Fastnacht', which takes place on Shrove Tuesday. In the Mainz Carnival, there are three days of celebrations from Saturday to the Monday before Lent (called Rose Monday).

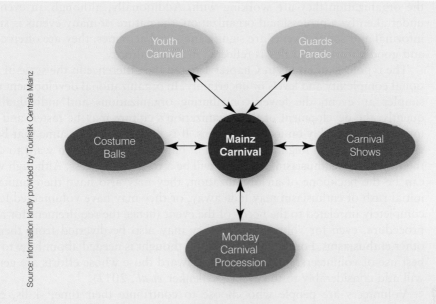

Source: information kindly provided by Touristik Centrale Mainz

The Mainz Carnival is organized by a carnival office (secretariat), the Mainzer Carneval Verein, formed in 1838. It co-ordinates the efforts of official bodies, professional organizations and the many volunteer carnival clubs. The carnival office has a small permanent staff, which is increased for the carnival itself by the addition of volunteers and additional casual staff who have many years' experience of running the event. Oversight of the Carnival is through a committee of almost 50 members with the City Mayor being an observer. Carnival organization officially begins in the previous October, to allow enough time for the complex work of providing the intensive three-day celebration in March. In practice, however, preparations and planning are more or less continuous throughout the year for such a large-scale activity.

The carnival organization is a combination of effort by public, voluntary and private sector bodies. Local government involvement helps provide tourist promotion and logistics support, whereas the private sector provides local business help with funding, sponsorship, displays and other support for the voluntary organizations involved. The voluntary element draws from the carnival clubs together with many other local clubs, societies and recreational organizations, and makes up a very significant part of the carnival effort. The clubs range from sporting to theatrical clubs, from music clubs to historical re-enactment societies and provide marchers in the procession, floats, displays and tableaux, ensuring that the carnival is loud and colourful. A very wide range of activities takes place in addition to the major carnival processions. These include carnival shows with stands and displays, as well as costumed and masked balls where participants, guests and visitors dress up, are wined and dined, dance and enjoy other social activities.

Discussion Questions

1   What role do the various voluntary organizations play in making the carnival a success?

2   What is the function of the carnival secretariat?

3   How does the existence of carnival clubs improve the standard of the carnival and the range of activities being put on?

4   Compare this organization with your own local carnival or annual festival: how do they differ?

Websites

For further information look up a marching band in the Rose Monday parade in Mainz at: **www.mainzer-carneval-verein.de/** and **http://www.mainzer-fastnacht.de/index.php**, and on YouTube, for example: **http://www.youtube.com/watch?v=bG47lCZkKII&feature=relmfu**.

the organization they are working with. Additionally, although an event may be undertaken by a professional organization, the nature of many events is still largely informal and social. Events are significant social activities; they are often communal and good natured, and this is reflected in their culture.

The typology of events in Chapter 1 noted the difference in the scale of organizational complexity and levels of uncertainty. In organizational development terms, the simpler an event, the fewer contributing organizations and individuals. Consequently, the development of the organization's culture may be faster, and may also impact more quickly on its effectiveness. It is rather easy to assume that because an events organization might be made up of happy volunteers who want to contribute their skills and enthusiasm, the event will be a runaway success. Although volunteers can be the backbone of an organization, they may also have their limitations: an initial rush of enthusiasm may fade away, or they may have volunteered for reasons completely unrelated to the needs of the event (hence the requirement for a selection procedure, even for volunteers), or they may also be diverted from their task by other enthusiasms. For this reason, careful thought is needed about how to make the best use of volunteers, but also how to reward those whose efforts are genuine and will add considerably to the event (Schlenker *et al.*, 2012).

Volunteers are people who choose to contribute their time, skills, effort and experience, without pay, to benefit a cause or the community in which they live. As such, their motives for volunteering are personal and possibly social, as by volunteering they may be involved in hobbies they enjoy, or be undertaking a role that enables them to meet new people, or to spend time with friends, or that might provide satisfaction or self-esteem. It might also enable them to exercise their skills, or to remain active if they are retired. These motives must be taken into account when volunteer labour is being used. In creating an effective volunteer organization or team, it will naturally help to know what their reasons are for being there, and what they hope to get out of it.

Brendan Howard/Shutterstock

Get a little help from your friends: Volunteer labour is used at many events.

Teams created and developed in short-life organizations, where situations may be unusual or new to them can vary in their effectiveness. The classic approach to team building is to go through a number of processes before teams become effective, for example, the 'forming, norming, storming and performing' scenario, bearing in mind that not all teams reach the performing stage. However, this approach pre-supposes that there is sufficient time to organize teams and for them to socialize through the process. In the case of special events, this method and approach to team building may not be appropriate or suitable. There may simply not be sufficient time to team build, in which case a participative style of management will be needed by the team leader. Additionally, since many events are reliant on volunteer staff, the timescale for organizing them and socializing them into the culture of the event organization may be very short indeed. In this case, the effectiveness of the organization may not rely on group development at all, but on a wide range of factors, some of which may ultimately be beyond the control of the organizing group (see Figure 11.4). It is also important to have an understanding of those matters which are important to the success of an event, the '**Critical Success Factors**' (Wanklin, 2005). These factors vary from event to event, but might include the nature of the core activity, ('a good performance') as well as a range of subsidiary issues from ease of access, to cleanliness, a lack of queuing and so on.

The event we have worked so hard to organize may not be a success. It may be a failure for any number of reasons, internal or external: success is sometimes elusive, for all our market research, for all the effort put in to producing something that we hope will be excellent. In the end, the public might not actually buy tickets, and the

> **Critical Success Factors**
> Those issues that are key to the success of an event, as laid down by its objectives, and that are criteria by which its success can be judged or measured.

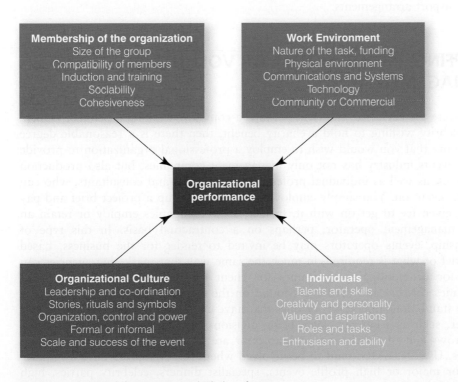

Figure 11.4 Framework for an event organization's performance

Source: adapted from Mullins, 1995, *Hospitality Management – A Human Resources Approach*, London: Pitman, pp 52-85

reasons for this might be beyond the control of the event organizers. However, let us assume that everything is going very well. We have a packed programme, enthusiastic and knowledgeable volunteers, advance sales of tickets have taken off and what we need to do is keep up the momentum. With volunteer staff, our effectiveness depends on good leadership, clear objectives, thorough communication and adequate support for the volunteers from the event organization. They should be given proper encouragement and praise for their efforts, be carefully listened to for their ideas and comments (and these should be acted on where they are appropriate), be given flexibility in how they can perform a task, if they require it, they should be in relatively small teams so that they can socialize and enjoy themselves, and be given suitable rewards. The emphasis with volunteer staff lies in the fact that they have volunteered because they are committed and interested, but they are unpaid. This lack of pay should be offset by careful thought about the support and rewards they get for doing the task. Support may range from providing proper meals for volunteers and their own dedicated facilities, to giving proper induction and basic training. Rewards could be anything from special uniforms, badges, custom-made sweatshirts or small gifts when they leave, to holding social events and parties, or giving celebrations and prizes for the volunteers at significant points during the event, rather than just a farewell party at the end, in order to recognize their efforts. It is also important that volunteers are mentioned in the internal and external marketing of the event, in newsletters and press releases, and that, following the close-down of the event, careful efforts are made to thank volunteers. It may also be necessary to provide some financial support in the form of payment for travel or other subsistence expenses, or the provision of travel passes when an event is so large that it has its own transport arrangements.

STAFFING: PROFESSIONAL OR VOLUNTEER MANAGEMENT?

If you were the client for an event, perhaps a company wanting a product launch, or a celebrity wishing to hold a charity benefit, then there is a reasonable degree of certainty that you would wish to employ a professional organization to provide it. The events industry has not only management companies, but also production companies, as well as individual professional organizers and consultants, who can put your event on. You simply employ one of these, set up a project brief and pay them a given fee to get on with it. In fact, some companies employ or retain an events management operator, perhaps on a contractual basis. In this type of relationship, events operators may be invited to tender for the business, based on a brief of what is required, in much the same way that marketing agencies can tender for promotional programmes for client companies. Event Management Companies (EMCs) and organizers found on the internet or by recommendation, may be stand-alone operations or ones that have developed out of a related service provider, such as a caterer (some being divisions of catering companies). Others have grown out of production companies or are part of hotel or venue booking agencies. Usually, EMCs tend to be involved where the organizers have a requirement for major or high profile events, specialist dinners, celebrity parties, high profile charity fund-raising events, or where an event demands specialist design, innovation or a major media impact.

Figure 11.5   Example job advert for an events co-ordinator

CREATIVITY

Events co-ordinator

We are a leading provider of corporate hospitality and event management services, working for a range of high profile companies in Europe. Our activities include sport, the arts, corporate incentives and conferences. We are seeking an experienced event co-ordinator with the following qualities: At least two years event management experience

- The ability to create imaginative programmes to meet specific briefs and budgets
- Must be confident, self reliant and mature
- Own vehicle essential
- Knowledge of French or a second language useful

Salary €20 000 plus attractive benefits package

For further information contact Trudi van Heater, Creativity Ltd, 150 Festival Park Road, Middleburg, SG1 3PP or phone us on 00 44 (0) 1786 123456. Closing date 1st March 2013

Source: adapted from an advert in the *Guardian* newspaper

Looking at an event, the organizing body, client or buyer may simply say: 'Our event requires a good professional organization. Let's get some quotations in and watch some presentations, then we will choose an organizer and pay them to get on with it'. However, the diversity of the events business is such that this is only one way of doing it. The alternative is that the organizers, clients or buyers do it themselves. This is extremely common and takes two forms. First, where the organizing body employs a full-time person or even has a department to undertake events organization. This is especially the case for trade activities, such as conference organization and fund-raising efforts among companies, associations and charities. It is also the type of structure found in public sector organizations such as town and city council tourism, leisure or economic development departments. These departments often have the task of providing events to support council aims, such as to increase tourism, community inclusion, economic expansion, etc. Second, where the activity is directly run, but not part of a separate department within the client's organization, it might be that whoever wants an event in an organization just gets on and does it themselves or with a group; this is often the case for conferences, staff parties, birthdays and so on.

Probably by far the most common type of events organization is none of these, but is the committee of volunteers. The committee might be in the position where it runs special events as part of its role. Alternatively, a special committee may be set up just to deal with a given event (we could even interpret the organization of a wedding by the respective families as a type of volunteer committee). But what if you have to start completely from scratch? You have a brief to organize an event, on your own. Most people, at this point will pick up the phone and ring their friends to ask who could lend a hand. Instinctively, you probably do two things:

- think about who you know has the ability to help;
- think about who you know might like to help.

In setting up something slightly more formal than a few friends putting together a dinner party, much the same approach can be considered, if in a rather more formalized way. You need to know some basic details about the event you are planning, but essentially you need to consider what talents or skills are needed and who might have them. Some people are good organizers, some are good communicators, some are good with their hands, some with figures, computers, or gathering resources or equipment. But it's not as simple as this. You will be putting together a team of volunteers, which means you will not necessarily get exactly the skills and talents you think you need, and you will most likely have a disparate group of people who want to be involved and who are enthusiastic, but who might have to undertake tasks they have never done before (although this can be one of the pleasures of volunteering). In short, you may simply have to assign by intuition the most suitable people to the various tasks you have identified.

On the other hand, you might look around your team and think, 'Now what?' First, this is a special event and you have a tight timescale; it might have to be enough that you have some helpers; and you will probably be thankful for them having just turned up. Also, for short-life organizations there is little time for group development, so you may wish to get this group of individuals to choose their own roles, thus ensuring that they are doing something they like or know a little about and will put their best efforts into. But a couple of things should be borne in mind: an individual is just that: one person's best effort will be completely different from the next person's best effort, and given their individual abilities and experience, you may get completely different results from two people doing the same job. Bearing in mind the limitations or scope of skills and talents that people have, in addition to letting helpers identify the jobs they would most like, you can divide up ancillary tasks among them to cover those things for which there might be no direct expertise in the group. In this way you should be able to deal with gaps in your group's knowledge and talents and so cover your original list of what needs to be done. After all, lots of people will probably be able to say: 'I can help out in the catering tent …', but you may not get anyone who says: 'I'm an expert at health and safety'.

A voluntary committee (or any committee) can vary considerably in its number of members and what they do, what their titles are and so on, but it will probably form the basic organization structure for many types of events (see Figure 11.6). It is

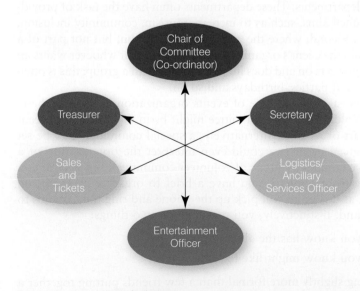

Figure 11.6   A committee of volunteers

important that the leader of a committee is the best person who can be found for the job. The best person will have enough time to undertake the role, should have previous experience of committee work and some knowledge of organizing events. The implication of this is that whoever sets up the committee to run an event, might not be the one who becomes the chair of it.

FACTORS INFLUENCING THE NUMBER AND TYPE OF STAFF

With the framework of the event organization up and running, the next stage is for the respective officers or heads of department to identify what type of and how many staff they need. This process is often based on experience, either of previous events or of members of the committee. Alternatively, a list of tasks can be drawn up (or the work break-down structure used) and the number of staff estimated. This will result in the basic outline of a staff plan, which can then be developed and costed into a staffing budget. Various factors will affect the number of staff each department needs to run the event (see Figure 11.7).

The size of the event

This is a simple enough place to start. How big is this event going to be? Can you put it on with a few friends and relatives, or will it need thousands? (The 2012 Olympic Games is said to have required over 176000 staff, a very large proportion being volunteers.) Do you know what the likely demand will be? (How many people will come?) Have you done any market research? Is your event limited by the capacity of your venue? If the site capacity is 300 people, or has licensing only for 300, then that is the maximum number of people you need to staff for. (See also logistics, especially for catering staff numbers.)

The balance between staffing types

There are variations between what your staff can achieve, given their expertise, ability, knowledge and experience. Full-time paid staff may have all these things in abundance, and one full-time staff member may be able to achieve what would

---

Figure 11.7   Factors influencing the number of staff required

- The size of the event, numbers attending, likely demand

- The balance between types of staff: paid, full-time, part-time, casual, volunteer

- The layout and components of the event

- The method by which the services are provided

- What functions are carried out 'in house' or contracted out

- The demand patterns and scheduling of staff, number of staff per activity

- The expertise required for the event

normally take two volunteers to do. (But this does not allow for enthusiasm: a volunteer is working at your event because he or she wants to be there and they may well work harder than a full-time member of staff who doesn't want to be there! This is a variable.) Perhaps you may have a choice about how the event will be staffed. Within the limits of your budget, you might decide you can afford three full-time staff to cover a particular task, say the information office. But that might mean – allowing for days off – that you might only be able to cover the Information Office with one person on a shift most of the time: if, for example, it is open 9 am to 9 pm and you know it will get busy in the afternoons, you have a range of choices:

- You can run it with the full-time staff, knowing that the one on duty in the afternoon will be swamped.
- You could use one member of full-time staff as supervisor and trainer have six volunteers to do the work and use the money you save for another task.
- You could have three full-time equivalents (this may mean six half-time staff), which might give you more flexibility to cover the tasks.
- You might not be able to get any full-time staff and you might finish up using a range of part-time, agency, casual or volunteer staff in various roles, to get the job done.

These alternatives depend largely on the circumstances you find yourself in. Full-time staff are not very common at the operational level of events, because running one event over a couple of days can hardly be described as full-time. Full-time staff are found mostly in festival cadres, or in those companies, such as contract or outdoor caterers, which have large numbers of events to put on, these staff, especially at a management or co-ordinator level, travel from one to another setting them up, running them and closing them down, then going on to the next one. In some companies, casual staff are taken on for a season, and can then be moved from event to event within a given geographical area. This saves time and money on training, and requires less overall effort on local recruitment. Casual staff are also often obtained via local agencies or through contacts at venues.

The location of activities and concentration of staff at key points

The location of the activities at an event can have a number of impacts on staffing as the wider the area that has to be covered, the more the staff that may be needed and the more difficult communication with them may become. Ideally, for their own safety and peace of mind, staff should not be alone in locations isolated from the main centre of activity without the means to communicate with it. The range of activities at an event is a major factor in staffing. In general, the more going on and the broader the range of services, facilities or components of an event, the larger the number of staff needed. In terms of physical layout, some events can be designed with ease of staffing in mind. It might be possible to concentrate all the services and activities on one central location, where the various staff, being multi-skilled, can do whatever needs doing. These 'service cores' tend to be centralized, so that fewer staff can operate and supervise a larger number of

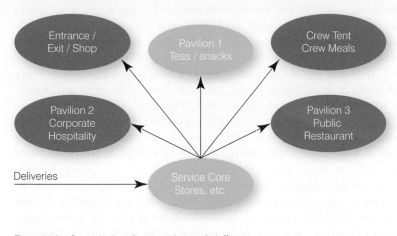

Figure 11.8   Concentration of core services and staff

activities. Concentration of design also reduces transit times for staff moving from one part of the venue to another and has the benefit of concentrating utility and store provision in one location (see Figure 11.8).

The method of provision

This is chiefly an issue of the provision of services such as catering or retail, where there are opportunities to provide the service 'in-house' (i.e. with your own staff or volunteers), as against contracting the activity to a specialist company. There are advantages and disadvantages of doing either, but in staffing terms, getting in a contractor will have the effect of relieving the organizers of having to bother about covering that particular task with their own staff. Related to this is the issue of quality. The contractor may have highly trained and expert staff and be able to provide something better than you could, within your limited resources. On the other hand, contracting sometimes leads to a loss of control and problems in the maintenance of quality.

The demand for, and scheduling of, staff

Demand is a baseline determinant of staffing. At any event, there will be a fixed level of staff below which it is not possible to fall (for example, one administrator may be required to be on duty at any time between 08.30 and 16.30 five days a week to deal with even a low level of business – visitors, general paperwork, enquiries by phone, email, etc.). The one administrator may be able to deal with greater demand only up to a certain level. Quite simply, as demand increases so too will staffing. The issue is often about how to schedule the staff to deal with peaks and dips in demand. For this, it will be essential to be aware of when the event is going to be busy and when it is not, and at those peak demand periods, which parts of the event will be most busy and need most staffing. Suppose the peak arrival time at our village fête is between 10.00 and 11.00, clearly we would need extra staff at the entrance selling tickets. The peak period in the catering tent might be between 13.00 and 14.00, so that spare staff could be transferred from the entrance to the catering tent. The peak period in the arena might be between 15.00 and 16.00, with visitors buying items at stalls and playing games, so spare staff could then be transferred there. This is a simple example, but illustrates the point that we need to give some thought to what parts of an event are busy and when and how we can deploy our staff to cope.

The control of the cost of staffing is also a major concern. Rosters are produced by management to schedule staff, yet cost control is as much dependent on effective forecasts of demand and careful rostering as it is on the sheer number of staff. A comparison of two managers compiling a roster for the same event, the same demand forecast and the same staff could still produce a significant variance in cost due to the ability of each to complete an appropriate roster effectively.

Paid staff might not be required. Even a relatively large-scale event can be accomplished by capable volunteers, provided it is both relatively simple in format and requires no major technical expertise. If we consider a play as an example, almost all the aspects of putting on a play, from preparing the stage sets to designing the costumes, could be done by experienced volunteers, but elements such as lighting or electrical systems would need expert volunteers. The concept of an expert volunteer might seem a little odd, but is perfectly common – the person volunteering to deal with the lighting of the play might be a lighting engineer in real life, or a retired one, or do it as a committed hobby.

The expertise required

This brings us to probably the most important issue for an events organizer – what kind of expertise is available for the planned event? The various tasks identified earlier should be developed into a series of job descriptions to help the matching process (an example job description form is given in Figure 11.9). The labour pool must be considered carefully at this stage: what staff are available, what are they capable of, what is their expertise, what things might need to be done for which either training is needed or professional help would have to be paid for? Even seemingly simple choices can have serious staffing complications, both in terms of staffing numbers and knowledge. This is often highlighted by catering issues, where an organizer might choose a dish that he or she particularly likes, only to find it not only completely unsuitable for, say, a wedding reception in a marquee, but also almost unproduceable for the numbers involved. Organizers have been known, for example, to put Crêpe Suzette on a function menu because they ate it once in a restaurant and liked it, only to find, on the day of the reception for 400 people, that only one member of the catering staff had ever prepared it before and had no chance whatsoever of producing more than 20 an hour. This is one reason why many function caterers will test dishes in advance for a customer who requests something unusual. Food is only one example of the problem of expertise. An events organizer is best advised to list the expert knowledge of regular staff, or to ask the team of volunteers what they can do, what they have experience of, what their normal job is and what their hobbies are. Such a list will help identify where the staffing expertise lies and where it does not.

Staffing is, therefore, as much an issue of identifying and utilizing the expertise that exists, as having large numbers of people to do things, unless, of course, the event actually requires large numbers of people to do very simple tasks – but these still have to be organized in some way.

Job Title _____

Department _____   Department Leader _____

Base location or area _____   Event Co-ordinator _____

Needed from _____ To _____

Hours of work _____ Work pattern _____

Duties and responsibilities

_____

_____

_____

Essential skills, talents or qualifications required

_____

_____

Desirable skills, talents or qualifications required

_____

_____

_____

Induction and training to be given:

Event Background and Tour   ☐   Date: _____   Given: ☐

Health, Safety and Fire   ☐   Date: _____   Given: ☐

Food Hygiene   ☐   Date: _____   Given: ☐

Hosting Skills   ☐   Date: _____   Given: ☐

Manual Handling and Lifting   ☐   Date: _____   Given: ☐

Specific task training (State):_____

Date: _____   Given: ☐

Rewards and benefits (Pay / expenses / transport / parking permit / meals / uniform / items in kind)

_____

_____

Any other comments

_____

_____

Copies: one to personnel file; one to Department Leader's file; one to the member of staff themselves

Figure 11.9   Job description form

FINDING STAFF

Recruiting paid staff

The recruitment of paid staff can be done in a relatively conventional way, through advertising in newspapers or events trade magazines. Marketing, tourism, leisure and hospitality magazines are also common sources of staff for events. Paid staff can also be found through employment (see Figure 11.5) and staffing agencies, some of which specialize in various types of personnel, and these can be identified from the phone book and websites. For large-scale events more than one agency may be needed, and it is common for contracts to be signed to ensure that both parties know what is required. The quality of agency staff varies. Some staff work for an agency regularly and are both experienced and flexible, while others may attend your event as their first-ever job for the agency. Sources of potential paid staff include colleges and universities, where students are not only looking for a job on graduation, but may also be seeking part-time work while they are studying, to boost their income. Paid staff can also be sought through the Internet (newspapers often duplicate job adverts on their websites) and via industry contacts. Many companies which operate in the events business, especially those in hospitality and catering, retain staff records for events and activities held in a particular location. This enables them to use people whom they have previously employed for repeat events, especially casual and part-time staff. Lists are kept by geographical area, so if a particular venue is used frequently for different events, there is an existing pool of staff that can be called on.

Getting staff may not always be easy for events companies. There are areas (towns and cities) where the local labour market is stretched as most people have jobs and in those towns and cities with low employment finding part-time or casual staff can be extremely difficult. In such cases, staff may have to be transported to the event from some distance away so adding to the labour cost.

Recruiting voluntary staff

This can be done informally, by asking around friends, colleagues, acquaintances and relatives. This might well yield a range of helpers. However, it will be useful to explore what skills or talents they have, so that where a conventional application form for a job might explore a person's background or job roles, an application form for volunteers should contain a 'talent and skills' section that will be significant in identifying what a volunteer can bring to your organization and event. This could include previous experiences of events: hobbies and pastimes; experience of groups, formal or informal, as a member or as part of a committee; whether they have even visited similar events, so that they know what one could be like (even if not how to run it); what the main elements of their normal work or daily roles are; what they did before they retired (if appropriate), and, most importantly of all, what they would be most interested in doing for the event as a volunteer (see Figure 11.10).

This means that as event organizers we have to look at the event to identify the range of jobs and tasks that need to be done, and seek to match our available volunteers to them. This matching is part of the selection process, and not all those who apply (even volunteers) are necessarily needed or suitable, with the result that some may have to be refused.

There are various sources of volunteer staff. First, volunteers immediately associated with an event or an event organization as part of their job or hobby. This type of volunteer may be a member of a society or a friend, relative or acquaintance of someone involved in that club or society. For example, an annual town flower show may be run by the Horticultural Club. In order to put on the event, members of the club will participate, members of its committee will organize friends and relatives of members may join in to help produce the show. Second, some events require large numbers of volunteers for which this type of informal personal networking approach

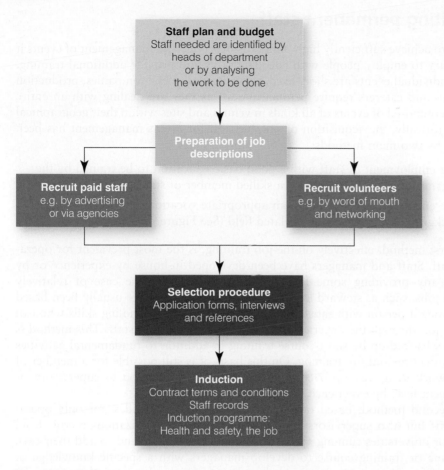

Figure 11.10   Staffing an event

may not be sufficient. In this case, a member of the organizing committee will have to be responsible for getting volunteer labour or the task may even have to be given to a recruitment agency. In either case we would have to seek to attract volunteers by advertising in the local media, by making presentations to other interested voluntary bodies, by networking (word of mouth or Facebook), or by organizing recruitment drives (i.e. preparing a comprehensive plan about how many people you need, how you will attract them, what sort of network you might need to do so, etc.) or by local advertising with small posters or leaflets at community centres, sports clubs, leisure centres, shop windows, other volunteer organizations, youth and retirement groups and local and special interest groups.

Finally, we have assumed up to this point that volunteers are individuals, but a large-scale event might involve not only the key organizing body, but also a range of voluntary bodies that wish to participate. This is the case with carnivals and festivals, where a central co-ordinating body may well be the focus for the activities of a wide range of participants, from commercial organizations to voluntary bodies, charitable organizations and so on. The success of staffing the event depends on the co-operation between them and may have to involve some orientation, meeting together and co-operative efforts.

Recruiting permanent staff

In order to achieve sufficiently high standards of service and management of events it is necessary to employ people with adequate skills and provide additional training. Even if individual events are short-lived, events management companies, production companies and caterers require permanent staff as they are dealing with an entire business composed of events of all kinds in venues and sites within their geographical area. Historically, the acquisition of suitable staff for events management has been achieved by two main methods:

- The employment of staff with a good basic education to be trained by the organization and developed as a skilled member of staff and/or as a manager.
- The employment of staff with an appropriate vocational and educational background in the field or a related field (See Figure 11.5).

The first method, effectively on-the-job training, is the most prevalent for operational staff. Staff and managers have been developed in-house by experience or by the company providing some form of basic training. In the case of relatively unskilled jobs, such as steward leaders or stage crew, these have usually been based on recruiting a person with satisfactory potential and good handling skills who can learn the job through the experience of working with existing staff. This method is sometimes backed up by short-course training in addition to fundamental activities such as induction and fire training. On this basis, it is still possible for a member of staff to work their way up over time through an organization to supervisory or management level by experience.

The second method, based on vocational education, provides not only operational staff but also supervisors and managers. Larger organizations recruit from colleges or universities running appropriate courses and then tend to add their own programme or training course to develop managers with a specific knowledge of their company. Yet it must be noted that there are limited event industry-specific further or higher education courses around Europe, although this is beginning to change quite rapidly. In order to recruit, say, a junior event co-ordinator, the most likely educational background would be vocational courses in the hospitality and catering field, in leisure and recreation, or in some business studies courses where the programme contains events management as a subject or module. These range from courses at the operations level to undergraduate courses at degree level. At degree level some colleges and universities include event management modules or events management pathways to their degrees, and some postgraduate programmes are offered too. Other potential sources of vocationally educated people are found in the field of: travel and tourism, sales and marketing, sport and leisure and business administration. Typically, people employed from these areas, particularly the hospitality field, will have a good background knowledge of business generally and some awareness of events as an activity, but will still need specific training, for two reasons:

- every organization is different;
- every job is different.

Even using graduates from those colleges and universities where the degree programme contains a specific events element, an events company will need to tailor the graduates employed to its particular organization and their role. Nevertheless, there is a good level of co-operation between educational establishments and events companies and bodies. This can involve industry co-operation with assignment work and field visits or even year-long paid placements for undergraduate students. By this method the events industry not only influences the curriculum content of courses, but also provides 'seed corn' for future employment among interested students. A number of the companies providing year placements may well employ some of the placement students ('interns') once the latter have completed their course. This symbiotic system is particularly well established between events venues and the larger hotel schools. Being mutually beneficial it is often seen as a model of good practice for other industries.

In addition to the above, the ebb and flow of employment in general provides a large number of staff and managers within the events business. People move jobs from one location to another or move into events management from related fields (e.g. hotels, tourism, retail, catering, business travel). Some are newly employed in their first job or are staff being transferred around larger, more diverse organizations that may include several divisions as well as types of events. All these methods contribute to the supply of potential staff. Some are better trained than others, but in all cases there is a good business argument for organizations to have a well-trained, well-motivated and well-managed staff (Conway, 2009). This also is the reason why many organizations have a defined staff development policy, progression routes and comprehensive staff training programmes, some of which are targeted at quality issues such as the, 'Investors in People programme' and are intended to achieve not only high levels of staff training and good service for visitors, but also to achieve public recognition in general.

RUNNING THE EVENT ON THE DAY

For all the considerable effort that goes into planning an event, running it on the day can still prove a challenge. The co-ordination of a wide range of disparate and even unusual activities, facilities and services can be overwhelming. Events management has to be effective, and events managers must be good communicators and good delegators in situations that may be constantly changing. Detailed and thorough planning plays an important role in reducing the variability and uncertainty of what takes place during the event and allows the event co-ordinator to prioritize those things that require attention. For the event co-ordinator some elements are essential on the day of the event:

- drink enough water so you don't dehydrate;
- eat enough, otherwise your decision-making and problem-solving abilities will decline;
- wear the most comfortable pair of shoes you've got; and
- keep a change of clothes somewhere convenient, because you never know if some fool is going to spill a drink all over you.

The nature of the event business is such that each occasion is unique, and a production line approach can rarely be adopted. The activities undertaken to provide one event effectively may not necessarily accomplish the next quite so effectively, although there are clearly common features. Thus, the recurrence of routine tends to be in the

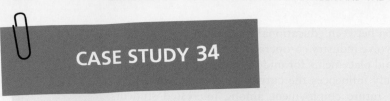

CASE STUDY 34

Organization at the Deventer Book Market

Deventer, The Netherlands

The city of Deventer on the River Ijssel

Ivonne Wierink/Shutterstock

- Deventer Boekenmarkt
- Attracts some 120 000 visitors
- 850 stalls with more than 6 km of shelves
- Has become the biggest book fair in Europe
- Associated activities include music, street theatre and an evening poetry festival in the gardens of the Bouwkunde Theatre

Learning Objectives

The aim of this case study is to examine the organization of an event with the following objectives:

To consider the way in which a modest event is organized and how many 'supervisory' staff it needs on its operating day(s)

To determine why the event is important to the calendar of activities of a particular location and how it fits in to an overall programme of annual events

To understand that not all events are suited to a single type of organization

The fine old eastern Dutch city of Deventer, in the province of Overijssel, famous for its history as a member of the Hanseatic League (an association of medieval trading cities in Northern Europe), holds a number of events each year. These include:

- the annual Book Market;
- the Christmas Dickens Festival;
- the international street-theatre festival:
- Deventer on Stilts; and
- 'Op Den Berghe' (a popular medieval festival).

The Book Market, held each year on the first Sunday in August, attracts not only the general public, but also booksellers and antiquarians from throughout the Netherlands and other parts of Europe.

The Deventer Book Market is organized by the events bureau of the Deventer Tourism Department (Vereniging voor Vreemdelingenverkeer: VVV). The department has the equivalent of some 12-and-a-half staff (some full-time and some part-time) who cover five departments. The organization and running of events is funded from a range of sources, including Deventer City Council; local business members of the organization, (such as catering, retail and market trade businesses), sponsoring organizations and through admission charges and related income, such as the sale of programmes, city maps, etc.

For the running of the event, an operating group of five to six key people, including the Director of the Bureau and his assistant, plus, at most, a further 15–20 helpers will be on the ground during the Book Market to co-ordinate activities. This is deliberately not a large number in order to prevent confusion. It also ensures that the Director can maintain informal contacts with participants, visitors, local businesses and officials to ensure the smooth running of the event. This process is, in effect, management by walking around. Contact is maintained by mobile phones and the Director is seen to be there.

The Book Market attracts between 90 000 and 120 000 people each year. This varies according to the weather and other incidental factors (e.g. alternative events). The measurement of attendance is done by comparison of data from sales outlets (e.g. comparing the event days' sales of ice cream against a normal day's sales), also from information supplied by the railway company Nederlandse Spoorwegen (which is able to report the difference in ticket sales to Deventer for the Sunday of the Book Market as against a normal summer Sunday). Knowing the number of people who travel to the market by rail, as a proportion of the total number, allows the total number to be estimated. However, the number of visitors is not always promoted in press releases, as the attendance clearly varies, and also the amount visitors spend. In one year there might be more visitors who spend less, and the next, fewer visitors who spend more – there is considerable variation, even though averages can be given, such as an average spend for day trippers of about €25 a day. (This helps prevent negative press coverage.)

The Book Market and the other major festivals, Dickens, Deventer on Stilts, Op Den Berghe and a smaller comedy festival, are key to the strategy that the events bureau operates.

This strategy has a number of central objectives:

- To stimulate cultural tourism in Deventer and its nearby region of Overijssel.
- To generate added value for tourists to Deventer.
- To improve the marketing and the image of the city.
- To generate positive publicity in order to attract tourists.

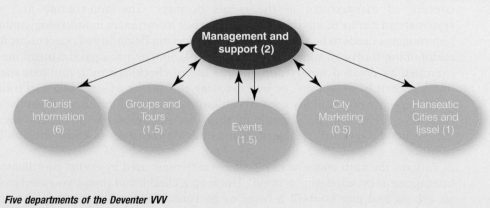

Five departments of the Deventer VVV
Source: kindly provided by Mr Hein te Riele, Director, Deventer VVV

- To highlight the strengths of historic Deventer and stimulate return visits.
- To make the city livelier.
- To improve the living and working environment.
- To encourage residents to be involved in the art and culture of the city.
- To encourage people to use the city for recreation and culture.

Discussion Questions

1 How is the organization of the Book Market undertaken? Is this type of organization suitable for all kinds of events?

2 In what way do the festivals in Deventer satisfy the strategic objectives of the VVV?

3 What reasons, including the weather, might there be for variations in visitor numbers and average spend at an event?

4 How might the media react to changes in published visitor numbers when headlining their stories, and would the view taken by the media make the strategic objectives difficult to fulfil?

5 Identify a festival or event in your district and consider how that event fits in with the style, environment, history or surroundings of the place.

Websites

For more information on *the* city of Deventer on the River Ijssel see: **www.vvvdeventer.nl/ and www. vvvdeventer.nl/deventerboekenmarkt/** and on YouTube **http://youtu.be/l_X9pwaaaE**.

framework – in the approach, organization and management, rather than in the implementation or the operation. On a simple level, the same ordering system can be used almost universally for all events; but the number of people, the timing, the amount of supplies and requirements will be unique for each event. It is this uniqueness that systems and staff must be sufficiently flexible to cope with. Systems and staff are intended to work hand in hand. In general, to reduce costs, especially labour costs, if an operation can be systematized or automated, it should be, but this supposes a more or less standard product. Nevertheless, many event-related activities, such as food production, can be systematized; whether this is cookery according to standard recipes or whether it is the buying in of a standard dish from a supplier.

The maintenance of standards in non-routine service activities is a significant concern of management in the events business. The non-routine and non-systematized nature of anything from site layout to variances in individual audience requirements needs to be accommodated by allowing flexibility of operations, while maintaining thorough supervision and control. Simple managerial control may be exercised by detailed supervision and the use of checklists; by techniques such as 'management by exception', or by improving the quality of staff and staff training to the level at which quality control can largely be placed in the hands of the staff themselves. This can be difficult in short-life organizations at events, because there is limited time for training staff and limited time to get to know what abilities they have.

Perhaps the most common management technique used by events coordinators is 'management by wandering around'. Draw up a checklist of things you need to keep an eye on and give yourself a route to go round, preferably covering your main department leaders and those places you regard as 'pinch points' – where things are likeliest to go wrong, or be busiest, or need support at crucial times. A regular events co-ordinator will know this from previous experience, but for the beginner, the best advice is to follow through what your potential visitors will do, including driving into the visitor's car park when you arrive and entering the site or venue through the same entrance that they will. In this way you will find out in time if locations are signposted badly, if the area is not clean enough, and so on. Do a walk-through of all the things a visitor will do, including the toilets. Test the things a visitor will ask for. For example, have a coffee in the catering tent – don't just get a coffee and walk out, take it and sit where the visitors will sit, because by doing so you will find unexpected aspects that can make or break people's experience of your event (see Figure 11.11).

Above all, communicate actively and frequently as you do your rounds. It is important that you delegate wherever you can, so that your regular staff learn to handle and solve problems for themselves; step in if you have to, but remember, you are the last resort, and you should not be trying to sort out minor problems when your staff could do so on their own. In fact, as a manager, if you have to do tasks that your people should be capable of, then you have failed: you have failed to educate them in their abilities and remits; you have failed to give them the resources and confidence to do their job.

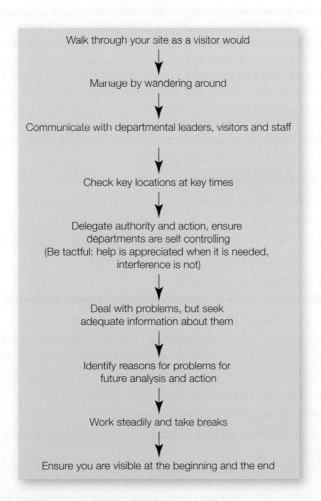

Figure 11.11   Activities on the day

ORGANIZATION AND BRIEFING OF STAFF, STEWARDS AND VOLUNTEERS

In running an event on the day, you cannot handle everything yourself, and will have a number of helpers, whether professional or volunteer. Your event needs to have a structure of organization, in effect a chain of command, in order to operate properly, as noted earlier in this chapter. On the day of the event you will have to rely on your heads of department and their management skills, as well as your own. For many events, however, you may have a large number of staff who are present only for the event itself. They will have to be properly briefed. If you have volunteers or casual staff they need to be orientated as effectively as full-time or regular staff. If you have an event where you have volunteers, you should have a Volunteer Co-ordinator to look after them, to orientate them via a briefing or short induction and to act as a point of contact for them during the event. You must take due care: volunteers need to be properly covered by insurance, by health and safety procedures and by the normal ways in which you would support regular staff, for example in terms of the provision of support facilities, rest areas, toilets and drinks and meals. Significantly, volunteer staff are often involved in events because the event has some charitable, philanthropic or community benefit and they may feel that their effort is benefitting that good cause. For this reason positive feedback should be given to volunteers about their contribution and efforts, and, where at all possible, there should be staff activities which bring enjoyment and pleasure. Get a laugh going. Remember you can sing. Have a pillow fight. Go to the bar afterwards, have a drink and tell jokes. At the end of an event or at some point in the course of a long-running event give your people some frivolous enjoyment, to encourage happiness and to celebrate what has been achieved.

The tasks which volunteers can help with vary according to the type of event, but can include:

- looking after charitable sales or stands;
- helping with raffles or games;
- selling programmes;
- directing cars to car parks or visitors to their seats;
- providing information;
- handing out leaflets or sitemaps;
- acting as welcome hosts to direct people and answer questions;
- acting as individual VIP liaison or disabled helpers;
- providing general visitor, spectator or crew services, such as staffing water stands;
- dealing with registration or cloakrooms;
- giving out samples or goody bags;
- timekeeping or marshalling at sports events;
- dealing with logistics, such as helping set up and break-down exhibitions or small shows;
- moving of small equipment or items to be displayed or put on show.

In the case of the latter they may need some training in manual handling.

Training and certification is also an issue in some other aspects of event organization, such as the provision of catering and food; the provision of first aid support; aspects of health and safety including crowd control and the care of lost children, or the operation of a crèche or children's area (for which special care in the selection of staff and the checking of their certifications must be made); as well as many smaller activities ranging from cashing up of tills to the use of cleaning equipment and materials. In all these cases it is important to remember the need for the member of staff to understand their duties, who to ask for advice and who the formal manager of an event is. We must bear in mind, however, that not everyone is suited to every task and with volunteers, in particular, their views must be closely listened to, and if they feel in any way incapable of performing a role they should be found a suitable alternative. It is also important that if we are using lots of volunteer staff, the heads of section or team leaders should be regular staff or at least more thoroughly trained, so that the section has some experience to it.

Let us consider some specifics in terms of, say, the Stewards Department. In order for the stewards and guides to work effectively, they must understand their role and responsibilities. This may be achieved through briefings prior to the event, or as part of a comprehensive induction or training session for all staff (records of which must be kept). In the case of a small event it could be done on the day. The briefing session would normally cover a number of key issues:

- Responsibilities for health and safety of visitors and participants, and the reporting mechanism for urgent problems, how to get help and the sequence of call-up of managers in an emergency.
- A tour of the layout of the site, highlighting emergency exits, assembly points, toilets, catering and other facilities, access for disabled visitors and for emergency vehicles or staff.
- Issues in crowd management; the operation, opening and closing of exits; ensuring that emergency exits are open throughout the event.
- How to direct and help the public, audience or participants and the need for a calm and courteous approach to all involved.
- How to recognize and act on signs of crowd or individual distress; how to deal with overcrowding by dispersal or by the opening of further exits or entrances to overflow space.
- What action to take in the event of an accumulation of rubbish or fire risk; action to take if a fire is found; how to raise the alarm; how to respond to a small fire or small emergency.
- The mechanism for communication between stewards and managers; the use of coded messages to identify types of emergencies and planned responses to them.

Stewards, guides and similar members of staff should be easy to identify by means of colourful or 'high-visibility' jackets, tabards or sashes. These may also carry easily identifiable numbers which should be clearly visible. No steward should be under 18 years of age, and there must be no consumption of alcohol or other substances while the steward is on duty, nor should any of them leave their allocated posts without permission or relief (HSE, 2012). The Chief Steward should have a rota in place so that no one spends too long a period doing the same repetitive job and to ensure that stewards are adequately provided for in terms of refreshment.

Problem-solving

In making decisions and solving problems, it is vital to be aware of the factors that have led to the problem and to be able to take the correct action. It may be that you have to take action first and ask questions later, but it is essential to ask the questions, otherwise you might fail again. By failing to identify the source and origin of a problem correctly, it will re-occur, and you may not be able to extricate yourself and the event from it the next time. A good decision is, therefore, dependent on the recognition of the right problem. Bear in mind the media reaction to disasters. At the Roskilde Music Festival, the media claimed that nine deaths were due to faulty loudspeakers. The loudspeakers were in perfect working order, and the cause was simply the weight of numbers of people at the front. In the 2000 Concorde airliner disaster in Paris, the media at first claimed that the catastrophic engine fire was caused by a faulty repair done hastily before the plane took off. The engines were working perfectly and the disaster was caused by a small piece of metal on the runway that led to a series of improbable but 'explosive' failures in the undercarriage, the wing, the fuel tanks and then the engines. In short, if you have an event problem be sure to try to identify the real cause, even if this means thinking about it later on and consulting others who were involved.

In your efforts to solve problems and make decisions, keep a notebook in your pocket and take a minute to write the problem down, as well as what you did to sort it out. For those events where you are running a new edition or a repeat of an event you have run before, make sure you take the time to look at last year's feedback notes and any questionnaires that were given out. In this way you can help avoid problems happening again, or concentrate resources in places where you think they might recur. Work steadily through the event, take breaks when you can, sit down when you can and take drinks when you can. It is important that you pace yourself.

SUMMARY

The organization and staffing of an event, its co-ordination and management, are all factors integral to its success. It is arguable that for certain kinds of events as much can be achieved with talented amateurs and enthusiastic volunteers as with professional paid staff. However, there is a place for both professional and volunteer staff in the events business. Events are varied and diverse, and their organization and staffing reflect this.

EVALUATION QUESTIONS

1 Identify two different kinds of organizations found at events, why are they different? Are there issues about funding, expertise, resources and willingness to consider?

2 How might you recruit paid and voluntary staff for an event?

3 Highlight some of the issues about event management 'on the day' – how are events being operated by managers or supervisors, what communication systems might exist, how do staff know what to do to run the event on the day?

REFERENCES

Conway, D. G. (2009) *The Event Manager's Bible: The Complete Guide to Planning and Organising a Voluntary or Public Event*, Oxford:How to Books, pp 172–92.

HSE (2012*) Guidance on running events safely* (up to date information replacing the *HSE Event Safety Guide*) see: http://www.hse.gov.uk/event-safety/index.htm (accessed 28th June 2012).

Schlencker, K., Edwards, D. and Wearing, S. in Page, S. J. and Connell, J., (2012) *The Routledge Handbook of Events*, New York:Routledge, pp 316–25.

Tum, J., Norton, P. and Nevan Wright, J. (2006) *Management of Event Operations*, Oxford:Butterworth Heinemann, pp 181–85.

Van der Wagen, L. (2005) *Event Management for Tourism, Cultural, Business and Sporting Events*, Frenchs Forest: Pearson Education Australia (2 edn) pp 220–31.

Wanklin, T. in Tassiopoulos, D. (ed) (2005) *Event Management: A Professional and Developmental Approach*, Lansdowne: Juta Academic (2 edn) pp 252–93.

CHAPTER 12

CLOSE-DOWN, EVALUATION AND LEGACIES

INTRODUCTION

It's three o'clock in the morning, your guests have just gone, having eaten you out of house and home, told assorted improbable stories and drunk all your best port. You are happy that the dinner party went well and also exhausted. Best to shut the door on the dining room and leave the washing up until tomorrow. Of course, if it's three in the morning and you are the co-ordinator at a major event venue where the guests have just gone, you might still have a whole night's work ahead of you. The close-down of an event should be approached in much the same structured way as it is set up, and remember the lesson often quoted in the mountain climbing world: most accidents don't happen on the way up, but on the way down. At the end of a long event, you and your staff will be tired, many will want to get cleared up and go home, but it is important to be able to handle the close-down and to clear up properly, and carefully.

Once the whole operation is closed down and handed back, there is still some administration to be done. This can be anything from filing to sorting out the accounts, paying the bills or collecting questionnaires. The final administrative details need to be completed, and the event – especially if it is to happen again in the future – should be properly evaluated to see what can be learned from it and what could be done better next time, not only from the visitors' point of view, but also from your own organizational point of view; it is valuable to look back and assess the outcome.

For some events there will be no next time. The purpose may have been strictly limited to a one–time–only activity, although in some of these cases, especially where the objective was economic or social in origin, there may be various legacies, some intended, some perhaps unintended. The significance of such legacies may have been carefully planned – this is particularly the case for regeneration events. Often, however, it is physical regeneration that is planned, and social regeneration comes as a surprise.

For those events that do have a next time they may continue to take place for many years. However, there are a range of reasons why even events that have been successful over a long period of time come to an end or are closed down. These can be anything from the loss of a key organizer to gradual attendance decline because of changes in the circumstances in which the event has been run.

CLOSE-DOWN

There are several elements to closing down an event. Besides clearing out the venue and closing the doors, there will be a range of administrative tasks to tie up. These will include the completion of the accounts, payment of final bills to contractors and final marketing activities such as closure press releases and providing information about future plans or next year's event, if there is to be one. There will also be various personnel issues to complete, in particular the final payments to all staff, the updating of staff records for future reference, together with the need to do some evaluation of the event (see Figure 12.1).

The most obvious close-down activities are the physical ones: the big clear-up once the doors have closed and the last visitors have gone. This should be approached in much the same way as the set-up. A work break-down schedule can be created, based

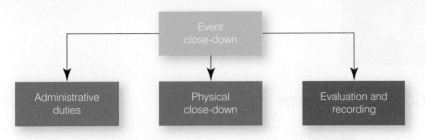

Figure 12.1   Final phase of event activities

in part on the activities leading up to the opening, but in reverse. Understanding that there is a sequence to follow for close-down is significant; otherwise people will make inappropriate attempts to get their gear out before it is safe to do so. In the same way that it is important for everyone to know how to set up, it is also essential for them to know how to break down. This information can be handed out in a summary sheet to staff during the event, and in a close-down briefing given over a meal immediately following the public's departure; otherwise you will be overrun with tired and frustrated people wanting to throw their stuff in a truck, without knowing that the truck doesn't arrive for another hour (Conway, 2009).

As a general rule, the clear–up operation moves from small items to large ones. You cannot get the stage down until you have cleared the equipment and the furniture. You cannot clear these items until you have cleared at least some of the litter, and collected and stored small valuable items. Staff should be properly briefed on this process, and control maintained till the very end, for reasons of safety and also for security of goods and equipment. Some tasks can be done in parallel (at the same time), providing there are enough staff to do them, and the various departmental leaders should continue to supervise these activities. Items of stock to be reused, such as catering stock, linen, consumables and small equipment should be returned to a central storage place prior to collection. Afterwards, this stock can then be returned to the stores, or to the supplier, or to your contractor's central depot.

Exit routes for goods, equipment and materials should ideally be separate from public exit routes, which might still be busy while the event is being closed down. Congestion is often a problem, particularly at large-scale outdoor events. The removal of utilities will also need to be carefully considered in terms of what goes last. Remember you will still have people on site clearing up, so don't cut off the power or remove all the toilets straightaway; see what can be removed first and what can wait until last. In many sites, there will be some permanent supplies and utilities, but it can be surprising how many do not have them, and this needs to be taken into account.

Where an event is being closed down it is important to leave the site or venue in the condition it was found, even if this means pictures of the site had to be taken before the event to ensure everything has been correctly replaced when it is over. It is also essential where there are existing facilities that these are restored to their correct standard before leaving, to ensure the cleaning has been done properly, that the consumable items have been re-stocked and that anything accidentally broken has been repaired or paid for. In many cases these functions are carried out by venue managements and organizations, but where an event has used an unusual sensitive site or venue, perhaps for a one-off activity particular care needs to be taken.

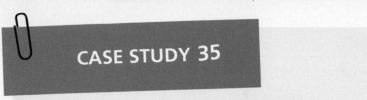

CASE STUDY 35

Clearing up: World Golf Championships

Valderrama, Spain

ClassicStock / Alamy

Spectators watching a golf tournament

- World Golf Championship 2000, Valderrama
- Three-day event involving 62 international players
- Large crowds to watch the golf
- Top prize of approximately €1 million

Learning Objectives

The aim of this case study is to examine the issues involved in the close down and clearing up of an event site. with the following objectives:

To examine the effect on the facilities or services of large numbers of the public being present at an event site

To highlight what issues might emerge in terms of wear and tear of a site and what steps can be taken to ensure wear and tear damage can be easily put right

To consider the how the closing sequence of an event should be planned and undertaken

Clearing an event site can be a major task. It can involve anything from the removal of large amounts of litter, debris and other general waste, to having to restore lawns, gardens and other natural features. Many events are run in locations that are sensitive to use by large numbers of people, and care has to be taken that crowds do not damage the area and its surroundings. This is particularly the case for open-air events.

The arrangements for major golf tournaments require particular care. Crowds of up to 100000 people are often possible, putting huge strain on the resources at golf courses. For major tournaments, stands have to be built, facilities provided for the media, including locations for broadcasts and media centres for journalists and other reporters. Additional facilities and power have to be provided, to cover catering and refreshments, first aid, toilets, retailing and so on. Thoughtful crowd control at Valderrama is absolutely essential, in order to prevent accidental damage from large numbers of people to the course itself, to the fairways and greens. As a consequence, most facilities, including parking, tend to be kept away from the main course, and walking routes for the crowd to watch the golf play are carefully set up, roped off and controlled by stewards. The course at Valderrama is extremely

well kept and is known for its ecological approach. This being the case, areas of the course are kept isolated from the public because of the presence of wildlife and rare plants.

Although the clear-up period is relatively short, as the site is more or less clear of its extra structures and equipment within a week, the repair to the areas used by large numbers of visitors, especially if there is damage to the ground as a result of heavy public use, takes the green-keepers and grounds people a great deal of time. For example, where the green areas have to be re-sown, the new grass may take up to six months to properly grow again.

The process of clearing up after a championship is quite intensive (see diagram):

Event finishes Public leaves Cash up	Cleaning begins	Litter picking, bagging, washing up (or removal), deal with laundry and linen, move items to a central collection point
	Clear down small items	Stocking and boxing up of consumables and small items, loading of transport for small items (may include removal of rubbish)
	'Bump-out' equipment and furniture	Technicians, caterers and media crews to remove their equipment etc.
	Cleaning and waste disposal	Collection of solid waste Recycling collection Emptying of tanks
	Removal of utilities	Stripping out of telecoms, electricity / gas (not at the same time), removal of temporary water supplies, temporary sewage, generators, etc.
	Removal of structures	Removal of rope-work and crowd barriers, removal of large items, tents, Portacabins, mobile refrigeration units, etc.
	Handover and site restoration	Removal of final waste skips, wash downs, check course for damage, green-keepers begin work on areas damaged by heavy use and wear and tear from public trampling

Event closedown processes

Discussion Questions

1 What are the effects, on a site, of having large numbers of the public present?

2 Because site damage is mainly caused accidentally, or because of the volume of people, how could you attempt to mitigate the effects of large crowds on open–air sites?

3 How can you plan the close-down of a site, and in what order should items be removed?

Websites

For more information see: **http://www.valderrama.com/** and **www.europeantour.com/**.

Be sufficiently prepared for the clear-up operation: consider not only the tasks, but also the number of people and equipment you will need to do the job. Many such operations are held up because of shortage of even the most basic equipment, such as brushes, mops, buckets, cleaning materials and refuse sacks. Have these various items stored and ready for collection at a specified time by department leaders, so that you can get the work done speedily.

Much of the equipment, materials and resources you use for your event will be recoverable for reuse. Ensure that you have an efficient and careful storekeeper to collect this material, record what has been returned, take stock and calculate any losses. Careful storekeeping and the ability to redeploy equipment and other materials may save a great deal of money and effort next time, especially for those things that are often overlooked at the planning stage, such as electrical extension leads, special signs and small administrative equipment. From the returned materials, experienced administrators will prepare 'ready boxes' of basic office supplies such as tape, scissors, staplers, glue, Blu-Tack, Velcro fixings, pens, etc., so that a box can be taken out of stores for the next event and used easily, without wasting time chasing round for a box of staples or a washable marker pen. Many contracting organizations take the same approach. Contract caterers will collect, wash, stock-take, then re-count and box items, such as crockery or cutlery (for example into batches of ten) ready for their next use.

If there is an element of organization that is neglected by venues and organizers, it is the close-down. This includes the fact that some effort should be made to ensure that all went well. Co-ordinators should be around to speak to visitors and VIPs on departure to obtain verbal feedback and pick up comments. Comments need noting as part of a quality control cycle, and can be recorded as part of the 'event history' to be referred to next time round. Even relatively simple issues such as the speakers preferring lapel microphones, or the need to have some spare umbrellas in the central office, while not being perceived as very serious, are significant to that event and one less worry at the next edition. In addition, particular care should be taken to record contact information about participants, exhibitors, presenters, stand providers and so on, in order to make the job of contacting people easier for a new edition (see Figure 12.2).

It is essential to thank all those involved, in particular key staff, in writing, 'as you never know who you might need again'. In any case, it is both good manners and a courtesy. In particular, thanks to volunteers and members of the community for their efforts are important, and this is also a matter of good relationship marketing for

Name of contact _____   Name of organization _____

Address _____   Phone number _____

_____   Mobile _____

email _____   Date made _____ / _____ / _____

Type of activity _____

Exhibition stand / stall / concession / entertainment / catering / retail / information / event support / emergency

service / other (specify) _____

Space required

Length _____ m   Width _____ m   Height _____ m

Power required

Type _____ voltage   Number of sockets _____ m

Shell scheme

Name on information board _____

Shell required: yes ☐ no ☐

Furniture: Chairs _____ m   Tables _____ (size)   Other _____ m

Linen: Tablecloths _____ (size)   Colour _____

Notes, history, remarks and special requirements

_____

_____

_____

_____

Figure 12.2   Event history contact record form

future events. On the subject of relationship marketing, if you are going to repeat this event, did you put the next date in the programmes and on the event website? You want people to return, so start by helping the process along. Again, various people may be interested in your event organization or the venue, and while they would not normally step out of their way to obtain information, can be asked for their business card or address as they leave and information can be despatched to them. A sales opportunity is a sales opportunity, and personal contact is far more effective than advertising.

The final administrative issues about event close-down are those regarding contract acquittal, dealing with outstanding bills and completing the accounts. Contract acquittal is not only a matter of making final payments to contractors and suppliers, but also of deciding, for the future, whether a supplier has done a good job. Key to our own success as event organizers is the ability to have the materials and supplies required, delivered in the way in which they were ordered, on time and correctly. A good relationship with contractors and suppliers is therefore vital, and one of the functions of contract acquittal is to identify those companies that will be retained for the future, and those that may have to be changed.

Preparation of the final accounts for the event will be a matter for the treasurer, financial officer or our own accountants. These final accounts will tell us how the event went financially. Where an event has run in the public domain (i.e. one that is not commercially sensitive) the accounts will need to be published as part of a final report to the client body, which might be government, local councils, or other funding or sponsoring bodies. In any case, a copy of the accounts should be included in our event history file for future reference and as an aid to planning any new edition.

EVALUATION

A short period after the close-down of the event, certainly within a month, there should be a meeting of the various interested parties (organizers, clients, sponsors, etc.) to evaluate the event. The evaluation should use all the various sources of information available (see Figure 12.3) and should consider not only the visitor's perception of the event, but also that of the organizers, because lessons may need to be learned from all points of view (Bowdin *et al.*, 2011). The potential sources of information are quite extensive. However, it should be noted that many events, especially smaller ones, record and keep very little information; sometimes only the number of people who bought tickets and what the various departments took or sold. This limitation is due in part to lack of expertise at recording or collecting useful information. For events management and similar companies, the need to get going with the next event can result in insufficient time to either collect information or review what has been collected. However, care in evaluation is an aid to future planning and should not be overlooked.

Figure 12.3 Types of information for evaluation of events	
QUANTITATIVE INFORMATION	**QUALITATIVE INFORMATION**
Visitor and participant data, sales	Visitor perceptions
Target market – visitor profiles	Questionnaires returned, exit surveys
Attendance statistics, market target information	Recorded (structured) chats or interviews
Financial reports and accounts	Staff and volunteer feedback
Financial balance sheet	Management notes and commentary
Economic impact analysis	Social impact analysis
General statistical information	Social benefi ts balance sheet

One of the limitations of evaluation is the inability to make use of the process. Most events organizations will have a meeting to review major events, but the process may end there. 'We had the meeting and we'll look at the minutes of it next year when we start planning the next edition...' (an intention that is then forgotten). The purpose of evaluation is for managers to learn how an event went and to be able to improve on it for the future. This 'improvement' can be looked at in several ways: first, there might be activities that went well but could be strengthened further; second, there are activities that went well in such a way that they are best left untouched; third, there are those activities that went badly and will need sorting out. These issues have to be evaluated, and even where only a modest amount of information is collected, perhaps by formal means (e.g. questionnaires), there might be a lot of underused information sources (see Figure 12.4).

There are quite a large number of sources of information, even for a small event where no formal research has been done. For example, a debriefing of stewards or the whole event staff together might lead to useful insights (Van der Wagen, 2005). However, where feedback or evaluation information is unstructured, we must be careful about its use, otherwise the analysis of it could be based on little other than someone's opinion, which may be worthless, without support. There are probably two key evaluation issues:

- Did the event meet its objectives?
- What can be improved for the next time (if there is going to be one)?

A review of the event objectives, in light of the information available, needs to be done, not only for the satisfaction of the event co-ordinator, but also to enable stakeholders to be reassured about the event's effectiveness. Also, if stakeholders

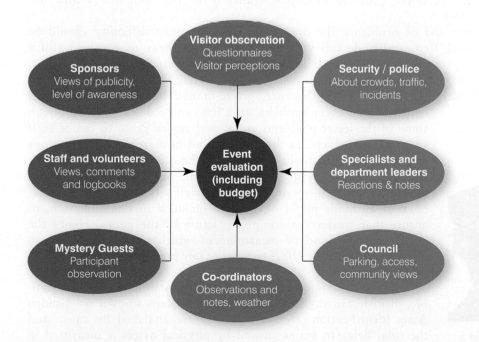

Figure 12.4   Sources of information for evaluation

such as councils, sponsors and clients put money into the event, that the money was well spent. This is the reason for the publication of final reports and accounts, particularly for big public events.

The usefulness of some formal or structured research and observation at events becomes most obvious when looking at what might need to be done for future editions. The identification and solving of problems can only be carried out properly if there is enough information to ascertain the real cause of a problem. It is no good saying: 'We had many complaints in the beer tent, when the beer ran out...'. We need to know the causal origin. If the apparent cause was the beer running out, why was this? Was it under-ordering, or high demand, or did the beer delivery get stuck in the mud? Without adequate information we cannot deal with this problem and prevent it happening again. Related to this is the question of how to allocate resources and time to solving problems. What were the major problems, were they serious and did they constitute critical failures in the eyes of our visitors?

In general, knowing what is best or worst about an event will help to increase satisfaction levels and reduce dissatisfaction – a process that may also help identify persistent problem areas that need time and effort to solve. By collecting and collating the 'problem area' information you can then rank the problems in order of priority or seriousness, 'Most serious to least serious' or 'Most frequently stated to least frequently stated'. Then, having set out this list of priorities, you can attack and sort out the most serious problems, so that in the next event edition, they will not reoccur. Or at least they will be less of an inconvenience for your visitors and you will have improved the visitor's experience of your event. Once a particular problem has been identified, it is best to give the task of sorting it out to one person who has the authority and the means to do so, or to a small sub-group of the organizing committee, than to have the problem discussed endlessly in big committees and not get solved.

In any list of problems, the ones that cause the most difficulty should be dealt with first, and to do this we need to be able to measure the impact of a problem. When we are looking informally at our list of problems, it might simply be down to a 'gut feeling' about which would be the best to solve, because, given limited management time and expertise, not every problem on a list can be dealt with. Although some of the lesser problems could perhaps be given to junior staff or volunteer helpers, as this might result in more creative solutions than professionals might provide. On the other hand, we might be running a major event again next year, and the effort put into evaluative problem-solving might be well worth the effort. Feedback of all kinds might have to be included in this approach, to ensure that we have a complete picture of the issues. Hence the need for some kind of measurement which would enable us to allocate resources or effort to solving key problems or issues which have emerged.

This type of approach is used in various industries. For example, British railway companies use a system known as Golden Asset Identification. Delays to trains are analyzed by cause and the total delay to trains caused by physical assets is measured in minutes. This is then costed, so that the total cost of an asset

A survey being conducted at a music festival

> ### Figure 12.5   Visitor Satisfaction at the Middleburg Music festival
>
> **VISITOR SATISFACTION ANALYSIS**
>
> Problems identified from structured interviews and post event questionnaires returned.
>
> Total attendance this year: 6400 visitors
>
> Most frequently stated problems: (sample of 138 responses)
>
> | | |
> |---|---|
> | Parking (exit congestion) | 48% |
> | Parking (general congestion) | 27% |
> | Catering | 26% |
> | Seating too far away from the stage | 10% |
> | Printed programme poor quality | 7% |
> | Not enough for kids to do | 4% |

failure or specific problem is known. Problems are then ranked by severity and the cost of solving them is compared with the cost of delays. By this method it has been found that very large delays (and costs) can sometimes be solved at very small cost indeed. Suppose that a set of points (track turn-outs) near a major station has been identified as the cause of regular delays – perhaps 20000 minutes of delays to trains up and down the line. The cost is €10 a minute (less than the real cost, but a convenient figure to use). The total cost of the problem is €200000 a year. The track engineers say that the wrong grease is being used to keep the points moving because someone decided to buy cheap grease that was €20 a can less expensive than the proper grease. In this case the cost of solving a €200000 problem is €20 a year, as one can of grease lasts a year. For those who think this is a fictitious problem, the set of points in question is just south of Purley in south London.

How can event managers use this approach? It might be felt that an event is more of a personal service activity than a railway, events being less dependent on physical assets, but it is a useful place to start. Here is a sample visitor satisfaction report from our good friends, the Middleburg Music Festival (Figure 12.5).

In this example there is a problem with parking. It might be a problem for several reasons: not enough space, not enough access, everyone leaves at once creating a queue and so on. In short, the problem may be quite complicated to solve and need several approaches. In order to solve it, we need more information from other sources, not just the visitor survey. In regard to the car park, there are two other sources of information. The first comes in the form of the 'mystery guest' reports (see Figure 12.6). The festival organizers employed six people from the local university (three lecturers and three students) to visit the festival as customers and prepare a structured report about their individual experiences.

In this example, the mystery guest report was corroborated from a second source, the Head Car Park Steward: 'Yes, the car park was a mess to get out of; you took

Figure 12.6   Mystery Guest Report (Extract)
QUESTION 2

Were access and parking arrangements adequate?

No, I found a great deal of difficulty getting out of the car park. Firstly, there was a huge queue as the car park was not properly marked out, so cars were not flowing in the right direction but crossing over each other before they could get to the exit. The exit was hard to see out of because of overgrown bushes on the roadside and it was amazing there were no accidents because of the speed of people coming down the main road and then being surprised by festival visitors trying to pull out of the car park.

your life in your hands when you pulled out onto the main road. We set up signs saying "concealed entrance slow down", but they didn't look official enough so many drivers on the main road ignored them'.

The problem is an obvious one, and has a safety issue, so action is essential, without a need to measure it. But the reader may wish to give some thought to how this kind of problem could be measured. The solution, in this example, may include better liaison with the road authority and the police to have a temporary speed restriction applied to the main road, have official signs put up and have the bushes cut back. Internally, we need to look at the car park layout, put up new signage and mark out the lines for the car park again, make the traffic flow simpler. It may also help to take some of the weight of cars away from the car park by providing a 'park and ride' bus to another car park, or a bus to the city centre or rail station; it might mean better signposting of the exits or staggering the finishing of different parts of the events to reduce the rush for the gates. The solutions that get the most management attention should be those that will have most impact on the problem, and then moving down the list of solutions to those that have respectively less but still positive effects. In the above example, we have supposed it has been identified only at the end, but monitoring should be going on during events, and where it takes place over more than one day, some urgent changes could be made once the event closes for the day, or overnight, or even during the event.

The costs of some problems and service failures may be hidden, perhaps because they deal with visitor satisfaction and enjoyment, or are not terribly obvious in some way. These costs might involve a hidden loss of revenue; the distraction of event managers from key activities while solving problems; time taken in dealing with complaints because the service was inadequate and so on. Consequently, the issue related to identifying the problems is to be able to identify satisfaction with events. In simple terms, people might have enjoyed the event, despite the problems they encountered, or alternatively, these irritations might have spoilt their experience altogether. We can make an event look pretty, have fancy marketing, have standardized management systems, provide smart uniforms, but if the event itself is no good, and our guests have not enjoyed themselves, all these mechanisms will not have enhanced guests' impressions of the event or guests' experience of it. You can go to see a play in a clean and well-kept theatre, with polite and efficient box office staff, prompt service at the bar during the interval and in company of good friends, but the play might still have been lousy. This is also true of events. What, then, affects people's impressions?

There is a view that visitors' impressions of an event are influenced by two sets of judgements, based on aspects of an event that satisfy them, and those that dissatisfy them. Things that work as satisfiers are the ambience, excitement, social involvement, relaxation and other positive emotional states, together with some service elements. Things that work as dissatisfiers tend to be physical and basic service features, such as the parking, the toilets, availability of information, queues, etc. In analyzing satisfaction levels using this approach, a formal method of research is needed, based on both questionnaires about the service quality features of an event as well as observations by trained observers. This kind of research could be done by a market research agency, but should result in the analysis of visitors' perceptions of the event and identification of those factors that were satisfiers, and were thus critical to its success; and those that were dissatisfiers and thus critical failure points.

It is important to recognize the limitations of what can be achieved in evaluating events. We are never going to achieve complete and total satisfaction. There will be, in the human nature of events, many factors that impinge on people's perception, even though we might go to considerable lengths to identify and deal with the critical incidents.

DIVESTMENT AND LEGACIES

Many events are repeat editions, others are not. Some events are designed for a single 'one-time-only' purpose; some do not normally recur in the same place twice, even though they may leave substantial legacies in terms of buildings and facilities; some events leave only social legacies. Many events leave no legacy except happiness and do not need to do any more than that.

If the event has been a one-off, with regeneration or reuse in mind as objectives for the site, the divestment needs to be planned into the process at the beginning. There will be a target date for the handover to the site's new owners or managers, and the site must be given over in the condition that the original objectives intended, or that the plans specified (unless this is done properly, financial or other penalties may be incurred in order to put things right). It will be essential to hand over not just the site, but also the knowledge that goes with it, about its nature, utilities, environment, problems and limitations. Consequently, a handover may not simply be a case of saying, 'Here are the keys', before leaping into your Ferrari.

There should be a period of overlap between the event organization closing down and departing, and the redevelopment organization, agency or new owners starting work. In some cases this may even mean the continuance of certain jobs or roles between the two organizations, perhaps for posts such as site manager

CASE STUDY 36

Event legacies: the Commonwealth Games

Manchester, England

Michael Bradley/Getty Images

Commonwealth Games Legacy: City of Manchester Stadium

- Commonwealth Games 2002, Manchester
- Television and sponsorship revenue exceeded €30 million, claimed as a record for a UK sport event
- 5650 athletes and team officials from 72 nations across 17 sports, with 15000 volunteers
- 1100 technical officials and 4500 accredited media
- 5000 new permanent jobs, derived from the Games, were forecast

Learning Objectives

The aim of this case study is to consider issues about the legacies which events can generate with the following objectives:

To examine what is most important about an event – the event or the legacy

To consider the way in which the legacy of the Commonwealth Games was an issue

To highlight why an event legacy might be important and why an event might be the mechanism to generate a legacy whose life span might prove to be far greater than the event itself

Irst held in Hamilton, Canada, during 1930, as the 'British Empire Games', this four-yearly event welcomes athletes from around the British Commonwealth. The run-up to the XVII Games were overshadowed by concerns as to whether the event could find a place in the crowded athletics calendar and media stories of government money 'bailing out' another flawed event. Manchester had prepared well, though, and the local community took an active interest – it was quickly hailed as the most important multi-sport event Britain had seen since the 1948 Olympics.

An intention to provide a lasting legacy from the Games, for Manchester and the Northwest of England, had been an explicit objective from the bidding stage, which had three themes:

- Ensuring the whole region benefited from hosting the Games.

- Ensuring that disadvantaged communities were, and felt, involved.

- Ensuring that businesses in the region benefitted from the activity generated by the Games and its potential spin-offs.

To this end, the, 'Commonwealth Games Opportunity and Legacy Partnership' was established three years prior to the event itself, bringing together such key agencies as the North West Arts Board and Sport England North West.

Following the XVII Games, some €103 million was quickly committed to Sportcity, in addition to the Games being a catalyst for a number of major physical improvements; including Piccadilly Plaza and Gardens, and the Ancoats Urban Village – plus a number of other developments across the region, including the €24.75 million investment of the Economic and Social Legacy programme. The regeneration of East Manchester was a key objective of Manchester City Council and of the development of Sportcity. With the City of Manchester Stadium – now converted to the new home of Manchester City football club – as its centrepiece, it was seen as critical to the area's regeneration strategy.

The volunteer programme was also seen as a great success and workshops were held to both confirm accreditation for this experience and to encourage individuals to build upon it; helping to provide a pool of volunteers for the region to draw upon – including the 10500 unsuccessful applicants which boosted the Post Games Volunteer Project to some 22000 people.

The Games benefitted from being able to use legacy venues from previous initiatives and event bids, such as the Manchester Evening News Arena (Europe's largest multi-purpose indoor entertainment and sports arena) and the Manchester Velodrome (developed as a joint venture between the English Sports Council, Manchester City Council and the British Cycling Federation). It remains to be seen whether the event will help to restore England's image as a venue for top-flight events, given the debacles of the Millennium Dome, Wembley Stadium and the Picket's Lock athletics stadium shambles. This reputation had to be restored if bids to hold the Olympic Games and the World Cup in England were to be treated seriously. The next games will be held in Delhi in 2010 and Glasgow in 2014.

Discussion Questions

1 What was more important: the Games or the legacy?

2 What was critical to Manchester leveraging a region-wide legacy from the event?

3 What was critical to leveraging a nation-wide legacy?

4 Are legacies something which every event can provide?

5 How has Manchester benefitted from the legacies of previous bids and events?

6 Do repeat editions of an event leave legacies, and if so, of what kind?

Websites

For more information see: **www.commonwealthgames.com** and for some academic background to the concept of legacies see: **http://www.slideshare.net/alanathomson/2010-thomson-leopkey-schlenker-and-schulenkorf-event-legacies**.

or marketing officer. This will improve the transfer of important information between the organizations concerned. Copies of important documentation will also be handed over, including copies of the final reports and the events history file (in case parts of the event occur again or certain suppliers need to be contacted). In some cases a formal handover ceremony may take place, with the media being present, to stress the change in the site's circumstances.

The type of post-event use of an event site, where regeneration or reuse has been planned, may vary, as may the kind of organization taking over the site. In the case of the event sites such as the Millennium Dome site and parts of the Hanover Expo site, development companies were allowed to purchase these with various projects in mind: in the case of the Dome, to eventually create the 02 Arena; in the case of parts of the Hanover site to create residential housing, an aspect that was planned at the beginning as a method of reuse of exhibitors' accommodation.

Reuse varies according to what facilities were provided for the event. The Commonwealth Games site in Manchester was reused primarily for sporting and leisure facilities. The objectives for the Hanover site stressed ecological sustainability, thus the Expo was intended to make use of existing on-site exhibition facilities rather than create new ones. For smaller-scale events, reuse may not actually imply any new use or a transfer of ownership. Where an event recurs year after year, the site may simply have to be restored to its normal condition, such as parkland or a public venue of some kind. The effort in these cases is mainly one of restoration and maintenance rather than any form of rebuilding.

The legacies of many kinds of events may not be conceived in physical terms, some being long-term, others indirect or subtle in their outcomes (Getz, 2007). Event-based regeneration activities are usually regarded as physical and economic, for example, transforming a derelict area into something useable, but this is outside the scope of most events. The impacts of an event whose aims are not targeted at re-use or some economic purpose are probably much more limited and social. They may be intended to improve the image of an area, or to sustain tourism by increasing awareness of a destination, or they may simply be to enhance social integration and improve the confidence of a community in itself. These social aims may be more than worthwhile, and may have more positive outcomes for a community than any physical legacies. It depends on what the event objectives were. Jago and Dwyer (2006) among others consider economic outcomes and various means of evaluation.

THE LIFE EXPIRY OF EVENTS

We have said that the range of events, from small personal ones to large commercial or sporting events is vast. Many events are single one-time activities but lots of events (annual festivals, carnivals, local traditional and folklore events, fêtes, shows, annual markets and sports days, exhibitions and pageants) are repeated year after year. Not all annual events go on forever. Some events that run every year for many years may simply end because the key organizing person or prime mover dies, retires and is not replaced, or tires of the constant effort. Even where an event has a tremendous tradition behind it, this is no guarantee of its survival over the longer term. The world changes, local circumstances and people change and what might once have been a great and popular event ceases to take place. In some cases the reasons why an event ceases or fails are not well understood. There may indeed be obvious reasons such as the loss of a key venue, the lack of money, the lack of people or volunteers to put the event on, the lack of resources such as equipment or the loss of a crucial sponsor.

There may, though, be less obvious reasons. The long-term decline of an event over several years may be due to a complicated series of factors which are only vaguely understood, such as a decline in attendance due to changing social attitudes or different age groups being attracted to other things. There may be a combination of factors ranging from poor organization or poor publicity to the combined effect of bad weather or competition over several years, or perhaps the loss of focus or loss of understanding by the organizers of the objective in running the event. In some cases where this happens the event organizers or an organizing committee may simply not understand why the event is failing or in decline, but may realize that the event cannot, even with goodwill, continue. Very often the only certain indication of the decline of an event may be increasing financial losses which either quickly, or eventually, cannot be sustained and reach a point where this problem is insurmountable.

We cannot say that the decision to close an event will be an easy one even where it is an obvious one. Many events, especially those run by volunteers, have a huge weight of commitment behind them, tremendous goodwill, and perhaps a long history or tradition. Nevertheless, events cannot be sustained just because of these reasons, and a decision to cease running an event might be best taken by evaluating carefully all the factors which bear on its operation, before a financial loss becomes a burden to the organizers. The decline or close of an event may need to be properly managed, the more so if an event is part of a programme of combined events of some kind, such as a series of different events put on in a town or city as part of its effort to attract tourists and visitors. Indeed each year the whole sequence of such a programme might have to be evaluated to see if all the events are to be kept, or some replaced, or some changed in order to safeguard the whole.

SUMMARY

Event close-down is one of those aspects of management that receives insufficient attention, as the temptation is to get cleared up and finished as soon as possible. But this can be a recipe for disaster, or at least for accidents. The large number of people milling round, moving heavy items or trying to get out of the venue in a hurry has to be overseen and reasonable control achieved. Once close-down is over, and the event team has had time to sit back and reflect; the opportunity should be taken to evaluate and to learn for the future. For repeat events, this process is both necessary and important to running a better event, or one at least as good, in the future. For some repeat events a decline in attendance or financial viability, perhaps over several years, may result in their termination.

For one-off events, there are still lessons that the team or individual can learn for their own benefit, and the evaluation process might also have to feed into some closing report or event history file, so that information should be collected and analyzed to help wrap up loose ends.

Some events leave a legacy. This may be in personal memories or friendly social contacts made at the event, or it may be in some item handed over – anything from a park bench, bought from the modest surplus of the village fête, or a donation for an honourable or charitable cause, to the grand arena built to regenerate a city. It may be transient or long-lasting. Either way, some thought should be given at the beginning to the setting of objectives for any planned legacy.

Where circumstances change over time, either in terms of individuals, committees or the market for an event, it may be found that an event will reach the end of its viable life. Not all events carry on year after year, exactly because things change. Difficulties may exist in recognising that change has affected the continuance of an event, and in deciding how and whether to manage the decline, shrinkage or termination an event.

If we have a final word it is this: there is a tendency to believe that events should be bigger, better, louder, more impressive or more profitable than their previous editions or their competitor events, and many pressures are exerted by commercial interests and the media to do this: but it is not so. Neither size alone, nor profit, nor vastness of noise should blind us to the true purpose of events – that of enjoyment, gentle pleasures, social well-being and a general and public affection for those around us.

EVALUATION QUESTIONS

1 What issues might be involved in closing down an event?

2 How are events evaluated and why, how can you obtain participant and visitor feedback?

3 What potential post-event uses are there of unique event sites? Could these uses be planned at the beginning, that is, could they be an outcome of putting the event on?

4 Why might an event decline or even close immediately after the previous edition?

REFERENCES

Bowdin, G., Allen, J., O'Toole, W., Harris, R. and McDonnell, I. (2011) *Events Management*, Oxford: Elsevier Butterworth Heinemann, pp 634–45.

Conway, D. G. (2009) *The Event Manager's Bible: The complete guide to planning and organising a voluntary or public event*, Oxford: How to Books, pp 266–78.

Getz, D. (2007) *Event Studies: Theory, research and policy for planned events*, Oxford: Butterworth Heinemann, pp 317–23.

Jago, L. and Dwyer, L. (2006) *Economic Evaluation of Special Events*, Gold Coast Australia: Co-operative Research centre for Sustainable Tourism.

Van der Wagen, L. (2005) *Event Management for Tourism, Cultural, Business and Sporting Events*, Frenchs Forest: Pearson Education Australia (2 edn) pp 337–45.

GLOSSARY

Assembly A large group of people gathered together, convention style, for deliberation, legislation, worship, lobbying or some community activity.

Attendees A group of people attending an event, for a range of purposes, from watching the event take place, to actively participating in some or all of the event's activities.

Audience The group of people engaged in watching an event or (usually) passively participating in some aspect of the event activities.

Backchannel An on-line real-time conversation among participants about an event or a presentation in progress.

Blag To attempt to get into an event by gate-crashing, or get tickets under false pretences.

Bowser A tanker designed to stand by at events to provide fresh water or other liquids.

Break-even The point at which an event's costs equal the revenue received for it.

Break-out session Where small groups formed of the delegates of a larger event work together, usually in separate areas or rooms, breaking out from the main event.

Break-down That part of the close-down activities of an event after load-out, when the final jobs of site clearance and dismantling of infrastructure are taking place.

Brief A document or specification prepared by a client that states the requirements for an event, which is used either as the basis for an EMC or PEO to tender for, or as a basis for the design of the event itself, or both.

Bump-in (also, **Load-in**) The arrival of equipment, stage crew, staging, materials, sound and lighting rigs and other various items of event set-up.

Bump-out (also, **Load-out**) As bump-in, but leaving.

Capacity The maximum number of people who can be accommodated at a venue.

Cash bar A bar set up during a function where the guests or delegates, rather than the host, pay for drinks individually.

Cherry picker A lorry with an extendable arm and platform on the end, used for reaching high places.

Chill-out room A place set aside for attendees (usually at events such as gigs) to cool off and relax in quieter surroundings than the main arena or stage area of an event.

Client The person or organization purchasing or specifying an event.

Concurrent sessions When sessions of a meeting are held at the same time in different rooms, usually allowing delegates to choose which to attend.

Conference A meeting whose purpose is the interchange of ideas.

Convention A conference gathering of greater importance, size and formality; perhaps with more than 300 people in attendance.

Corporate hospitality (or **Corporate entertaining**) Inviting groups of people, usually clients of a company or high profile organization, to public events.

Critical path The key time-limited route through a number of time-critical activities in the planning of an event.

Critical Success Factors Those issues that are key to the success of an event, as laid down by its objectives, and that are criteria by which its success can be judged or measured.

Critical tasks Those tasks or jobs that must be completed in a sequence, before any other, or all other tasks, can be done.

Cut-off date The designated date on which an organizer must release reserved but unconfirmed space, or confirm a booking by payment.

Cut-off points The points at which something ceases to apply.

Day delegate rate Is the price quoted by conference venues for providing one delegate with meeting facilities and refreshments, such as morning coffee, lunch and afternoon tea, normally for a single 09.00 to 17.00 session.

Delegates The main term used to describe people who attend conferences, seminars, workshops and similar events.

Delegate day This is a measure of the number of people attending a conference each day. Thus, ten people attending a conference for one day is ten delegate days.

Dumper truck A truck used at building sites for moving heavy stuff around, such as sand or gravel, usually painted yellow.

EMC Event Management Company.

Event co-ordinator (see also **PEO**) The individual who manages an event on behalf of a client.

Event organizer The individual, or organization, who promotes and manages an event.

External dependencies A task performed by a person or an organization outside the direct control of the event organizer, perhaps by a contractor or supplier.

External events An event arranged by an organization, particularly in the corporate market, to disseminate information to external audiences (e.g. to wholesalers, distributors, dealers, consumers, the press).

Final Exit The termination of an escape route from an event site in the case of an emergency, giving exit to a place of safety or dispersal to an open space (e.g. in case of fire).

Gantt chart A project planning chart that resembles a horizontal bar diagram.

Gig A concert of rock, pop, house or other popular musical style.

Green Room A room in a theatre, studio or arena in which performers can relax or prepare when they are not performing.

Guaranteed number The minimum number of guests at an event, for which the host has paid or will pay, irrespective of the actual number attending.

Head count The actual number of people attending a function or event.

Hierarchy of controls A process to assist in choosing the most effective control measure to minimize a risk.

Incentive An event designed to be a perk or reward for staff in an organization. Although some incentives have a serious element, the principal purpose is to motivate, encourage or reward. Incentives are often for salespeople (and may include their partners).

Internal events These are events where attendance is confined to personnel inside the organization, such as the sales force, workforce, departments and groups, and to people attending internal – as opposed to external – training courses (thus 'in-house' or 'in-company').

Letter of agreement A document that confirms all the requirements, services and costs that have been agreed between the organizer and the venue. In effect, a contract.

Load-in (also **Bump-in**) The arrival of equipment, stage crew, staging, materials, sound and lighting rigs and other various items of event set-up.

Load-out (also **Bump-out**) As load-in, but leaving.

Logistics The discipline of planning and organizing the flow of goods, equipment and people to their point of use.

Means of escape A structured way of providing a safe route for people to travel from any point in a building or site, to a place of safety, without assistance (such as a marked corridor, or pathway enclosed by rope).

Moshpit The place at the front of a gig audience where the liveliest activity takes place.

Occupant capacity The maximum number of people who can safely be accommodated at a venue.

PEO Personal Event Organizer - a person who organizes private events such as weddings or birthday parties.

PERT Programme Evaluation and Review Technique. A project management planning technique for plotting work to be done in a given timescale, generally in a computer programme.

Participant A person attending an event who is actively taking part in it, or in some activity related to it.

'Pear-shaped' Description of something which goes wrong or turns into a shambles.

Pit The place immediately in front of a stage, that provides a gap between the audience and the performers.

Production schedule The scheme of work to be done, in time order, to ensure an event is set up properly.

Product launch A 'show' to introduce an audience, such as the media, to a new product or service. It may also be aimed at an organization's internal management and staff, sales force or external dealers and customers.

PPE Personal Protective Equipment. Generally includes safety helmets, goggles, hard toe boots, fall protection equipment such as harnesses, gloves and ear defenders.

Public event An event attended by members of the general public.

Roadshow When the same event is staged in several different geographical locations.

Seminar Describes small gatherings similar to the break-out sessions, where a group, but not the whole plenary, will discuss an issue.

Set The performance given by one individual or group at a concert or gig.

Set-up time The time needed to arrange, or rearrange after a previous function, the necessary facilities for the next event.

Show A full sequence of sets, or more simply, the event itself, in terms of musical, artistic or similar activities.

Skip A large waste or rubbish container that is moved by lorry.

Special event The phenomenon arising from non-routine occasions that have leisure, cultural, personal or organizational objectives set apart from the normal activity of daily life, and whose purpose is to enlighten, celebrate, entertain or challenge the experience of a group of people.

Syndicate see break-out session.

Ticket Tout A person who resells a ticket for an event at greater than the price of the face value of the ticket, also sometimes called a **Scalper**.

Trade show A gathering for a trade or competitive exhibition, often with accompanying social events, a conference or workshops and entertainment, which is probably not open to the general public.

VIP Very Important Person, may also appear as **CIP** Corporately Important Person (i.e. someone who is important to a given business).

Wheelie Bin A large rubbish container which can be pushed around by hand, also sometimes called (by Americans) a Dumpster.

Work Breakdown Structure A schedule of the various jobs that have to be done to complete an event.

Workshop A small gathering of people to discuss a specific topic, exchange ideas or solve a particular problem.

INDEX